THE BEST OF ITALIAN AMERICANA

WILD DREAMS

Edited by Carol Bonomo Albright
and Joanna Clapps Herman

FORDHAM UNIVERSITY PRESS   NEW YORK   2008

Fordham University Press has no responsibility for the persistence or accuracy of URLs for external or third-party Internet websites referred to in this publication and does not guarantee that any content on such websites is, or will remain, accurate or appropriate.

Library of Congress Cataloging-in-Publication Data

Wild dreams : the best of Italian Americana / edited by Carol Bonomo Albright and Joanna Clapps Herman.
    p.   cm.
  ISBN 978-0-8232-2910-9 (pbk. : alk. paper)
    1. Italian Americans.   2. Italian Americans—Social life and customs.   3. Italian Americans—Literary collections.   I. Albright, Carol Bonomo.   II. Herman, Joanna Clapps. III. Italian Americana.
  E184.I8W55   2008
  973'.0451—dc22

                                                                          2008032091

Printed in the United States of America

10 09 08   5 4 3 2 1

First edition

CONTENTS

Art and Self

For my grandchildren, Bennett, Zachary, Max, Sam, Harry, and Charlie, who will carry on the tradition.

—C.B.A.

For my Italian son, James Paul Herman, who has his own wild dreams.

—J.C.H.

ACKNOWLEDGMENTS

JOANNA CLAPPS HERMAN AND I would like to acknowledge the Order Sons of Italy and the National Italian American Foundation (NIAF), not only for their financial support of this project but also for their dedication over the years to similar endeavors. For example, both organizations have contributed prize money to the John Ciardi Award for Lifetime Achievement in Poetry. This annual prize of $1,000, which is awarded through *Italian Americana,* recognizes an Italian-American poet who has not only published books of poetry but who has also written critical essays and promoted the reading of poetry. Past honorees include Felix Stefanile, Lewis Turco, Jonathan Galassi, Sandra Gilbert, Jay Parini, Kim Addonizio, Daniela Gioseffi, and Lawrence Ferlinghetti.

We would like to single out a woman who has worked for both NIAF and the Order Sons of Italy, for her competence, integrity, and devotion to things Italian American. That woman is Dona DeSanctis. She is always on the front lines—as was her late husband—in working to further the ideals of Italian-American culture.

The journal owes a great deal to the vision of Joseph DeAngelis, the former Speaker of the House of Representatives of Rhode Island. When *Italian Americana* lost its support at Queens College, the journal, as a result of Mr. DeAngelis's efforts, was able to resume publication at the University of Rhode Island/Providence. My gratitude to Richard Gambino, the founder of the journal, for trusting me to continue his journal, is boundless. To former dean Walter Crocker at URI/Providence, for having me publish out of the university, and to current vice-provost John McCray, for continuing this undertaking, my humble thanks.

No book of this sort would be possible without the gifted authors who found their way to *Italian Americana.* I am in awe of their talent. Nor would this book be possible without Robert Oppedisano's belief in the project. He was a dream to work with.

Last, but hardly least, my thanks go to my family: to my parents, who understood the power of a good education; to my grandmother, some of whose great courage rubbed off on me; to my brother Tom and his wife, Lorrie, for all their support over the years; to my children, Ed and Sally, who continue the best of the tradition, and their children, Bennett, Max, Harry, Zachary, Sam, and Charlie, who bring such energy and joy into my life; and to my dear husband, Birge, who accompanies me on this journey of Italian-American culture.

Carol Bonomo Albright

FIRST AND FOREMOST I want to thank Carol Bonomo Albright for the opportunity to work with her on this project. I have encountered or reencountered a body of work that I have been thrilled to read, reread, consider, think about, enjoy, and help to contextualize. It has been a deep pleasure. Carol holds up an important corner of our Italian-American intellectual life, in our community and with her tireless work on *Italian Americana*.

Without Robert Oppedisano, *Wild Dreams: The Best of Italian Americana* simply wouldn't be. His strong and positive response to our proposal meant the world to Carol and me. Both Nick Frankovich and Mary-Lou Elias Peña provided us with kind, helpful, quick, professional attention throughout this project. Carol Bonomo Albright and I thank both of them. Daria Masullo, my dear friend and quasi-nipota, took the manuscript over this summer and made it into a polished whole.

Personally I want to thank Edi Giunta for creating a joyous Italian world for so many of us. Her generosity of spirit brings intellectual riches, friendship, and joy wherever she is. My life is better for having Edvige Giunta as my dear friend. My lunches with Maria Laurino have made my life larger and better, with our hours of talk of books, films, writing, and especially of raising our sons. But most of all I want to acknowledge my wonderful family: my husband, Bill, without whom I could not have brought this book to completion, and James, whose writing and work I am watching arrive in the world alongside his father's and mother's.

Joanna Clapps Herman

WILD DREAMS

INTRODUCTION

Prose—Achieving an Authentic Identity

IN 1974 RICHARD GAMBINO, together with Ernest Falbo and Bruno Arcudi, founded *Italian Americana*. This historical and cultural journal followed the wave of interest in Italian Americans that had been building in the previous decade and that became particularly strong that year owing to Gambino's book, *Blood of My Blood: The Dilemma of the Italian-Americans*. He elucidated the culture of the family and community in the lives of Italian Americans and wove personal experiences "typical and illustrative of the Italian-American saga" through his historical and sociological scholarship (vii). He particularly feared that young Italian Americans, not knowing the foundations of their heritage, had no means of achieving an authentic identity.

Blood of My Blood received rave reviews from the *New York Times Book Review*, the *New Republic*, and other influential papers and magazines. As the *New York Times Book Review* wrote, "With greater impact than any other nonfiction book on the subject has achieved to date, it weaves together the history, sociology and psychology of first, second, and third generation Italian-Americans." Michael Novak commented, "It sets the cultural agenda for the seventies." Like any classic, *Blood of My Blood* remains pertinent today.

With the rise of the civil rights movement and the great popularity of the television program *Roots*, based on the book by Alex Haley, ethnics began to explore their own heritage and were willing to talk publicly about it—something new to Italian Americans whose parents urged them to keep everything *about* the family *in* the family. Additionally, by then Italian Americans in sufficient numbers had received Ph.D.s and were represented in the academy. Already in the late 1960s, a small group of Italian-American scholars had met at the initiative of Rudolph Vecoli to discuss forming an academic association devoted to Italian-American studies. This resulted in the founding of the American Italian Historical Association (AIHA) in 1969.

The time seemed right to ride the crest of this wave and publish a journal devoted to the Italian-American experience, wherein Italian Americans would record and document their history, literature, and culture. The journal, *Italian Americana*, was housed at Queens College, where Gambino taught, and was not at first connected to AIHA. From its beginning, *Italian Americana* brought out not only the historical articles and book reviews that other such newly initiated ethnic journals published but also included fiction, memoirs, and poetry. Gambino reasoned that this latter trio of genres filled out in a human way what history teaches us about a group. In a word, literature puts meat on the bones of history.

In 1989 the two remaining founders of *Italian Americana* turned over the publication and editorship of the journal to me, Carol Bonomo Albright. It was to be published in cooperation with the University of Rhode Island, which, through the office of the then–Rhode Island Speaker of the House, Joseph DeAngelis, had received a modest legislative grant to fund publication. Professor Bruno Arcudi, the other founding member, would continue at the journal as associate editor. John Paul Russo was, and remains, book review editor. Later I invited Dana Gioia to be poetry editor. He served from 1994 until 2003, when he stepped down to become chairman of the National Endowment for the Arts. Mr. Gioia selected the poems published during those years, while Michael Palma, his successor, is responsible for selecting the poems after 2003. The date at the beginning of each selection in this anthology refers to the year *Italian Americana* published the piece.

After an intermittent publishing schedule and a three-and-a-half-year hiatus, *Italian Americana* resumed publication in the fall of 1990. I gladly continued Gambino's policy of presenting history, fiction, memoirs, poetry, and reviews, adding a play and an opera libretto, together with an interview of the composer of the opera (which went on to win a National Opera Association competition). The opera reflected Italian Americans' expanding entry into all the arts occurring during the years in which *Italian Americana* was publishing.

Meanwhile, AIHA had grown to include all disciplines connected with Italian Americans, including literary analysis. In the late 1980s, led by Professor Richard Juliani, the board of AIHA decided that the journal under my editorship would be published in cooperation with the association but would receive no funding from it.

The publication of the twenty-fifth volume, in the magazine's thirty-third year of its existence, should be recognized not only to celebrate its occurrence but also to provide an opportunity to reflect on the past and the changing nature of Italian-American literature. While *Italian Americana* has published hundreds of works, including historical articles as well as literature, I felt that this anthology should reprint in one volume a sampling of Italian-American literature exemplifying the best work the journal has published, great literature that could easily be included in ethnic studies and American literature as well as composition and writing courses, and that would be of interest to the general public.

Not only have programs in Italian-American studies spread across the country, they are also now moving across the ocean to what our ancestors called "the other side"—Italy. The general public, I am sure, will find the literature compelling, not only because everyone loves a good story, well told (and which can be read on a number of levels), but also because, with society's growing emphasis on diversity, readers will perceive an authentic experience of what it means to be Italian American in the twenty-first century, in all its various manifestations.

The authors in this anthology are some of the people who shaped such a literature. By juxtaposing canonical writers like John Fante with emerging writers in this volume, we not only illustrate the dynamic process by which a literature is formed but also demonstrate a solid tradition that has continued within an evolutionary flowering. But beyond describing this evolutionary process, from its beginnings the authors displayed, in referring to Europe and Italy in particular, a cosmopolitanism that American authors rarely reflect. Dana Gioia discusses this quality most especially in Italian-American poetry in his article "What Is Italian-American Poetry?" in the *Academy of American Poets* newsletter.

Both these characteristics, evolution and cosmopolitanism, are seen in Ben Morreale's "The Prince of Racalmuto" and Michael Maschio's "The Actor Prepares." Evolutionary differences are seen in the treatment of the same subject matter, that of identity. The early authors do not question their Italian identity, while today's authors, in their search for integration, must recover its meaning. The Prince of Racalmuto tries to maintain an identity while suffering its loss in grappling with three languages: standard Italian, Sicilian, and English. This trifurcation, together with the protagonist's hatred of Mussolini for closing off his option of returning to Italy, is literally driving him insane.

By way of contrast, present-day author Michael Maschio's suburban-bred narrator needs to recover the Italian part of his identity—he achieves this through his relationship with his immigrant grandfather—and to integrate it into his all-American persona. Called the Actor, the narrator frames his search for identity metaphorically. Cut off from his heritage, he "acts" an inauthentic role. Tellingly, the Actor refers to a Sean O'Casey play and to Stanislavski's method. Maschio's story cannot but make us reflect on the kind of literature that future generations of Italian-American authors, who will not know an original immigrant, will produce.

Another evolution seen in the most recent Italian-American literature is the use of avant-garde modes of expression. We have included in this anthology two authors who write in this manner. Though the authors are third-generation (Caponegro) and second-generation (Palermo Stevenson) Italian Americans, their mode of expression perhaps points the way to one kind of Italian-American literature that will develop further in the future. Both stories, Mary Caponegro's acclaimed "The Etruscan Catechism," with its look at pre-Roman culture—Caponegro became intrigued by the Etruscans during her stay at the American Academy in Rome—and the other, by Rosalind Palermo Stevenson, "The Guest," with its modernist approach to Mussolini, nonetheless reflect their Italian-American backgrounds.

At the other extreme of expression is Tony Ardizzone's prizewinning "Lamb Soup," written in the style of a folktale with proletarian undertones. Using a fable form in lieu of an avant-garde mode, the story equally demonstrates high creative experimentation within a framework of continuity with the Southern Italian folk tradition. Salvatore La Puma also experiments in much of his fiction, sometimes using magical realism, as does Paola Corso.

Feminist themes, exemplified most directly by Louisa Ermelino, Tony Ardizzone, Kenny Marotta, Christine Palamidessi Moore, and Paola Corso, are also a new development. These authors present not only female protagonists but also ones who construct their own futures. This ties in with another major change in the Italian-American literary landscape: Many more women are writing and getting published.

The emergence of the comic spirit seen in Kenny Marotta's "Permanent Waves" also marks a fast-growing trend in Italian-American literature—a literature so often filled in its early manifestations with the *miseria* of the immigrants. Rita Ciresi in "Big Heart" and Tony Zurlo in "Marco Marcoroni," a satiric parody of academia, continue that comic vein.

With the exception of Ann Hood's memoir, the memoirs in this volume act as glosses on the classics of Italian-American literature: Jerre Mangione bears witness to the deathbed of one of the two uncles who reigned supreme over the spirited table of *Mount Allegro*; William Foote Whyte, while not Italian American himself, reports on his Italian-American cornerboy informant for his sociological study, *Street Corner Society*; Christina Bevilacqua interviews Camille Paglia, who responds in her intellectually provocative manner in the aftermath of the publication of her book *Sexual Personae*; and Dennis Barone identifies and provides a photo of the real-life counterpart of the young Jewish intellectual in Pietro di Donato's *Christ in Concrete*, while my story, with a boiling vat causing a character's death, references this same novel.

A word needs to be said about the basis for our selections: Our first and foremost consideration was aesthetic excellence; next we considered stylistic variety, ranging from traditional storytelling and poetic expression to the avant-garde; historical significance was also considered; and finally we included a range of subject matter—among others, intergenerational conflict as seen in Joseph Papaleo's "Sizes"; loss of innocence in Albert Di Bartolomeo's "Against Gravity"; women as practitioners of the oral tradition in Joanna Clapps Herman's "Perfect Hatred"; religious subversion in John Fante's "My Father's God" and spiritual redemption in Antonio Costabile's folktale; moral considerations in Philip Cioffari's "Sanctifying Grace"; and maternal love in Paola Corso's "Unraveled." One last consideration was, alas, space restrictions, which prevented us from including more of the works that *Italian Americana* published in its first twenty-five volumes. Only the possibility of a future anthology eases that limitation.

—*Carol Bonomo Albright*

Poetry—The Aesthetic of *Alto Basso*

AS I HAVE WORKED on this collection with Carol Bonomo Albright, I have come to think of this cultural heritage as *alto basso,* the simultaneous expression of the high and the low. Italian Americans lay claim to this high aesthetic *and* to the archetypal ordinary. In their lives and art they call upon and refer to a classical tradition—from Greek temples and ruined theaters (and the raw emotions of their severe drama), epic storytelling, mouth to ear, and the voice of opera, their native creation, that is heard in the tiniest Italian town square as well as on the radio in their American kitchens. Add to these their long history with the Church, which gave southern Italy Greek and Latin liturgies, art, and music, and they take the everyday to high ground.

Dana Gioia is the former poetry editor of *Italian Americana*—indeed, the man responsible for bringing many of the poems collected here into print. In his poem "Planting a Sequoia," a family with earth on their hands calls on an ancient Sicilian ritual of planting a tree for a firstborn with a lock of his hair. Earthbound, they hold on to where they came from, but here they plant not a fig or olive or lemon tree but a giant, terribly American sequoia. An air of loss pervades this elegy: the loss of one's ancestral home and a past way of life, but most of all the loss of a first-born child brings a sweep of terrible beauty to the poem. In reading the last line, "Silently keeping the secret of your birth," we feel the devastation of this planting and undoing.

In Robert Viscusi's "Autobiography," Italy is perfectly monumentalized as an immense, intrusive elephant living in the family home. "We painted her sides with huge pink flowers . . . rented her out for parties / wrote papers about her in school." But she, this Italy, this elephant, made practical, made use of, made into art, will never die—not for the Viscusi family or for any Italian Americans.

Italian-American authors, such as those collected here, live in the continuous present with Italy. She's their history, their burden, their God, that which transports them. She is "a fossil, like leaves in coal" (Joseph Salemi); "[her] songs stay with you, still" (Gerard Mancini). Alas, she is also "a gnarled, spindly intruder, / the transplanted heart / of an old conjure woman" (Peter Covino).

John Ciardi's poem "Tea at Aunt's" and Jay Parini's "Grandmother in Heaven" make poetry through incantation. The lists of their living and of their dead are raised through the device of the Homeric catalog: "Mrs. Clossen died of cancer . . . Mabel Sinclair's girl Kathleen / . . . / . . . / she married that boy that used to bring / The paper—you remember him" (John Ciardi). "Her little Gino, who went down the mines / and whom they had to dig all week to find; / that willow,

Tony, who became so thin" (Parini). Each poem brings together the living and the dead and places them onto the same breathing plane. This is normal for Italian Americans: the living and the dead, the blessed and the damned, the ancient and the modern, side by side, or perhaps at one with one another.

In George Guida's poem "Mother," a classic Italian mother, moved by something she's seen on the History Channel, has been transformed into an amalgam of a Buddhist, a Shinto priestess, and a televisionist who, with the fervor that only an Italian mother can call up, has turned to ancestor worship. "'Wipe your feet, and keep quiet,' she said/'I'm worshipping Great Aunt Tessie.'" No normal modern demarcations, borders, categories do for Italians. Although Italian Americans write poetry and create art, their strength is that art and life are not separate.

As Kevin di Camillo is driving his Alfa Romeo around Nantucket "roads smoked with sand. Maria was with me/listening to the only music: Verdi's operas." At the end of this poem, he, the Alfa Romeo, Maria, and Verdi lift up and "drive towards the sun, the ocean, Italy." Cars have an aesthetic of design along with Verdi's aesthetic. It's important to have the name of their loved one in the poem. And when all of this rises in the poetry, out of this ordinary comes a lift toward the gods and inevitably toward that sacred horizon, Italy.

In Sandra Gilbert's poem "In the Golden Sala," "the great sala of the ruined palazzo" has "gold leaf, gold moldings, shredding tapestries with gold threads." But the palazzo is in ruins: Clothes hang on the line of the terrace; animals wander in and out of this grand palazzo while a baby is born into splashing water in the "light of Agrigento."

In Italian hands, inhabiting the ordinary becomes a fine art. It is precisely what they are loved for: "These people know how to live!" The world flocks to Italian shores precisely to see some of the most important art and culture that exist in the West—and to have a perfectly made cup of coffee.

This juxtaposition *and* intertwining of these two, the high aesthetic and the low everyday, are apparent in the poetry you will read here. Side by side, we find angels and animals, the sacred and the profane, damnation and ecstasy. The *alto* cultural heritage ranges from Alexander Theroux's references to the Aghlabites' mosques to Gerard Mancini's mention of Aeneas, Sybil, Keats, Bernini's fountain, and Montale's poetry, to Mary Jo Salter's *Madame Butterfly* and Lewis Turco's quotation from Don De Lillo's novel *Libra*. For Italian Americans, artistic life has not been partitioned off and placed in a museum-ready world, but lives in their bones.

The opera of the everyday is also a commonplace for them. Not only are Verdi and Puccini playing in the background, but there also exists the melodrama of women clutching their breast, of men posturing, and people swooning with love. As Camille Paglia has said, "the vendetta, the loyalty, the blood brother. . . . There's something Italian, Italian American . . . that has a fierce attack quality to it." All of this is part of the air Italian Americans breathe. And so when they write they call upon all of this.

In these poems there is fire and ice, then waters and wind, the elements made into words that beat in Italian Americans. The fire and ice are an intense core of their work. But there are winds and waters to refresh and calm Italian Americans enough to love and write, and think and assemble anthologies.

—*Joanna Clapps Herman*

ANCESTORS

PROSE

My Father's God

John Fante

Fiction (1975)

UPON THE DEATH of old Father Ambrose, the Bishop of Denver assigned a new priest to St. Catherine's parish. He was Father Bruno Ramponi, a young Dominican from Boston. Father Ramponi's picture appeared on the front page of the Boulder *Herald*. Actually there were two pictures—one of a swarthy, short-necked prelate bulging inside a black suit and reversed collar, the other an action shot of Father Ramponi in football gear leaping with outstretched hands for a forward pass. Our new pastor was famous. He had been a football star, an All-American halfback from Boston College.

My father studied the pictures at the supper table.

"A Sicilian," he decided. "Look how black he is."

"How can he be a Sicilian?" my mother asked. "The paper says he was born in Boston."

"I don't care where he was born. I know a Sicilian when I see one." His brows quivered like caterpillars as he studied the face of Father Ramponi. "I don't want any trouble with this priest," he brooded.

It was an ominous reminder of the many futile years Father Ambrose had tried to bring my father back to the church. "The glorious return to divine grace," Father Ambrose had called it. "The prodigal son falling into the arms of his heavenly father." On the job or in the street, at band concerts and in the pool hall, the old pastor constantly swooped down on my father with these pious objurations

Reprinted by permission of HarperCollins.

which only served to drive him deeper among the heathens, so that the priest's death brought a gasp of relief.

But in Father Ramponi he sensed a renewal of the tedious struggle for his soul, for it was only a question of time before the new priest discovered that my father never attended Mass. Not that my mother and we four kids didn't make up for his absences. He insisted that it had to be that way, and every Sunday, through rain, sleet and snow he watched us trek off to St. Catherine's ten blocks away, his conscience vicariously soothed, his own cop-out veiled in righteous paternalism.

The day after the announcement of Father Ramponi's appointment, St. Catherine's School droned like an agitated beehive with rumors about our new priest. Gathered in clusters along the halls, the nuns whispered breathlessly. On the playground the boys set aside the usual touchball game to crowd into the lavatory and relate wild reports. The older boys did all the talking, cigarettes dangling from their lips, while second graders like myself listened with bulging eyes.

It was said that Father Ramponi was so powerful that he could bring down a bull with one punch, that he was structured like a gorilla, and that his nose had been kicked in on an historic Saturday afternoon when he had torn apart the Notre Dame line. We younger kids stiffened in fear and awe. After the gentle Father Ambrose, the thought of being hauled before Father Ramponi for discipline was too ghastly to contemplate. When the first bell rang we rushed to our classrooms, dreading the sudden, unexpected appearance of Father Ramponi in the halls.

At 11:30, in the midst of arithmetic, the classroom door opened and our principal, Sister Mary Justinus, entered. Her cheeks shone like apples. Her eyes glittered with excitement.

"The class will please rise," she announced.

We got to our feet and caught sight of him in the hall. This was it. The awesome Father Ramponi was about to make his debut before the second-grade class.

"Children," Sister Justinus fluttered. "I want you to say 'Good morning,' to your new pastor, Father Bruno Ramponi." She raised her hands like a symphony conductor and brought them down briskly as we chanted, "Good morning, Father," and the priest stepped into the room. He moved forward to stand before us with massive hands clasped at his waist, a grin kneading his broken face. All the rumors about him were true—a bull of a man with dark skin and wide, crushed nostrils out of which black hairs flared. His jaw was as square as a brickbat, his short neck like a creosoted telephone pole. From out of his coat sleeves small bouquets of black hair burst over his wrists.

"Please be seated," he smiled.

The moment he uttered those three words the myth of his ferocity vanished. For his voice was small and sibilant, surprisingly sweet and uncertain, a mighty lion with the roar of a kitten. The whole class breathed a sigh of deliverance as we sat down.

For twenty seconds he stood there lost for words, his large face oozing perspiration. With the uncanny intuition of children we were on to him, knowing somehow that this colossus of the gridiron would never loose his terrible wrath upon us, that he was as docile as a cow and harmless as a butterfly.

Drawing a handkerchief from his pocket, he dabbed at his moist neck and we grew uneasy and embarrassed waiting for him to say more, but he was locked to the spot, his tongue bolted down.

Finally Sister Justinus came to his rescue, breaking the silence with a brisk slap of her hands. "Now children, I want each of you to rise and give Father your name so that he can greet you personally."

One at a time we stood and pronounced our names, and in each instance Father Ramponi nodded and said, "How do you do, Tom," or "How do you do, Mary," or "How do you do, Patrick."

At my turn I rose and spoke my name.

"Paisan," the priest grinned.

I managed a smile.

"Tell your folks I'll be around to meet them soon."

Even though he told most of the students the same thing, I sat there in a state of shock. There were some things I could tell my father, and others I preferred to delete, but there was one thing I didn't dare tell him—that a priest was coming to visit him.

With my mother it didn't matter, and upon hearing that Father Ramponi was coming she lifted her eyes to heaven and moaned.

"Oh, my God," she said. "Whatever you do, don't tell your father. We might lose him for good."

It was our secret, my mother's and mine, and we paid the price, especially Mama. All that was required of me was to keep the front yard clean, raking the October leaves and sweeping the front porch every day. She took on the rest of the house alone, and in the days that followed she washed the walls and ceilings, she washed the windows, she laundered and ironed the curtains, she waxed the linoleum, she dragged the frazzled rugs out to the back yard, flung them over the clothesline and beat them with a broom.

Every evening, home from work, my father strode through the house and paused, the smell of ammonia in his nostrils as he looked around and found some small new change. The gas heater in the living room polished and shining, its chrome gleaming like a band of dazzling silver, the furniture luminous as dark mirrors, the broken rocker repaired, the worn needlepoint replaced with a piece of blue wool from an old coat.

He crossed the linoleum that sparkled like a sheet of ice. "What's happening?" he asked. "What's going on around here?"

"House cleaning," my mother said, her face careworn, her hair coming loose from the bun in back, her bones aching. He frowned at her curiously.

"Take it easy. What's the good of a clean house if you end up in the hospital?"

Days passed and November showed up, bringing the first snow of winter. But Father Ramponi did not visit us. I saw him almost every day at school and he always tossed a word or two my way, but he made no mention of the visit.

The snow fell steadily. The streets disappeared. The windows frosted. My mother strung clotheslines around the stove in the living room, in order to dry the washing. The cold weather confined the little ones indoors. Crayons were crushed underfoot, toys kicked beneath the furniture. My brother spilled a bottle of ink on the linoleum, my sister drew a pumpkin face with black crayon on the best wall in the front room. Then she melted the crayon against the side of the hot stove. Mama threw up her hands in defeat. If Father Ramponi ever visited us, he would have to take us for what we were—just plain, stupid peasants.

The snow was my father's deadly enemy, burying his job in desolate white mounds, engulfing brick, cement and scaffolding, robbing him of his livelihood and sending him home with an unopened lunch pail. He became a prisoner in his own house.

Nor was he the loving husband a woman could enjoy through long winter days. He insisted on taking command of a ship that was already on course through rough waters. Lounging in the kitchen he watched my mother's every move as she prepared meals, finding fault with everything. More salt, too much pepper, turn up the oven, turn down the oven, watch the potatoes, add some onion, where's the oregano, fry some garlic, and finally, "Let me do that!" She flung down her apron and stalked out of the kitchen to join us in the living room, her arms folded, her eyes blazing. Oh God! If Father Ramponi didn't arrive soon she would be driven to the rectory to see him herself.

Our house on Sunday morning was chaos. I can still see my frantic mother dashing from bedroom to bedroom in her pink slip, her braided hair piled atop her head, as she got us dressed for ten o'clock Mass. She polished our shoes, fashioned knots in our neckties, sewed buttons, patched holes, prepared breakfast, ironed pleats in my sister's dress, raced from one of us to the other, picking up a shoe on the way, a toy. Armed with a washcloth, she inspected our ears and the backs of our necks, scraping away dirt, my sister screaming, "You're cruel, cruel!"

Lastly, in the final moments before we departed, she slapped talcum powder over her face and came out to the front room where my oblivious father sprawled reading the Denver *Post*. She turned her back for him to button up her dress.

"Fix me."

Chewing a cigar, he squinted as the curling smoke blurred his eyes and he worked the buttons through the holes with blunt fingers. It was the only contribution he made to those hectic mornings.

"Why don't you come to Mass with us?" she often asked.

"What for?"

"To worship God. To set an example for your children."

"God sees my family at church. That's enough. He knows I sent them."

"Wouldn't it be better if God saw you there too?"

"God's everywhere, so why do I have to see Him in a church? He's right here too, in this house, this room. He's in my hand. Look." He opened and closed his fist. "He's right in there. In my eyes, my mouth, my ears, my blood. So what's the sense of walking eight blocks through the snow, when all I got to do is sit right here with God in my own house."

We children stood listening enthralled at this great and refreshing piece of theology, our collars pinching, our eyes moving to the window as the silent snow drifted down, shivering at the thought of plowing through the drifts to the cold church.

"Papa's right," I said. "God is everywhere. It says so in the catechism."

We looked imploringly at my mother as she put on her wool coat with the rabbit fur collar, and there was a sob in my sister's voice as she begged, "Can't we all just kneel down here and pray for awhile? God won't mind."

"You see!" my mother glared at my father.

"Nobody prays here but me," he said. "The rest of you get going."

"It's not fair!" I yelled. "Who're *you*?"

"I'll tell you who I am," he said threateningly. "I'm the owner of this house. I come and go as I please. I can throw you out any time I feel like it. Now get going!" He rose in a towering fury and pointed at the door, and we filed out like humble serfs, heads bowed, trudging through snow a foot deep. God, it was cold! And so unfair. I clenched my fists and longed for the day I would become a man and knock my father's brains out.

IN THE SEVENTH WEEK of his pastorate Father Ramponi finally visited our house. He came in the darkness of evening, through a roaring storm, his arrival presaged by the heavy pounding of his overshoes on the front porch as he kicked off the clinging snow. It shook the house.

My father sat at the dining room table drinking wine and I sat across from him, doing my homework. We both stared as the wine in the carafe tossed like a small red sea. Mama and Grandma came startled from the kitchen. We heard the rap of knuckles on the front door.

"Come in!" my father shouted.

Father Ramponi loomed in the doorway, hat in hand, so tall he barely made it through the door. Had the President of the United States entered, we could not have been more surprised.

"Good evening," he smiled.

"Whaddya say there," Papa said, too astonished for amenities as Father Ramponi walked deeper into the house. All atwitter, my mother's face tingled with excitement as she hurried to take the priest's overcoat. He laid it across her arms like a massive black rug, so large that it dragged over the floor as she hauled it away to the bedroom.

By now the rest of us were on our feet, staring at the towering priest. Everything shrank proportionately, the room, the furniture, and the members of our family. Suddenly we were a tribe of pygmies confronted by a giant explorer from the outside world.

As they shook hands, Father Ramponi lowered a friendly paw on Papa's shoulder and spoke in his high, gentle voice.

"They tell me you're the finest stonemason in Colorado. Is it true?" My father's face blossomed like a sunflower.

"That's the truth, Father."

"Fine, fine. I like a man who's not ashamed of his worth." Reeling with flattery, Papa turned and ordered the room cleared. "Everybody out!"

With grand pretensions of authority Mama herded us into the living room, which didn't in the least add to the privacy since the two rooms were separated by French doors, only there weren't any doors. Just the hinges. The doors were out in the garage, for reasons nobody ever questioned.

We kids flung ourselves on the floor near the stove and Mama settled into the rocking chair. Presently Grandma appeared, a black shawl around her shoulders, the rosary twined in her fingers, and she too found a chair. No more than four feet away, Papa and Father Ramponi had the entire dining room to themselves.

Those were the days of Prohibition and Papa's routine with guests never changed. Every caller was invited down into the earthen cellar where four fifty-gallon barrels of wine were stored—a hundred gallons matured, and a hundred in the fermentation process.

Through the trapdoor in the pantry he and Father Ramponi disappeared into the cellar. We listened to them down there under the house, their voices muffled, their laughter rumbling in the ground. Patiently we waited for them to reappear, like an audience expecting the return of the players to the stage.

As they came back Papa carried a fresh pitcher of wine, the beaded foam still bubbling. They sat at the table beneath light pouring down from a green metal shade. Papa filled two tumblers with wine and Father Ramponi lit a cigarette.

Raising his glass, the priest proposed a toast. "To Florence, city of your birth."

Pleased but dubious, my father shook his head. "I come from Abruzzi, Father. From Torcelli Peligna."

It surprised Father Ramponi. "Is that so? Now where did I get the idea you were a Florentine?"

"Never been there in my life."

"Maybe your relatives came from there."

"Maybe," Papa shrugged.

"You *look* like a Florentine."

"You think so?"

"A true Florentine, a craftsman in the tradition of that great city." He drained his tumbler.

We watched Papa expand with a sense of importance. It was as if Father Ramponi had sprinkled him with a holy water of magic powers. From that moment he was Father Ramponi's pigeon, eating corn from the good priest's hand. Then the subject matter changed quickly, and the real reason for the priest's visit became apparent.

"Nick," he said with a new familiarity, his voice softer than ever. "Why is it that I never find you at Mass on Sunday morning?"

Mama and Grandma nodded at one another smugly. My father was a long time answering, kneading a kink in his neck, smiling as he sensed a trap.

"I been thinking about that," he said.

"Thinking about it?"

"About going."

"You should. As an example to your children."

There was an uncomfortable silence. My father put the tip of his fingernail in the wine glass and twirled it absently. "We'll talk about it some other time," he said.

"Come to the rectory tomorrow," Father Ramponi suggested.

"I'm gonna be pretty busy tomorrow."

"How about the day after tomorrow?"

"I'm pretty busy, Father."

"In this wretched weather?"

"Lots of figuring to do. Getting ready for spring."

"Shall we make it next week?"

Papa frowned, rubbed his chin. "Too far ahead. You never know, one day to the next."

The priest sighed, lifted his hands. "Then I leave it entirely up to you. When would it be most convenient?"

My father found a cigar butt in the ashtray and went to a lot of trouble scraping and lighting it. "Let me think about it, Father." He produced clouds of smoke that hid his face. Then, to everyone's surprise, he said, "Let's make it tomorrow."

Mama's gulp of delight sounded like a shout.

Father Ramponi rose and offered his hand. He was smiling in triumph and my father shook hands and squinted at him skeptically. Having committed himself, he seemed to regret it.

"Two o'clock tomorrow?" Father Ramponi asked.

"Not possible," Papa said.

"Three, then? Four?"

"Can't make it."

"Would you prefer to come in the morning?"

"How can I come in the morning? You don't understand, Father! I got things to do, people to see. I'm a busy man. All the time. Day and night!"

The priest did not press it. "I leave it up to you. Come when you can."

Papa nodded bleakly. "We'll see. I can't promise anything. I'll do the best I can."

THE VERY NEXT DAY my father began a series of talks at the rectory with Father Ramponi. The meetings left him in a somber mood, and a brooding calm settled over our house. We tiptoed around him, we talked in whispers. During meals he was completely silent, tearing bread and holding it uneaten in his hand. Even my little sister felt his melancholy.

"Are you sick, Papa?" she asked.

"Shhh!" Mama said.

My father exhaled a sigh and stared, his forkful of macaroni dangling limply in midair.

Every day he wore his Sunday clothes with a white shirt and a necktie. So intent was his concentration that he stopped talking altogether and merely gestured when he had some request. A wave of his hand could clear the room. A nod at his feet summoned his slippers. A flat stare and talking ceased among us. Moving furtively in the background, my mother and grandmother watched him with sympathetic, adoring eyes. The man of the house was in crisis, grappling with the devil, and the decision was in doubt. Every night at bedtime we left him alone in the dining room, seated under the light, sipping wine and writing on a jumbo school tablet with a stubby pencil.

A week of this, and suddenly the saturnine atmosphere of our home was shattered and my father was himself again. We awoke to hear him in the front yard, shoveling snow. Mama called him to breakfast. He bounded into the house with scarlet cheeks and purple ears, his eyes snow-bright as he slapped his hands hungrily and sat down before his scrambled eggs. One mouthful and he scowled.

"Can't you even fry eggs?" he said.

We were happy again. Papa was complaining like his old self.

As I prepared for school, my mother followed me into the living room and brought my mackinaw from the closet. She buttoned me up while my father stood watching. He had a bulky envelope in his hand.

"Give this to Father Ramponi," he said, handing it to me. I said okay and folded it to the size of my pocket.

"Not like that," he said, taking it from me. He opened the mackinaw and stuffed the envelope under my T-shirt. "Guard it with your life," he warned.

"What the heck is it?"

"Never mind. Just give it to Father Ramponi."

"Tell him," Mama said. "So he'll know how important it is."

"You talk too much!" he snapped.

"It's your father's confession," Mama said.

I suddenly felt it there against my flesh, and sucked in my stomach. It was incredible, impossible, sacrilegious.

"You can't write your confession!" I wailed. "You have to tell it. In the confessional!"

"Who says so?"

"It's the rule. Everybody knows that!"

"He won't get me in that confession box."

"It's the rule!" I cried, ready to burst into tears. "Mama! Tell him, please! He doesn't understand!"

"That shows how much you know," Papa said. "He told me to write it: so what do you think of that!"

I searched my mother's face for the truth. She smiled. "Father Ramponi said it was all right this way."

I looked at my father accusingly.

"Why can't you be like everybody else?"

"No, sir. You can't get me in that box!"

Dazed and angry and disgusted, I walked out into the cold morning, my lunch pail rigid in one hand, my books in the other, my father's cold envelope freezing my stomach. Who the hell did he think he was? Why didn't he take his damned confession to the priest himself? Why should I be forced to walk the streets with it? They weren't my sins, they were his, so let him carry them to the priest.

The frozen air took my breath and whirled it into ostrich plumes and I walked afraid, like a glass vial, fearful of spilling my burden. I knew my father had not been to confession for thirty years, not since he was a boy of my age.

All of this wickedness, every human being he had injured, every sin against God's commandments were congealed in a block of ice burning against my stomach as I crossed town, under dripping maple trees, around grey mounds of mud-splattered snow, my toes picking their way with the delicacy of bird's feet, across the town, the awful responsibility of my burden hurting my flesh, too sacred, too heavy for my life.

As I REACHED St. Catherine's Father Ramponi drove up and parked in front of the stone steps leading to the main entrance. I waited for him to step out, pulling the envelope from under my shirt as the bell sounded and stragglers raced up the stairs.

"Oh, yes," he smiled, taking the envelope. "Thank you." He seemed in a great hurry and at a loss as to what to do with the envelope. Opening the car door, he tossed the envelope on the seat and dashed away, taking the stairs three at a time.

I watched in dismay as he disappeared. How could he do such a thing? That document was no trifling thing. It was my father's confession, a matter sacred to God, and there it lay on the car seat, cast aside like a rag.

What if someone came by and filched it—one of the older boys? The school was full of thieves who stole anything not nailed down. Suddenly I was in a panic as I imagined the confession being passed around, being read in the lavatory, touching off raucous laughter spilling into the halls, the streets, as the whole town laughed at my father's sins.

Guard it with your life, my father had warned, and guard it I did. For three hours I posted myself beside Father Ramponi's car, my feet numbed with cold, my ears burning like ice cubes as I stayed out of school and scorned the wrath of Sister Justinus.

At last the noon bell sounded and the students burst from the doors and down the stairs. I concealed myself as Father Ramponi appeared. He slid under the steering wheel and drove away, and the minuscule pinching pain in my stomach vanished at last.

That night Father Ramponi made his second visit to our house. It was very late and Papa was turning out the lights when the priest knocked. Papa welcomed him and they came into the dining room. Through the open bedroom door I saw them as I lay beside my sleeping brother.

Father Ramponi stood huge as a black bear under the green lampshade. Then my father noticed the open bedroom door and he closed it, and I was in darkness save for a ribbon of light under the threshold. I slipped out of bed and peered through the keyhole.

Papa had seated himself before the wine, but Father Ramponi was still on his feet. He drew the envelope from his overcoat and tossed it on the table.

"You deceived me," he said quietly.

My father lifted the envelope and tested it in his fist. "It's all there, Father. I didn't forget a thing."

"It's long enough, God knows."

"Some things I wrote, they were very hard, but it's all there, over thirty years, the bad things in a man's life."

"But you wrote it in Italian. . . ."

"What's wrong with that?"

Father Ramponi sank gloomily into a chair, his hands thrust deeply into his overcoat pockets. "I don't speak Italian," he sighed. "Or read it. Or write it. Or understand it."

My father stared.

"Bruno Ramponi, and you don't speak Italian? That's terrible."

The priest sank deeper in his chair and covered one eye. "It simply never entered my mind that you'd make your confession in Italian."

"The Pope speaks Italian," my father said. "The cardinals, they speak Italian. The saints speak Italian. Even God speaks Italian. But you, Father Bruno Ramponi, don't speak Italian."

A moan from the priest. He pushed the envelope toward my father. "Burn it."

"Burn it?"

"Burn it. Now."

It was an order, angry and incontrovertible. My father rose and took the envelope into the kitchen. I heard the lid of the stove open, then close, and then he returned to the dining room where Father Ramponi now stood and draped a purple stole around his neck.

"Please kneel for penance and absolution," he said.

My father's joints cracked like sticks as he knelt on the linoleum. He clasped his hands together and lowered his eyes. Father Ramponi made the sign of the cross over him and murmured a Latin prayer. Then he touched my father's shoulder.

"As a penance, I want you to say The Lord's Prayer once a day until Christmas."

My father lifted his eyes.

"Until Christmas, Father? That's sixty days."

"You can say it in Italian."

It pleased my father and he lowered his eyes. Father Ramponi absolved and blessed him, and the little ceremony was concluded. My father got to his feet.

"Thank you, Father. How about a glass of wine?"

The priest declined. They moved toward the front door. Suddenly my father laughed. "I feel good," he said. "Real good, Father."

"Next time I'll expect you to come to the church for your confession."

"We'll see, Father."

"And I'll expect you at Mass Sunday."

"I'll try and make it, Father."

They said good night and the door closed. I heard Father Ramponi's car drive away. My father returned to the dining room. Through the keyhole I watched him pour a glass of wine. He raised it heavenward and drank. Then he turned out the light and all was darkness.

The Actor Prepares

Michael Maschio

Fiction (1994)

FOR INSTANCE, the Actor awakes to an empty bed. He has been drifting in and out of consciousness and has followed the dead-end trails of every dream he might have dreamt reluctantly, even heartlessly. At the moment, he cannot sleep: his mind is attentive, less restless than focused, like a microscope or camera lens, ready to render the angles of his life to death if need be.

A voice within reminds him, "You're alone."

The Actor's response is a mumbled "I don't care," while he stands and looks down at the messed side of his double bed. He wants to be alone—he tells himself this surely and assumes that he will take advantage of his solitude to assess his career, which has spanned eight years, as well as to find a way to come to terms with Leigh, his lover of three. But he does not have time—it is almost ten o'clock and his scene partner, Carol, will soon arrive—and he has yet to make his living room into the set of Sean O'Casey's burlesque *Bedtime Story*, from which they will rehearse a scene for their acting class.

The Actor's body is stiff. Blinking, he wanders into the living room and throws a white sheet over the coffee table, to make it a bed, thumbtacks a dark sheet over the kitchen doorway, to make it a front doorway, arranges pots squarely on the kitchen table, to make it a stove, and puts two kitchen chairs together, to form a couch. The Actor will play John Jo Mulligan, a bachelor, and Carol, recently a mother, will play Angelica Nightingale, a gay lass. According to O'Casey, she has spent the night or part of it and the ensuing action centers around her leaving before dawn; however, Angelica's love is unrequited. She wants their intimacy to be discovered. Spiteful, she sings, *"I don't care what becomes of me, I don't care cos' I'm on the spree,"* at the top of her lungs, flustering John Jo, who is to be portrayed cyclically—as flattered, ambivalent, uninterested and expedient. Yet, at the moment, the Actor is mad. He does not know Carol well but knows that she works and acts and is married and wonders if her husband is taking care of her baby. He surveys his apartment: a cracked ceiling, an aqua rug, two dying plants, one plastic shade, and concludes that he does not want to be a house husband—he does not want to be a husband at all. He loathes thinking of himself as being anything but an actor; but he is losing his confidence gradually, unmistakably, senses its diminution as discontent and regrets it.

He lowers the shade and lights a candle. Its flame blackens the wick, yet barely grows while he feels himself slide, or fall, into character: his heart picks up pace, he holds his breath, expectant. The doorbell buzzes. "Come in, lass," he tells Miss Nightingale, and sees, when she does so, clutched in her hand, a yellow, white, orange and blue bouquet.

"For me?" he asks.

Carol is taken aback by the sound of his voice—by its bright tone, which belongs to John Jo Mulligan. She blushes, purses her lips and flutters her lashes, in character, before nodding yes.

But while John Jo Mulligan starts to deliver his next line, the Actor plainly sees Carol as Carol-being-insincere: her emotions are false, her flowers are for their scene. The Actor's concentration breaks. He feels beside himself: twenty years younger or fifty years older, less shocked than disillusioned—retroactively disillusioned. That condition, that circumspect burnout, makes sense to him and is seconded by losses—loss of youth, time, love. He is sweating. A cold point emanates from his spine and expands into a chill, which spreads to all of his skin, not to change, but to reclaim his facade. He wants to go back to his bedroom. He has a line to deliver. He clears his throat, parts his mouth, but can say nothing.

IT IS WELL KNOWN that Brando rode the subways to study people, so as to perfect his craft. At noon, the Actor takes the N train from the Theater District, where he lives, to Bensonhurst, where his grandfather has lived for forty years. During his ride the Actor eats his breakfast: a bagel and an apple, reads unsolicited mail and studies the script of *The Daring and the Deceitful*, the soap opera for which he will play a bartender. In real life, the Actor is a bartender—part-time, at the Lincoln Center Grill. He met Leigh there three years ago—along with the opera crowd, she and two friends came in, sat at the bar and drank margaritas. Leigh did not drink, she talked to the Actor—about the ballet she had just seen, about her apartment on Riverside Drive, about East Lyme, Connecticut, where she had grown up, about her mother, a title searcher turned real estate lawyer, and her father, also a lawyer, living in California. When she left, she left her phone number on her check. The Actor was breathless. Leigh was persistent. She moved in at the end of that year and appeased his pride by letting him pay the larger share of the rent until his trust ran out.

Today, the Actor avoids her calls (she is in Dallas working on a bankruptcy proceeding), in order to find within himself another character: Willie, a gay-basher who, in an upcoming NYU film, comes to terms with his identity. But the Actor is forcing the part: he can neither alter his perspective nor redirect his emotions away from himself or his failure, which he feels is real—indeed, he feels that he has jeopardized everything he started with when he embarked on his career during his last year at Yale. Since then he has spent his days looking for work, his nights temping and his late nights preparing spaghetti dinners, watching reruns of the local news and falling asleep to the munch and beep of garbage trucks. Each morning he awakens late, rushes through a rehearsal, a shower and a meal before he runs out in black boots or work boots or penny loafers or whatever the audition requires. And each afternoon, after he has been told that he is not right for the part, he goes to the YMCA, plays basketball with kids half his age, showers, buys a hero and returns to his apartment to sit in front of the TV and tell himself there is no purpose to his routine, no end, just this day and the next. As a result, the Actor is mean when he is not distant or sulking. He reads great plays incessantly, thinks about writing his own one-man show or starting a theater company—he researches the government grants for which he is eligible, but usually ends up napping with his papers spread about his bed.

At the moment, he bows his head. He would like to be taken to a trading post, where he can swap his method for an attainable goal and a good start, have his slate wiped clean and be allotted the time he has lost. He would like it all done privately, too, so that no one would ever know and he could forget. He closes his eyes, lets his senses drift. The sound of the subway train, the thrust and unsettling kachungt, surrounds him, confines him, as if he is a prisoner or an exile—he knows better how he got where he is than how he can get out.

The train goes over the bridge. Light, in random blocks, falls across his chest, drawing his attention. Squinting, he looks through the dirty window, across the water: blue, calm and rippled uniformly—looks at the farther and larger Twin Tower, candle-like, where his father works. Less like a son than like a brother, or, say, like a friend, the Actor thinks about being like his father. He would be a lawyer then, work with people his own age, for people with families, make money. But because he is disdainful instinctively or habitually of the work, he believes being a lawyer is playing a part. His acting teacher, Stanislavski, once said, "You must live the part."

"How wise is it to live a bad part?" the Actor wonders.

He has no answer. Rather, he has his experience. And before he can compare that to the "bad part," or even stand to change his seat, the train goes into the tunnel and he notices his reflection in the dark glass. There, he looks different: his hair appears jet black and matted but is really brown and fine, his pupils have either expanded or the whites have receded into the circles surrounding his now colorless eyes; his nose, normally prominent, dominates his cheeks, which look glued on and pale. He believes he is distorting himself purposely, testing himself: his tolerance for himself, his ability to rationalize or transform that which appears distasteful and ugly. The belief that his life will be different if he changes is supplanted by the reality that his life will continue to change if he stays the way he is. He wants to pause, cease and desist, declare a truce between his thoughts and experiences so that he can formulate a recovery, a rescue plan, write his own self-help book or pamphlet, so to speak.

The train stops. Before him, a young mother holding her daughter's hand barely makes it into the subway car, but leaves her other child, an older girl, on the platform. The doors will reopen, the Actor is sure. But they do not reopen. So he stands. But the train moves, making him stumble while he sees, through the gray window, the girl on the platform freeze, her finger in her mouth, the sudden draft in the station making her hair flutter. He is speechless—he steps toward her, but then she is gone—or he is gone, into the tunnel.

Meanwhile, beside him, the smaller girl is screaming, "Let me go, let me go, let me go!" while her mother pulls her off the floor and into a seat. Also in the car are two men, old and raptly interested, looking at the Actor in particular. He feels he has to do something. The woman is oblivious to her crisis. The Actor touches her arm, tells her what has happened and offers to go back. But she takes her daughter and moves to the other end of the car.

The Actor is stunned. He thinks that she just does not understand—that she just does not realize what she has let happen. At the next stop he follows her off. But she walks quickly to a far bench, where she sits and waits for the next train. The Actor: hunched, mouth agape, mind locked into readiness, feels two-dimensional. He tries to compose himself: to relax the muscles of his face, arms and legs, slow his heartbeat, breathe regularly. But he becomes self-conscious and tense, static and jittery in tandem spurts. He half-turns, as if he will turn in place (to take a second look), but sprints up to the street instead and continues back toward the previous station, as if racing: arms bent at their elbows sharply, knees rising straight and high, until he loses his sense of direction and stops, catches his breath and lets himself hate the woman for not having let him help her.

It feels good to hate her, good in his heart, then bad—very bad. The Actor believes that he is guilty. He becomes nauseous. He steps right, and then left and then right until he loses his strength, bows his head and feels the high sun thicken his hair, making his head feel heavy and his body feel small. The Actor was born in Brooklyn, but moved to the suburbs when he was four; therefore, he is lost, or thinks he is lost or feels lost emotionally. His spirit is low. Dejected, he looks at the two-story, two-family houses: close together, row upon row of red brick, for as far as he can see. Strangely, the uniformity, the nascent familiarity, clears his mind, while his heart, which has been running, slows to a regular beat. He feels fine, balanced, yet light on his feet, as if drugged or sedated. In seconds, from someone, he finds out where he is, and then walks past the houses, wondering how much one might cost.

ON THE SET OF *The Daring and the Deceitful* the Actor serves white wine to Gwen, a model, and former model in real life. She thanks him, takes a sip and places her drink on the bar. Then Dex grabs her arm. Dex is a real estate mogul. "What did you do?" he demands.

She got pregnant—by him, on purpose, he suspects. He wants her to get an abortion. However Dan, the actor who plays Dex, cannot convey a sense of urgency. His hair sprayed, his fit frame wrapped in an Armani suit, in real life he is a family man from Brooklyn who started acting just that year. He has taken a liking to the Actor. "All you need is a break," he's told him.

Meanwhile, frustrated, her heart pounding beneath her leather jacket, her eyes glassy and defiant, Gwen does not answer Dex's question directly. Rather, looking up at him, she pauses for a close-up, which fades to a commercial.

The Actor thinks the scene went well. But the director, wearing a red jump-suit and cowboy boots, is unsatisfied with the sequence. She tells Gwen to flirt with the bartender for a beat, so as to add fuel to Dex's fire.

"Should I say something?" the Actor wonders. It is not his place to speak, but he feels at ease behind the bar.

"Yes," the director says. "You smile . . . and you take her order and make her drink . . . be sure you make a good impression on her—You're not really a bartender, you're trying to become a pilot—and you serve her, and lean toward her . . . and you whisper . . . something. But make sure we don't pick it up—and then, Gwen, you smile, and . . . no, you blush. And then we cut to Dex and let the tension build."

Being an extra, the Actor wants a line. "Dex is gonna threaten her. I could sense that and give him a standoffish look, or I could ask Gwen, 'Is he with you?' or 'Do you know this guy?' And she'll say, 'You mean Mr. Dexter Bondsman? He's my fiancé,' even though they're not engaged—but everyone knows that she wants to marry him, so it'll make matters worse and build tension."

Without further consideration, the director decides that Dex will become disgusted when he sees Gwen flirting with the bartender. Subsequently, Gwen will leave her drink, run after Dex, grab his arm, turn him about and force him into a public kiss. "It's about time we saw something like that," the director comments.

AT HIS GRANDFATHER'S HOUSE, having eaten his fill of macaroni, the Actor is slouched on the couch, watching the Yankees game. Quietly, even derisively, he delivers stray lines until he notices, on the coffee table and beside the phone, a stack of photographs, warped, or cupped like hands. Shuffling through them, he recognizes his extended family, gathered around a tree, before a small house, all on a vast, undeveloped field. There is the patriarch: Great-Grandfather Finale, six feet tall, white mustachioed, pipe in mouth—he retired when he was forty and lived off of his children until he was ninety. Thinking about that makes a wound, long closed, open inside the Actor's heart. He adjusts his pose, holds the photograph at a distance, then close to his eyes for contrast. But his eyes close and across his mind a stage, low to the ground and dark, becomes apparent. There, the Actor sees himself encircled by a spotlight, poised to deliver the line, "The readiness is all." But this image of himself playing Hamlet is tiresome and, he concludes, beyond his grasp. Presently, he is unwilling to see silver linings: he knows that he will never be able to take care of his father and that he is living off of his girlfriend. Ashamed, he dislikes himself, his apartment, his resume, his scene partner, as well as Brando, Robert De Niro and Kenneth Branagh. He would like to clear his mind, to empty it or shake it up, so that memories and wishes would merge, his body being a laboratory and he a scientist who has botched an experiment. He looks at the photograph—at his grandfather: about age thirty (his age), a filterless cigarette, a crooked smile. When his grandfather got the chance, he sold his summerhouse in order to create a trust for the Actor. "I am I," Stanislavski once said, "but if I was (fill in the blank), then I would (fill in the blank)." Using this formula, known as The Magic If, the Actor considers: what if I had been my grandfather . . . then I would not have sold our house . . . then I could live there . . . marry Leigh.

His hand is supporting his head while he considers this—he looks interrupted or frozen like a video image on pause. His grandfather comes in, smiling, his teeth out, his glasses off, a cup of espresso in each hand. Yet his long smile flattens quickly when he sees his eldest grandson locked into glum inattentiveness. It baffles him, makes him wonder why such a smart, handsome boy is letting some silly thing get the better of him.

He wants to know what's wrong and does not hesitate to ask, "What's wrong?"

The Actor breaks his pose, takes a cup of espresso and bluffs by telling his grandfather the score of the game. But then he has nothing to say. So he picks up another photograph and recognizes himself, standing beside a tree. "The man had no recollections of the place at all. He remembered only the emotions he left," Stanislavski, in reference to his theory of Emotion Memory, once said. Recalling it now, the Actor feels secure, cared for. "I was at our summerhouse?" he asks and does not know that he has spoken aloud.

"That's you, Tony." His grandfather points to the photograph.

But that is not Tony. Rather, Tony is holding the photograph, he is not *in* the photograph—he understands this intellectually. Yet he is connected to the photograph emotionally, or he is connected to his emotions. He looks at his grandfather and thinks about his grandmother, who, one morning, less than a year ago, was unable to get out of bed. She complained. His grandfather called the hospital. She refused to go. When the ambulance arrived, she was embarrassed for the paramedics. She sat in the back, but stopped breathing before long—and could not be resuscitated.

Tony tells himself, "It's terrible for Grandpa to have to live without Grandpa," but then corrects himself, "I mean Grandma," yet thinks his initial mistake was closer to the mark. He believes that he has been living without himself.

"Are you staying tonight?" his grandfather asks.

Tony said that he would, but does not know if he should. He withholds his answer, puts the photograph in his breast pocket and tells his grandfather that he has to make a telephone call.

After many rings, Leigh answers.

Tony apologizes. "I woke you up. I didn't know if you were home yet."

"I saw what you left me," she says.

"What?"

"I put them in water. Where did you buy them?"

"When did you get home?"

"A little while ago," she yawns.

She must be under the covers, talking on the cordless phone, Tony assumes. But he is wrong—she is in their living room, standing, legs crossed, in the dark, by the open window, wearing nothing at all, twirling, beneath her small nose, the petals of an orange flower that his scene partner, Carol, brought over that morning. Without a doubt, Leigh thinks the flower is for her, from him. "When're you coming home?"

In his mind, Tony is home. "I'm leaving now."

"Wake me up."

Tony barely hears her words. Rather, he realizes that he will stop acting—not quit, but move on—and not backwards, looking back like a novelist, but forward, looking ahead—less like a visionary than a "normal" person. In his opinion, he has not been that for a long time—and he wants it—the normalcy, the I'm-with-you-ness that he despised unwisely when he started to remake himself.

He loves Leigh and he loves, too, the person who loves her—*he* is that person. He understands this now and decides that he will try to remain that person. But then his heart tightens. He is afraid that he will never see Leigh again. Sharply, he tells her, "Don't go to sleep without me," and finally lowers his voice to say, "All day I've missed you."

The Night Maggie Saw God and Sal Barnum Too

Carol Bonomo Albright

Fiction (1994)

MAGGIE, PEGGY, MARGIE. These were all names Michela had assumed in her quest to become American. Born Michela Guerrisi, she said, "I died. I wanted to hide under my desk and never come out when my teacher called my name for the roll in school." But she didn't die—though in her own mind, she always remained "in-between." And within that in-betweenness there was one night when Maggie saw God and Sal Barnum too.

Maggie had gone to Parrazza's funeral home on Bleecker Street, where the southern Italians were buried from, for Vito's wake.

On the day he died, Vito was helping a ragman deliver his merchandise to a factory, which was understaffed because people were dropping like flies from the flu. The ragman, arms outstretched, head down, forced to stare at the cobblestones he walked on, maneuvered his cart from behind. The faded wagon was piled high with rags, slabs of cardboard, felt, bits and pieces of stuff, too dirty to know what the original was. Today the wagon was so overloaded that he couldn't put it down without toppling half its contents.

The ragman turned his head towards the sidewalk and saw Vito, a well-built kid in his twenties. "Hey, kid, I give you a penny. You come 'ere help me."

Vito agreed. It was better than staying upstairs and stringing tags, a thousand for twenty cents, which his mother would want him to do, along with his two brothers and sister, when she got home from work. The whole family poked a short piece of thin string, which they then knotted, through a hole on price tags for clothing. Not that he minded so much, but since Jesse was no longer being sent to the movie house during the day to tell the rest of them the story at night, the tag-stringing had grown boring. True, Lucy was pretty good at telling ghost stories, but this offer seemed like an easy penny to make—outside, where he wanted to be anyway.

Vito thought he might see Maggie on Thompson Street. Maybe she hadn't gone to work yet at Reo Cars. She was a looker. Mary Pickford, they called her in the neighborhood. She took his breath away.

Vito, alongside the ragman, walked from Canal to Eighth Street without incident and without seeing Maggie. They avoided Washington Square Park and snaked their way up Sullivan and MacDougal instead, passing St. Anthony's Church.

Vito liked St. Anthony's, especially the lower church with its flickering candles in the red glass containers, its statues in their niches, six on either side of the altar, its paintings on the walls. Vito himself had drawn some pictures. He drew one of St. Michael, the archangel, who when you died, weighed your good and bad deeds on his scale to decide if you belonged in heaven or hell. But he had put Maggie's face on the picture he drew. Vito thought Maggie held his fate in the balance. A smile from her sent him to heaven. Though Maggie was quiet and had a sweet smile, she had courage too. Hadn't she been the first Italian to be hired as a secretary by Reo Cars uptown? Vito knew the archangel wouldn't mind having Maggie's face on the drawing. It was only the face Vito had changed. He kept the hair the same—long and wavy like Maggie's.

Vito liked to draw. The fish man with the basement store, he drew as St. Peter—even though the fish man wasn't Catholic. After all, St. Peter was a Jew once too. Vito didn't know anyone who was a carpenter, so he put a pickax in St. Joseph's hands and drew his Uncle Tedor's face. Vito sometimes thought his mother had an extra set of eyes outside her head, so St. Lucy with her eyes on a platter had his mother's face. And Pino with the fruit and vegetable pushcart on Spring Street, Vito dressed as St. Francis, walking in the fields among the olive trees and artichokes. Maggie's mother Teresina, who made her own wine and anisette, he drew as St. Theresa of the Little Flower and the midwife 'Magala became St. Anne. Gabriel, the other archangel holding a balance, Vito painted with the face of the butcher, Biaggio the bulldog—his big thumb pressing down heavily on the scale. Vito's mother laughed when she saw that picture instead of yelling at him for wasting his time drawing and dreaming.

He and the ragman continued their walk uptown. They stopped at the curb by the entrance to the building. "Help me get this up the curbstone," the ragman mumbled through his gray beard, dotted with specks of dust.

Vito walked to the front of the wagon, bent over, and hunched his shoulders under its bottom. As the ragman pushed, Vito lifted with his shoulders and back. He heaved. The ragman pushed one more time. The wagon teetered. They steadied it, lifted and pushed again; the wheels rose over the curb. They quickly steered the wagon into the main room of the factory and started to unload it. Two temporary employees weighed the rags; the boss paid the ragman. Vito got his penny.

The factory owner offered Vito a nickel to wash the rags before shipping them out. Vito whistled. A nickel was two hundred strung tags. He agreed. Actually, he didn't mind working. It would all help put Dominic through medical school. Dominic was the smart one . . . remembered everything he learned. Any work Vito got helped the whole family.

He climbed the stairs and stood on the narrow platform surrounding the large vat, grabbed the paddle and began to walk along the platform, stirring and agitating the bubbling water and rags as the boss had shown him. It was harder work than he thought. The rising steam enveloped him. He was sweating heavily. He peered down into the soapy water. Pieces of cloth, their colors just becoming visible—maroon, tan, blue—bobbed up and down. Vito put the paddle down, wiped his brow and leaned over the vat from the waist—the upper half of his body hanging over the rim of the vat—staring intently at one glittering piece of cloth. It would make a pretty bow for Maggie's hair.

The penny in his shirt pocket fell out. He had worked hard for that penny. Dominic would appreciate it. Vito grabbed for it but he lost his footing on the soapy, wet floor. He tried to right himself, grabbing for the rim. It slipped from his grasp; his fingers stretched and hooked again.

AT LUNCHTIME the boss came by on his way to eat. "Where the hell is that kid?" he muttered, staring up at the platform. By the time they found him—he had never learned to swim and besides the water was boiling hot—Vito was dead.

His mother's boss called her away from the table where she was packing chocolate-covered cherries to identify him. She put down the half-filled box and wiped her hands on her green apron. Gondolpha, a coworker who was wrapping her 8,347th piece of hard candy of the day, gave a quick twist to the cellophane and shelved her box to accompany Magdalena. Following the paesan, who came over to say he thought it was Vito who was in an accident, they trudged over to the building, looked at the body, half blue from drowning and half red from the boiling water, with harlequin patches of cloth rags clinging to it. His mother screamed and scratched at her face, then fainted.

The paesan went to get Dominic to claim Vito's body and make arrangements with the undertaker. Vito's body lay on the platform surrounding the tub. Dominic, staring in anguish at his brother, waited for the undertaker to arrive. Dominic stepped closer to look at Vito's fingers, which had drawn so many pictures. He lifted one of his brother's hands gingerly, shuddered slightly, and then held it in both his own. He rubbed the now cold skin as tears fogged his glasses. He removed his glasses and wiped his eyes with the back of his hand. He let out a thin sigh. His breath seemed to be caught in his chest, beating against his ribs.

A fly buzzed by Dominic's ear. He swatted at it, but missed, coming down heavily on the side of his head. His ear rang; his heart pounded like a volcano. With a heavy step, he moved back from Vito to make way for the undertaker, but he didn't let go of Vito's hand. He walked alongside his brother, rhythmically patting Vito's hand, then caressing it. He choked back a sob, until the gray dusk became night.

WHEN MAGGIE joined the mourners at Parrazzo's, she paid her respects to Vito's mother and to Lucy, whom she had gone to school with at PS 8. She was about to offer her condolences to Dominic, but she faltered, startled: he stared intently at the casket and seemed not to know where he was. His glasses, slightly askew on his face, magnified his red-rimmed eyes. Maggie turned and kneeled in front of the casket and said a prayer—not only for Vito but for Dominic too. His poor mother, she thought. Vito dead and Dominic looking more dead than alive. Vito had been good to his mother, who needed all the help she could get with four children to raise. Maggie knew Ralphie, Magdalena's husband, angry in the morning, angry at night when he returned home, cursing along the hallways as he lumbered to their fifth-floor apartment. Why do the good always die? Maggie wondered.

Maggie made way for the paid mourners, three women in black, hired in case no one showed up for the wake. She sat in the last row of folding chairs and watched the others who came to pay their respects. And that was when she saw a god and Sal Barnum too. His name wasn't really Sal Barnum. It was Salvatore Barone, also known as Sal Barnum, a Castle Garden official's best transcription of his father's name when he entered New York in 1883.

Sal wore a navy blue suit. His auburn hair was smoothed back, sleek. She saw him in profile, with a cigarette between his lips. The small mole on his straight nose made him look distinguished.

She didn't realize she was staring at him. She had been brought up not to look at boys. Her mother beat her once because she thought Maggie was wearing rouge, but she wasn't: she always had a high complexion. She caught herself staring and forced her eyes away from this man who looked like a god to her.

As Sal rose from the kneeler, he too walked to the last row of chairs. He sat next to Maggie and nodded to her. "I hope my cigarette doesn't bother you."

Maggie assured him it didn't. They sat for a while longer. He couldn't think of anything else to say. Her looks were making him tongue-tied. Rose, her older married sister, lived in his building so he knew Maggie even though he had never spoken to her before. Rose was a beauty too. Olive skin with cheeks a rosy tinge that made her name appropriate. But Maggie was something else: blonde, fair, high cheekbones, a serenity in her hazel eyes that made you want to know more about her and the mysteries she held.

When she rose from her chair and smoothed her skirt, Sal stood up too. He put out his cigarette and turned to face her, peering into her eyes. She gave just a hint of a shy smile. Was that an invitation?

"I live in the same building as your sister Rose," he began. "Can I walk you home?" She nodded. He took out another cigarette and tapped it on its silver case. "Sure you don't mind?" He held the cigarette in his lips, unlit, until they reached the sidewalk. Then he stopped, cupped his hand over the tip and lit up. The orange-red glow of the cigarette burned bright in the darkness. The night air was pleasant and the sky was particularly inky. Fireflies had drifted away from the park to send out their light to attract a mate.

Sal and Maggie walked along silently, his heart pounding. She mumbled something about how in the daytime the fireflies kept cool in the trees in the park. He murmured his agreement, though what he agreed to he didn't know. He was so nervous he was having trouble hearing. Or was it that his heart was pounding so loud. He could barely keep his cigarette from shaking and moved it swiftly from hand to hand. The burning tip streaked across the night like the glow of a firefly in motion.

"Look at that sliver of moon," he began. "It sure is beautiful."

Maggie nodded. "That's why the fireflies are out. . . . It's a dark night and they're here where it's darker than in the park with its lamplights," she said.

Their elbows touched; they continued strolling along in silence for a while, taking pleasure in being together and in the fireflies. The streets were mostly deserted except for an occasional neighbor sitting on a stoop enjoying the nighttime breeze and the evening hush. Sal and Maggie could hear faint strains of the aria, *Mi chiamano Mimi*, floating through an open window. Maggie hummed along softly. Sal cleared his throat.

"It's too bad about Vito," Sal said. "He was a hard worker. Who knows what he would have become?" He stared at the ground, thinking about Vito's lost future. He shook himself out of his reverie and then added, "His brother Dominic wants to be a doctor. But tonight he looked more like he needed one." Sal felt he was rambling.

They had reached Thompson Street where Maggie lived. "Isn't that the tenement where Fiorello La Guardia lives?" Sal asked, pointing to the one next door to Maggie's building.

Maggie said yes. "He's for people like us," she said. "He's making a name for himself . . . got elected to Congress."

"Who would have guessed it," Sal responded, "with a name like that, Fiorello? These names we have, they don't sound American. I dropped the 'e' off Salvatore to make it more American. And even though I was registered in school as Sal Barnum, I knew my name was Barone. I wouldn't change that."

Just as they reached the stoop of Maggie's tenement, Rocco seemed to come out of nowhere. Sal jumped back and made way for him. He quickly removed his hat in an exaggerated tip to Rocco.

"Maggie, I've been looking for you. Your mother said you'd be along any minute." He muscled Sal out of the way. Sal took another step back, faltered and dropped his half-smoked cigarette.

"Maggie," Rocco whispered, "I got something for you." He followed her up the steps. Sal hung back. Rocco stood a step below Maggie, his back to Sal. Maggie's face was visible over Rocco's head. She was looking intently at whatever it was Rocco was holding.

"Oh no," Sal heard Maggie saying. "That's awfully nice of you, Rocco, but what would *I* do with something like that?" She smiled sweetly.

Rocco moved up a step, on the same level now as Maggie. As he turned sideways, Sal could see the small jewelry box in his hand. "Here," he said emphatically, "take it. Whadaya mean, what would you do with it? You'd put it on your finger."

Maggie protested.

Sal took the stairs two at a time. "Isn't that your brother Louie out the window?" he asked. They all looked up. Sal put himself between Maggie and Rocco, careful to give him no offense. All three peered at the third story of the building.

Louie was indeed there. Maggie waved. Rocco retreated. Sal moved closer to Maggie. The fireflies glowed against the red brick building. He cupped his hands and caught one. He held it over her slim fingers like a living jewel, the heart of God beating between them. He wanted that moment to go on forever and only reluctantly let the firefly go.

Sal took Maggie's hands and enclosed them. His hands were trembling just a bit, but they were trembling. "You did a very brave thing, coming between me and that Rocco—and him a married man. You were smart about it . . . the way you said my brother was watching from the window. Not even Rocco would be disrespectful to a girl in front of her brother."

Sal said nothing. He motioned Maggie to keep her hands cupped. Then he caught another firefly and put it in her hands before opening the door for her. "I enjoyed our walk together."

"Oh, I did too," Maggie said. "So much. Thanks for walking me home."

Sal was encouraged. "Maybe we could go out another time . . . I know a nice restaurant."

Maggie said she'd like that a lot. He assured her he'd be in touch. Maggie whispered a good night. Her throat felt dry.

She had always wanted to hold a firefly, to see its light close up. Nobody had ever done that for her. She gazed at the firefly, glowing with life. Then she peeked out of the doorway and watched Sal walking down the street until he faded into the darkness, no longer visible. But it seemed to Maggie as if he had never left her and never would leave her. The firefly was the proof of the beauty in her life, a gift from heaven.

The wind came up, swirling the street debris of cloth scraps in ever faster and tighter circles and twists and chasing the fireflies back to the park with its trees, banging the cellar door and rattling the bakery store window until rain beat against the pavement.

Maggie took the firefly upstairs and placed it in a jar. The rain had abated a bit, falling more gently than before. She opened the window, unscrewed the lid of the jar and let the glowworm fly free to join its mates. As she watched its little light blinking in the navy sky, she was sure that her action would please Vito, and he'd be happy to know too that on this night Maggie had met Sal "Barnum" Barone and would no longer feel in-between.

Sizes

Joseph Papaleo

Fiction (1994)

"I DON'T CARE what you heard your girlfriend Mary told you. I don't think the Escort or the Chevette or the Rabbit or even the Cockroach, and I don't care what else you call them in Japanese, is not the right size, any of them."

"But I want a small car, Pa. You understand, *I want* a *small car* and not a big bazoom—though if you wanted to buy me a Merc, I wouldn't fight you."

"You, my dear, you think everything is the style and the color. Even the size to you is the style. But I am not talking about what's in style. I am talking about a chassis, a protection in the car you drive that's not just the pieces pasted together. *Gabeesh?*"

"Yes, I *gabeesh*," she said, her voice going down.

Her father did not pick up the appeasement in the tone and kept on. "A small car is like a paper tiger, you know what I mean? Pretty on the outside and tissue paper if you hit a dog." Her father assumed a stance. She knew it was his way of making the mood lighter. Denise examined him. She looked away from the wrinkles around his chin, like small knife cuts—the way a sheet of typing paper makes a cut. She watched the driveway lined with cars, her mother's large Mercury, Johnny's Camaro, and, at the end, her father's big black Mercedes. Her father was pacing before her like the dog when it wanted to go out.

She saw his tuxedo jacket pulling at his sides, as if he had two hip guards in place there. But he looked handsome in his white jacket. He had that look. He loved to go formal.

"Where is it you went out today?" she asked.

"Today was the first Cotillion at the club." The words were uncomfortable for him. "Your mother's vice president this year, so I had 'a look dressy. I didn't have a choice. It was daylight on the lawn."

"Don't kid me, you love it," Denise said.

He walked across the kitchen to his daughter and leaned down, almost touching her face: "And how come you know everything, you little peanut?"

She put her right finger on his nose. "Because I'm smarter than you, that's why. Didn't you know women are the superior breed?"

"That's what they tell me. Except with cars. How long before you all become automotive engineers?"

He walked to the refrigerator and opened the brown door. "Will you tell me if your mother still does any shopping around here? I can't find a glass of mineral water in here."

She saw his face lit up, left her chair and pushed him away from the door. "I knew it would be right in front of your nose. What is this green bottle?"

"The San Pellegrino."

"The San Pellegrino." Her repetition made her father smile like a boy, and she continued. "Listen, you are damn lucky I didn't ask you for a Mazda RX or a 280Z."

Her father sat where she had been sitting and watched her pour a glass full of the water. "You bet your sweet life," he said. "And you would get a Jap car over my dead body. This much I'll tell you right now. Nobody will take me on *that* trip again." He had the glass in the air and was shaking it for emphasis. "There's one mechanic who fixes it, he's in South Jersey, and the parts—they're in Poughkeepsie. For ten times the price of what we got here."

"But I still don't want a big load. I haven't starting smoking cigars yet, you know." She moved back by instinct and let her weight fall back on the sink.

Mr. Polero drank his water slowly and made her sweat. Then he said, "And now I got another comedian in the family. Listen to me, Joan Rivers. A medium car is not a big load, you know. Take a two-door. Go out and see some Chevvies. Take a look inside. GM is a sensible car."

Denise walked to the white archway that led to the dining room and the hallway. "And some little ones are sensible, too. Didn't Johnnie have a Fiat Brava a long time?"

"*Him*? *Him* you don't look at. And the Fiat Brava they don't even dare import anymore. But your brother and his friends, they can handle a breakdown on the road, they can tune a car, they can change points on the spot. For you, you want a dependable, solid thing in your hands."

"All right. But I read up on the Escort and the Lynx, which is the Mercury version. They have *heft*."

Her father assumed the pose again: she called him Mussolini many times when he was like this. "*Heft*?" he said. "And where did you learn that one?"

"Wouldn't you like to know?" Denise said.

"Look, Denise, do me a favor, will you? Don't get me too excited for once? And listen to me once in a while, at least about men things. Like maybe I had more *experience* in cars than your friend Mary has. And that I buy ten trucks at a time for my stores and maybe through the years I learned a little about cars you don't have to read up on?"

"I showed you the *Consumer's Guide*, Pa. And I asked you to discuss it. They have testers, engineers or whatever. Remember what they said first about the Honda, and then everybody who bought one said the same thing."

"And I'm telling you years of experience is worth more than some little magazine you buy. Don't you think those magazines take a little payoff from a company now and then to help the sales?"

"You said that about Ralph Nader, also without any facts. These organizations get letters every day from car owners—about what the cars do—and then they test—and test—"

"Denise, I swear to you." Mr. Polero stood up and placed his glass neatly on the cloth and looked at it. He said, slowly looking up, "Denise, let me tell you, I do not shoot my mouth off. I have talked many years with mechanics, friends of mine. I have thirty years of retailing under my belt. I talk when I *know* about something. The question I ask of *you* is why don't you trust me?"

She had begun to pace as he had earlier. "Because this is not a trust thing, Pop. You haven't yet said one bad factual thing about a small car. Not one thing. Give me a list of things that show they are worse than mid-size, for example. That's all I ask, give me a list. But your mind was made up in nineteen seventy-one. Nothing good could come out after then. So you don't even look at the little cars of today; you just condemn them."

"So is that what you think I am? He who condemns without looking?"

"No, I don't *think* that. I've been your daughter twenty-three years. And just go ask Momma."

"Ask your mother *what*? Ask the lasagna expert about compact and mid-size cars? Sometimes you make me sick, you know that? You all make me sick. No spit."

"Don't bring everybody into this. This is a simple thing between me and you."

"Me and you?" He looked at her, trying to feel his feelings. They all said she was his image in every way, but he did not see it. "You are a twenty-year-old snotnose—"

"Twenty-three and a half," she interrupted.

"Who talks to your father like he was an illiterate ditch digger too stupid to know the *Consumer's Union* which I knew before you was born."

"There he goes. Every time we have a disagreement, you pull out the wop stuff—"

"Don't use that word in my house."

"You taught me that word."

"Denise, I taught you nothing. No words to say to me like spit in my face."

"Thank God you taught me nothing, then."

"What did you just say?"

"I'm sorry, but that word came into my ears in this house, and I did not invent it. I never even knew I *was* something else."

"And what does that mean, *something else*?"

"Italian."

"You damn right you never knew. Because you never made one move for us."

"Who's *us*? Come on, what is this *us*? Don't put that one on me. There is no us, and you know it."

"I know it, but you don't believe it. Because it's not in Ralph Nader's book; they didn't review it in the *Consumer's*; it wasn't on sale this week in Caldor."

Denise stepped closer to the kitchen table and to her father. "Pop, sometimes I wish I could get you a good kick in the a—."

"Oh, very nice."

Denise turned on his words and went for the staircase, her steps becoming silent as she hit the rugs.

Her father followed; she stopped at the landing as he pointed a finger at her. "To a father, a girl says that right to his face. What should I say? I should say at least she's honest. I wonder, is there one thing left that I might know better about from experience than you? Like maybe how to flatten you on the floor with one punch? And the big mistake is that we stopped slapping your little fannies when you were growing up. You wouldn't of had those words inside your head to say to me."

"And maybe you just don't like it that I *have* the words to tell you that what you tell me about cars is unproved, undocumented—"

He held up both arms, hands out to her. "Stop with those words. Please? You are going too far. I feel my hands moving without me. I'm choking. I swear to God. I will lose my control. I will break your head open if you can't talk right to me."

"*Right*? What's *right* to you? You know what you mean by *right*? Forget it, I'm not saying it. I don't want you to get a stroke. Just forget the new car, all right, will you? Just forget the whole thing. I wanted to get the best buy. It's my money this time. I just wanted something that could take me to the hospital. Transportation. With no repair trouble. Which they all said was Toyota. And then the war started."

"Transportation. And that's what I want, too. That's all I always wanted." Mr. Polero was feeling dizzy. "Denise, that's why I went with you."

"But you wouldn't let me buy it. You didn't let me sign. You put your hand over the contract—"

"Because. Because I am trying to tell you that you was buying a little piece of junk. With paper dashboard and plastic grille."

"You do not buy a dashboard and grille for getting there."

Mr. Polero had reached the steps; now he smiled and stepped back, letting her go up a few steps. "You see, my dear, I did not want to buy it and feel humiliated in that showroom where I knew that man was giving you the business."

"And how did you think I felt?" She leaned over the banister. "How nice, the salesmen must have said. This little bird is his slave. This parrot. She buys whatever *he* wants. But I am paying this one off myself."

Denise continued up the steps. "It's better. If I need a little more, I'll take a loan."

"You know what?" His voice was calm as he looked upwards; the raising of his head calmed him somewhat. "They once told me, no matter what you do for them, they'll knife you in the end. They'll pick a stranger over you. And listen to *him*."

"And don't think I don't know what you think of *me*. You disapprove of everything I do. You're on my back as if I'm training to be a hooker. You spy on me like I'm in a drug ring. You look at Billy when he comes into this house—when he used to come because now I meet him outside this house. You treat him like he's some form of puke."

"There is no answer, my daughter. You just said you hate me, too. Listen to your own words. And you used to accuse me of causing all the troubles of the black man in this country because I never hired enough of them. I only tried to tell you what I learned from my mother and father. Either you live by a few things that are supposed to last or you go down the drain."

Denise stood on one carpeted step and looked ahead, taking her hands off the banister. "I just don't understand what you're talking about, so what's the use? Why bother? All we do is fight. We fight even when we're not fighting. I have to go to work tonight so I'm going up to do my hair and get dressed for work."

"Go right ahead, I'm not touching you."

He watched her go silently to the top landing and down the white hall. He turned and walked back to the kitchen. Then, still festering from the words, he walked out to the back garden and looked at the late afternoon light, a new redness that meant summer was on its way.

From the corner of his eye he picked up the spot glistening from the medallion of his Mercedes and walked to it at the back of the line of cars. He looked at it and the others and shook his head and walked back to the door and around the house to the front lawn. Up through the window above the entrance, he could see Denise in her room. He turned away quickly when he saw she was in her underwear with no top. He felt his face red and flushed. He went to the side of the house for the hose. He found it in the grass coiled near the spigot. He began spraying the lawn and put his head down when he came 'round front again.

When the water would not sink through the grass anymore, he shut off the hose and came inside and stood at the head of the staircase, quiet a few minutes before calling his daughter.

She came out; she was dressed and made up and looked like Blanche at that age. He spoke with as much calm as he could find: "I'll go with you for a car whenever you want. And keep my mouth shut all the time."

"What could we do, then, Pop? I don't want a big load, and you don't want a little dink."

He was smiling at her tone. "All right, why don't we take a look at the new mid-size Pontiac and the Olds they call Omega. They're supposed to be solid and also trimmed down small."

"You want to go *again*? Now?"

"I could drop you off at the hospital after we shop around, and you could take a cab tonight. Or I'll come get you."

Denise went for her purse in the kitchen and came back to the front, thinking plans. "Actually, you don't have to pick me up. I'll get Billy to do it. He's working late."

"Working? Late?"

"He's bartending at Mario's."

Mr. Polero turned his face away as soon as he was aware of his expression, but Denise caught it. She smiled and shook her head slowly. He mimicked her by nodding just as slowly. They both laughed. Then Denise put out her hand. "Peace? Shake," she said, and her father began to shake hands.

But as he took her right hand, she yanked him to her and kissed his right cheek. "I'm going to wait," she said, "as long as it takes for you to grow up."

He began his guilty boy's laugh again as he led her to his Mercedes at the end of the driveway.

An Etruscan Catechism

Mary Caponegro

Fiction (1997)

THE PRIEST PLOWS a straight line with the assistance of one white ox and one white cow, the furrow he makes acknowledged by all Etruscans as a sacred boundary. The city stands watching, reverent, attentive; the engineers stand ready to build and to tunnel. Then what sprouts up from the new-plowed earth? A flower? A rock? A colony of worms? No, a head; a baby's head, or rather face, grafted onto a white-haired head, is birthed from the earth, but attached to this head is a dwarf's stunted body. The body's hand thrusts something toward us: a book.

IT IS WRITTEN in The Book of Tages that the liver of the sacrificed sheep will be divided into four sections, which are each in turn divided into four, and these comprise the organ's outer edge only, within which still more divisions occur, repeating some of those found in the sixteen. The whole of the liver's houses' sum is forty-four, and each is affiliated with particular gods in the heavens.

WHO IS TAGES?

He is the source of Etruscan sacred law. He is unmistakable: a creature with the body of a dwarf, the smooth face of a child, and the head of an old man, who emerged from the soil like a beetle or worm to deliver our sacred knowledge.

WHAT IS THE NUMBER OF GODS IN THE HEAVENS?

The sum of our gods is sixteen.

WHERE ARE THE GODS LOCATED ON THE LIVER?

In all three regions of the northeastern quadrant we find Tinia, whose head squeezed out his goddess daughter, Menvra, at birth, winged and in full armor, bearing a shield. The liver's seat, meanwhile, is occupied by Ani Thne and Mulciber. Cetha is in the eighth, while Letham in the twelfth and thirteenth, comprises the Fates. In the sixteenth dwells Nocturnus, god of night. After many years of tactile practice, the haruspex's fingers know one god from another, even without the assistance of his eyes.

WHERE ARE THE SUN AND MOON LOCATED?

On the liver's underside which is divided into the two major divinities of sun and moon: Usils and Tivr.

HOW ARE THE BOLTS ASSIGNED TO THE VARIOUS GODS?

Nine gods are designated to hurl one or more of the eleven kinds of thunderbolts available. Tinia hurls three thunderbolts whereas Uni his wife hurls one.

WHEN DO THEY PERFORM THEIR ACTIVITY?

Menvra Cilens, guardian of the gates, hurls by night, and Sethlans and Mars participate as well. A trained haruspex does not have to make an equation but will know when the rumble or flash occurs, that this is the hand of Mars, or Tinia, that this bolt is Uni's sign. There will be no need to convert, it will be as quick as the flash itself, just as the calculation of a temple's length is automatic when its width is known, just as ejaculation of the gods is sure to send white shooting through the sky and cause the body of the mortal who receives it to tingle in a corresponding manner.

WHAT CAN THE GODS DO?

In addition to the hurling of thunderbolts and lightning, they are responsible for all fortune, good and ill, of mortals.

They can also do injury to each other, as did Sethlans—to his mother Uni— imprisoning her in the throne he built, and from which later he released her. They can decorate the sky in a variety of ways: make it awash with light, as when sleeping Hera's breast was wrenched in astonishment from the lips of full-grown suckling Hercules, spawning the milky way, or they can sear it with a lightning bolt from any arbitrary quadrant.

WHAT CAN AN ETRUSCAN DO?

Many things, both remarkable and unremarkable. An Etruscan can build and plan and drain, change the course of rivers, irrigate, navigate, play and dance persuasively enough to drive away the plague, if for instance called upon by unsuccessful Roman neighbors, less renowned in arts of movement, creativity and divination—neighbors who might prove useful in Etruscan games when blood is required to appease the ghosts of our ancestors. This is required only on special occasions, however, whereas on any given day an Etruscan, male or female, is likely to wear a tebennos if a man, and a chiton only partially covering his body; a lightweight longer pleated tunic if a woman. Both are likely to step every morning into handsome red shoes high in back and pointy in front, or bronze thonged high-soled sandals. A man might have a beard or shave, perhaps wear a toque; a woman might braid or coil her hair, or have tight curls to frame her face, or plaited hair tucked into a cap. She would likely toast her husband and his friends, drink wine, write and read. But there is more than this to what Etruscans, male and female, do. He or she can import joy to every movement. He or she can make of any gesture music. He or she can even make a dance of defecation.

IS THERE ANYTHING AN ETRUSCAN CANNOT DO?

An Etruscan cannot avoid the will of the gods. He or she cannot see the dawn rise over the sea. In certain instances he cannot avoid the aggression of animals if the gods will his defeat or if he is distracted by more urgent sensations than his fear. For example, he cannot defeat a dog if the dog is at his heel and driven by another man, while his senses are impeded by a hood over his head. It is without question better to wear a head punctuated by a haruspex's pointy hat, aligned with heaven, than to wear a hat of humiliation, that shrouds the victim's face, and makes vulnerable the entire body underneath. Even more desirable would be to have the head of a god which sprouts another fully formed tiny god as hat, a hat which thus has limbs and wings and shield and even helmet.

But one might wish to have no head at all, when in the midst of being entered from behind, he suddenly finds himself nearly face-to-face with the horn of an oncoming bull. In such instances irony might cause an Etruscan to smile, displaying the beautifully worked gold dentistry for which we are widely known. For no other reason, in fact, than to bridge his teeth may an Etruscan import gold into his tomb. And most importantly of all, golden-mouthed or otherwise, an Etruscan cannot under any circumstances avoid abduction to the underworld by the fierce pair Charun and Telulcha. Irony might cause an Etruscan to smile, when after importing her many bronze mirrors and cosmetic boxes, spatulae and jewels, and carefully plaiting her hair, her escort to the underworld is a harpy-haired creature whose hideous snakes snarl her braids, whose donkey ears and vulture face and blue skin are far more dramatic than any style she could concoct by means of the aforementioned accouterments. If the hammer in Charun's hand suspended over her skull paralyzes her in fear, however, she is unlikely to smile, swiftly noting that the persuasiveness of his tool makes a mockery of any weapon bulging from the tomb's wall, articles all carefully fashioned for her comfort and protection, as she surrenders to an irony more literally striking.

WHAT CAN A HARUSPEX DO TO MEDIATE
BETWEEN THE GODS AND MEN?

In general, observe, interpret and advise, and from these three come all the more specific gestures. He relies upon his hands and eyes, to read the signs that populate the sky and to interpret with his fingers imperfections on the liver's surface.

LET US REVIEW.

By the height of his hat a haruspex connects us to heaven. By the breadth of his knowledge he answers our questions: reminds us the length and the width of our temple is equal; he records the location and number of birds in the sky at all times, the number of bolts thrown from heaven between dusk and dawn by the gods. Furthermore he distinguishes which god threw which bolt; furthermore he is never in error.

HOW DOES HE AVOID ERROR?

Would you mistake a cock for a turd, simply because one enters where the other exits, or because the posture of a man receiving the former and excreting the latter is in some cases similar? Would you mistake a dwarf for a haruspex, or a horse for a fish, or a whip for a flute, or the earth for the sea, simply because you inhabit land and water with equal pleasure? Surely you would not confuse west with east or you could never be a haruspex (for all Etruscans know that good fortune derives from the east, and all that derives from the west is unfavorable). Can a bird be a fish? And yet there are times when a horse becomes fish: when each lends half its nature to a third hybrid creature. A man is, however, less likely to ride such a beast; his knees might lose their grip and his body slide off; instead of meeting the barrier of horse's haunches he'd find himself straddling a slippery tapering cylinder. That is our mascot: hippocampus. There are, however, far worse fates than to feel the horse between one's legs become fish, for an Etruscan is also intimate with water, and rides its waves as well as he rides land. It is preferable, for instance, to ride a hippocampus than to be a slave in disfavor, although even a slave in disfavor is not denied the lyre's consolations. One need not be a haruspex to know that in Etruruia no scourging occurs unaccompanied by double flute or lyre or castanets, though perhaps this is custom rather than law. And yet when the creature who emerges from the soil to give our sacred laws has an old man's head, a dwarf's body and the smooth unlined face of a child, we know a force of strangeness drives the world, a force we raise our arms and leap into the air to meet; we bend our bodies forward, even contort ourselves to greet the strangeness that compels us as our nature.

IS THE HARUSPEX EXCLUDED FROM THESE REVELS?

The haruspex is not excluded from our revels, but he cannot be a full participant in celebration, as we have designated him observer. His eye must miss nothing, and his hands must not be occupied with trifles, not with kneading or beating time for he must count the duration of thunderclaps, and his feet cannot either be captured by music, for they must be placed one at right angle to the other on the boulder that likely as not is a meteor sent us from heaven. Thus he must at all times offer full attention to his sacred tasks. He must observe all that pertains to his concerns, and of line—be it crooked or jagged or straight—he remains the undisputed legislator.

BUT TELL ME WHAT USE HAS THE HARUSPEX
FOR THE CURVE OF A CAPE?

Its red fabric draped over shoulder or hip, what use for the curve of a wrestler's firm thigh harmonized with the elegant shapely libation dish placed between himself and his opponent: two wrestlers who lock forearms as they struggle to declare the victor, gazing only at each other, and not at the birds overhead or the augur gesturing toward the birds as he interprets their flight, or the pair of less equally matched opponents to his right: one sighted, one blinded, a dog in between, the latter clearly disadvantaged: one man at the mercy of man and beast?

Indeed, what would cause a haruspex to dwell on the convexity of the boxer's belly, a curve which to the Romans is displeasing, suspicious—like the curve of our slightly slanted eyes—but to us, Etruscans, sensuous, perhaps less relevant to the haruspex than the surprising convexity of an implement or artifact that protrudes from the wall, placed there by those we love, to give ballast as we approach the underworld.

IS IT THE TASK OF THE HARUSPEX TO FURNISH
OR DECORATE THE TOMB? IS IT HE WHO
CHOOSES ITS OCCUPANTS?

No, he only counsels, he does not choose the wreath or vase or parasol, those greaves or axe or helmet, rope or wooden tray, and he might echo our sentiments when we remark, how curious to find a wall tumescent instead of flat. For what is a wall if not a surface to lean against after too much dancing or too much wine, after the exertion of blowing into the mouth of the bronze trumpet or dispatching a rapid succession of exhalations into the double flute, or in the wake of a sensation of communion so overwhelming that it makes of two humans for moments a third hybrid creature, and whose aftermath of closure requires a surface to lean upon in order to reconstitute their separate selves.

HOW CURIOUS INDEED THAT THE UNFLAT
WALL ERUPTS IN SHAPES

which I do not mean to disconcert but to console, such as the shield to protect from the blows of Charun's hammer which is poised to deliver the blow that abducts her to the underworld, against which there is very little even the haruspex can do to intervene, as it was not he, in the first place, if what you say is true, who deposited her there.

This is exactly so. For all his powers of concentration, all his knowledge and training, he cannot change the will of Herc or Menvra, Fulfuns, Uni; the gods will what the gods will, and the role of the haruspex is not to intercede but to advise. "Abase yourself to Silens who sent this bolt," he might suggest, or "Beg mercy from Sethlans who is displeased with you, perhaps because of where you stood a certain time of day, and do not forget that lightning could strike twice from different sectors, for some gods, like Tinia, occupy more than one house."

BUT WAS THAT NOT HE WHO SEATED
THE COUPLE AT THE TABLE?

Or reclined them on their brocaded banquet couch; was that not the curve of her body in his arms, drapery of her tunic flowing, as he set her on the sarcophagus, was he not placing her upon the hard bed, laying her head gently on the stone pillow? I heard he even set the banquet table, fastening the miniature cluster of grapes made of bronze at her earlobe, and braided her hair, and placed a book in her hand for her journey.

You are mistaken, for all the while he stands with left foot on boulder, left hand on left knee, right foot at right angle while right hand reads the dark eviscerated meat. The only ornament he touches is the fibula he fastens at his neck. The only fabric draping is his own pleated tunic; he never fingered the soft fleshy part of her lower ear, he holds only the lobes of the liver draped over his palm.

YOU ARE SO CERTAIN OF THE HARUSPEX'S ACTIONS. TELL
ME THEN AND BY WHAT METHODS EXACTLY, AS HE HOLDS
THE LOBES, MIGHT HE AVOID ERROR?

It is a matter of comparison, when over and over a sheep submits to slaughter, such that liver begets liver and organ after organ is compared with the memory of another, prior, repository of signs, which in contrast to what the uninitiated might suspect, do not blend, and become one, but rather gain distinction in their sequence; each astoundingly unique. Thus while other citizens before dawn dream in bed or linger at the banquet table, noting only casually, for beauty's sake, the moon and stars' illumination, cast upon the delicate divergences of flesh rotating wife to servant, husband, lover, toasting each other with bucchero cups and libation dishes, consuming grains and olives, fish and game, then still sated, arranging themselves on their couches or retiring to their private chambers drinking from more secret vessels, thinking in their lovers' hubris, in one organ I can read the universe; even more so can the haruspex who, elsewhere stands, solitary, angled in dawn's nascent light to touch again and again that extracted organ divided meticulously into houses though removed from its own house.

BUT WHAT THEN IS A BODY?
A WHOLE DIVIDED INTO PARTS?

A body is, in part, the breast or testicle the festive lover weighs in a hand and exclaims over, boasting, to the other banqueting guests, although it can also be that of her which is hidden under a costume's folds when dancing, that of him more likely visible, or the part of Hera which the mouth of Hercules sought even full grown (and which ejaculated milk into the sky as statement of surprise) or the four burgeoning pendulous udders of the leopard who has borrowed the teats of the cow.

In certain instances a body is comprised of both twinned parts of the creature that supports itself erect in front with legs and swims behind, galloping and flapping in a single gesture.

IF A BODY IS DIVIDED INTO PARTS THEN CAN A SINGLE PART ITSELF DIVIDE?

Yes, for instance, a head can be both that which sprouts snakes from a vulture's face and droops a donkey's ears, in the case of the creature who is half of the pair that escorts an unfortunate Etruscan to the underworld: a creature who proliferates parts, for he wears many beasts as a head: a head that perhaps might continue to undulate while his body reposed, were he ever to sleep, and give our people respite from intimidation.

Alternatively, one part can flower into a secondary whole, as in the story of the god who excreted a goddess from his head in birth. Whereas usually we find wedged between the head and feet a trunk; in this case head supports another's feet and not the feet one's own head.

More disquieting still is a situation in which a man finds himself in the center of a collision from both ends as he faces a charging bull, when that part of another man behind him which visits his rear is divided itself into body and head; is a rod with a hat and its hat called head, so that man in the middle serves as a wedge between horned head of beast and headed horn of a man, the latter which in effect fastens for moments a tail to the man's tail (as the two men fleetingly craft of themselves a third hybrid creature that is, alas, even in its ingenuity hardly a match for the bull). Thus all of the man between tail and head comprises a wedge between two forces, one brutal, one benign.

BUT COULD IT NOT BE THAT THE HUMAN PLEASURE IS ATTRIBUTABLE ONLY TO THE SECOND MAN?

And that he in fact forces that pleasure on the first man, and that perhaps the bull, sensing the victim's distress, approaches to lick his face and not to ravage? Perhaps he will leap over him to assault the man behind him? Furthermore, what of the considerably paler third creature, faintly visible, whose back is supported by the back of the kneeling man. Is it woman, man, or beast?

I can see nothing you describe, although it compels. But allow me to finish. Most curiously, and disturbingly of all, a head can be more than divided, erased: when it is that part of an Etruscan which is hardly visible because it is covered with a hood, as in the case of a participant in funeral games: a man pursued by a dog who tugs at the leash held by a second man who follows close behind and seems to make no effort to restrain the creature whose teeth sear the flesh of the barefoot man's calf—the second man seeming in fact to use the leash of the dog to restrain not the dog but the man, who cannot—despite the all but useless cudgel in his hand, entangled, as it is, like ankle, shoulder, wrist in a red rope that flowers in the collar around the dog's neck—arrest this abuse, retaliate or defend himself, in part because his senses are impeded by the hood which he, not by his own choice surely, has covered his head, and which like ankle, shoulder and wrist, is ensnared by the binding red line.

CAN A DOUBLE FLUTE WALK?

Two cylinders poked with holes? More easily than can this man after his arduous participation in the game the gods chose for him to play and we sought fit to set to music.

AND WHAT OF THE HARUSPEX WHO PLUCKS FROM ONE WHOLE ONE PART, ONLY FURTHER TO DIVIDE HIS PRIZE, OSTENSIBLY TO REPRESENT A GREATER WHOLE? WHAT IS HIS RELATION TO THESE PARTS?

Obviously a haruspex would have less desire to ride the exuberant curve of a dolphin's sleek back as it decorates the sea, than to attend to the arc of the bird that the augur, hand to forehead in a gesture of mourning, watches, beside the doors to the underworld. What use for the arc of the stone that is hurled from the boy's slingshot, as he stands poised with bent knee behind him and the toe of the forward leg curling over a precipice, without fear or awkwardness, at the bird about to be eliminated from the flock which soars above him, and may in its diminution bode ill for his future, but only the haruspex can discern, not the boy, surely not the boy, as he stands joyfully oblivious on a precipice above the boat over whose hull leans another boy who dangles his red, precisely measured line, held slack between two hands, pinched at each termination between thumb and forefinger, lowered into the green of the sea's banquet, while from another precipice plunges the diver's body, headfirst, about to penetrate the wet surface adjacent to the site of the boy's line as his feet uphold the sky. He does not question if the water will receive him; he assumes his welcome, like a fish.

WHAT SIGNIFICANCE IS ASCRIBED TO THE HEIGHT OF A HAT, THE LENGTH OF A COCK, THE NUMBER OF BIRDS OR OF BOLTS IN THE SKY,

the duration of rumbling over our heads that our feet feel, our ears hear but that cannot be seen? The length and the width of the temple, the depth of the tomb—

itself a product of skilled engineering—the distance from object to object affixed to the wall of the tomb, the depth of the diver's plunge into the sea, the distance the stone in the boy's slingshot travels, the size of the dancing man's turd, the duration of and distance between each pitch when the subulo places his mouth on the hole and sends breath through to please us, to balance the sound of the whip's repetition, the cries of the woman or man being beaten, the moans of the boar and the deer as the net ensnares?

Your questions, your questions, I am suddenly weary of so many questions!

WHAT IS THE SIGNIFICANCE OF THE
NUMBER OF PRISONERS TAKEN IN BATTLE

and only later slaughtered as offering to appease the ancestors, and thus indirectly the gods, in the hope that less lightning derive from the west, that the shed blood of Romans will mitigate wrath and elicit their favor, that the shed blood of Romans will serve as deterrent, as surrogate, sparing Etruscan blood?

I do know that no activity, be it brutal or benign, should lack the sweetness of music. Music can act as the smooth unlined face of a child to sweeten a stunted withered body; music can make a whole of a half-horse half-fish.

AND WHAT IS THE RELATION OF THE HARUSPEX TO MUSIC?

While all around him move in a continuum of revelry and celebration, performing ordinary daily gestures, in attitudes of reverence, love, or recklessness, brutality and viciousness, exalted or quotidian, he is stationary; he does not beat with sticks or flutter fingers clicking castanets, or thrum a lyre. Nor does he bake or knead or stir or drop a line into the sea. He does not hurl a stone at bird or fish or beat with club or wrestle an opponent. Neither does he sip from a libation dish at banquet table; he is unlikely to enfold a man or woman in his bed, and does not dance unless the subtle movements of his fingers are a dance.

WHAT ARE THE QUESTIONS MOST OFTEN ASKED OF THE
HARUSPEX, AND WHAT IS THEIR TONE?

Desperate or importunate, most likely. For example: "What shall I place in my tomb to accompany me to the life below, and to whom shall I make a votive offering so as to right the consequences of the thunder's damage, and what tune shall I bid the subulo play as I scourge the servant for his misdeeds, and where shall we place the sacred furrow to declare the boundaries of the city . . . ?"

THESE ARE RELENTLESS. ARE THERE NO
SOFTER VOICES FOR THE HARUSPEX TO HEAR?

At times, he might hear voices such as this: O haruspex, I seek your counsel: tell me, if you hear, what sector of which god's will has led me to this place? What is its name? All is familiar yet I feel unmoored, unsure. Shall I have my parasol in my tomb? My comb, how many mirrors, haruspex? My lovely boxes of cosmetics in the shape of beasts? My earrings? Bracelets? Diadem? Will it ever again be warm enough to warrant my unfolding the fan folded into this wall of my tomb, my tomb, like some vertical table which houses familiar objects that comfort? Am I one among the dead then? When will life turn to death turn again? Will it turn to the Styx and return me from that brackish mirror to gaze in the one whose polished surface will offer a woman some centuries older, whose hair worn in ringlets, is now worn in braids, whose hair is coiled round, whose myths etched in bronze on the backs of these mirrors have entertained her for all the hours she spent of her lives braiding or coiling or curling, adorning neck and wrists, fastening jewelry and painting her face more often than not for the man who once done with the nubile obliging servants would find her again in the bed, interrupting her reading, to read all the lines of her flesh. And she said to him often, I confess to you now, "your hands are so knowing, so gentle, if I loved the Etruscans, my people, more than my own pleasure I would insist you enter the vocation of the haruspex, caressing the liver of sheep after sheep as intently, as tenderly, sensuously, as you caress me."

LET US REVIEW.

Again and again you plunge your hand into the interior cavity. Dawn and again you enter, another dawn and you enter to find yet another answer to a question not yet formulated; forage with your practiced hand in a warmth that still remembers life though life has left it, a life whose bleating you recall beseeching you, you who cannot spare one or another creature when the gods require you read a larger picture quietly encoded on the surface of this particular liver that once ruled its body now a larger measure: index of the universe. A sheep cannot expel the liver without the stewardship of your practiced hand, and thus you enter to inseminate and exit immediately with an afterbirth that is, in effect, your only child.

WHAT RESPONSES IS A HARUSPEX LIKELY TO GIVE TO THOSE ETRUSCANS WHO ARE BESET BY MISFORTUNE?

He must be sober but not lugubrious, for one can always abase oneself and hope for better in the future. It is necessary to remind the aggrieved who seek his counsel that all heaven's light cannot be from the east, and neither will all be from the west; misfortune will befall some citizens as surely as the dice will eventually display each of its faces: each of the letters that spell out our numbers, and for each misfortune and each fortune there is origin and we must honor all signs that come from the gods; we must not favor only those which favor us, for that would comprise only half a cosmos.

IS THE ACCRETION OF MISFORTUNES BURDENSOME TO THE
HARUSPEX? FOR EXAMPLE, DOES HE NEVER WISH IF TIME
ALLOWED HIM TO INDULGE IN PLAY AS OTHER CITIZENS,
PERHAPS TO RECOMMEND TO THEM THESE DISTRACTIONS
IN CONJUNCTION WITH THEIR OFFERINGS TO THE GODS?

What possible use to the haruspex, who performs specialized tasks of gravity, to
follow the curve of the discus thrown by a young man who eventually with great
skill will extinguish the candle's flame in this manner, competing with his friends
who take their turns to accomplish the questionable objective until the room is
dark, altogether dark, with no bright tongue flickering to draw the eye; this is
indeed an idle game and he would not disparage it, but he would have time neither
to participate nor observe the haphazard curve in the earth made by the violent
wheels steered by the charioteer, who if he is a young reckless man wraps the
reins about his waist, causing them to encircle his form rather than be pulled taut
and straight, thus creating a crease in the earth chaotic in comparison to the
sacred furrow of the haruspex with his one white bull one white cow as he sits
somber under his tall hat driving a straight path almost all the way to the gates,
clods turning inward always toward the city, knowing that Tages once greeted
our people through just such earth to give the laws that dictate the very line he
now creates. Clearly a man who drives the sacred plow does not perform ostenta-
tious feats for entertainment or for competition; his concern is rather that
unswerving line carefully etched into soil and terminated just short of the gates,
so as to allow the unclean gods entrance and exit, for in this manner are the
boundaries designed, and the city consecrated.

DOES THE HARUSPEX SEE ALL THINGS?

A haruspex, though mediator to them, is neither god nor godlike in his perspicac-
ity, focused on the signs before his eyes; all that is peripheral is useless to him:
the crowds gathered to celebrate the city's consecration do not divert his gaze
from the furrow. For instance, he would not once squint into the distance beyond
these newly designated city limits, to take notice of the horizontal horn of a
man's lower body as it enters from the west the furrow of the curved buttocks of
the man who, bent before him, faces the horn of a beast from the east, an oncom
ing bull who was never yoked to the plow of the haruspex; in any case, it is as if
the pleasure of what enters from behind could save the man from what confronts
him face to face perhaps to rend his chest—although in another situation the
beast might just as easily turn away disinterested in the spectacle before him
when he reaches the man, now on his knees before his thrusting partner, who on
first glance thrusts in air, but upon closer scrutiny enters a very pale figure barely
visible, whose back is supported by the kneeling man. In any case, and in all, it is
for the gods to dictate.

WHY WOULD THIS MAN NOT ATTEMPT TO FLEE?

He will not likely flee, the man, for we are a people who roll the dice even as famine demands more sober measures, even as the thunder in our bellies competes with the sky, for we know that pleasure must never concede to danger or hardship. We play before planning, leap in lamenting; we'd rather dance to drive away the plague than mourn. This is our solution, our equation, just as length and width of temple is a given, so this measure offers balance. And while there is perhaps no respite for the middle man, he would nonetheless prefer to remain as he is, bent and yielding, vulnerable and aroused, to keep his position intact rather than exchange his fate for the fate of the man with shrouded head who has pleasure neither from creature nor human. Even the feeble reed the buggered man clutches is more solid than the cudgel held by the hooded man, entangled in the long red line that, while it blossoms in the canine collar, baits him, without mercy, like a fish.

AND WHAT OF YET ANOTHER MAN ON THE OTHER SIDE SIMILARLY POSTURED, BENT FORWARD BUTTOCKS JUTTING, HIS FOOT RAISED AS IF TO INITIATE SOME RHYTHMIC SEQUENCE? IS HIS ACTIVITY OF CONCERN TO THE HARUSPEX?

Continue to observe that man and you will see he merely augments the soil by offering to earth his plosive turd (as the brass trumpet somewhere sounds) not to be confused with the clods of soil turned always inward, lifted and moved if they fall outside the city's boundaries. However, if the haruspex, as he turned all the clods of soil in toward the city, discovered the careless man's turd, you can be sure his finger would find later, on the next liver over which he lingered, a mark indicting him.

CAN FATE TRULY BE DETERMINED THROUGH THESE SUBTLE INDICATORS?

Yes, from a mark on the liver or streak in the sky, swiftly etched and then just as swiftly retracted by the gods, never fixed in the manner of an image etched on a mirror's bronze back or letters scratched in papyrus: written, rather, in air; all the signs written in air on a tablet so dark and soft it has no edge, with a shape neither round nor square, a texture between solid and liquid, a substance consisting entirely of contour.

THEN IT TRULY IS OF CONSEQUENCE WHICH PART OF SKY THE BIRDS INSCRIBE AT DUSK, AT DAWN?

This question you can answer for yourself by now. We must conclude. I must be about my business.

I WILL ASK NO MORE IF YOU WILL TELL ME WHAT IS THE MOST TERRIBLE SECRET HARBORED BY THE HARUSPEX?

If you must be sated, I will answer. When the lightning tells him more than we might wish to know and when the birds squawk even at night and when the liver seems too densely inscribed with signs then who is he, he wonders, mere haruspex, to tell them that the very gold that crowns her teeth will one day, after Etruscans are no longer, be extracted like a liver from a sheep and all the carefully selected items plundered, subtracted one by one; the sweet, diverting stories borrowed from the Greek etched on the back of her bronze mirrors silenced as they melt back down to metal, their lump sum of origin; in the same manner that a trumpet's blustering wind might obliterate the ephemeral intoning of the lyre's strings, these stories will succumb to the bold raw lettering that spells SUTHINA on the polished surface. For is it not an indivisible sum and the most reliable of measures, that we who are expert at navigation and manipulation of all waters, at tunneling, sewage and hydraulics, cannot for all our mastery, divert the course of the River Styx?

Lamb Soup

Tony Ardizzone

Fiction (1997)

Ciccina Agneddina

EVER SINCE NONNA NEDDA, the toothless, blind old grandma who could fore-tell your marital future after you prepared for her a bowl of soup, informed my dear mamma that I was destined by age eighteen to marry a man riding a dappled horse, I feared that I'd end up with the disgusting *gabbillotu*.

You had to stir the soup with your little finger after the broth was poured into a bowl. This was after you invited the old woman to your house. You had to sweep the floor and shoo out all your brothers and sisters as well as any animals. Even though she could see less well than a moss-covered rock, if you had a rack of candles Nonna Nedda expected them to be lit. She sat on your best chair, and for an hour you were supposed to engage her in gossip while the soup that was about to reveal your fate simmered over the fire. Mamma had me tend the pot. In it she'd put a whole onion and some herbs and three handfuls of beans. Nonna Nedda was said to prefer bean soup over broth made with only a bit of onion and greens. That's what we usually ate: soup made of boiled onion and greens.

The women chatted about one of the village's farmers, Don Ricci, who owned a piece of extremely good land and whose goats that past spring were said to have had seven babies.

"Seven goats!" Mamma announced brightly, as if she'd given birth to them herself.

"Humph," Nonna Nedda said, perched on our three-legged stool. The black dress she perpetually wore clung to her rolls of fat like a shadow. Stuffed in their black stockings, her legs hung down to the ground like a pair of dark sticks. "You've seen these goats with your own eyes?"

"No, Nonna," Mamma said, "but he's shown all seven to others I know in the village."

"His goats had ten or more," said Nonna Nedda. She rolled her head wildly, then sniffed the air like a hound. "At least three real strong ones, which he keeps out of sight."

"Ahh," my mamma said, nodding. "The hen's unseen eggs are never stolen."

"He throws the stone," Nonna Nedda said, "yet hides his hand." She flut-tered her dead eyes. A finger stretched out across the room and pointed out at me. "The beans are nearly soft enough. Bring me your little lamb."

Agneddina, Little Lamb, was my nickname, an endearment my father bestowed on me when I was still on all fours. He gave each of my brothers and sisters nicknames of animals, too. In our family there was Little Monkey, Little Butterfly, Little Parrot, Little Owl Eyes, Little Weevil, Little Bat, Little Turkey, Little Red Fox, Little Gray Mouse. Sometimes when he called all of us into the house you'd think he was wise Noah loading the ark. If ever I tarried or came near to disobeying him he'd put on a serious face, point to my hair, and ask if I wished to be fleeced.

"Shall I pour Nonna the bowl of soup now, Mamma?" I called.

She didn't answer. Instead the fat old crow on the stool wagged her head no, then curled her gnarled fingers in the air. Her fingers were the tips of branches of trees that were too ancient and dry to bear any more leaves. Her arms were rotting tree trunks that wanted to leap out of the forest and fall on top of you. I stood before the old sausage, trying not to stare at the straggly dark whiskers sprouting on her chin and the thick tufts of hair generously protruding from her ears as well as the gaping nostrils of her immense nose.

She ran her claws up my arms, over my shoulders and across my chest, down my back and rump, over my hips, then between the middle of my legs, all the time saying, "My, my, my." Believe me, I don't think the old woman had ever known a washtub. Behind me Mamma smiled with approval as she spooned all the beans she could gather into the woman's bowl.

"She's fine," announced Nonna Nedda, "though quite far from perfect. She's too skinny, though she's getting nice and firm on top here where you want a young girl to be round. But these hips—" She stuck her tongue forward and smacked her gums. "These hips should be a bit broader. Warn the midwife. She'll be in for a hard time with the first baby." Again she clawed my arms. "She's fourteen years, you say? She'll be plucked and gone from your tree in four more. Already I can tell her plum's ripe and sweet." The old thing's talons patted me between my legs, then gave my cheek a fierce pinch.

"I was skinny at her age, too," my mamma said.

"She's skin and bones," Nonna Nedda sneered.

"She never goes without. We feed her all we can."

"And what do you do when all is not enough?" The old woman paused. "Tell me, does she eat dirt at night?"

"Never," I said.

"A spoonful every now and then would help her bones." She pointed around the room, then patted my shoulders. "Look for a nice soft spot in the wall. You don't have to eat a lot. A mouthful twice a week will be enough. With it, drink fresh water until you feel your belly swell."

The thought of eating the walls of the house was so ridiculous I put my hand to my mouth and laughed.

By this time Mamma had ladled out the bowl of soup. I stirred it with my little finger before handing it to the old witch, praying that she would say I was destined to marry someone gentle and handsome, with kind eyes, like my papa, whose skin was as clear as the inside of an almond shell, and whose drooping moustache tickled whenever he kissed me, and who at night sometimes would comb out my long hair and not hurt me by pulling the comb's teeth too quickly down through the thousand and one snarls in my hair. As the old woman took the first sip of soup, I prayed that she'd predict that the man would be from a village nearby rather than from somewhere far away so that I could visit my family as often as I wanted and care for my parents when they were old or if ever one of them were to be alone.

Instead Nonna Nedda said she saw water, and lots of it, so much that it was gathered in great white-tipped waves that rolled and spilled wildly back and forth on top of themselves.

I immediately guessed she meant the African Sea, which my eyes had never actually seen but about which my ears had heard numerous tales. Monsters with eight long arms and a thousand and one mouths were said to live within the sea, along with creatures with wings so huge some men used them as sails. There were fish whose top fins were as sharp as saws, able to cut boats in half. Other fish had swords as snouts. Some fish had such big bellies and mouths they could swallow a whole house. I knew the story about Nick Fish, the famous boy from Messina whose mother's accidental curse transformed him into half fish, half human. Perhaps I'd wed a boy like him, I thought. Perhaps I'd marry a *piscaturi*.

At once Nonna Nedda shook her head no, as if in answer to my thoughts. She opened her eyelids and held the sides of my head, her sightless white eyeballs spinning up and down inside her skull.

"He rides a dappled horse," she said. "He's a man of belly, *un'omu di panza*. There is even more water."

"Blackest of days!" I cried. "A dappled horse!"

My poor mamma gasped, fell back several steps, then crossed herself.

I pictured the only dappled horse in the province, the overseer's dappled gelding. I fell to my knees, at once sobbing. "No!" I cried, "not the *gabbillotu*! No, no, not him! Oh, Nonna Nedda, please say it's anyone but him!"

"*Sali*," was all she would reply.

All the blind crow would say further was to ask my anguished mother for a pinch of salt for the beans and onion that lay heaped in the bottom of her bowl like the mound of stones topping a grave.

EVEN THE WALLS one is told to eat have ears. Within the day, word of my cursed fortune spread. The fastest animal on one leg is the gossip's tongue.

With the exception of the old baron, the *gabbillotu* was the most evil man in the village. Like a piece of thickly varnished wood, the *gabbillotu* acquired his many layers of evil gradually, coat by coat by coat. It was said that as a boy he had a penchant for inventing torments for the Almighty's most helpless creatures. He captured the happy cricket and pulled off its notched legs. He set fire to the butterfly's wings. He netted the contented cod and chortled as it thrashed and drowned in the horrible air. He cracked the proud, noble shell of the land turtle's house. With a sharpened stick he poked holes in the eggs of songbirds, then filled the shells with ants. He fashioned a whip of thorned vines and tortured the passing mole, field mouse, and hedgehog. Whenever he came across someone younger or smaller, he threw dirt in the child's eyes, then beat the poor thing's face until the child cried.

To become a *gabbillotu* you have to convince the estate owner that you can be vicious enough with the peasants to squeeze them of every last measure of their labor. You have to turn your living heart from flesh to leather, then from leather into the most unfeeling stone. This path begins with mistreating God's most helpless creatures.

Years ago the baron noticed the boy's talents and asked if he ever considered becoming an overseer. The baron invited the boy to take the test each *gabbillotu* apprentice must pass. The boy was ordered to tend a garden of nettles and thorns, in the middle of which lay a gentle tomcat whom the baron commanded to assist the apprentice in whatever ways he could. Each day for a month the apprentice carefully watered the weeds and pulled up the roots of any stray wildflowers that happened to blow in on the edge of summer's hot winds. Then the master denied the apprentice all further use of his well. The weeds immediately began to wither in the sun and constant heat.

"Oh, what shall I do?" cried the apprentice.

From the center of the nettles the cat answered. "Have you any human feelings?"

"Yes," replied the apprentice, looking perhaps for the first time into his soul. "I have sorrow and sorrow's expression, tears." So the boy thought of the dying weeds and wept, and in this way was able to water the baron's garden. The apprentice's tears lasted for three days. But after he'd drained himself empty, the master's weeds again began to wilt.

"Oh, what shall I do?" cried the apprentice.

From the center of the nettles the cat answered. "Have you any human feelings?"

"Yes," replied the boy, looking again into his soul. "I have empathy and its metaphor and expression, blood." So the apprentice thought of the thirsty nettles and cut open his chest and bared his heart, and in this way was able to water the garden. Again this lasted for three days. But after he'd drained himself empty, the master's weeds again began to wilt.

"Oh, what shall I do?" cried the apprentice.

From the center of the nettles the cat answered. "Have you any human feelings?"

"No," replied the apprentice, looking into the now-dark void where once his soul resided. "I have no more sorrow or tears. I have no more empathy or blood. All is dry and withered within me. I am a desert of endless sand. I have no liquid left in me, nothing wet within my soul with which I might be able to water the master's weeds."

"If you have no human feelings, then perhaps you're no longer an apprentice. Perhaps you've become a *gabbillotu*," said the cat, who lay in the center of the withering weeds proudly licking the shiny coats of his seven kittens.

The apprentice overheard the smallest kitten's gentle mewing. He stepped deliberately through the garden, careful that his boots not fall on any of his master's weeds, until he came to the center where the cat lay. One by one the apprentice took the kittens in his hands, twisting their necks until their little bones snapped, and then he crushed each of the seven limp bodies against the hard earth with his heels.

"Indeed, you have no human feelings," cried the cat, whose copious tears of sorrow watered the master's garden so well that all of the wicked weeds grew tall and immediately bore seed.

"Indeed," said the baron, seeing the seeds of his many foul weeds take wing and fill the air. "Indeed, you've passed the test and become a *gabbillotu*."

So IT WAS THAT Don Babbuinu, the *gabbillotu*, came to live in the absentee landlord's extravagant house, more of a mansion really, or now that I've seen one I should say more of a museum, a place where exotic objects from the mainland of Italia were set on display in cabinets made of the finest wood, all of it smothering beneath a thick coating of dust.

But I'm getting ahead of my story. Before my eyes were to view the many treasures the cabinets held, word of Nonna Nedda's prediction reached Don Babbuinu's ears.

"What?" he shouted, hands flying up and over his head.

Don Babbuinu thought the woman's prophecy absurd. The very idea of marrying a poor girl from the village was so ludicrous that even on the far edge of the forest the deaf gatherer of moss and mushrooms could hear the overseer's roaring laughter.

Now, Don Babbuinu was exceptionally vain. It was said that he shaved twice daily and perfumed his thick and matted hair with oils from France, which the old baron sent special from Roma. Don Babbuinu wore white silk shirts with a useless splash of frill at the neck and tight black britches, which he tucked into his boots. He could often be seen scratching himself, then holding between his fingernails whatever guilty party—usually a tick or flea—he'd discovered. He carried a whip which he used on the peasants all too frequently. He dwelled in the mansion with the sad old tomcat everyone called Don Gattu out of respect for his advanced age.

Since Don Gattu had belonged to the baron, the old cat had no other alternative but to be Don Babbuinu's companion in the house. Don Gattu wept so copiously over witnessing his seven children killed that his tears cut ridges through the gray fur on his cheeks, which perpetually dripped with sorrow wherever he would go. If he stayed in one place for more than a few moments, Don Gattu soon stood in a puddle of tears. One could always find him by following his brackish trail, in which starfish stretched their arms and frogs and toads laid twisting strings of eggs and a flock of ravens could usually be found bathing.

It is said that the mourning dove acquired its melancholy coat and mournful call by drinking too frequently from Don Gattu's river.

The old cat was tantalized by the idea of a peasant girl whose destiny dared to take her to live in the *baruni's* house. "Perhaps we should invite the young girl of the prophecy here," Don Gattu said to Don Babbuinu that evening during dinner. "Have you no curiosity? How could you not want to meet her?"

"If I wanted another fly at my table, all I need do is open the door," replied Don Babbuinu, leaning back in his chair and scratching his hairy belly.

"You don't know that the girl's a fly," said the cat. "She might be fair."

"And roses might grow out of your ass!" Don Babbuinu guffawed. "I could invite my horse in here, too, and he could give the little gnat and her whole family a fresh, steamy pile to feast on!"

Don Gattu patiently dripped his sorrow onto the floor. A pair of tadpoles leapt over his tail. "But you can't just sit by idly. You must do something about this prediction. It certainly would be prudent if you at least were to break bread with the girl's father."

"It certainly would be prudent of me if I were to break my thickest strap across her father's lazy, useless back!"

Don Gattu started a new puddle. "You don't know that he's lazy."

"All peasants are lazy," Don Babbuinu said. "It's only logical. That's why they're peasants."

"Your logic's circular," replied Don Gattu.

"Circular?" Don Babbuinu roared. "So's my ass! So what? If my ass was square or triangle, it wouldn't stink any less. If peasants weren't lazy, they wouldn't be peasants! They'd be landowners. Some might even be rich."

"You know that's not true," said Don Gattu. "No amount of work alone can possibly lift their lives out of *miseria*."

"Leave what's true or false to the judges and lawyers," Don Babbuinu said. "All that matters to me is the way a thing is, which as far as my philosophy stretches is the way it's destined to be, for now and for ever and always, until the end of the illusion we call time."

"The way a thing is, you say?" countered the cat. "Well, the thing of this prophecy is that you end up marrying a peasant girl."

"My wise old Ziu Culu has two words for that," replied Don Babbuinu. He lifted one haunch. "Brrrp! Brrrp!"

Don Gattu stepped back quickly, one paw waving the air in front of his nose. He stopped in the room's far corner, where he began another puddle. "But everyone knows that the blind woman has never been wrong."

"Brrrp!" Don Babbuinu farted. "Brrrp! Brrrrrp-ppa-paa!" Sitting back in his soft chair he strummed his fingers on his full belly and sighed a contented, "Ahh."

"Has the tuba completed its after-dinner recital?" said Don Gattu after the air had cleared.

"Only if you first amuse me with the recitation of rhyme."

"Had I both wit and time," Don Gattu said and bowed, "my words might be more sublime. Tell me, Babbuinu, what will you do if this fortune proves true?"

"Rue the day I heard of the shrew's words." The overseer scratched his armpit, then behind his ear and knee.

"Her reputation," replied Don Gattu, "is regarded highly through the nation."

Don Babbuinu held up to a candle a fat flea. "As mine would be sure to decline, were I to wed swine."

"Or perhaps pearl. The girl's face, if washed, might display charm and grace. Sir, I see no gain by remaining still. What harm lies in greeting the girl? Or consider this. Switch, and meet the witch?"

Don Babbuinu's nails sliced the struggling bug in two. "Perhaps, perhaps. I know not what to do!"

"Glue your doubts to actions! Doesn't this prediction make you curious?"

"Enough!" shouted Don Babbuinu. Furious, he dropped both fractions of the flea into the flame. "God's name, I'll put a gag on this matter!" He gestured for the bold cat to come near. "Call the old hag here! Then all this chatter about my future will be clear!"

SO THE CAT LED OLD Nonna Nedda up the hill to the baron's mansion, where Don Babbuinu prepared his pot of soup. In another room Don Gattu and a newly hired stableboy boiled second and third pots of soup, at Don Babbuinu's instruction, stirring them every now and then with the tips of their little fingers, or, in Don Gattu's case, with the least of his claws.

Bowing nearly to the floor, Don Babbuinu offered Nonna Nedda his finest chair, then pulled at his nose and said, "Let's dispense with the chit-chat and proceed straight to the hocus-pocus." He poured out a bowl of soup from the pot he had made, stirring the stock ceremoniously with his little finger.

"This is for you, dear Nonna Nedda," Don Babbuinu said, offering her the bowl.

At that moment there was a loud crash from the next room. "Nobody move!" Don Babbuinu shouted. He whirled and rushed after the noise, carrying his bowl.

A few moments later he returned to the room. "Forgive me, Nonna Nedda, it was nothing, just the wind." In his hands he now carried a bowl of the stableboy's soup.

After Nonna Nedda took the first sip, she smiled and said, "Now here's an untamed, spicy broth! I could drink this soup all day!" Her thick tongue lapped her lips. "This soup tastes of the hills and the forest and its wildest rivers! I sense that like a river the maker of this soup knows when to meander through the meadows and go slow, when to be furious and fast, when to dip, when to bend, when to curve, when to fall, when to rush and be foamy and surging and reckless!"

"*Bravu!*" cried Don Gattu from the doorway, his tears forming a pair of sudden waterfalls from the twin ruts on his cheeks down to the floor.

Don Babbuinu yanked the bowl from the old woman's hands and threw it against the far wall. "Very well, you old charlatan, you've passed the first test. That soup was made by one of the stableboys."

"Any mare under his care must be most content," the old woman said.

"Now for the second bowl," Don Babbuinu growled.

"Please," said Nonna Nedda, twisting her gnarled arms into a knot, then pointing to her mouth, "bring me a little something to clear the palate."

"What would you like?" cried Don Gattu.

"Only a teeny tiny something."

"Only a teeny tiny something," minced Don Babbuinu.

"Sure," Nonna Nedda said, "whatever you've got."

Well, in the master's mansion when a guest asks for her palate to be cleared it stays clear for a long time. Nonna Nedda ate a plate of roasted chickpeas, a bowl of olives, some peppers, cheese, eggplant, zucchini, a platter of ziti, several boiled eggs, a couple of loaves of bread, a leg of lamb, *braciola*, a bowl of couscous, *calamari*, eel, anchovies, tuna, more ziti, and an entire sardine and macaroni pie, all washed down by glass after glass of red wine and prepared in Don Babbuinu's kitchen by the new stableboy.

The *gabbillotu* again poured the old woman a bowl of soup from the pot he had prepared, stirring the steamy liquid with his little finger. "This is for you, dear Nonna Nedda," Don Babbuinu again said, offering her the bowl.

And again at that moment the sound of a loud crash. "Nobody move!" Don Babbuinu again shouted, whirling and rushing out of the room, carrying his bowl.

When he returned he said, "Forgive me a second time, Nonna Nedda. It was nothing, just the wind." In his hands he carried a bowl of the soup made by Don Gattu.

As Nonna Nedda sipped this bowl, she began to cry. With the next sip she moaned and wept so openly that the room's marble floor soon was covered by her tears, and all of Don Gattu's water creatures had a much bigger pond in which to splash. The sky outside darkened and the air grew strangely cold, and from the distance everyone in the village and out in the fields heard the tolling of church bells even though there were no churches with bells for leagues, and all the *genti di campagna* fell to their knees as if they'd just been informed that someone they dearly cherished had died, and everyone wept and moaned and began reciting the doleful verses of the *rèpitu*. Then the disconsolate sky opened its eyes, and it stormed for seven days and nights in sorrow and pain and the keenest misery.

Don Gattu knelt at Nonna Nedda's feet. "Mother," he cried, placing a paw on her knee, "forgive me for sharing my life's sadness with you."

Nonna Nedda took the cat up into her arms. "Oh, puss puss puss," she said, "how I wish I could lift even an ounce of your heavy pain."

"Take me to live with you," Don Gattu whispered into her ear. "Oh, please, I beg you, I've been waiting for someone like you to rescue me for what seems like a thousand years! Look at him closely! He's not a man! He's a baboon! Demand me as payment for telling him these fortunes."

And so it was that Nonna Nedda came to be the companion of the old gray tomcat, who continued to weep wherever he went until the dawn of the day that his ninth life expired, when his heart filled with the hope that he would again be united with his seven children. And it's said that this pair—Don Gattu and Nonna Nedda—joined the parade of others making their way up the road to Palermu and the New World, and that their tears, combined with the tears of all those leaving and all those left behind, created new rivers and streams that tumbled sorrowfully and swelled the banks of the Tyrrhenian Sea.

After the week of rain stopped and Nonna Nedda again had cleared her palate, this time ordering the new stableboy in the kitchen to fill thirty wheelbarrows with food for the people in the nearby village, and after she'd been granted custody of Don Gattu and momentarily dried the ridges in his cheeks with the hem of her black skirt, she agreed to taste the bitter brew in Don Babbuinu's bowl.

"This is for you, you greedy shrew," hooted Don Babbuinu as he handed her the bowl of soup he himself had spent his life making and in which floated remnants of each of his life's foul deeds.

The old woman lifted the bowl to her lips and took a sip. At once she gave out a terrified shriek and fell to all fours, braying in unimaginable pain and agony. Her long head wagged in exaggerated fashion. She squealed pitiably, mimicking perfectly a donkey trying to kick someone standing behind it, someone doing it a disservice forbidden by both nature and God, the obvious cause of the miserable beast's distress.

After several moments Nonna Nedda's body went still. Then her eyelids fluttered like a pair of beating wings, and her white eyes twitched in rolling spasms of apprehension and terror. Her mouth gaped wide as she vomited out onto the floor a snake and seven scorpions, which scuttled at the baboon's feet and then climbed up the legs of his black britches and beneath his white blouse to the flesh covering what would have been his heart, if he had one.

The snake formed a circle around Don Babbuinu, holding its tail in its mouth and rolling sideways up and down like a fallen ring, preventing the overseer from wringing the necks of the old blind woman and the gray tomcat, who fled out the door into the nearby hills and forest, never to be seen by the people of our village again.

WELL, YOU REMEMBER what I said about walls having ears. From that day on, whenever Don Babbuinu turned his back the peasants brayed like a donkey and made loud kissing sounds.

With so much laughter in the fields during the day, nights in the village became particularly noisy and active. Soon the belly of every woman in the village inflated like a bouquet of balloons. Perhaps Don Babbuinu's humiliation piqued the virility of even the village's most timid. Perhaps it was some scent or seed floating through the night air, a spell Nonna Nedda placed on us before she left.

No matter. But then two events took place.

To replace Don Gattu, the old baron in Roma sent three wild dogs who arrived the next day on sleek Arabians. And then, to regain some small shred of dignity and to disprove Nonna Nedda's prediction that his marital future involved the rape of a donkey, Don Babbuinu began to woo me.

Now, in our village back then this otherwise romantic matter was undertaken by the mothers of the boy and girl. After all, only the fool thinks he knows more than his mother. There is no sense more sound than a woman's. So, in accordance with the rules of this ancient arrangement, a certain ritual would be played out. One of the mothers, usually the boy's, would approach the other, and after the introduction of her child and the proper passage of time the daughter would be introduced and the match discussed. But, to displace the possibility of rejection, the boy's mother would lay a disguise over the topic of her conversation. Instead of directly discussing the attributes of her son and risking the other mother's rejection of him, the woman requesting the match would ask the other mother if she preferred, say, a comb with sixteen teeth, or was she content using a comb with teeth amounting to nine.

It's the numbers used by the women that are the key to this play. In the Sicilian dialect sixteen is sìdici, nine is nòve, with the first syllables stressed in these instances to stand for sì or nò, yes or no.

"Yes, I'm most happy to say I'd very much like a comb with sì-dici teeth," the girl's mother might answer, "and I'd be most pleased if you would look at my comb tomorrow afternoon," meaning that the second mother finds the son agreeable and is willing to introduce her daughter to the pair the following day.

Or, "No, I'm so very sorry to say I prefer nò-ve teeth on a comb," the mother could answer, meaning that she isn't agreeable to the match. This drama allows both the women and their children to save face and uphold their honor within the community. Or at least it was how this thing had always been done, which back then was reason enough to do anything.

NOW, WITH NO MOTHER to speak for him, Don Babbuinu risked revealing himself even more publicly as a buffoon. Sure enough, early one evening my family heard the sound of approaching hooves outside our hut, then a reckless shout.

"Mother of Agneddina," Don Babbuinu yelled from the saddle of his dappled horse, "hear me! Hear me, mother of the Little Lamb! The master has sent me several barrels of fine wine, which I wish to share with you and your family. Tell me, do you prefer a barrel made of sixteen wooden slats, or a barrel made of only nine?"

The twelve of us were sitting near the fire, sipping our evening soup of onions and greens. After hearing the overseer's voice, Mamma made a horn of her fingers, spat between them, and pointed the horn at the door. Then all my brothers and sisters, even the one at my mamma's breast, did likewise. The rude overseer got the horns from the Little Parrot, the Little Monkey, the Little Butterfly, Little Owl Eyes, Little Bat, Little Weevil, Little Turkey, Little Gray Mouse, and Little Red Fox. I shot him the horns, too, as my papa stood, hesitating as if in thought, then put a finger to his lips and leapt out the back window.

"Mother of Agneddina," Don Babbuinu shouted, "speak to me! Is it sixteen or nine?"

We remained as silent as a forgotten aunt.

"Answer me or I'll knock down your door!" the voice again roared. "*Sìdici o nòve?* Sixteen or nine?"

Then we heard Papa's voice, disguising itself as a woman's.

"Kindest sir," Papa called out, falsetto, "I'm right here with my daughter, gentle sir."

We snuck a peek out the door. Papa had borrowed and donned a woman's cap and long apron, and led a neighbor's donkey by its harness. "Permit me to introduce her, gentle sir," he called. "Yes, I like a barrel made of sixteen slats. Sixteen, do you hear me, kind sir?"

The overseer's face contorted with fury as chuckles burst from a nearby hut. Within moments the laughter spread from one hut to the next. The villagers gazed out a window or doorway, giggling, hiding their glee with a hand over their mouths. Soon everyone stood in front of their huts, roaring and pointing alternately at the *gabbillotu* and my papa dressed in women's clothes.

"There's an agreement," shouted one of the villagers from his door. "You heard the fair woman's reply!"

"If that woman be fair," shouted another, "Don Babbuinu's destiny is certainly foul!"

"*Sìdici*, Don Babbuinu! *Sì, sì, sìdici!*"

"Hee-haw! Hee-haw!"

"They'll call their firstborn son *lu sceccu-omu!*"

"No, *l'omu-sceccu*, since his father is the bigger ass!"

"Such a long nose on that bride!"

"Every nose has a face to match!"

"Oh, he'll soon have her smiling!"

"Hee-haw! Hee-haw!"

"*Sì, sì, sìdici!*"

From the north a second man appeared dressed in a woman's cap and apron, leading a donkey by its harness, and singing in a high voice, "Don Babbuinu, what about *my* fair daughter?" Then from the south a third man appeared in the same disguise, calling out the same. From the east and west appeared two others, likewise dressed.

"What about *my* daughter?"

"No, kind sir, *my* daughter!"

"*Sìdici*, Don Babbuinu! *Sì, sì!*"

"Choose *my* daughter! Mine!"

"Hee-haw! Hee-haw!"

"The truth is in the soup!"

"The proverbs of the ancients never lie!"

Don Babbuinu slammed his heels into his horse's dappled sides, then jerked the reins sideways and rode away. The villagers stayed where they were, in their doorways, still silly with laughter. I think we wanted the moment never to end.

Night was falling fast. One of the men grabbed his wife's cap and put it on his head, and someone else shouted, "*Sì, sì, sìdici!*" and that made us laugh all over again. It was good to hear the women and men laugh. Soon one of the peasants was throwing down wood for a fire, and another joined him, and I smiled, knowing it would be one of those nights when all the people sat around a fire together making rhymes and telling stories.

I squeezed Mamma's hand, all at once frightened. Now I knew that the overseer really did want to marry me. And now that we'd ridiculed him, I thought, he'd want me three times more. The thing denied always grows in beauty. Even worse, I feared that it truly was my destiny to be his wife.

I pictured his horse, remembering how roughly he'd kicked its sides. I could still see the animal's wild eye rolling upwards in its skull as the man's rough hands pulled mercilessly on the reins. I didn't want to become something saddled and reined. Something in my soul feared that I wasn't really a girl at all but was instead actually a donkey, as foretold by Nonna Nedda's prediction.

I pushed my head against my mother's belly and filled my nose with her smell. I tried to bury my face inside her. I wanted to crawl back up inside her and suck my thumb and curl up deep in her belly and feel safe again.

I pushed against her so forcefully that I must have caused her pain. Her hands shoved me away and I fell back, tripping over my feet, into the dust. I think that was the first moment the cord between us felt truly cut, when I first felt separate from her, curiously apart, suddenly aware of the air surrounding my isolated and individual body. Looking back I think she already could sense what was going to happen to my father. Though his actions that night spared me from the promise of marriage, his joke strayed beyond humor into insult.

Nearly all the men now were wearing their wives' caps. Mamma's hands pushed me and the other children into the circle around the fire. Already a voice was beginning to give form to the story of my bold papa and Nonna Nedda's prediction and Don Babbuinu.

The fire in our midst surged brightly against the darkness. I sat next to my papa, holding his hand. I wanted the night to last forever. I knew we would not be alone for as long as it was night and the fire remained lit.

THE SOLDIERS ARRIVED on the third morning.

They pushed my father down to the ground, kicking him as he fell, then pulled him back up and punched his face and chest. Then they bound his hands with rope. I wondered why they pushed him down only to pull him back up again. Was it just because they could, as a display of their power? Still, they didn't dare look into our eyes. Mamma hurled curses at them and threatened them with a pitchfork but put it down after they pointed their rifles first at her and then at the heads of my brothers. The soldiers had my papa march between them as they took him away. He kept shouting out his love for us until his voice faded into the wind.

My brothers took up his work in the fields. Two mornings later Mamma found a gold coin inside her apron pocket. The day after that, a fat young chicken scratched the dust outside our door. Every day from then on there was something for us.

Then we heard word that the night that Don Babbuinu came to ask for my hand the old baron's estate had been robbed of all its livestock and gold. According to the rumors, the mansion had been looted of its finery and burned to the ground. It was said that my father had organized the raid. We heard that there were witnesses who had sworn that he was absent from the village that evening. The four others who'd dressed as women and came from east and west and north and south to mock Don Babbuinu were named as my father's accomplices. Knowing the authorities were searching for them, the four fled to the hills. We were told that after the court pronounced my papa guilty, he'd be hanged by the neck until dead.

There was little laughter in the fields during these days.

I lost hunger, then all desire, until I realized that the knife could cut both ways. There was only one path before me, only one road my fate could take. So the next afternoon while my mother worked with the other women and tended to my brothers and sisters, I made ready to leave.

Before departing I gave blessing to the hut's walls—may these good walls remain strong and never again hear the footsteps of soldiers—and to the floor—may this good earth remain clean and never again be asked to drink the tears of my family's sorrow and grief—and to the thatched ceiling—may this good roof keep out the wind and rain and never again look down on my family's hunger or need. I blessed the hearth and pot and pitchfork and the three-legged stool. I gave blessing to our bowls. I ordered any spirits or little demons lurking in the corners of the hut to jump into the fire and take their mischief up with the smoke. I put my finger to my lips and told the house to be quiet and not tell my mamma or brothers or sisters my plan.

Then I set out on the road toward the remains of the baron's mansion, where I would agree to marry Don Babbuinu in exchange for my papa's life.

CONTRARY TO RUMOR, the great house had not been burned. Indeed, it hardly looked touched, although I noticed immediately that the livestock pens stood silent and empty. The estate as well was oddly quiet. There were no chirping insects in the grass. Not even the smallest sparrow sang from the least tree.

At the front door I was met by a dog who introduced himself as Don Cani. He pushed past me and growled in the direction of the village and snapped his teeth for several minutes, then invited me inside, licking his chops.

"Follow me," he said, his nails clicking on the marble floor as he scampered in circles and then, as if he could not contain himself any longer, raced wildly from one room to the next.

The walls of each room were lined with cabinets and wooden shelves stacked with riches and frills. I took my time walking about. There was one room filled completely with magnificent bowls and platters on which were painted various scenes of dance and costume, hunting and horses and dogs so lavish that my mind could barely believe or contain them all. One showed a wolf and a wild dog embracing in a fight to the death. I walked past rows of delicate teacups and saucers and gold-rimmed goblets. The next room displayed shelf after shelf of exquisitely fashioned glass. A third room was devoted to embroideries and velvets. I ran my fingertips across a swath of black velvet whose nap was so deep that my shoulders tingled with delight. When I put my cheek against the cloth I thought I'd faint. In the next room were a thousand and one porcelain dolls dressed as lushly as any king or queen. I swear each painted face held living eyes that could see me. I crossed myself and ran from that room to the next, in which more lions and tigers than I could count stood waiting for me, silent and still, threatening to devour me. Around them the walls were decorated with the heads of all the lower beasts they'd already feasted upon.

"My two brothers will very much enjoy meeting you," Don Cani said as I ran from that room.

I stopped in a marble hallway near the front door. "I'm here to speak to Don Babbuinu," I replied.

"The baboon's gone," snarled a second dog, stepping out from behind the drapery, in all appearance the twin of Don Cani.

Then their triplet emerged behind me. "We haven't the slightest idea when he'll return," the third dog announced, "but we'll be most happy to entertain you while he's gone."

"Extremely happy to entertain you," said the first Don Cani, pacing closer to me.

"Happier than you can imagine," said the second.

"Oh, how I drool just to think about it," said the third, panting so heavily that his breath was like a hot oven against my hand.

They circled me, sniffing my legs, then began pushing their snouts up beneath the hem of my skirt. I slapped their noses away and made the sign of the Cross in the air above their heads saying, "In the name of Mary, Mother of God, and all the holy saints, I banish thee to Hell!" Still, the three demons persisted, revolving in an ever-tightening circle around my legs, backing me up against one or the other until I tripped over one of their backs and toppled to the floor.

I kicked and slapped them and tried to claw their eyes. "Hail Mary," I shouted, "blessed are you, among all women born! Keep me chaste and pure, untouched and untorn!"

At that moment I heard a howl so loud and long it made the moon spin. The dogs froze, all wide eyes and twitching ears. No one breathed. Then something sudden and loud and mighty kicked open the mansion's front door. It slammed solidly against the wall, then creaked eerily back on its hinges. There was the distinct smell of lemons on the cool evening breeze.

Into the room stepped a powerful wolf.

The three dogs dropped their heads, ears flattened, and stepped slowly back and away from me. No one moved. Then one by one they bared their teeth and leapt at the wolf, who pulled out from beneath his cloak a twin stick of fire and made it explode once and then twice, stopping in midair the first two dogs who'd charged him. The room grew hazy with smoke. The dogs' bodies flew backward, slamming against the walls where they bled to what I hope were painful deaths.

Don Cani, the first dog, remained, timing his leap for the moment that the wolf dropped his magic stick. The dog and wolf struggled, leg to leg, paw to paw, until the strength of their forces balanced the other so evenly that their motions hardened into the peculiar tableau vivant painted on the master's bowls and platters.

Then Don Cani yelped and fell back, his front paws holding his throat. His throat was gashed wide open and red. Don Cani's paws worked against it, furiously moving up and down, back and forth, as if trying to push back together the separate flaps of his skin. His blood surged from between his paws in bright, hardy spurts, then in weaker and ever more feeble arcs in the air.

The wolf put the handle of the bloody knife in the paw of one of the first two dogs, then said to me, "Don't be afraid." He took the shotgun and cradled it in the front legs of Don Cani, whose bloody, still figure no longer resembled anything painted on the master's platter. The wolf grasped my hand and helped me to stand, modestly looking away from my eyes.

"Did they injure you?" he asked me in a soft voice.

I shook my head no. My heart thumped so furiously that I wanted to laugh or scream. He held my hands in his.

"Look at your feet, not at their bodies," he told me as we walked out the door into the cool evening, careful not to step into any of the blood.

The black sky had swallowed the stars and nearly all of the moon. I thought of the velvet that I'd held up to my cheek. It was much too dark to see.

"There's a storm approaching," he said. He led me to his horse, which was tied to a post outside the mansion. Then he washed his paws and muzzle and all the blood from the fur on his chest and legs in the trough from which the horses drank. He moved easily, without hurry, as if we had all the world's time, as if there was nothing to be afraid of.

Around us, as if suddenly awakened, the countless insects of the fields released their cries.

THE SAINTS MUST HAVE BEEN with us, the wolf said, as we rode together on the horse back to my village. The shotgun was old, he told me, and old shotguns were known sometimes to explode in the hands of those who fire them. The dog's knife, he said, hovered between their throats for so long that he nearly felt his strength give out. Then a strange thing happened, he told me. In his mind he saw the knife's keen blade slice the dog's throat open, and then the knife leapt from his hand as if it had a will of its own and did precisely as his mind had imagined.

He spoke in long, lively, delirious sentences. At times his voice grew so jittery and shrill that it broke and he had to pause and howl at the moon. At other times he had to stop and gulp down breaths of air as if he couldn't breathe. Then he'd start to shake all over. I sat behind him on the saddle, holding tightly onto his coat. All the while I could feel his body trembling.

"It's hard to believe what I did," he said after a while. "I'm really only a cook and stableboy, and not really much of either, to tell you the truth. A few months ago I was sent to the mansion to spy. Really, we'd planned only on taking the *baruni's* livestock once it had fattened." He began to wheeze.

"You don't have to talk," I said, stroking his back. I'd never before stroked a wolf's back. It wasn't unpleasant. Once I began to talk I couldn't stop. "May the Mother of God bless you. May Jesù Cristu bless you. May all the saints bless you. Blessings on your mother and father and family."

He wheezed more loudly, then nodded his snout in thanks.

"My family owes you my life," I said. "Those dogs certainly would have killed me."

"They would have done far worse," he said. "Forgive me for saying so but it was foolish of you to go there."

"I wanted to save my father," I said.

The horse pulled up. Now we were just outside my village. "Don't worry about your father," he said. "He'll be just fine."

"But the *gabbillotu*—"

"Don't worry about the *gabbillotu*. Others"—he gestured a paw toward the hills—"have more than taken care of his needs."

"But my father—" I began.

"Listen to me," he said as he helped me down from the horse. "I give you my word. They won't hang your father."

"I pray you're right," I said.

"You have my solemn promise," he said, swinging himself down from the saddle, "in exchange for one thing. Your name."

After I told him Agneddina, he laughed and said it was a name more fit for a child. We stood alongside his horse. It was starting to storm. I could see his features begin to fade from a wolf's back into a man's, as if he'd once been one. I wanted to ask him why I was no longer a child. I wanted to touch his cheek, even to kiss it. As his eyes held mine, then took my measure, he asked my true age and what name had been uttered when I was baptized.

"Remember me, Ciccina," he said just before he changed back to a wolf and rode off on the dappled horse toward the hills and forest.

THE FOLLOWING DAY a few of the villagers scavenging for greens at the edge of the forest found the body of Don Babbuinu. What drew them to it, they said, was the spiral of vultures winging the air. The villagers' versions of what they saw expanded in detail from one telling to the next, but on three facts all witnesses agree. The *gabbillotu*'s corpse was lying belly-down on a rock, his throat slit from ear to ear. Both of his hands had been chopped off. Around his head had been placed a donkey's harness.

Later that day we heard word that inside the baron's mansion Don Cani had shot and killed his two friends, one of whom apparently attacked him with a knife. In the bloody struggle Don Cani had died, too.

It took a few more days for the remainder of the story to take shape. Soon everyone believed that Don Cani and his two friends had stolen the baron's gold and livestock, then fought over how the bounty would be divided, murdering one another in the process. The proof was that a bag of the baron's missing gold was found hidden in Don Cani's belongings, and nearly all the stolen livestock was found in the forest not too far away in makeshift pens. An inked map to these pens was discovered in Don Cani's pocket.

Of course I told no one what I knew.

A month later the baron's first son journeyed to our village from Roma and declared Don Babbuinu a great hero. The baron's son had us gather one noon out in the hot sun to listen to him recite a speech, though his northern dialect was so strange and weak we could hardly comprehend a word of what he said.

What the men around that night's fire pieced together was that Babbuinu had uncovered Cani's plot and as a result been murdered by Cani and his vicious partners, who in their greed over the baron's riches then turned on one another.

The baron's son also announced that as a result of the tragic incident he was hereby increasing his share of the year's harvest as a tithe toward the construction of a statue which would be erected in Babbuinu's honor. The new *gabbillotu* translated this portion of the speech in a dialect so clear and masculine that we each understood that we had no alternative but to suffer yet another new tax.

Three days later, as the wolf had promised, my dear father was set free.

OVER TIME I CAME to believe the villagers' story. I accepted the possibility that in my distress over my father's imprisonment I must have dreamed up the story of the wolf who knocked down the mansion door and rescued me. But since we all knew and despised Don Babbuinu, how could a tale about his murder be told in anything less than heroic light?

With each retelling, Don Cani's actions grew more honorable in the storyteller's eyes. Soon the stories told around the fire suggested that the wicked Babbuinu was in conspiracy with the two traitorous dogs, who'd plotted against and tried to deceive Cani, their trusting, noble friend, who would have befriended the peasants and taken their side, as the gentle Don Gattu had, if only given the chance.

And just as the baron's son promised, a statue of Don Babbuinu was erected on the mansion's grounds.

Again all the peasants of our village had to stand in the noon sun and endure an incomprehensible speech before the peacock from Roma pulled a rope that lifted a huge veil and revealed to all eyes the statue.

The statue's legs stood apart, one arm thrust toward the sky, the other crooked out at the elbow and back to the waist, which was girlishly thin and nothing at all like Babbuinu's ample girth. The statue wore shoes instead of boots, and a pair of fine pantaloons rather than a *gabbillotu*'s rough britches. We circled the statue looking for Babbuinu's long whip, which he was never in his life seen without, and which even the midwives claimed he was born holding, and which he used on his mother whenever she was slow in pulling down her blouse or when her breasts did not supply him with milk in his desired temperature and quantity, but on the statue there was no whip. As for the face, it resembled no one we had ever seen.

Indeed, the likeness was so crude and our hatred of Don Babbuinu so severe that among ourselves we referred to it only as the statue, then a year or so later as Don Cani's statue. After all, we observed, hadn't Don Cani's waist been nearly as thin as a girl's? Didn't he wear pantaloons from Roma? Weren't those buckled shoes on both of his hind paws?

By the following spring it was not uncommon to hear mothers tell their sons to be as true when they grew up as the martyred Don Cani. Indeed some went so far as to pray to the statue, leaving it offerings of flowers and herbs, candles and trinkets and lockets of their sick children's hair, believing in their hearts that the Almighty had turned the noble, martyred dog into a holy saint.

I WAS NEARLY EIGHTEEN YEARS and on the verge of accepting these beliefs when early one evening as we sipped our modest soup of onions and wild greens I heard the sound of approaching hooves, then a shout.

"Mother of Ciccina," a voice yelled, "kindly hear me!"

My heart stopped still in my chest.

"Being both friend and stranger to your family," the voice continued, "and lacking a mother nearby to give voice to my deepest hopes, please allow me to propose a question."

By now Mamma stood at the doorway. "It's Babbuinu's dappled horse!" she cried. Immediately she made a horn of her fingers, spat, and pointed the horn out the door.

"Mother of Ciccina," the voice shouted as the speaker dismounted and took a step toward our door, "if a boy from a nearby village, the second son of a man named Santuzzu from the province they call Girgenti, came calling with his sweet mother Adriana, and you learned that he'd worked as a stableboy and sometimes as a cook, and now he was on his way with his sister Carla across the wide sea to the Promised Land they call *La Merica*, and if Adriana told you that years ago her son had also made soup for Nonna Nedda and stirred it with the little finger of his hand, and that he'd been of secret aid to your family that same season while in disguise, and these were secrets that could not easily be given voice to but were true in God the Father's sight and in Jesù Cristu's most holy Name, and true as well before the gentle eyes of Mari, his holy mother, as well as all of the saints and spirits who walk unseen across this land, then what would you say if she asked if you preferred a pie whose crust was knit with sixteen strips of dough or a pie topped only by nine?"

Before I could stop him Papa grabbed my mother's cap, put a finger to his lips, then slipped out the back window.

"Mother of Ciccina," said the voice a third time, "kindly answer me and at the wedding feast I'll steam just for you a big pot of couscous, and I'll roast for your whole family one of Don Ricci's finest lambs!"

"*Sidici!*" I cried. I couldn't wait a moment longer for my dumb mother to speak. She stood as still and as silent as the statue on the mansion grounds. I dared not wait for my father in disguise to interfere.

"*Sidici!*" I shouted again as loudly as I could. I was eighteen and sure that I could make my own match. In the doorway I now stood taller than my own mother, whom I was easily able to step past.

"*Sì!*" I cried, walking toward the dappled horse to meet the man who'd come to call on me. "*Sì, sì, sidici!*"

Thus Nonna Nedda's bold prophecy came true.

I wed Luigi of Girgenti, second son of Santuzzu.

Marco's Marcoroni

Tony Zurlo

Fiction (1999)

AT A RECENT CONFERENCE of maverick scholars in far western China the well-known Italian sage, Giovanni Topolino, presented the thesis that the Chinese were the Italians of the Orient. Before he had a chance to dot his exclamation point, Lu Po, a famous philosopher from Beijing, jumped to his feet and declared direct lineage to the Italian adventurer and Mongolian spy Marco Polo.

"Look at me," he shouted, pirouetting while pointing to his prominent nose. "And check out this curly hair. Can you deny my authenticity? My eminent friend and scholar from Italy, you've got it reversed," Lu Po howled with emotion. "The Italians are the Chinese of the Occident."

At that point Topolino lost the audience and a verbal melee ensued. The conferees were immediately corralled by uniformed Chinese police who hauled the unruly scholars down to the village chief's detox tank for a free night's lodging. For several hours, the police questioned both men, first separately and then together, demanding to know where this suspicious mystery man, Marco Polo, was hiding out. The answer "He's dead" simply annoyed the interrogators and they tossed the two scholars into a cell by themselves.

When word circulated that such substantial cerebral energy had assembled in a public building, the homeless and unemployed from miles around congregated just outside the barred windows of the public jail and clamored for their story. So the village authorities decided to give the two sages a chance at concurrent self-confession and reeducation.

Topolino and Lu Po conferred in animated whispers for a couple of minutes, stepped back and bowed to each other, and Topolino advanced to the window bars and sang in his high tenor into a stilled desert air, as the crescent moon retreated into the Mountains of Heaven. "The true story of Marco Polo," he began, "must be publicized." But the mob fell silent. No one understood Italian. So Lu Po with the Polo nose took his friend's hand and demonstrated their unity for all to see by planting a kiss on Topolino's cheek.

Together they began Marco's story, the operatic melody of high-tone Italian vibrating the villagers' hearts, and the counterpoint tones of Mandarin Chinese spinning their brains.

MORE THAN SEVEN CENTURIES AGO, twenty-one-year-old Marco Polo, his father Nicolo, and his uncle Maffeo, led a group of Venetians on a tour of the Orient via the Silk Road. Highway robbers, weather, and disease had claimed most of the tourists. So the Polos set up their first camp in the heart of the Middle

Kingdom near the First Emperor's tombs and devised a scheme to make a fortune by introducing polo, their family sport, to the Chinese.

As they passed through Xinjiang Province, they had captured a herd of miniature horses and rode them into the famous city Changan (Xian). While waiting for an audience with the mayor, they convinced the government ministers and Confucian scholars to play a practice game. After propping the Chinese dignitaries on the horses, the Polos armed them with croquet mallets and tossed a bocce ball onto the field, but the scholars collapsed and passed on to the Pure Land Paradise from all the paraphernalia: gowns, caps, tassels, etc. The game had to be postponed until they could all be reincarnated with the same level of intelligence.

Before the Buddhist monks could be convinced that the reincarnation had to be speeded up, all the minister polo players were executed for plotting against the eunuchs, who had boasted they would beat any team in the land at polo and they'd do it riding the little ponies bareback.

Then the eunuchs were executed for consulting Daoist priests about secret restorative potions and herbs. Discouraged by the revolving door of government, Poppa and Uncle Polo rode away on their tiny ponies, strumming their mandolins and harmonizing to "The Yellow River Blues." Then they sighted their rival Dante Alighieri sailing up the Grand Canal researching for his new trilogy about living within commuter distance of Heaven and Hell. Intimidated by Dante's reputation, Poppa and Uncle Polo grabbed a camel train and headed north to link up with Marco near the Beijing Duck Restaurant south of the Great Wall.

Marco followed a more northern course toward the mysterious capital of Cambaluc in the kingdom of Cathay. On the long journey, he studied conversational Chinese, and by the time he arrived at the Khan mansion, Marco could speak Chinese as well as any Mongolian. When Marco lost a marathon mahjong match with Khubilai Khan, Marco paid off his debt by becoming a spy for the Khan family. Khubilai Khan renamed him "Marco Khan Du" and sent him out to do background checks on potential concubines.

On a bright, cool, autumn morning, Marco had a breakfast date with one of the calendar girls that Khubilai had his eye on. Meeting the female candidate at an expensive Chinese restaurant, Marco ordered Chop Suey, but the chef said he'd never heard of it. So Marco agreed to try the house specialty: noodles. For the next three hours, he overdosed on boiled, fried, dried, and baked noodles; noodles with fish, noodles with sauces, and noodles with wine; so many varieties of noodles, in fact, that he finally requisitioned a horsey bag to take back to his tent. Smacking his lips, he told the chef that King Khan expected either the recipe or the chef's head. Although the calendar girl jotted down the characters, Marco couldn't read. Because of the chef's dialect, Marco misheard the name and called the noodles Marcoroni.

When he reported back to Khubilai, he kept the recipe a secret. And having taken a fancy to the calendar girl, Marco told the Khan that the young lady of his majesty's eye might have a nomadic gene. The Khan's temper flared like a sunspot and Marco, Nicolo, Maffeo, and the young lady grabbed all the packages of Marcoroni their little ponies could carry and galloped off into the Gobi Desert. When they stopped over in Teheran, Persia, for R and R, vandals ambushed them and demanded the Polo cargo. Marco, with eyes always alert for doing business, cooked up a plate of his Marcoroni and served it with a sample of the Khan's primo vino. The vandals accepted the wine for a lead camel, and Marco led the Polos back to Italy with their stash of Marcoroni and the calendar girl.

After his release from prison in Genoa, Marco married the calendar girl and established a chain of Marcoroni restaurants at Polo stadiums throughout Italy called Noodles Khan-Polo. Marco's great-grandson, Stronza Polo, traveled to China to set up a joint venture with Khubilai's great grandson, but then that's another story.

Marco wrote a song about his adventures, which is still sung today by Venetian gondoliers. He later introduced his hit song to Columbus, who used it to soothe his sailors' soulful moods on the holy trinity ships crossing the Atlantic: the Nintendo, the Palo Pinto, and the Momma Mia Maria. The song goes like this:

Marco Polo came to town
astride a midget pony;
stuck a feather in his hat
and called it Marcoroni.
Marco Polo restaurateur
lures with garlic odor;
saturates with olive oil
and calls it Marco's cure.

The Guest

Rosalind Palermo Stevenson

Fiction (2005)

Before the Arrival

IT IS THE BUSTLING OF C—the excitement that the guest is coming. He will stay a full day and one night in our city. Because my father is Padrone, the *ras* of our region, the guest will stay with us—he will eat at our table and sleep in our bed.

Grandmother orders Zinnea to scrub the floor three times in just one day and clip the arbia to the windows. Even the saints on the walls get scrubbed. I, too, will be drawn into the cleaning frenzy and forced to scrub or polish if I don't stay hidden in the recess on the stairs—or else go down to Fox Lake, or out to the Z, where no one goes. Grandmother marches through the house examining this corner and that corner and finding this undone and that undone and seeing dust still on the furniture and places on the floors without a high enough shine. The dogs, who never come inside the house, have also been bathed—the white of the beagle shining brighter than I've ever seen it.

Scent was put in the water and the dogs now have the odor of citrus, a new collar was found for the basset hound, it is red and made of leather and makes the hound look elegant and pampered.

Before the Arrival

IT HAS BEEN DECIDED—the stop in C will be made. It is this town no larger than a pea that will secure my future.

My name will rise above all others. Already in the north, the Districts acclaim me. The children there wear my initial. The little girls run after me with peaches and flowers, the *M* of my surname pinned high on their dresses. They smile when they see me and dream of me at night the way they someday will a lover. I have possessed their hearts and their souls. The boys imitate my walk and copy my gestures. They part their hair the way mine is parted and practice at their boxing in the hope that I will notice.

C, too, will follow suit—will soon ally with the Party. And when it yields, the reformists will be humbled. It is I, it will be said, who embodies true reform.

Itten, Sabattini, Milo, Facta—and the henchman, Balbo.

The hills, the rock, the sparseness of the shrubs and trees, the rock, the redness of the soil. I see the ramparts in the distance and there arises in me a desire to go out to them, to linger

When the women are not busy with their cleaning they are cooking. They have cooked all the dishes of C and the pots are stored in the rear pantry. There are sausages of wild pig, canapes of chicken liver, flanks of beef sliced thin in strips and soaked in marinade to be put on the open fire, roasts of veal and chicken, grilled cockerel, rabbits in pimento sauce. Less perishable foods are sitting out on shelves: haricot beans, smoked meats, dry cakes, elaborate swirls of confection in the shape of figure eights, tarts and pies and mounds of chocolate and roasted chestnuts. More food has been prepared for the guest than for all the holidays and weddings of C. George, who is the younger of my brothers, made sure to find me and to show me a bag so large he had to drag it, filled to the top with the heads of chickens, and with their feet too and feathers, on his way to burn them.

This morning I examined the room where the guest will sleep. He will have the one called Aarlat room on the south side of the house with the windows that face out to Fox Lake. The room is called Aarlat room because it used to belong to Aarlat when he lived here with his wife from Fiume and their first baby, my cousin Thomas. It has a large bed and a sleeping balcony with an iron railing, just big enough for one person (or two at most) to stand on and gaze out to the lake or down to the garden below.

The garden too is being scrubbed— pruned and manicured in preparation

among the walls, the ruins, the burial grounds—all that is left of what was built so long ago. The hills remind me of my mother, that dear once-living being, her breast that nourished me, the flesh of her breast in my hand, my mouth pulling for the warm stream of milk. I can almost remember . . . the ramparts, the walls, the burial grounds.

Two cypress trees at the top of a hill. The barren ground, and off beyond the hill the Z, a forgotten land that stretches to the north, the dead and buried from a thousand centuries ago. The strength of this land is in its dead, those souls who watch, those armies past, their battles waged with strength and cunning.

I have taken Parliament. No counter influence remains that is strong enough to stop me—to reverse the tide, the sweep of events that will deliver the country to me. Hundreds signed their names on my *listone*—and from all the factions—not only those already in the Party. Hundreds asked to be placed as candidates for deputy positions, hundreds more gave their endorsement.

Even Croce, high priest of the liberals, gave his blessing to the Party. I am positioned now for full ascent, for final rule. With the unification of C, Salandra will yield, will give me my due . . . and so will Facta.

We marched from the north to the seat of power, and with our march claimed victory. 3,000 fell. The martyrs of the Party. But Balbo is restless now. I for the visit. The ground is strewn with leaves and branches chopped from the poplars to make them round and tame. The gardener takes no notice of the nest of swallow eggs that falls to the ground with the branches.

I go out to the Z—to the Edge where the hives are kept. The hives are father's who has taken them on from Grandfather who is partially blind now and no longer strong enough to take the honeycombs in or to put the racks up or move the frames into place. Nor can he take the basket filled with smoke to coax a swarm into a hive. Grandfather knows the bees so well he can tell by the hum of just one bee which hive it belongs to, or if the worker is old or young, the condition of the queen, the number of the foragers, all from the humming of a single bee. It is called the Edge because there are cavernous holes that open up in front of you—it is as if the earth has run out of space there—as if the flat surface has come up to its end . . .

The bed is high where the guest will sleep. Most of the beds in our house are low to the ground in the style of C, but this one came from Veii and had to be shipped by rail and dragged up to the house on a flatbed constructed to hold it. When they had dragged it to the door, all of the men of the household formed a lift and carried it up the stairs and into Aarlat's room. The frame of the bed was hand-carved by an artisan in Veii, carved with the figures we see in sleep: winged fish, chariots drawn through the air by birds of prey, a woman looking in a mirror,

cannot hold him back much longer. He nervously fingers the trigger. I remind him that Vittorio Emmanuele has already acceded, has given full support and conferred his authority. The rest will follow. After C there will be nothing that can stop us.

Again the breeze, the smell from off the Z, the warmer air of this part of the country. The arid ground, the clay hills, the yellow flowers that grow on the shrubs. The smell that is found only here in this region of my childhood.

So early and already so hot. The heat hangs in the air like a sheet of glass. The sun bears down to crush the earth—waves of heat float in front of the windshield. Boratto drives and keeps quiet. He understands the uselessness of conversation. He watches the road, fixes his eyes straight ahead, holds his back erect and his thoughts in silence. An image on the waves of heat: the face of the widow in Forli. She lifted her skirts for me when I was a boy. Closer, she begged me, come closer. I went beneath her skirts with my hands like claws. With my eyes like magnifying glasses. Exploding the veins that stood out against her flesh, the blue lines that marked the flesh of her thighs, her thighs as thick as my waist. I went closer. Crawled underneath her skirts, between her legs, scrutinizing every inch of her flesh, making my way to her sex, slamming my fist into her, and then slamming in my manhood. Returning to her every afternoon. I was fourteen at the time. It was her hair plaited, a dog at her feet, dwarfed creatures peeking out of shadows, turtles, the signs of the zodiac, sibyls and lyres and inscriptions and veiled dancers and angels and the heads of demons. The mattress is the thickest in the house and stands more than a foot up from the frame. Before Zinnea covers it with sheets, I climb on top to see how it will feel to the guest—lying there with my face pointed up to the ceiling, to the ripple of clouds in the plaster, the breeze off Fox Lake drawing in through the window, touching my face the way it will soon touch his, waking him perhaps, calling him out from sleep, his body massive, heavy with sleep, and living here with us (if only for one night), all of C knowing he is sleeping in our bed, the breeze dragging him gently out of sleep in the morning, playing with him, teasing him to wakefulness, to the breakfast table heavy with creams and breads and fruits and ham and pieces of veal and hard cooked eggs and honey and shelled almonds and hazelnuts and orange and lemon rind and exotic spices and the smell of coffee.

I place a vase filled with honeysuckle on the table near the guest's bed.

There was an incident right after lunch that disrupted the preparations— Uncle Ugo was stabbed by one of Zinnea's sewing needles. It had been lost somehow among the pillows on the sofa in the parlor where Zinnea was last doing hand-sewing. Uncle Ugo sat on it, driving it into the folds of the

before they sent me to the school at Faenza.

Back now in this region of my childhood. Among the ramparts, the stone, the arid earth on which the sun beats down, the ancient temples housing gods, gates like the gates of cities, roads known only as the "ways," a region of hills carved out of earth and stone. Boratto keeps his eyes fixed on the road. The town where I was born is some small distance to my left— born—the infusion of the life spark— and out of it the destiny of man.

And what am I if not the destiny of man? The destiny of the nation? What is it that moves me if not the force of destiny itself?

The new day has dawned. A day so new it must be dated in a new year— recorded not as anno domini, but *anno primo* . . . forever to be remembered as the *first year.*

I will rise to meet the fire of the sun. Where others are devoured by its flames, melted and annihilated by the intensity of its heat, I will be strengthened. I will join my will to that of the sun. I will join to the sun the way the people join to me. The people will follow in obedience to the rules handed down by the Party. Soon it will be said that through me the country has become cleansed and purified of all that previously defiled it . . . That through my leadership the people have become one with the nation . . . They will say it is my self-sacrifice that has flesh on his ass. His screams were louder than the pigs and his curses and threats could be heard all over the house. Zinnea was also screaming and crying and hitting herself with her fists. Grandmother tended the wound with special medicines and kept telling everyone to be quiet and said that the wound was not so bad and that Uncle Ugo was lucky because the point of the needle had not broken off.

The family is divided on the subject of the guest, though most of us are for him. Uncle Nicholas takes up the lead of those who are opposed and stands back from the preparations. He has no face, Uncle Nicholas says. He is a reed that bends in the direction of the wind—his spine is no more solid than the grasses in the marsh. He is a jackal. A peasant happy sleeping in a ditch. He is a scoundrel who will bring us all to ruin. He is a recreant.

In the distance I can hear the buzzing from the hives—I can see the bees flying in their elaborate formations. The guest's room smells of the honeysuckle. I can no longer climb onto his bed because Zinnea has put the sheets on it—the sheets are so white that they startle the eyes and there is just a small bit of crochet work at the edges. The pillowcases match the sheets and both have the clean smell of wash soap and sun. The folding stand for the guest's valise has been opened at the foot of the bed. A painting of the young Christ hangs over the headboard.

brought this great nation into being . . . that I am its center . . . its source . . . its throbbing heart . . .

Already in the streets they follow chanting *Duce* . . .

Arrival

The guest has arrived—his face is red with sunburn and his hair is black and flat against his head. He wears a white linen suit which makes him look dignified. When it is my turn to be introduced he takes my hand just as he does with the others and does not smile patronizingly or condescend or humor me. His fingers are short and thick, and he wears no rings. It is late morning and the heat is rising off the Z—Grandmother has ordered the trays with the cold meats and the bottles of mineral water and cold white wine.

The guest does not eat with the fastidiousness Aunt Luz predicted—a fastidiousness she claims befitting an exalted man. He eats like Uncle Ugo, tearing at his food, gulping down the wine in perfunctory swallows, talking as he chews so that the cold meat appears in all its stages of mastication, the cold meat clings to his teeth as he talks with father. He has not shaved—there is a dark bristle of hair on his face, a bristle that stands straight up and gives him a brooding appearance. He pushes his chin forward and stares directly at father, his eyes narrow. They talk of Facta's failure to declare an emergency or to call in the army reserves, of the way that Facta's reticence gave the Party the advantage it needed.

The guest makes strange grimaces when he speaks. His brow furrows and his teeth clench behind his open lips. He moves his head and waves his arms and gestures with his hands.

Arrival

I am not surprised by the family. The opulent house. The table laden with food. The women buzzing like the bees that are kept on the Z. A house full of women. Soft and ample flesh. And the men, too, have the same softness. It is the softness of the full belly. Their bellies are full and their minds contrive loosely the principles of democracy and individual freedom— the principles of a humanity good and bad, made up of angels or demons, saints or beasts.

The child is the only one who is thin. Her face is like a fox. Narrow eyes that look inward at the corners. The brow furrowed. She stares at me from underneath her brow. She appears to be staring at me even when she's looking elsewhere. Like a bird with eyes on the sides of its head.

The ras does not know I know that one of his sons is a traitor. That his son, Nicholas, opposes the Party. That he is active in the reform movement. Balbo favors open vindication. He likes the taste of blood—likes to taste it in advance.

I will wait and see—bide my time. From C to the south, to Rieti and L'Aquila. The unification of C will serve as a model. The son's contempt must be overlooked for now. Events write themselves.

The child is thin. Like a peasant child. Hungry and furtive.

His forefinger underscores the points he makes. Father's face is red with excitement. He agrees with the guest that the people must be focused, that they must be directed, that the aim of the Party must be towards unification.

If we are to err [the guest says] let it be on the side of severity. Too much force and not too little. This is the time for a firm hand, harsh if must be.

Traitors must be treated as traitors [the guest says]. A good beating never does any harm. Although I would not wish to stain with blood what is essentially the spiritual nature of the movement I lead to victory.

But what a handsome house [the guest says] and what a charming family.

Day

The rally in the square will begin promptly at noon. Father will give a speech to introduce the guest. Father will wear the suit of his office and his shirt with the wing collar and all the men of the family will stand alongside him in declaration of the solidarity of C. Even Uncle Nicholas will stand there. This after much discussion and persuasion and promises and threats. It is time to set politics aside, father told him—to put the good of the family first.

The women will sit in the front row that has been roped off and reserved for them. Mother had a special dress

From the window in my room I can see the Z, the garden below, the lake they call Fox Lake. I hate lakes—they are not seas, they are not rivers—they give me the sensation of betrayal.

Day

The one called Luz does not stop looking in my direction, she bores holes in me with her eyes, her face is powdered, the cut of her dress shows the flesh that rises just above her breasts. She offers me the tray of *panforte*, brings the tray to me herself, leans over with it in front of me and in a husky voice encourages me to eat. I tell her that too much is made of eating, that we must grow lean with the desire for national unity, that our stomachs must growl and we must not take notice, that our vigilance must replace our hunger until the last citizen of the country has taken his place in the ranks. She smiles as I speak. Nods her head continuously made—all eyes will be on her. The aunts, Luz and Octavia and Vida and Marcella and Lucy and Olivia will be to her left, but I am to sit on her right, between her and Grandmother. My dress is blue which mother says becomes me, and in the chemise style that women wear (not the high-waisted dresses made for children). Mother brushed my hair herself this morning until it felt like silk and fell straight down to my shoulders.

Aunt Octavia is telling how the guest came up from poor origins, how his father was an idealist and could not earn a living, how when the guest was a child there was never enough food on the table and he often had to go hungry, how his mother nursed him until he was four years old to supplement the cupboard . . . how his father instilled in him a passion for reform, how he has always lived his life by his ideals without regard for money or for comfort, how he even once lived under a bridge, in a packing case with a woman, and that the woman was so crazy for him she drowned herself when he had finished with her.

There is an incident on the way to the square—an attempt on the life of the guest. A man, slight in stature and armed only with a pistol, rushes the guest's car in the motorcade. Within a few minutes the man is dead, riddled with holes from the police bullets. Father orders that the man be left in the road like refuse to be picked up later. That we not even look at him. That he be left with the stocking on his face he wore to hide his identify.

in agreement. A habit she has—to bob her head up and down like a partridge when she listens. She would like nothing better than for me to take her. To catch her underneath the stairs inside the house or down in the cellar. Outdoors perhaps, in the garden behind the house, on the stretch of ground that leads to the Z, or on the Z itself among the hives, alongside the ancient graves, among the remains of the dead armies. Yes, she would like nothing better than for me to catch her, to rip her dress from her, to throw her down, to take her, and in that way—even if for only a few minutes—to make her mine.

Father says this will underscore the disdain of C for insurgents.

The Rally

The incident leaves the guest undaunted—his speech is more majestic than any heard before. He is a man of holy purpose—a man of mystic force, an almost sacred being. He is the man of the century. We are privileged to live in the time of the guest.

The people of C scream in admiration. They stamp their feet. They surge forward. The women push their children in front of them to receive the guest's blessing. He places his hand on the children's heads.

Our family and the guards have flocked around him. We move with some difficulty through the crowd to the cars that will take us home.

The guest catches my eyes—his eyes rise up to examine my eyebrows. I feel embarrassed, like my eyes will start to tear, or I might laugh or lose my balance, so I quickly look away. He turns directly to father then and says, the children, too, must be included in the workings of the Party.

Later in the Afternoon

I have kept my chemise dress on but have taken my shoes and knee stockings off—the silk catches at my legs—the pale blue of the dress clings just below my knees—my toes are in a straight row of equal length and I squash them in the wool of the runner that covers the floor

The Rally

The moment has arrived when the arrow must leave the bow, or the cord, too far stretched, will break . . .

What is it that stirs you when you hear the song of the Piave? It is that the Piave does not mark an end, it marks a beginning . . .

For ours is the permanent revolution. Ours is the profound political, moral and social revolution that will leave nothing—or almost nothing of the past still in existence . . .

For ours is the permanent revolution— the mystical and spiritual revolution . . .

And you shall become the synthesis of every negation and every affirmation; the embodiment of beauty and courage and love and risk . . .

Later in the Afternoon

The family is taking its rest now, the house is quiet. The papers are filled with news of my recent triumphs— the papers of the Party reach into every district and speak only of the inevitability of me—of me and my place at the head of the Nation.

of the hallway—it is hot—at least 100 degrees—everyone is resting—the guest, too, in his room—behind his closed door—the room still smelling of honeysuckle—and he perhaps at the desk deciding important matters, making notes in his ledger journal, or deep in thought, in front of the window—or standing on the sleeping balcony, the clay hills just visible out beyond the Z, hills which from the distance look like hives—the bees at their work, industrious even in this heat—the guest, too, at his work—more tireless than the bees—working now in our house the way they say he works in his office in the north—the light in his office burning eighteen, twenty hours at a stretch—once the light was said to burn around the clock for several days— a woman brings his meals, but he barely eats—he does not live like other men— he lives sustained by duty.

A commotion! The golden finch which we placed in its cage out on the guest's balcony has been mysteriously murdered. It was the guest himself who found it—handed the cage to Zinnea when she was bringing the fresh linens—told her to please remove it . . . to not replace it. Zinnea has come running from the room, the cage in her hand, the dead bird inside, and she, of course weeping and thrashing. The doors of the other rooms begin to open, first my oldest brother, Maso, then Grandmother, then mother and father, then Aunt Marcella, Aunt Lucy and Aunt Luz, with everyone soon in the hall—except the guest who remains inside his room. They are talking excitedly about the bird and what happened, and

Soon not a voice will dare to rise against me.

It is hot, so hot, the heat bakes the flesh, reduces the blood to ash—the leaves on the shrubs in the garden below have turned brown and parched in the sun.

The hysteria that engulfs a living being—the rush to defense of the life force—the impulse to continue—it is the same impulse in all of life, in everything that lives—in people, in animals, in insects, even in the squid— old or young, it does not matter, nothing wants annihilation. We cannot imagine without imagining ourselves.

Marianna Stabile resisted like the bird—the blue of the veins in her neck were straining—as if to push Balbo's hand away—her heart beating like the bird's against her chest—the look in her eyes of disbelief—Balbo waving me away with his free hand—he would take care of it, he said—he would take her away—the arrangements had already been made for her permanent confinement—she would not come back to make a claim one day—for herself or for the child.

The bird's black eyes—a ring of red around the neck feathers—the deep circle of red against the yellow.

What is it that they want? Marianna Stabile so insistent in her demand—in her claim to a right to be jealous—in her claim and in her rage. What is the right of a woman to rage? What is a woman beyond the capacity to love?

Aunt Luz who loved the bird is crying and Zinnea is in hysterics. It is the work of the Reformists, Uncle Ugo says and father immediately agrees with him. An attempt at intimidation.

(*But who? Who would do such a thing to the bird?*)

Shortly after there are whispers in the parlor—father and Uncle Ugo and my brother Maso. Uncle Nicholas has just returned from town, agitated. He has to be restrained from raising his voice, from heaving the side board against the window. The guest has joined them in the parlor. He pivots around on the heel of his shoe, makes faces, pushes his chin forward, opens his eyes very wide as he listens. At one point Uncle Nicholas looks like he might attack the guest, but this is checked by a gesture from father. Then Maso moves in closer to Uncle Nicholas' side—to restrain Uncle Nicholas if necessary. Father and the guest talk in hushed tones— occasional exclamations rise above the whispers. Uncle Nicholas' face is red, but he is now composed. Father's voice is still low and his expression grave, the guest waves his hand as if to wave away concern, he smiles broadly, a glint of light from the window bounces off his teeth. It seems the man who tried to shoot the guest was not a man at all—but a young woman dressed as a man—a member of the reform movement of C.

It is nothing, it is nothing [the guest says]. She was nothing . . . a scorned lover, a common whore, a mad woman.

And what is her life if not dominated by that love—for her children—for her husband—for her lover. Is it not that love which defines her? Still those tantrums hurled so frequently at me. The insistent demand that I reflect something back. Marianna pounded my chest with her fists—for the child—the boy she claimed was mine. How could I be certain he is mine (though his face was my own)? Even so, what significance can it have—this woman, this child against the destiny of man.

My destiny confirmed by the shooting star—the star which crossed the sky the very night, the very moment the victory of my march was proclaimed. The shooting star which crossed the heavens as a sign, an omen, a signature of God.

I have again caught the eyes of the
guest. This time I do not look away.
He opens his eyes very wide at me. He
does not smile, but he parts his lips.

Night

Grandfather says the bee dance is done
inside the hive, in the dark on the cell
of the honeycomb—the dancer leads as
in a tarantella, moving her abdomen
the way a bellydancer moves her hips,
changing positions, dancing to the
rhythms of the moon, making
sweeping movements, pointing and
dipping and fanning her wings.

*I have sometimes tried to imitate
the dance.*

The bee dance is nothing like the dance
Grandmother does. Grandmother holds
the skirt of her dress just above her
knees. Smiles. Moves the fabric of the
skirt back and forth in front of her like
the sailcloth on a sailing ship. Sways
her hips in time to the music. Smiles.
Gives the impression she is kicking her
legs up, high in the air, the way she did
when she was just a girl, when she
danced better than all the other girls.

It is the spider dance, she tells me,
come, like this, kick your legs, move
your hips. And don't forget your face,
the dance is also the expression on
your face. Kick your legs, she tells me,
show your little ankle.

The night is black. There is no moon.

Are the bees sleeping? Is the brood
curled up—each new egg in its cell?

Night

What is it in this countryside, in the air.
I can smell it, I can feel it, on my skin.
It gets in my lungs—in my eyes—in my
hair. What is it that comes up off the Z?
And what is the voice that gets in my
head? That I hear when I stand at the
window. I cannot sleep for the sound of
it. Is it the buzzing of bees? It cannot be
at this hour. The middle of the night.
What is that sound?

Nothing but blackness broken by the
light of stars.

Horses—a muted neighing—the low-
ering of hooves—

The sound of footsteps in the hall.
The trailing of a nightdress? One of the
women? A woman? The pause at my
door. The dark night sky. A woman.
Her nightdress trailing behind her. Or
is it the son, Nicholas, come to take
his aim at me, to take his turn, to set
right what was botched by his female
companion? Or is it only a woman?
Perhaps the one called Luz who could
not take her eyes off me, plump, fleshy
arms, enormous breasts—a sweet salt
taste to her flesh—the crease showing
between her breasts— her nipples
stained dark in the shadows. Has she
dared to come to me?

If it is Nicholas, do I slaughter him?
Will that turn the opinion of C

Has the humming of the guardian bees stopped for now? Is it as quiet in the hive as in this house? And the guest? Is he also sleeping?

There is a light beneath his door.

Even the night is hot. The floor warm to the touch of my feet. And the touch of my feet is light. I am the breeze that blows off the Z. I am air against the guest's door. I can move through his door as if by magic. Like the spirits Aunt Octavia sees. Like the hand that came to her but had no sub-stance. Like the hand her own hand moved through when she reached to touch it.

The guest sits hunched over a great heap of papers. He works while the others sleep. The night is hot so he wears no shirt. His back is wet with perspiration. I can see the little hairs that grow along his shoulders. He can-not see me, but he knows I am near.

He dips his pen again and again in the inkwell.

 As I approach, the guest shivers. A ripple runs across his back. His back is broad. His arms are thick with muscles.

I am the angel that whispers in his ear.

In just an instant he is standing before me. Bending to bring his face near to mine. What is it I want to tell him? What has driven me to seek him? I cannot speak. It is as though the night has stolen my voice.

against me? Even though an act of self defense? I believe a more generous tack is called for. A conduct befitting a great man. I will spare his life and let everyone see him for what he is. A man who attacks while the other is sleeping. A man who comes in the night like a common thief. A traitor to his family and his country. I will insist on mercy out of respect for the family. Out of respect for the people of C.

If it is the woman, Luz, will I take her under the nose of her own household? On this bed? Against the wall? Or out on the terrace cloaked by the night? Or in a corner against the wall behind the door the way I did that girl so many years ago in Forli? Catching her on the stairs and throwing her into a corner where I went ahead and made her mine. Her tears streamed down when she got up. She hurled her indignity at me. She said that I had robbed her of her honor. What kind of honor could she have meant? Is it the woman, Luz? In her nightgown with her robe open, with the flesh of her thighs showing through the transparent film of her nightdress, the high crease visible just above her breasts, two handfuls of flesh spilling over.

The steps have stopped outside my door. There is a hesitant turn of the knob.

It is the child.

It is the child who has come. Who presents herself so unself-consciously

In an instant he stands before me. Towers above me. Bends to bring his eyes level with mine.

His hand brushes my cheek and I am a statue. I am the statue in the square—the lady with the smooth white face—with arms that fold across her chest. The guest brushes my cheek with his hand.

He stands up straight and is tall as a mountain. As solid as mountain rock. He wears no shirt and there is hair on his chest and beads of sweat that glisten on the hair. The guest's nipples are dark and hard at the tips.

I would reach up and touch him if I were not a statue.

His hands are hot and wet on my shoulders—they leave their impression on the fabric of my nightdress. He turns me back in the direction of the hallway. His hand on the top of my head.

The hallway is filled with light now—it is as bright as the spotlight the dancer stands in on the stage in the variety shows at Forli. It is the band of light thrown from the lamp on the guest's desk. I step into the light in the hallway.

Come, kick your legs, move your hips, show your little ankle.

Departure

A breakfast feast is prepared for the guest. A pig roasted whole, platters filled with hens and squab, pans of

to me. It is the child who moves towards me—like a shadow, like a wraith. She is so thin. To touch her is to break her.

Her eyes are open and yet I think she is sleeping. Perhaps sleeping. Perhaps just walking in her sleep. Her jaw is square like that of a boxer. Yet she is delicate. I think both delicate and wild. Her eyes are open and she stares as if with purpose. Intent perhaps on the purpose of her visit. Her visit. This child (for she *is* a child) has come to my room in the night.

I should lift her and return her to her room. How intent her stare is. Such a little bit of flesh. She is more like a soul than a child.

Like a soul without the boundaries of the flesh. Undisciplined and wild. Like the staghorn, the amaranth, the bristle and the panic grass. Like things that grow. The skin of her face pulled so taut against her chin.

Heat radiates from her neck, from her shoulders. The skin on her shoulders is barely covered by her nightdress. She frowns as if in concentration—as if she would speak—tell me why she has come—what it is that she has in her mind.

In a year—two at most—she will have lost this delicacy.

Departure

The *ras* is powerful and yet a buffoon. He still believes that compromise is trout and eels and sweet-water crabs, *panforte* and dry cakes everywhere. He eats his fill and then makes his good-bye. The family gathers and thanks him for the honor. They give him presents to take away with him—a pen of solid gold, a crystal inkwell, baskets of fruit from our trees, bread from our ovens, honey taken from our hives. The guest, too, gives parting gifts. Chocolates for the women. Whiskey and cigars for the men. And for me a ruby red *M*, the initial of his surname, a pin which the guest affixes to my blouse. He says I am now Figlia della Lupa, the daughter of the she-wolf of Rome. He says that he himself had been fed from the milk of the she-wolf. And then he places his hand on the top of my head.

Father tells the guest the visit has been a success. The unification of C is now certain. The reform movement will be crippled. The city of C will stand firmly behind the Party. Aunt Luz weeps as the guest departs. She walks following his car until it is long out of sight.

Father tells me I will be a member of the Children's Party. I will march in formation with the other children and we will form a big M and sing songs in honor of the guest and of our country.

For our Duce,
For our Blessed Duce,
We are ready . . .

I go out to the Z where the hives are kept, to the hives and the cavernous holes. I hear a sound I've never heard before but recognize from Grandfather's description, it is the sound of a hive

possible. He embraces and defends the ideals of the Party, but leans secretly towards acquiescence with the principles of individuality. He is soft at his center though he would appear the man of iron. He is soft like the women who dominate this household—as soft as the flesh on their bodies. He thinks to strike down one insurgent, to leave him with his face still covered with a stocking like a rabid dog in the street, is enough of a show of strength to those who would further dissent. He does not in his heart believe that it is only through the persistent repetition of violent action against all who would dissent, against those who would even in their thoughts dissent, that the disintegration of the nation will be prevented and we will see the rise to full power of the Party. I have watched the way he caters to the fancies of the women in this household . . . the way he tolerates the rebelliousness of the son, Nicholas. In the end this *ras* must be ousted, his compliant nature must be abolished.

Yes, in the end this house must fall. There must be a final end to the over-intellectualization of the bourgeoisie. A final end to their neutral intellectual speculation. A final end to everything that grows wild and undisciplined and in direct contradiction to the interest of National unity. An end to the sermonizing and to the lecturing of which we have already heard too much, too much for this and a thousand lifetimes. An end to all the unnecessary functions of the State, to all the masks behind which there are no faces, to all

when the queen has died, and only the
orphans are left, and they mourn the
queen with a song, each singing in
turn, a single low note slowly merging,
rising and falling at dissonant inter-
vals, and then simply falling, decreas-
ing steadily in volume until it is so
faint I almost cannot hear it, but still
the bees are singing, in turn and in
unison, the long and dying note.

the scaffoldings behind which there are
no buildings . . .

an end, an end, a final end.

ANCESTORS

POETRY

East River Nocturne

Felix Stefanile

(1974)

The sun is setting over the dirty channel:
in the slant light the sun glows, soft as suede,
and stinks to holy heaven. Here I am.
I had to sail a thousand miles of grass,
past sky-scrapers of corn, grain elevators
the meadows heaving like a golden main,
to get to where time's all at sea again:
this muck-and-mutter of my childhood home
caught in the mangle of the incoming tide
of old Atlantic, dead, polluted water
swirling south of the Queensborough Bridge,
a stream as dark as Styx, as dirty as history.

Back home in Indiana, the grand goose goes
like a white sloop, riding a choppy sea
of bean and squash; the tassels clack their dry bells
and the stalks bend their backs in the rolling wave,
their colors changing, rolling in the wind,
the way an ocean changes, green to gray
to flecks of dark and yellow, back to green.
Often, in the soft, mid-western haze

of field and village, an old dream returns,
and I think of this shore, its rubble of broken water,
its haul of cities like bones on a beach,
the cowrie-glimmer of the light, the smell
of grease and smoke, the burning of a world,
and then it seems I've dreamed the corn-fields up.

When I was a boy we swam this cluttered river:
Before we dived we called out to our friends,
"Here's half-moon on the Hudson!" and jumped in,
Bare buttocks up. Everybody laughed.
Sometimes the girls observed us from the park
A street away, beyond the breakwater.
Their mewing sounded like the complaining gulls
barred from the gleaming flats by the sprawled beast
of our proud adolescence, Pure Disease.
I marvel now that danger never struck:
dead men still ride these waves, the broken glass
glints from the bottoms, bright as Spanish treasure,
the whirlpool gurgles its gay, drunken song.

The memory is rich, but is it real?
Did something only happen, as is said,
in anecdote, a half-remembered chat
in the gray past, a thing your mother said
you did, until with years the saying made
a certain dream, a memory now yours?
Or did you dream it sure enough one night
and waken suddenly, amazed with fear,
and then times later, when the dream came back
it brought no nightmare you could know it by,
and now that you've forgotten you forgot
you can remember, and it didn't happen?
Dreams, fears, shameless fantasies,
the past's that kind of rainbow, dust and light,
a prism for the solipsistic eye,
an art of seeing. The past is bad art:
my art's astonishment, not piety.

A nightmare's plenty, we had dreams enough:
we proved our bravery raiding the coal-yards.
Fleet of foot, we leaped the barbed-wire fences,
empty coal-sacks fastened to our belts,

and when the old watchman shook a fist at us,
like Polyphemus hurled his stones, we hooted,
gathered up the heaps, our bloody harvest.
Or else we raced across the roofs for a glory,
leaping from alley to alley, mountaineers
tilting over the rusty tenement Alps
of pigeon-coop eyries, peaks of pitch and tar.
Once my father chased me up and down
and whaled the daylights out of me. And once
Tully fell and broke his neck. And once
we knocked out all the windows of Platt's Works
on Tenth Street, which was fun, and hard work too.
Sal was caught by Clancy and didn't snitch;
his father whaled the daylights out of him.
And some weeks later Clancy caught him again
At the cellar-window of the hardware store,
and Clancy whaled the daylights out of him.
That made Sal's father angry. He went to court
to say that Clancy had no right, and then Sal's father
whaled the daylights out of Sal once more.

Years: wind in a shell, and what's unclean
gleaming, gleaming, ripped fish on a pier,
the half-moon foundered, like a broken bottle,
at the tide's edge, in a rank, glittering place
of horse-shoes, razor clams, the crazy morgue
of an auto-dump, a ziggurat of waste.
Some boys have built a look-out at the top,
a tent of swaying tin. They've hoisted flags
made out of burlap bags and a bed-sheet,
and scrawled in paint their insolent emblems:
a skull-and-bones, a woman with monster breasts.
This shore's their neutral ground, a no-mans' land
to contemplate the world, the dirty sea,
the waves forever rolling toward the land
from what far-flung, untamable beginnings.
They play at being pirates, spy the dogs,
the gulls, the crows, at a calm work of salvage
to glean the pittance that the tide casts up.
There's not a flattery here; they bay like hounds,
whistling and hooting at the strolling cop
who tips his cap at them from a fair distance.

And here I am, without a tourist's eye
my one good ear not good enough to hear
the siren-flimmer of sentiment's movie-score:
no spirit-lifting floating orchestra
perched in its moon-spot magic helicopter's
technicolor-window, zeroes in
on dome and cupola, cosmetic sweeps
of arches, bridges, splat geometries
of piers and culverts glossed to satin sheen
of lens-cured waters, then the argon flash
of a saw toothed horizon blotting out
the nearest stars, and the rich dark of space,
while the rich hero kisses his slum-days sweetheart.
Beneath that dome and cupola, that sweep
Of crazily canted cables, power-lines
cupping the city in their spider-pouch,
right in the center of the epic, there!
next to the cannery and the soda-plant
that looms like the Parthenon by my dim wharf,
off to the side, kink-angled, like a crate
slipped from a truck and splintered in the street,
a patch of window-fleck in the neon's flame,
my childhood home leans to, like shipwreck stalled
in a montage of miracle and mud.

Where is the past lean to, for connections?
Those Hoosier fields—those corrugated meadows—
my art's astonishment, not piety.
At thirteen, Carmen tried to kill herself;
"tired of the job," she told the doctor.
Too inexperienced with death to die
she lived her small death through, and at fifteen
was married, and her child was born that year,
and her husband sent to prison. ". . . for the car.
The car broke down. He couldn't pay for it;
the company was suing him for it.
He forged a check. The baby's all I had,
and that was lonelier than death. I hustled:
I wouldn't go for less than twenty dollars.
It only takes, be nice. You just be nice."
Behind McSorley's Alley, where he'd gone
to forage in the junk, as he often did,
an old man found her, among the crates and cartons.

Roses red and yellow at the hem,
she was the flowered dress that caught his eye.

I listen to the hooting of the boys.
All day their rasp was in the city's ears:
the first remark of the gutters, mimic roosters,
they whistled their flags up, hauled their small parades
even before the sun had come to shine.
They took up all the free seats in my mind
with their gabble on garbage-cans, by telephone-poles,
dust in the wind, cinders to fleck an alley.
They're raucous, and inexpensive, and rather useless,
Their cheep as thin as a nail, or a querulous chirping
As of old women out of breath, and scolding.
Lost in the rumble of trucks, the policeman's siren,
their little hordes small matter to the world
and the world—for that—no audience they need
who sing because they sing, and not for supper,
somehow they've made it, made it to this evening
where searchlights scrawl their tigerstripes in the sky,
and the river, like Ophelia, dances silver.

The Chrysler Building spits St. Elmo's fire
right in my capering eye; across the channel
the sand heaves up its hoard of beer-cans and stars,
like a council of lost friends, the houses
rise out of shadow, all their helmets gleaming.
A tug-boat's horn, that trails its skein of gulls
to flutter in its wake, like banners streaming,
sounds elegies. The music gets to me,
racked shore, rock-gleam of tides, the creaking pier,
and in my heart these words to answer back.

On the Square

Anne Paolucci

(1974)

We'll sit a while. The sun
Is setting behind the Baron's house,
And church bells ring tired
Old women to vespers. Here comes
The overseer, back from the fields,
His boots all caked with mud,
A wide hat shadowing his face;
In silence he passes by, confidence
In every step that rings
Against the cobblestones.
Toothless old men greet him
From their place beside the wall;
From the shadows of the lane
Comes the rumble of a cart
Returning from its morning
In the fields.

This hour of dusk recalls
Other men with other children
By the hand, strolling
Under a young sky and savoring
Familiar Sunday smells.
I too once had an old man
To call home from the square
As the day set and church bells
Rang to rest another sun.

Autobiography

Robert Viscusi

(1991)

in my house we had an elephant named Italy
grazed the parlor for peanuts
stroked the back of your neck with the thumb of her trunk
kept sitting on the chairs and breaking them
when we went out she stayed home and threw straw all over the floor
we didn't know what to do with her
there was no group for people stuck with an elephant
the social worker took one look and left.
we painted her sides with huge pink flowers
marched her in the parade
rented her out for parties
wrote papers about her in school
waiting for her to die, we bought sacks of lead shot
to stuff her with but she refused to go.
we have had to reinforce the floors three times
and are always putting in another sidewalk.

Tea at Aunt's

John Ciardi

(1994)

Mrs. Clossen died of cancer.
Irene's married to a dancer.
Bill Kerr runs the hardware store.
Joe-that-used-to-live-next-door
Lost his job and moved away.
Jeb? Saw him just yesterday—
The picture of health at eighty-three,
God bless him. Try these with your tea.

Mrs. Alvi's Victor's home—
He's with the consulate at Rome.
She says he likes that line of work.
Renaldo's living in New York.
Grace and Terri bought a house.
They have two girls. But Mr. Kraus
Needs nurse's care—it costs a lot
To stay alive. Who would have thought
A man like that would have a stroke?
"Work for the doctors and you die broke,"
Your uncle always used to say,
God rest his soul—ten years next May.
Well, everyone has his load to bear
He'd say, poor soul. Here! I declare
You haven't eaten a thing! Try these—
Time was when you and Eloise
Couldn't even wait to let them cool.
Landsakes now, where'd I put my spool?
Thank you. I'm glad you're still some use
Though you can't eat. That's no excuse—
Your health comes first. I wish you'd seen
Mabel Sinclair's girl Kathleen,
The mess she made herself, poor thing,
With all this fancy dieting.
She married that boy that used to bring
The paper—you remember him.
It's little he married, but it's slim—

I agree that's everything nowadays.
I swear I can't keep up with ways
And times and people. There's that Le Roy
Something or other, the fireman's boy—
Married, divorced, and married. Why
He wasn't more than two feet high
Last time I looked. And Clara's Johnny
A major in the army. And Sonny
Gone for a pilot. Time runs away.
Landsakes it seems like yesterday
I wiped his nose. Well, that's how 't is.
And now you eat a piece of this.

Cento at Dawn

Daniela Gioseffi

(1995)

The wind blows out of the gates of the day.
Let the night keep what the night takes away,
dreamt in a dream the heavy soul, somewhere
struck suddenly and dark down to its knees,
sighs as a griffon sighs off in the orphic air—
awakes as morning at the brown brink eastward springs
and the whole landscape flushes on a sudden at a sound—
the clang of waking life; the streets are stirred,
    birds fly to the glistening roofs and sing;
an omnibus across the bridge
    crawls like a yellow butterfly,
while I stand on the roadway and on the pavement grey
and dream that beauty passes like a dream
    fastened to a dying animal.

Cento is an Italian form of verse in which lines and refrains from poets of the past are deliberately used and combined into a new poem.

L'Esiliatu

Al Poeta Francesco Greco

Domenico Adamo

(1996)

Chissà è la terra dduve sugnu natu,
pocu me 'mporta chillu che diciti
Si 'ngratamente m'aviti cacciatu
Vena lu juernu chi vine pentiti.

Nente vala ssa pompa chi portati
E tutta s'arruganza chi teniti
Vue de rapina e farsità
E la povere gente l'affrigiti.

Siti a stu mundu sulu mu'ngrassati
A dannu de li schiavi chi teniti
Supra li furti de i vuestri antinati
Vacabbundi: De grolia ve pasciti.

The Exile

After the Poet Francesco Greco

Translated by Joseph D. Adams

(1996)

This is the land where I was born—
Little it matters what you say
As you drive me unappreciated away—
The day will come when you will
mourn.

Your imperious array has no worth
Nor does your display of smug
disdain—
From plunder comes all that you attain
And the impoverished you crush to the
earth.

You exist only to fatten your gut
On abuse of the serfs you oppress
Expanding your pirate parents'
excess—
Vagrants all: you relish your glut.

The Cellar Twenty Years Later

W. S. Di Piero

(1997)

The twelve goofed wooden steps
even now try to shrug me off,
as I duck under the lintel,
the cockeyed timber, where years ago
we nailed the yellow horseshoe's horns,
tips down, to beat bad luck.

That's how we gave the Devil back
his own smart gilded work.
I must have passed beneath this sign
a hundred times, baffled in the force
stretched tight between rooms upstairs
and dark-shining zones below.

Hugging the wall, I can feel the coal trap
snap and shutter wide, then flint-streams
flashing light half left outside
cheered down the chute into the bin.
I stood aslant myself, neatly pitching
off the stairs into the phaseless dark.

But the horseshoe did its work, holding me
in place, saved me from the fall
into merely real mineral gravity.
It also fixed me in this middle range,
homeless, off balance, listening
to odd faint sounds above my head.

Minotaur

Lewis Turco

(1999)

In my dream there is light
in the underground passage
turning between stone block walls.
The floor is a shallow stream.

How have I come to be
here in this place with my son,
not yet a yearling? Danger
waits nearby—one can feel it.

He must be preserved. At
the end of the passage there
is safety—another thing
I know, but cannot tell how.

The water moves slowly,
but it can bear him in this
frail shell in which I place him.
And he has been set afloat.

As he drifts through stone, through
light, he rises, leans upon
the rim to fathom water.
It is true: Pain is depthless.

My feet move to follow,
to set my child again, but
the fluid drags at my flesh.
I call; he does not look back.

As he diminishes
in the curve of his passage,
I sense the beast I have feared
in the distance between us.

The Garden of the Apocalypse

Vincent Ferrini

(2000)

The black man has no premium
on color and enslavement
neither has the yellow man, nor the white
nor the brown skinned

each person
carries a civil war within him

who wedding the contraries
in himself
already is on his way
pioneering the new civilization

flags are obsolete
and so are countries and creeds

we are witnesses and participants
ending an interregnum
tomorrow, no today
Earth is the begetter of the universe
and Love, the only kingdom
which is not by fiat

a man is in it
outside it
or approaching the gates

In the Golden Sala

Sandra Mortola Gilbert

(2002)

Sun of Sicilian hillside,
heat of poppies opening like fierce
boutonnieres of Apollo,
light of Agrigento, fretting the sea and the seaside cliffs—
light of the golden *sala,*
the great *sala* of the ruined *palazzo*
where my Sicilian grandmother and her nine children
camped outside Palermo.

Gold leaf, gold moldings,
shredded tapestries with gold threads.
"Once it belonged to a prince
Mama kept chickens on the terrace
but they came in sometimes, and the donkey too."
Gold chairs, gilt around the windows,
angels with shining hair and empty eyes
staring from the ceiling.

"Mama made our beds in the corners:
the big room scared us, we thought
the prince's ghost was there."
Gold railings where her laundry hung,
gold curtains, new eggs under them.
Her cooking fire in a corner,
the center of the *sala* a cave of gold
for spankings and scoldings.

"Mama was a midwife, knew everything
about herbs and births.
The peasant women came from farms around Palermo
so she could help them."
On floors still streaked with gold
she made them spaces
in the dazzling spaces where the prince once walked.
Gold of forgotten dances, tattered rugs.

When a new baby slid out in a splash of water
he must have looked up, dazed,

toward the prince's Apollonian light,
and the black eyes of the midwife
and the black eyes of the midwife's nine black-haired children
would have looked quizzically down,
as if from a high cliff by the sea
hot and yellow with new poppies.

Father's Days

Gerard Malanga

(2004)

Yeah, nevermind with the whole weight of history behind you.
Allen Street Orchard Street the El overhead.
Nevermind the snapshots you with me
on your knee in Poe Park. The graininess of spring into summer.
A vacant lot in the dusty afternoon light.
Clotheslines crisscrossing the alley.
Nevermind the dashed dreams.
Your mind in a trance notating numbers that never add up.
The scores of little red notebooks piled up and forgotten.
Nevermind the day you vanished without a trace.
Nevermind how things turned out.
Tutto questo tempo.
We ride the subways forever, counting the stations
lugging bundles of drygoods staring into the faces.
Nevermind the clothes you sewed by hand,
the new suit for Easter. Time rapidly passes.
Uno due tre cente nove
The tracks that ascend and lead nowhere.
Nevermind how things turned out.
Nevermind the daemons.
The daemons consumed you, the darkness surrounds you.
Nevermind I didn't take my pill this morning.
Nevermind some people have all the luck.

In Tunis I Walked through Halfaween

Alexander Theroux

(2004)

In Tunis, I walked through Halfaween,
A slum quarter, trays of sweets, impudent
  spiels, toothachy candy, bedouin in

from the *bled*, streaks of children,
urchins pandemonic, coffee vendors clacking
  cups in your face like castanets,

liquids as yellow as pencils, red as
medicine, green as dye. I solve a riddle
  under the white sun, while I watch

at noon under a minaret and courtyard
of mosques erected by the Aghlabites. A man
  who kisses his forefinger in greeting

at a table gathers a woman to him,
surrendering to whispers. All cities are
  founded in fear. What are the Tunis

afraid of? The sea. I watched them,
as I saw Byrsa, Dido's mountain, recalling
  in her loveliness loosing his lust,

while she drew her *ha'ik* tight
across her back and under her buttocks
  which to the Tunisian male

is the focus of voluptuousness,
how colorfully candy-like a lovely woman,
  like Dido, won't be trifled with,

for colors, red, yellow, and green,
her impudent spiels, her castanets, ringing
  in the air, make not just magic

of her unsolvable mystery,
giving her unquestionably an aura of
  real danger like the sea.

Shinto Mama

George Guida

(2004)

She converted after five-thirty mass,
while watching The History Channel.

She had the gilt-framed family photos
down from the paneled wall.

"Wipe your feet, and keep quiet," she said.
"I'm worshipping Great Aunt Tessie."

"Aunt Tessie, Aunt Tessie!
Give the little *sfacim'* my daughter some common sense."

My mother hovers at an altar to
sere images of housecoated women
frowning, upon the brick stoops of Brooklyn.

She chants staccato,
"Ohm, ohm, ohm-ohm-ohm,"
semi-automatic.

My poor sisters in miniature,
made of excess tinsel and *presepio* figurines,
sit in her hands.

Her kimono the size of Sicily,
my mother has gone
Japanese, converse *Madama Butterfly*.

The narrator has told her
a Shinto priestess can summon spirits
of ancestors bound to serve their own.

She understands this guilt by blood.

"Uncle Martin, Uncle Martin!
Let my cheapskate brother, that *murte fam,*

pick up a check now and then.
What do I look like,
a friggin' Brinks truck?"

Her prayers rouse suburbs from slumber.

Italian women with direct lines to
their *stramort'* are legion.
They conjure the dead,
whenever we don't behave.

Their pleas still empty streets,
resound to us in dreams,
they already our gods.

Spanish Steps

Gerald Mancini

(2006)

Maybe you can get away,
maybe the whole long story
has a place after all—sure Greco says,
like the two young women who threw
drinks in your face
the night you told them
a little truth, they wanted to get back
somehow, the way talk
goes from bad to worse.
And now it's just these friends
who've led you back
through crowds,
the march for *pace*
over, the streets closed off.
You walked all the way
to find the little chapel of San Silvestro
where nuns sang a cappella the chants
of peace, the tiny wooden door
opening to take the change—and later
the church of the Quattro Coronati,
and then the piazza,
the streets leading down again.
Those songs stay with you still,
hymns to a stillness, unheard
and sweet.
Oh, how many years
since a boy stood on the edge of the dark
and asked you to come back?
Howard Camp, where the crop was almost in,
the season ended,
the workers on the move again.
How many times have you gone back
to stand alone in that growing dark
and ask the same things, waiting for the truck
to come. The crew boss angry
that you'd stayed too late.
You still see his hands.

Pilgrims, your Italian friends say,
pilgrims who've come to see the barque,
Bernini's fountain beneath the rooms
where Keats and Severn stayed.
I lost my son here once you tell them,
he ran ahead of us, down into the crowds at night.
He was six years old then, panic hit.
And there below, at last
we saw him—
playing chess with older Roman boys
who'd gathered to watch him play.
It's like that really, the quick
sting of loss that comes
because you're honest and don't know how
to cover up. A death so sharp and quick
it takes your breath away, an infant son's death,
his hands so small they cling to your finger
holding on for life. You cannot
turn away.
We took our sons to Cumae,
to see the cave where Aeneas
asked the Sybil for advice,
we saw the sea beyond
the caves, and climbed the stairs.
How sad Montale said
memory at its fullest
has no one to hold it back.
And still this small hand reaches out
like foreign voices chanting songs of peace,
a view from shuttered rooms along a river,
silver coins tossed into a moving stream.

Nana's Earrings

Tina Tocco

(2007)

My nana wears clip-on earrings.
They are costume pearls, real
to her and to me. They lie low on lobes almost as big,
flapping a hand span away as she chatters
at the end of the day
in the after-dinner tints
of the milk glass lamp.

At her rosewood vanity, she slips them off
with a click from each, a green streak
left where their globes had been. The gobs are handed off to me—
to quieting hands and quieting pleas—
if I say that I have been good.
They nip a bit when they sink in to skin
of still a fragile width.
I strut the room like Rita Hayworth,
hoping they will pierce.

My nana claps her hands at me and I run
to them for her to take the heavy balls and lay them
in their special sleeping place—
a box that came from somewhere far
with empty pockets meant for things my nana
doesn't know to want.

THE SACRED AND PROFANE

PROSE

Against Gravity

Albert Di Bartolomeo

Fiction (1991)

MY FATHER SAT behind the wheel of the immense white Buick, driving us patiently through the city streets toward the Walt Whitman Bridge, and then, after we had crossed it, swiftly through New Jersey beneath a wide cataract sky, the light that day tremulous from the dense August heat. He was quiet as always, and gave off his familiar aura of distance and private suffering. My mother sat across from him close to the door. She hummed or sang bits of songs, appearing cheerful, well-adjusted, and not at all like the madwoman who, just the other day, had chased Jamie around the house with a spatula raised up above her head like a tomahawk, shouting obscenities.

We were heading toward the annual cookout at the house of my Aunt Marie, my mother's favorite sister. The rest of my mother's family would be there, too, including her parents, and that made my mother happy. The cookouts were usually outings of great fun and warm pleasures, and they always left me with fond memories. But with that day's strange and somber close, I became aware for the first time in my life that, beneath the everyday motions of adult activity, there was a shadow world of mysteries and emotional labyrinths so complex they could scarcely be comprehended by the very men and women who created them.

Jamie and I sat in the back seat, the cooler of potato salad and our little brother Ted between us. A docile kid with dark, gloomy eyes, Ted didn't say much, content to gaze out the windows at the scenery. I sat directly behind my mother. My window was closed because there was a hole in the door panel where the handle should have been and I couldn't roll the window down for a breeze. My father bought the rust-splotched car from a pal of his "real cheap," but shortly after getting it we found the car one morning with a wide puddle beneath it of red fluid that had leaked copiously from the car's underbelly. I knew that was bad from the way my father stood looking solemnly at the car as though at someone with a terminal illness. "Transmission," he had said. The car sat in the same spot for months before my father scraped together enough money to have it repaired.

The window on my mother's side was closed, too, but that was to keep the wind from disturbing her hair, which was shaped into a beehive and sprayed so heavily that Jamie remarked it would stay in place even in a typhoon.

"I'm hot," I said, soon after leaving the city.

My mother said nothing.

"Mom, can't you roll down the window a little bit?"

"Aren't you getting enough air from the other side?"

"No. Jamie's blocking it."

Jamie said, "Would you please stop moving." My sister held a large sketch pad in her lap as she drew my portrait with a stick of charcoal.

"You said to be natural."

"I said to be natural, but I didn't say you could dance."

"I don't want to be drawn anyway," I said.

"Come on, sit still. I'm almost finished."

"Mom, I'm suffocating back here."

"We'll be there soon," my mother said, patting her rigid column of hair as if checking to see that it had not listed off the vertical.

"Switch seats with me, Jamie?" I asked.

"I can't. I'm drawing you."

"How about switching when you're done?"

"Maybe. Now why don't you look at your magazine and be still."

"I'm too hot to be still," I said, but took from the floor a recent copy of *Life* magazine that featured the Mexico City Olympics, which I had watched on television. I turned to the photographs of Bob Beamon, who shattered the world long jump record by nearly two feet and then fell to his knees, hands over his face in disbelief. The text repeated what the television announcer had said: that Beamon's jump was an astounding feat not likely ever to be matched, that he had jumped at the very edge of human capability and that any farther would surely result in injury. The announcer had been awestruck, his voice quivering. I was awestruck, too. Beamon had jumped nearly ten yards, more than twice the width of our living room, a leap that seemed unreal, superhuman, and as I watched the jump again and again on the television, goose bumps formed on my skin. Beamon's achievement had the look of the magical, something influenced by a spiritual hand, and that's what awed and chilled me.

When the program ended, I took my father's tape measure and went outside. Every day since witnessing Beamon's miraculous jump, I had been sprinting and leaping in the park near our house for hours, desperate to create a miracle like that of my own.

I put the magazine down. "It's so hot, I can't breathe," I said, feeling warm and clammy.

"Be a man," Jamie said.

"You be a man."

"That would be difficult." Jamie blew a large purple bubble with her grape gum and immediately burst it. "Listen," she said, removing the gum from the tip of her nose and about her mouth, "the voice of a giraffe," and she made a noise that originated near her adenoids.

"What?"

"It's a game."

"Animals don't have voices."

"That's the idea. You have to imagine what it would sound like." She showed me the drawing. "What do you think?"

"Pretty good," I said, too uncomfortable from the heat to be impressed, even though the drawing looked like me quite a bit. "Will you switch seats with me now?"

She popped her gum. "I don't like to sweat."

"You're a creep." I turned away from Jamie and looked around to see if Lillian Walsh and her family were still following us. They were.

The previous month, we rented a bungalow at the New Jersey shore with the Walshes. On the last afternoon of our week stay, while the others ate lunch on the boardwalk, Jamie and I watched from the blanket as Lillian and one of her kids jumped around in the surf like seals. My father, holding Teddy's hand, stood at the ocean's edge in the wet sand and watched.

"Who does she think she is?" Jamie had said. She turned from the water, threw herself on her stomach, and began to draw with furious strokes. "I don't think she's so hot, do you?"

"No," I said, but when Lillian came from the water and lay glistening on the blanket with her face to the sun, I thought of the freckles scattered about her cleavage as crumbs sticking to my tongue.

Thinking about her in her bathing suit, I waved to Lillian through the back window of our car. Lillian drove a sky-blue convertible, and her hair whipped about her head in the breeze. She smiled broadly at me and waved back. I felt an electric tingle in my belly, not too different from what I felt at night when thinking of Lillian. She had been asked to these cookouts before, but this was the first one she had attended. Her husband had taken a job across the state and the Walshes were moving away in several weeks, so I had to act fast and boldly that day, or soon, if I was going to experience what I only now imagined.

I couldn't sleep the night before because I kept thinking about Lillian and how I would go about meeting her tomorrow in some secluded spot at my aunt's house so I could kiss and touch her. That I was thirteen and Lillian somewhere in her thirties didn't seem to matter. I knew she liked me. Hadn't she already kissed me on the back of the neck when she came in the house the other day to share a cup of coffee with my mother? Wasn't she always saying how cute I was? So I fully believed Lillian would not be outraged if I pressed my feverish body against her in some hidden spot there in New Jersey; she would understand.

"The voice of a duck-billed platypus," Jamie said, making snorting noises.

"That sounds like a pig."

"You don't even know what a duck-billed platypus is."

"It's your twin."

She punched me in the leg.

After crossing the railroad tracks, then driving another quarter-mile down an unnamed road with only a house here and there to the sides of it, we arrived at my Aunt Marie's place. She and her family lived in a wood-framed house with cock-eyed windows and the paint peeling from the clapboard like mange; they owned only the acre the house stood on but no one ever troubled them or us when we hiked through the surrounding fields or woods. With its snakes, toads, tomato fields, orchards, ponds, and old wooden musty houses like my aunt's, New Jersey, next to the city's unrelenting rectilinear shapes and combustion odors, always struck me as strange and exotic and like no other place I knew yet.

Dust rose about the car as we turned into the dirt driveway. Aunt Marie's dogs, tied to the peach tree with long ropes, barked at us, half mad already with the smell of meat sitting on a chair just out of reach beside the grill. A group of my uncles surrounded the grill, trying to light it. Beyond them, I saw small children, cousins, playing in the dilapidated gazebo near the trees.

When we emptied from the car, my Uncle Dave appeared from the detached garage, a spark plug in his teeth. Dave drove tractor-trailers across the country and was often away from home for weeks at a stretch. He was a large man and smelled of engines. When I was much younger, Dave would put me on his shoulders and lift me into the peach tree where, dangling from a limb ten feet off the ground, I'd call to my mother just to hear her scream.

Dave started over, but just then my mother's sisters spilled squealing and laughing from the house and he held back as they swarmed us. My father made his greetings brief and went toward the grill, as if the lighting of the fire were an adult male ritual he must witness. Wanting to escape the women myself, I put the cooler of potato salad on the hood of the car, squeezed out of the huddle, and followed Uncle Dave back to the garage.

Dave's sons were there, helping him work on a car.

"Long time, no see," Eddie said when I came up. He grabbed my hand with his black and greasy one.

"What's broken?" I asked.

"What's *not* broken, you mean," Ralph said. "Hey, you want to help us?"

"That's okay," I said. I had no interest in cars.

"Come on. Afraid to get dirty?"

"No." But that was exactly why. Looking at my cousins' blackened arms and smudged clothing, I did not want to spend the rest of the day resembling them. "I didn't see Grandmom and Grandpop yet."

"Then step aside, junior." Eddie shoved me and squatted at the front wheel.

I left the smelly garage and walked back into the sun.

My mother, her sisters, and Lillian still stood at the car, grouped together like a tribe, but Jamie had detached herself. I saw her by the shaded side of the house where my grandparents sat in beach chairs. They sat in those chairs practically all day, shooing flies and receiving homage like royalty. Jamie held her drawing pad under her arm, and I wondered, as I walked over, how long it would take her to tell my grandparents that she wanted to draw them. Not long. After I went around saying hello to everyone and returned to my grandparents, Jamie was sitting across from them doing their portraits in pencil. I stood talking to them for a time while Jamie drew, then my Uncle Louie asked me if I wanted to play horseshoes. As I walked off, my grandfather warned his son about his aim, my Uncle Louie having brained one of the dogs last summer with an errant toss.

An hour later, Jamie organized the customary softball game, always a comical affair because of the quirky efforts the women made with the bat and their wild parabolic throws. She made up the sides, dividing the men and women and boys and girls evenly. Uncle Dave umpired, his voice booming with each call. My father never played softball, preferring instead to stand on the sidelines and play mora with my grandfather. I glanced over at them from my first base position now and then, watching them throw their hands at each other, my grandfather animated and vigorous, my father as contained as when he played solitaire. But most of my attention during the game that day went to Lillian. She wore tight shorts, no shoes, and a halter top that hugged the marvelous shapes beneath.

When Lillian hit the ball her first time at bat, I intentionally dropped it after Jamie threw it to me from second base. I hadn't seen Lillian alone all day, and giving her the single would keep her with me at first for a minute or two.

"You can broad jump better than you can catch," Jamie called.

I ignored her and turned to Lillian, watching her heaving chest before I spoke.

"That was a good hit," I said, moving closer to Lillian and feeling a little giddy in the stomach.

"You think so, Vincent? Thanks."

"You swing better than the other girls."

"And you're a good batter, too."

One of my cousins struck out and my Aunt Marie came up to bat. She had always been the most athletic of my mother's sisters and was likely to hit the ball, sending Lillian toward second base, so I would have to act fast.

"You smell good," I blurted.

"Excuse me?"

I felt myself redden. "Your perfume."

"Oh. I don't think I have any on, but thanks." She put her hands to her mouth. "Hit a homer, Marie!"

My aunt hit a pitiful pop fly that the pitcher, her son, caught to end the inning. Lillian said, "See you later," took my glove, and trotted to short-stop. She failed to hit the ball again and, sadly, I didn't speak to her the rest of the game.

Late in the afternoon, I found my father and several uncles playing pinochle at a round table beneath my Aunt Marie's oak tree. I watched the game for a while, thinking about the night before when I couldn't sleep, not because of the August heat or the cornerhangers making a racket in front of the hairdresser's, but because of Lillian Walsh.

Giving up on sleep, I went downstairs around twelve o'clock and found my father at the kitchen table playing gin rummy against himself. He did not look up when I drew near, and I thought that I could be a burglar or a killer and he would still appear to fish cards with the apathy of the doomed.

I stood close to him for a few moments, watching the game and his jaws, clenching now and then as if upon rage or heartache, though maybe neither, or nothing he would admit to. Because of the warm night, he wore only his boxer shorts. He looked thinner than I had ever seen him, but I didn't give his health much thought. His fickle illness these last years, which he never complained about or spoke of, had become so much a part of our lives that we were reminded of it only when he went into sugar shock or into the hospital.

"I'm hungry," I had said.

My father put down his hand of cards and lifted the one opposite him. He studied the hand briefly, then fished a card from the deck and threw away one of his own.

"Is that why you can't sleep?"

"Yeah." I wasn't about to confess my yearnings for Lillian to him. "You?"

He kept his head pointed downward at the cards and didn't answer. I hadn't expected him to. Getting him to explain about anything was difficult enough, let alone whatever kept him awake and quiet.

I shrugged and went around his woolly back to gather what I needed. A few discards later, I sat across from him at the table eating a bowl of corn flakes and a banana. My father continued to play against a phantom and only glanced at me between hands, not much expression in his face. These silences and his dull looks were as much a part of him as his great nose and one eye, and I was not offended by them.

"Play?" my father asked when I finished my snack.

He surprised me. "Sure."

He immediately dealt me a hand of cards and we began to play gin. He had taught all of us to play the game years ago, though only my sister Jamie was a match for him; she actually beat him a few times. I never did, and that night was no different. We played until two o'clock in the morning, saying little to each other. I won three hands, but my father won every game.

"Better practice," he said when I had enough.

"I'll play against myself like you."

"No, don't." He gathered together the cards. "You should go to bed now."

"Are you?"

"No."

I lingered for a minute, watching his coarse plumber's hands and his flexing jaws, then I left him. As I walked up the stairs, with an image of Lillian forming in my head, I heard the cards being shuffled.

After the softball game, I hiked to the slimy pond with several of my cousins and threw stones into the green water. We later rode bicycles down the quiet lanes and on the path that ran into a wide arc behind the house and through the fields. Returning, we ate more charred hotdogs and hamburgers, the potato salad, and chunks of warm watermelon.

When night fell, the mosquitoes came out in force and drove everyone inside but Jamie, who had stayed out to collect fireflies in a mayonnaise jar. Eddie and Ralph vanished. The women gathered in the kitchen to talk and the men and older boys like me filled the dim living room to watch the ball game on television; the children were spread evenly between. I sat next to my father on the sofa; from my seat, I could see into the kitchen where Lillian sat at the end of a table. Looking at her a number of times, I caught her glancing my way, and there was an intensity in her eyes, though fleeting, that I had not seen before. When she stood up from the table and walked out of sight to either the powder room or the door to the porch, I decided it was to the door.

I waited a half minute, then left the living room, walking casually to the screen door and outside onto the front porch, pausing there to gaze into the dark before walking into it.

No moon shone that night and there were no street lamps near my aunt's house; the light from the windows cast only a few feet before the darkness became solid. I thought I heard the lid of Jamie's jar clap near the garage, where I wished and feared Lillian might be, but saw nothing when I reached it. I circled the garage to face the house and saw heads in the kitchen window without making out whose they were. The dogs growled in my direction, and one of them let out a single half-hearted bark.

I heard the clap of the lid again, but still couldn't tell from where. I walked slowly toward the gazebo, thinking that might be a place where Lillian would go. The sound of the crickets seemed to increase and the drifting fireflies thickened the closer I moved toward the trees.

At the gazebo, I heard whistling that could have been Jamie, but I could not tell whether the sound was coming closer, moving away, or stationary. I stood on the back side of the gazebo, opposite the arched entrance that faced the house, and waited, straining to hear Lillian's step above the crickets.

I heard the jar again and, looking toward the sound, I saw a ball of light hovering above the ground a distance away that I could not gauge. I watched the ball move sharply upward, heard the clap of the lid, then watched the ball drop and hover again. I quietly worked my way toward the light, but not quietly enough.

"Who's that?" my sister asked, hearing me.

"The bogeyman."

"Trying to scare me?"

"Would I do that?" I grabbed her arm.

"Hey! You almost made me drop the jar."

"What are you going to do with them, anyway, those bugs?"

"Take them home and let them out in the dark basement."

"That's crazy."

"It would be pretty."

"They'll just die. Besides, Mom'll kill you."

"Shhhh! Somebody's coming."

Jamie drew me against the gazebo. The sound of footsteps came from the other side. Looking through the wooden slats of the gazebo and the vines that clung to them, I glimpsed a dark form approaching. The person took the two steps up into the gazebo and came within an arm's length of us. Because of the vines, I could only see the legs, and those not too clearly.

Then I heard footsteps again in the grass, and again they came from the side of the gazebo that faced the house.

"Are you there?"

I shuddered, felt my heart leap. It was not any of my cousins, not my mother or one of her sisters, not a grandparent or uncle. It was her.

"I thought you weren't going to be here," Lillian said, stepping into the gazebo.

"I shouldn't be." My father's voice hit me like a punch in the stomach and made me gasp.

"I'm glad you are." Lillian's feet shuffled on the wooden floorboards. "It was getting unbearable in there, knowing you were so close, but not being able to touch you." She moved. "Hold me."

"No."

"What's wrong?"

"You shouldn't have come today."

"I'm leaving in two weeks. I had to see you."

"What good would it do?"

"I just wanted to be near you one last time."

"We made a mistake. Can't you just let it go, like me?"

"But you haven't."

"I have so."

"I don't believe that."

Dead silence now, not even their breathing.

"I'm going back to the house," my father said.

"Not yet, please."

"They'll wonder."

"Just let me hold you for a moment."

"You want to hold me? Go ahead, hold me. Touch me, feel my ribs, put your arms around a dying man."

"Don't, Jimmy. Please."

"Everything's over now. Everything. Do I have to spell it out for you?" My father stepped quickly from the gazebo and went toward the house. Lillian called his name once, faintly, then her breath caught at the back of her throat.

I felt a throbbing pressure in my head and chest.

Lillian had taken one step toward the house when Jamie left my side and went around to the other side of the gazebo. I remained in the dark, feeling paralyzed.

"Who's that? Jamie? Jamie, what are you doing out here by yourself? Oh, I see, gathering fireflies. What you have there is called a Japanese lantern. Did you know?"

"I heard all that," Jamie said.

"Excuse me?" Lillian seemed to stop breathing.

"I heard everything."

"You don't understand, Jamie. Your father and I were just talking."

"I'm a kid, but I'm not stupid."

Lillian paused, and the sound of the crickets went louder. Someone's laugh came from the house.

"I'm so sorry," Lillian said, the words choking her.

That's when I bolted. I leaped into the trees and ran full-speed. Low branches whipped my face for some distance, and then I tripped over an unburied root, crashed into a tree, spun completely around, kept running, crashed into another and fell. In the momentary stillness, I heard someone behind me.

"Vincent?" Jamie called.

I scrambled to my feet and began to run again. I collided with another tree before I broke into the clearing and onto the path that ran behind the house. I could see the path dimly stretching into the night, knowing that it eventually connected with the road, and I ran on it as fast as I could.

Jamie called me again.

I looked over my shoulder and saw only that dancing ball of light, the fireflies in the jar. My sister had run after me, but she ran far behind and would never catch me, I thought. She would tire long before I did.

At the end of the path where it joined the road, the ball of light still chased me, but it was closer now. I turned onto the macadam road and ran through the bend and past the house there, dark except for a pale yellow light on the porch. I kept running, wanting to run through the night into the day, run until too exhausted to think of my ridiculous yearnings to embrace Lillian or to imagine my father with Lillian, remember what they had said in the gazebo, what it meant.

I wanted to run forever. But my side began to ache, my throat burned, and my legs started to weaken. I slowed from the pain and fatigue and stopped. With my chest heaving for air, my head about to explode with too much blood and anguish of a sort I had not experienced until now, I sat down in the road.

Jamie did not come up as soon as I thought she would. I looked behind me and saw nothing but the night. I looked into the fields on one side of the road and into the clump of trees on the other, but there was no sign of her.

My breath slowed and my heart had nearly returned to normal when I heard something on the road coming from the direction of my aunt's house. Turning, I saw the light jerking against the darkness, and, moments later, Jamie's blurred arms and legs as she came straight toward me in a sprint.

Two strides before Jamie reached me, she leaped into the air over my head, the jar of fireflies in hand, and flew as far as my best jump back in the city.

She landed on her feet and turned to me. "Beat that."

"What?"

"Bet you can't."

"I don't feel like jumping."

"Come on, Vincent, jump."

"Didn't you hear them back there? He's—" But I could not say anything, because I did not know how I felt about him, my shame and anger confused by what he had said about dying.

"I heard."

"Well?"

"You're afraid I'll beat you."

I paused and looked away. "I know what you're doing."

"I'm challenging you."

"That's a goddamn laugh."

"I want to know who's best."

"Not you."

"Prove it."

I looked at her for a long time before moving, then I got up from the road, walked fifteen paces in the direction of the house and turned. Jamie set the jar of fireflies on the road as a take-off mark before I sprinted toward her and leaped. I easily beat her jump. Jamie marked the length of my jump with a stone from the roadside, walked a distance up the road, turned, ran toward me, and jumped. She sailed a foot past the stone. I said nothing, moved the stone to where her heels had come down, and started up the road. We did this over and over, running and jumping in the deep New Jersey night. We did not speak and ignored the voices in the black distance calling out our names, ignored fatigue and the crash of our feet and knees against the coarse macadam, ignored everything but the need to jump. Jamie and I were caught in something, temporarily doomed, unable to free ourselves from the repetition of jumping. Why, I did not yet have the words to

name. That would not come until years later, long after my father had been buried, and I had finally, after years of resisting, visited his grave, where I stood
staring at the chiseled stone, remembering that manic night. The headlights of
his car had come groping into the darkness and lighted upon Jamie and me. My
father slowed the car to a stop, but he did not step out, beep the horn, or call to
us; instead, he let the engine idle as he sat alone watching us from behind the
windshield, muted and still, as we threw ourselves over and over against gravity.

My Friend, Angelo Ralph Orlandella

William Foote Whyte

Memoir (1995)

MY MEETING WITH Angelo Ralph Orlandella in 1938 began a friendship and collaboration that has continued and grown stronger for more than fifty years. At the time, I was a twenty-four-year-old Junior Fellow at Harvard University, carrying out a sociological study of the North End slum district of Boston, which, at the time, was populated almost exclusively by first- and second-generation Italian Americans.

Angelo Ralph Orlandella was then a nineteen-year-old high school dropout. (I have always called him Ralph because that was what his friends in the North End called him. Many years later, when his immediate boss was named Ralph, Orlandella went back to his first name of Angelo so as to avoid confusion.)

Our backgrounds were completely different. I am the only child of John Whyte, a university professor of German, and my mother, Isabel VanSickle Whyte, who had a master's degree in German and who had taught that subject in high school. Her forebears were Dutch and English who came to this country in the eighteenth century. I am named after my grandfather, William Foote Whyte, who came with his family from Scotland to Wisconsin when he was three years old.

My parents, and especially my mother, were socially concerned people, worried about the plight of the poor, especially in big-city slum districts, but I had had no prior experience with slums before entering the North End. I had grown up in small towns, Caldwell, New Jersey, and Bronxville, New York. I had had many casual friendships, but I had never had anyone I could call a pal or had been a member of any tightly knit informal group, anything like the street corner gangs I found in the North End. My mother used to say with pride that I was becoming a self-sufficient person, by which she meant that I could get so absorbed in what I was doing that I did not need anyone else to entertain or interest me. Perhaps that was true to some extent, but there were times when I was bored or lonely.

I was fascinated by the leadership and structure of street corner gangs. I had made a start as a participant observer, carrying out a study of the North Bennett Street gang of men in their mid- to late twenties. Its informal leader was Ernest Peed, whom I called "Doc" in *Street Corner Society*. To generalize my findings, I needed to study other street corner gangs.

By this time, I had already lived eighteen months in the district yet I still had not figured out what I was doing. I had accumulated files of interviewing and observational materials on a wide variety of topics for what I intended to be a community study, but still I could not see how it might all fit together. It was through the further study of street corner gangs that I began to see the overall shape of the book I was to write.

In 1938 I had learned that Frank Havey, head of the North End Union settlement house, had secured a grant to finance three storefront recreation centers. I had found that the settlement houses did not attract street corner gangs. For young men, they served primarily to attract those who were striving to move up and out of the district. This effort to reach the street corner boys on their corners interested me.

For the three center director positions, I urged Frank Havey to choose current or former street corner gang leaders. I was only partly successful. He appointed two men with master's degrees in social work and my first choice, Ernest Pecci.

It was Pecci who introduced me to Ralph Orlandella (whom I called Sam Franco in *SCS*). On the first night Pecci's center opened, Ralph came in as emissary of his Endicott Street gang. After a brief conversation with Pecci, he went out and brought his gang in. By the second night, Ralph had become Pecci's informal and unpaid assistant director of the center. Pecci knew a few people in this part of the district, but Ralph knew everybody.

Pecci suggested that Ralph could help me to extend my studies of street corner gangs. I invited Ralph to come up to the North End apartment where Kathleen and I lived from 1938 to 1940. He came with his scrapbook of clippings on the district and background material on his own gang. He had started the scrapbook in 1935, without encouragement from any adult. One part of this scrapbook particularly interested me. For his own gang, he had a page for each member. At the top of the page was a sketch (from memory) of the individual, and then he wrote in such points as age, address, education, job, and ambition.

I complimented Ralph but suggested he look beyond individuals to see them in terms of their relations with each other. I had only begun my explanation when Ralph got the point and accepted it with enthusiasm. Of course, this was the sort of thing he knew; he had so taken it for granted that it had not occurred to him how important it might be. From this point until the end of my study, Ralph was my research assistant. I even managed to get Harvard to pay him $100 for his research services.

Since I now had two sharp social observers working with me, I asked Ralph and Pecci to pick the leaders of the other gangs that were frequenting the center. On twelve or more gangs, they were in complete agreement, except for one case. Pecci claimed that Carl was the leader, and Ralph insisted that it was Tommy. Each man presented incidents he had observed that supported his choice, but they remained deadlocked.

As I left the center, I told myself that an agreement on over ninety percent of the cases spoke well for their abilities to identify group leaders, but still I wondered about that one unresolved case. And then came one of the most exciting moments of my research. The following morning while Kathleen and I were still at breakfast, Ralph came thundering up the steps to our second-floor apartment and came in with this breathless message: "You know what happened last night? Carl and Tommy nearly had it out. They got into a big argument, and now the gang is split into two parts with some of them going with Carl and the rest going with Tommy." So Pecci's and Ralph's conflicting views turned out to be an accurate representation of what was happening in the gang.

Some months later, these group leadership studies led me to an action project, which was far from what I had originally planned. My fellowship was designed to support basic research, and sociologists who wandered into applied projects were thought to allow their values to contaminate their empirical findings. I was too troubled by the serious economic and social problems all around me to stick to the pure science model.

I deviated on two occasions. The first occurred when I persuaded Frank Havey to appoint a corner gang leader, Ernest Pecci, to direct one of the three centers. The results turned out as I had predicted. Pecci's center ran smoothly, with a full set of activities largely organized by the young men themselves throughout the six-month duration of the project. Within two weeks' time, the centers directed by MSW degree social workers had to be shut down. They were unable to maintain order.

I had heard innumerable complaints about how the district was forgotten by politicians, how no improvements ever got made, how the politicians just tried to get themselves and their friends ahead. The only park in the district had no covering beyond bare earth, and grounders hit so many rocks that fielding them required daring and luck as well as skill. Garbage collections were erratic, but the bitterest complaint concerned the public bathhouse, where in the summer of 1939 as well as in several earlier summers, there was no hot water available. In a district where only twelve percent of the flats had baths, this was serious.

It occurred to me that what Ralph, Pecci, and I knew about street corner gang leadership could provide a lever for action. Among the three of us, we knew most of the North End gangs and had identified their leaders.

I suggested to Ralph that we organize a protest march on the mayor's office in City Hall. He welcomed the idea and was eager to help organize the march.

The mayor was out of town, but we could not wait, so we marched on the acting mayor. I called the newspapers, and they had reporters and photographers out to follow us. We assembled in the Prince St. playground and then marched up Hanover St. We had to march faster than planned, because many of the younger boys had joined the crowd and wanted to get toward the front. I took up my position toward the back. We stopped traffic along the way, but the police stood by to let us pass.

We assembled again in the City Hall courtyard. While our ten committee members went up to the mayor's office, the other marchers sang "God Bless America" and other songs to the accompaniment of an improvised band. The acting mayor got a list of names of the committee members and a list of our grievances. As our members began to speak, I heard Ralph saying behind me in a low voice: "Get out of here, you cheap racketeer." I turned to see a local politician, Joseph Russo, elbowing his way in. Russo stood his ground, and, at the first opportunity, said, "I would like to add my voice to the protest as a private citizen. . . ." Ralph interrupted, calling out: "He's got nothin' to do with us. He's just trying to chisel in." The acting mayor stated that he would not hear Russo at this time. While the speaking was going on, I distributed a statement to the reporters. The acting mayor said that all of our protests would be taken seriously and some actions would follow.

The next day's newspapers carried big stories with pictures of our march. Among the various papers, we were given credit for having mobilized 300 to 1,500 marchers. The fellows happily accepted the highest figure, but I suspect 300 was closer to the mark.

The day after the demonstration, engineers were examining the boilers in the bathhouse, and in less than a week we had hot water. The street cleaning and garbage collections seemed to be improved, at least for a time.

What next? We had got an organization together and staged a spectacular event that got results. Anything after that must have seemed a comedown, but we wanted to use our initial organization as a base for getting the young men of the North End working together on other community projects. The committee members were not used to working together, and we could not agree on any new projects.

It seemed at the time that our march had been an isolated event, without any follow-up. The following spring, Ralph organized a softball league that built on and extended our protest organization. The league came to fruition in the summer of 1940, after I had left the North End.

I completed the first draft of *Street Corner Society* while living in the North End. From 1940 to 1942, Kathleen and I were at the University of Chicago, where I completed my studies for a Ph.D. in sociology. In December 1942 Ralph enlisted in the Marine Corps.

When *Street Corner Society* was published in November 1943, Kathleen and I were in Georgia Warm Springs Foundation, where I was recovering from an attack of polio. I wrote Ralph to ask if I could send him a copy. He replied that he was about to be shipped out to the South Pacific and he could not take books. He asked me to send it to his wife, Rose.

I thought that might be the end of our joint story, but he survived three island assaults. The island ordeals inflicted only minor physical wounds, but he spent two years recovering his emotional equilibrium in the San Diego Marine Hospital. Shortly after he reached San Diego, he sent us a postcard that appeared confused and not fully comprehensible. Two days later, we got a long letter that was clear and eloquent. He had just read the book Rose had sent him, and *Street Corner Society* had reinforced his desire to resume his studies of leadership and organization.

At the time of my retirement ceremonies in 1980, the Dean of Cornell University's New York State School of Industrial and Labor Relations suggested I invite seven former research associates or students to come and speak about their own work in relation to mine. I invited six behavioral scientists and Angelo Ralph Orlandella. Ralph spoke so effectively that several people in the audience said that his remarks should be published.

That gave me an idea. The second edition of *SCS* had contained an appendix describing my experiences in doing the North End study. That appendix kept the book alive. For the third edition in 1981, the main addition was appendix B, "The Whyte Impact on an Underdog." I was particularly moved by one passage describing Ralph's feelings as the U.S.S. Middleton approached the island of Eniwetok.

> The close sea and air support was a hurricane of flame, steel, and black smoke, which permeated the air with a strong odor of explosives and diesel fuel. In a "rolling barrage," battleships, cruisers, destroyers, rocket ships, and a host of smaller ships, together with navy and marine aircraft, shelled, bombed, and strafed the atoll in a relentless attack. The tremors and noise sounded like a sustained thunderclap and kettledrums magnified a million times.
>
> The tension inside of me mounted with the intensity of the operation. A new sensation gripped me with a wild, desperate feeling in the depth of my stomach. It was at this very instant that a flashback of my whole world came before my eyes: Rose, my parents and sisters, and Bill Whyte.

He goes on to describe the transfer to the landing barge to go in with the first wave of the assault.

> As we lay face down on the bottom of the barge, I checked the safety on my rifle with my hand and also assured myself that the bayonet was in place and thought to myself, "I will never see my loved ones again, nor ever get to read Bill's book."

We next saw Ralph and Rose in the fall of 1950, when they were living with two young sons in Burlington, Massachusetts, where they had settled in his last Marine Corps assignment before retiring from the active service. This was a gloomy meeting. Still in the Marine Corps Reserve, Ralph had just received notification that he was being called back to active service. Soon he would have to go to Parris Island for some weeks of advanced training at the First Sergeants' School before being sent into combat in the Korean War. He felt that a marine could not reasonably expect to survive three South Pacific island assaults, and now in Korea his chances would have run out. To take care of the family, he had put all his savings into an insurance policy on his own life. Survival was the main thing, but then he knew this would also be the end of his ambition to build a career in social research.

I sympathized with his plight, but I also felt a sense of social injustice. If a man had risked his life in three deadly island assaults, he should now be granted the opportunity to serve his country in other ways through his exceptional talents.

I had recently joined a group of behavioral science advisors to the Human Relations Research Institute at Maxwell Air Force Base in Alabama. I told Ralph about this assignment and mentioned that the army and the navy also had social research units. What about the Marine Corps? He shook his head. "No, in the marines we just fight." As I groped for words, Ralph added that there was such a thing as "detached duty" whereby a man could be transferred from one branch of the service to another, but added that he had never heard of it being done. That seemed like grasping at straws, but I said I would give it a try.

By this time, I had attended only one meeting of our advisory group at Maxwell, and Raymond Bowers, the civilian social psychologist who headed the Human Resources Research Institute at Maxwell Air Force Base, was no more than a casual acquaintance. Nevertheless I wrote Ray a long letter, describing what Ralph had done with me on the North End research and suggesting that he had special skills of observation and interviewing that could contribute importantly to HRRI.

I assumed that was the end of the story. Several weeks later, I got a call from Camp Lejeune, where Ralph was now a first sergeant assigned to the Sixth Marines, Second Marine Division. Ralph told me breathlessly, "Bill, it's just like the movies! Yesterday I got orders to ship out to Korea, and today I got a message from higher headquarters redirecting that I report to the Air University at Maxwell Air Force Base on detached duty."

As I learned later, for such a transfer to take place, it had to be requested by the commanding general of the air force and approved by the commanding general of the marines. Any student of the military bureaucracy would tell you that the chance of that happening on the initiative of someone who had no important political or military contacts was practically zero—but it did happen.

After 1950, my next meeting with Ralph occurred in March 1976, at a Boston meeting of the Eastern Sociological Society. I had been invited to give a "didactic seminar" on participant observation as a research method. I invited Ralph to join me in the presentation and discussion. People seemed fascinated with having the observer and one of those observed (who became a co-participant observer) telling the story. When I had the same assignment later that year, we took our show to New York City for the national meeting of the American Sociological Association.

Our next meeting was on June 17, 1977, when Kathleen and I attended the dinner honoring Ralph upon his retirement after seven years as Superintendent of Public Works for the town of Burlington, Massachusetts. We were impressed by the large crowd that turned out to honor Ralph and by the enthusiastic statements of town officials, the superintendent of schools and president of the Rotary Club, and other prominent local citizens.

With the 1981 edition, I thought I was through with *SCS*, but in 1991 and 1992 there was a sudden revival of scholarly interest in the book. Five behavioral scientists edited *Reframing Organizational Culture*, which devoted a major section of the book to "Exploring an Exemplar of Organizational Culture Research." That part begins with a long excerpt from my appendix of my North End field experiences. The third edition of *Street Corner Society* not only includes Ralph's appendix, but the paperback cover is based on a photograph of Ralph's street corner gang. Then there are four essays by behavioral scientists on *SCS* and finally my "Comments for the *SCS* Critics."

The April 1992 issue of *Journal of Contemporary Ethnography* is entirely devoted to *SCS*. After an introduction by the editors, it leads off with a long paper by W. A. Marianne Boelen, who made several visits to the North End thirty-five to forty-five years after I had left it. She found and interviewed some of the people I had known then and some others and, on the basis of their recollections, challenged my interpretations and my professional ethics.

Without comment, I sent the Boelen essay to Ralph. After reading it, he phoned me in high dudgeon, over what he considered a distorted and mean-spirited attack. I suggested he write me some notes on his reactions and he went on to write a full essay. Thus the issue contains not only my "In Defense of *Street Corner Society*" but also Ralph's essay "Boelen May Know Holland, Boelen May Know Barzini, but Boelen Doesn't Know Diddle about the North End." Also included in the issue are commentaries by social anthropologist Arthur Vidich and sociologists Laurel Richardson and Norman Denzin.

I wrote the University of Chicago Press to suggest that the renewed scholarly interest in *SCS* could be the basis of publishing a fourth edition of the book on the fiftieth anniversary of the first edition. For the 1993 edition, I added a summary of the charges made by Boelen and the points raised by the behavioral scientists, and then wrote my own commentary.

In May 1992, Ralph phoned to tell me that Rose had died. For years she had suffered from rheumatoid arthritis and had been in and out of the hospital for operations and medical treatments. When we had visited them in 1977, Rose had been up and around with hands and feet already partly crippled, but she insisted on cooking for us and helping Kathleen to make the beds. As her condition grew steadily worse, Ralph had to assume more and more of the care for her and the operation of the household. She was a lovely person to whom he was deeply attached. For many years, her illness severely limited his social life. We had invited them to visit us, but Rose could not travel, and he could not leave her. Except for one son, Frank, who lived nearby, he had no family support. Now her death was not only a great sorrow but also seemed the loss of all he had to live for. Ralph phoned me shortly after her death. He was severely shaken, and his doctor had put him on medication to help him through the crisis.

When I called to tell him that the plenary session on *Street Corner Society* had been scheduled for the March 1993 meeting of the Eastern Sociological Society, he told me of a new idea. Many years ago his son Ralph Angelo had received a $4,000 scholarship to Holy Cross College. Now Angelo Ralph proposed to give back to society the support his family had received by giving $5,000 as a grant to a graduate student who planned to make a sociological study of the problems of inner city youth. This was a rare and possibly unique case in which a person who became involved first as a subject of a field study and later became a co-participant observer in the study now proposed to provide grant money to support future social research. I was overwhelmed. Ralph was not a rich man. I assumed that he had been living on his military pension and his pension from the Town of Burlington. While his military health insurance had covered some of the major costs of Rose's long illness, there must have been other large costs that were not covered.

For the *SCS* plenary, I had visualized an author-meets-critics session. I felt I could not propose Ralph as a critic, since he was intimately involved in the study, but moderator Peter Rose invited Ralph to join the platform speakers.

Ralph made no claims to being a sociologist, but several people gathered around him after the session to tell him, "You are a sociological practitioner." John Hudson, a sociological consultant himself, invited Ralph to speak on methods of dealing with street corner gangs at a meeting of the New England Sociological Society in April at Bryant College in Rhode Island.

That talk went so well that he was then invited to talk to several sociology classes, and Hudson and others urged him to put his ideas in writing. That got him working on "A More Effective Strategy for Dealing with Inner City Street Corner Gangs."

The message is simple but fundamental. If you want to work with (and influence) street corner gangs, you don't approach them on a mass basis. First you identify the informal leader and work with the gang through him.

How do you identify the informal leader? In any group who meets together often over an extended period of time, the informal leader is the one who frequently (but not always) initiates changes in group activities. When anyone else makes a proposal for a change in activities, no change is observed unless the leader gives his approval.

Ralph did not learn from me how to pick leaders of corner gangs in his neighborhood. Intuitively he already knew that. What I taught him was a way to formalize that skill, so that it could be applied in a short time to groups he had not met before.

This has turned out to be a mutual learning process. I taught Ralph a research method, and he has been showing me (and others) how that method can be applied in practice by social workers, local policemen, and others who might want to help corner gangs to find activities that would have more long run payoffs for them and their communities than just hanging on the corner.

Finally, Ralph has a special value to me as a participant observer. In a community or organization, when you use that method, making friends becomes a technique. You try to develop friendly relations so that some key informants will want to help you in your research. But friendship is not supposed to be just a device. You try to be helpful to your friends when you are with them, but what happens when you leave the field? Do they then feel that you have exploited that friendship? After leaving the field, I have kept in touch with various key informants and collaborators for several years, but my relationship with Ralph goes far beyond just keeping in touch. After more than fifty years, we continue to learn from each other and to work on new projects together.

That Winter Evening

Antonio Costabile (Translated by Lucia Mudd)

Fiction (2002)

Prologue

THIS STORY, presented as a framed engraving of its time, is in truth a pretext for remembering and describing the life of our old village and its people—real or imagined—in that small corner of the world where we spent the most beautiful years of our lives.

In that remote, never forsaken corner of the world, where pigs wandered blissfully and hens flapped in the dust and sang the praises of a newly laid egg, where asses brayed with hunger, thirst, or love, and dogs coupled freely in our streets, which were littered with piles of manure and innumerable flies, unknowingly, we acquired the necessary antibodies that would protect us from every contagion, political, moral, or environmental. There, with the war and its subsequent upheavals, we were tempered to confront the grave adversities that the future reserved for our generation.

Nevertheless, like most studious young people then, we, too, were idealistic, romantic, and a little poetic.

On the marvelous nights of the full moon, next to the little church, "Purgatorio," we faced each other across balconies and, with our favorite poet, Leopardi, interrogated the moon that shone in the sky above Pazzano.

And, even if a sudden creak of a rusty shutter broke the silence of the evening, and then, the night soil flung onto the cobblestones fouled the air and forced us to shut ourselves behind the balcony windows, even then, the shining moon, silent and full of mystery, continued to light our fantasies and illuminate our dreams from beyond the glass.

And now, after man has stepped onto that heavenly body, and scientific progress has swept away romance, dreams, religious beliefs, secular errors and all the wretchedness of the past, now one dares to believe that there is no longer anyone who might look toward heaven and, with the poet, pose our naïve questions of yesterday.

Prometheus, the Titan who stole the spark from Jove and will ever represent the enduring progress of mankind, has prevailed and carried the spark of modern life even to that remote corner of the world—our home town.

Yes it is beautiful, believe me, to think about the moral and material miseries of the past in this marvelous present.

MECCA, SHORT FOR DOMENICA, lived in the neighborhood of the old castle, near the little church, Purgatorio, in a narrow, dirty street that some patriots of the past had proudly dedicated to a victorious battle of the second war for Italian independence, Via Palestra. She occupied a room on the ground floor, which was at one time the stable of an old noble's palace. There weren't any windows, and the air and light filtered in through the upper half of the so-called "mezzaporta," the half door, which was, out of necessity, always left open. The cat and the hens went in and out freely through a special, circular opening.

Inside the house on the left was a hearth, black and shiny from old smoke. The walls of the hearth were marked with mysterious Egyptian-like hieroglyphics from macaroni which had been thrown there as part of the traditional Christmas Eve vigil, the same night that rings of dough were fried in new oil to make the famous "scurpedde," as they're called in the local dialect.

That night, a large pot hung from a chain in the fireplace. Boiling water was readied to receive the "manate," a local homemade pasta white with semolina flour, which was spread on plastic sheets everywhere—across the bed, on the big chest, all over the table—indicative of the appetites of those about to sit together at the table.

Vito di Ciullo, the temporary sacristan (who, along with Vito Zucarieddo, was the only one who still wore "cotori," the traditional, calf-length, leather boots), had just rung the bells for the Ave Maria at the small neighborhood church, and everyone had already returned to their homes.

Damp air forecast the coming snow. Thick smoke from olivewood burning in fireplaces rose above the low rooftops and mixed with fog and the odor of garlic and oil being fried for the peasants' suppers.

In Mecca's house there weren't any electric lights. They cost too much. And just that night by sheer coincidence, the oil lantern wasn't working because the wick was all used up. Mecca had gone around to all the little shops in the neighborhood, from Luigi Milinari's to Vito Lafica's, but no one had wicks to sell because they were by now obsolete. Even "Pizzitacchio," normally the best supplied of shopkeepers, didn't have any, although he had solemnly promised with that eunuch's cackle of his that he would get them even if he had to bring them from Naples.

Mecca, who was used to doing without, did not lose heart and was resigned to thinking that that night, like so many others in the past, she would have to content herself with the light from the fireplace, which after all created greater intimacy. Because in Mecca's house that evening, notwithstanding the small setbacks, there was an unusual feeling in the air, gay and full of promise.

And the flame from the fireplace, which bore sole responsibility for providing light, performed its task better than one could have hoped. With cheerful cracking sounds and a fantastic mixture of blue, yellow, red, green and turquoise fireworks, so beautiful to behold (these last were attributed to the malicious tongues of the neighbors and were, in truth, not welcome and were immediately extinguished with a quick jet of water), the fire lit up the house magnificently and projected onto the walls the enlarged profiles of the three people seated around the hearth, as in Plato's famous "myth of the cave."

She, Mecca. Her daughter, Maddalena. He, Rocco, Maddalena's fiancé.

Maddalena was a big girl with a freckled face, red hair rubbed with oil, and shining black eyes. Well built and round as a jar, she had the large and low hips of a peasant girl.

Rocco, who was called "Il Casalese" because he lived below in the Casale neighborhood, the most populated part of town just above the Barricani (the ancient gates that barred the dogs, i.e., non-Christians), Rocco was a tall, athletic young man with the legs of a horseman, the gray eyes of a falcon, an aquiline nose, the olive coloring of an Arab, and a mustache like Charlie Chaplin's. He was a shepherd.

And you could tell at a distance that he was a shepherd, because of that certain scent of the woods, almost animalistic, a synthesis of wild flowers, the pig pen, smoke, the den, the fox, the asphodella, a species of the lily family, and sour milk, that characteristic odor, in short, that was referred to in the dialect by the word "cacchime," which cannot be translated into Italian without denigration. It goes without saying that to the fine nose of Maddalena his scent was a perfume more inebriating than the incense of the solemn ceremonies of the church and more exciting than any drug.

Mecca, like most people, had a "soprannome," Mecca Ponente, meaning Westward Mecca. No one knew why. Ponente couldn't have meant west as in the setting sun, because she was neither declining nor waning. Mecca attributed it to that far-off place west of town by the river, below Rossano, where she went on foot with a basket on her head, her hands at her side, toward the rise, the so-called "scirscitora," a place for washing clothes, and then, while these were drying in the sun on the thorn bushes, she would undress, stretch, rinse and refresh herself in the fresh water without inhibition.

She was exactly like Diana of mythology, indifferent to any shepherd who might spy on her, and thus be condemned to be an involuntary Acteon. Mecca was no longer young, but she was bursting with health. She was well built, radiant, and sensuous. In her traditional dress with the flowered bodice, wrapped sash, and long skirt, she diligently kept the best of herself hidden.

She was said to be almost a widow, and talking to the neighbors she would compare herself, melancholically, to the fields lying fallow, waiting in vain for the blessed rains. For Mecca, those dry days continued, a drought without end. In short, she felt the weight of solitude and bore the passing of everyday events with resignation, repressing the natural instincts. With every new event, however, she hoped for the unforeseen and the unforeseeable.

She lived alone with Maddalena because her husband, Caniuccio, had been in prison for a long time and would remain there for many more years; she didn't know how many, ten, fifteen, a lifetime. During the festival of San Rocco, the patron saint of the town, he had been involved in a swindle that ended in murder.

Maddalena and Rocco had met each other at the Sanctuario di Fondi, where they had both gone on a procession for penitence in the month of May. They had lost no time in becoming engaged. Together they made the ritual three turns around the church holding each other's hands. Then together they had gone into the woods and flung themselves on the swing that Rocco had hung from an oak tree and, finally, tired and happy, had stretched themselves out blissfully in a green field like young heifers out in the world and ate a simple breakfast. Together, yes, but always under the watchful eye of Mecca.

That winter evening, Rocco "had come to fifteen," as they used to say, that is, he had returned from the fields for his fortnightly time off and went to call on Maddalena, who waited for him feverishly. Side by side, the two young people looked at each other meaningfully in the light of the fire. Sitting close, they inflamed each other with desire, while Mecca, pretending indifference, prepared dinner.

The minestra was seasoned that night without sparing the rich tomato conserva, or the pecorino cheese brought by Rocco, or the hot pepper, that aphrodisiac which makes one restless. Mecca dished up the steaming minestra and invited the young people to come to the table for the evening supper. Now, with the cauldron removed, the light from the fire was clearer and illuminated the faces and the table, which was set out with the steaming pot of soup and a towering double-handled jug of good wine for the occasion; the wine came from Comare Paolina Giordano, the proprietress of the wine cellar below the Arch of the Towers. She knew how to pour out the real thing, not the watered-down stuff.

The walls of the house, better lit, showed themselves to be bare and poor. In one corner was a large chest that was everything for Mecca, reliquary, pantry, wardrobe, strongbox, file and desk. At the center of the house was a bed standing like an enormous catafalque on iron legs covered for the occasion by a red comforter, which was gaudy and still smelled of mothballs. The uniform roughness of the walls, which hadn't been plastered for years, was interrupted only above the bed by an old colored print of the patron saint of the town, the glorious San Rocco.

That print, now blackened by smoke and rendered more valuable by the lacework of fly excrement, had been bought by Mecca many years before under the Arch of the Towers from the vendors, who for decades came from the Abruzzi to sell sacred and profane pictures, cult objects and popular books. But she had immediately regretted her acquisition, because she felt that the saint in that effigy didn't resemble the beautiful, smiling statue in the church at all.

In this picture, no offense intended, San Rocco looked more like a Calabrese brigand, or at least like an old officer of the carabinieri, the kind who turned up every once in a while at the local barracks in full uniform. In Mecca's picture, San Rocco wore a three-cornered hat that was missing its colored feather; he had a drooping back mustache, a coarse and ill-mannered stare, and, with the index finger of his right hand, he pointed in a menacing gesture to the enormous, scarlet ulcer on his leg.

In the silence of the house, only the cracking of the burning coals could be heard, along with the rhythmic sounds made by those three table companions swallowing the "manate" in its hot and savory broth. Each in turn drank deeply from the wine jug, exhaled profoundly, sounding like the inner tube of a car going flat.

Meanwhile, under the narrow table, the hostilities, so to speak, had begun. The wandering knees of Rocco and Maddalena sought each other out and in a sensual contact full of promise pressed against each other until it hurt. Once in a while, Rocco's knee, trespassing, would touch Mecca's, but in truth she wouldn't withdraw, even if a sudden shiver that was certainly not from cold ran through her body from her head to her foot.

Outside, it was silent. It was snowing. Not a living soul was to be seen in the street, not even Canio d'Erario, who was always the last to return from the fields in the dark of late evening. He had passed a while ago, with his horse noisily pawing the slippery cobblestones.

All the many neighbors—Pasquale Pisciafuoco, Caniuccio, Ciccantonio, Rocco Granninio, Peppuccio Roccuzzo, Mecca Miranda, Filomena Mustazzo, Antonio Furtucone, Marietta Spaccone, and finally, Rocco La Massariola, who was always the last—had already been sleeping awhile. The dogs, the real bosses of the night, though normally roaming free, were neither barking nor running around. That night, only the cats gathered. In the darkness of big doorways and in the streets, the female cats meowed sinisterly and carried on a dialogue with the toms without restraint. In their own way, they were negotiating love pacts, alternating long laments with sudden lacerating cries, flights and quick returns— expression of promise, consent and repulsion. Until suddenly, male and female would quickly couple, rolling around in the snow now hot under the furious scuffle. Desire was mysteriously in the air that evening in everything, in the animals, in the people, in the warm intimacy of the hovels blackened with smoke.

It snowed without interruption for hours. Gusts of wind, like invisible ghosts in flight, sped through the narrow alleys banging shutters, raising spirals of powdery snow and finally quieting down, leaving silence to reign in the night. By now the snow, which had spread its white lace on the church, on the bell tower of Purgatorio, on the houses next door, hid the crumbling ruins of a house that had fallen a century before and never been rebuilt; by now the snow had conferred on that remote corner of the town an unusual reality, one of the fairies and of dreams. Even the solitary lantern hanging from a brace in the corner of Palazzo Perrone, its faint light almost afraid of offending the dark, was beating out the rhythm of the wind for the dance of the snowflakes.

A little further away, the ancient stone masks (two big, chubby, sculptured faces with iron rings in their teeth, which at one time only knew the reins of finely bred horses and now only those of the whore's donkey) were also white with snow. By now it was deep in the night. The bell in the clock tower near the Florenzano Arch, below the Palazzo Amato, had tolled the hours with a sound softened by the snow, but no one, neither Rocco, nor Mecca, nor Maddalena, had counted them. How many hours? Ten, eleven, twelve, twenty, who knew? That exceptional medieval clock, at one time the official town clock, had lost all credibility because, now and then, because of indifferent maintenance, it tolled all the hours of the day at one time and then went silent.

For Mecca, Maddalena, and Rocco, who were used to going to bed with the hens at the tolling of the Ave Maria, their vigil seemed more like Christmas Eve. And why was it important to know the time or the hour? They had eaten, drunk, and were sated. They were finally happy. Mecca knew that only when one is sated is one happy. Only when one is sated and happy does one go, as they said in the town, in search of the "erba vento," the magic herb. Because it is then, in truth, that one's suppressed desires, renounced in solitude, are awakened.

That night for once Mecca felt happy while Maddalena dreamt with her eyes open. Rocco, as if waking from a long hibernation, from a spell, suddenly stirred himself. He got up. He wanted to go home. He went to the entrance, opened the door, looked out, and immediately came back, bringing a wave of cold air in with him.

"So much snow," he exclaimed. "It's late and I have to go."

Mecca immediately reproached him. "Are you crazy? Where do you want to go at this hour? How do you expect to get to the Barricani? You can't even see the streets. Stay here. We'll get along as best we can. "

There was in that voice a certain tone of persuasiveness, invitation, warmth, motherliness and, at the same time, mysterious sensuality. Maddalena nodded in agreement, her cheeks red, her eyes hopeful. Rocco had a moment of uncertainty and timidity. He knew that a fiancé doesn't ever sleep in the house of his betrothed before the wedding. In the dim light, however, he turned his glance fleetingly towards the two women and then towards the big chest. He would have to sleep up there, on top of the chest. Being used to the sacrifices of the shepherd, one night in those conditions wouldn't be the end of the world.

Mecca, who had intuited everything, immediately cut him off and speaking for her daughter too, said to him, "No, dear Rocco, we can't let you sleep on the chest like a dog. All year long you sleep in the sheepfold without being able to rest your bones in a bed. Now that you are in our house, we can't let you twist and turn up there. Ours is a small house," she added, "but the bed, as you see, is as large as the Piazza Fontana, and we can stay there comfortably, all of us, each in his own place. Are we, or are we not, one family?" And then, almost to drive away any lingering doubts or confusion, she added, "After all, at this hour and with this weather, who will see us? Rocco, go undress yourself, and get in on the edge of the bed," she said to him in a peremptory tone.

Rocco did not respond. He was confused, bewildered. Even if the decision of his future mother-in-law seemed absurd to him—a man in the same bed with two women—nevertheless he felt unable to refuse. A refusal might seem like a denial of their familial connection, an offense to their hospitality, even a lack of affection toward his fiancée, and also, in keeping with the morals of the times, cowardice. "And then, at this hour, with this weather, who will see us?" These last words of Mecca resounded in his head like an invitation, a precautionary absolution.

All three of them undressed in silence in the room which was by now almost dark. Maddalena jumped like a colt into the left side of the bed trying not to crunch the dry corn husks that filled the large mattress in place of wool. Rocco, instead, sank in noisily, like an avalanche at the extreme opposite side, rigorously respecting the command he had received. Both Rocco and Maddalena disappeared under the red comforter at far sides of the bed, turning their shoulders away in modesty.

Only Mecca remained at the foot of the bed, undecided about what to do. Should she lie down in the middle, to make a barrier between her daughter and son-in-law, or stretch out across the foot of the bed? Or, should she sacrifice herself and spend the night by the fireplace?

None of these ideas was possible. There were no other covers. The fire was spent. There wasn't any light and, truth be told, she didn't want to spend a cold and endless night like that away from her own bed. And what if there were an accident? Leaving those two alone in the same bed was impossible. Mecca knew from experience that if a man and a woman were alone, unseen by anyone, a coupling was inevitable; it was almost a law of nature. Imagine then, these favorable conditions, in the dark, in the same bed, with the fire that smoldered in the bodies of those two. A shiver of cold forced the only decision possible—the bed. She got up on the chair on Rocco's side, lifted the comforter, and energetically pushed him over with her body. Without making any noise, she made herself comfortable, as they say, like a bird in a nest.

That contact, skin to skin, with the hairy body of a man, the heat of the bed, and the glow she still felt from their indulgent consumption of wine and minestra, along with the long forced abstinence, suddenly stunned her. A hundred bells began to sound a warning in her head. Her heart beat now with a frenetic rhythm as if wanting to escape from her skin. She had the impression that someone wanted to suffocate her, while a strange tingling sensation ran through her body from her head to her foot.

And what heat she felt! Sant'Antonio, what heat! The coals that were dying on the hearth were suddenly on her cheeks, on her lips, inside her body, igniting a desire that she could not remember having known before. She wanted to cry out and call for help, but she was out of breath and her head was filled with incredible confusion. She needed to resist; resist at all cost. But how?

Thinking of her husband so far away, of the neighbors in their houses, of the world and all the saints. She felt unable to reason anymore; she no longer understood a thing. To the devil with everyone. Even if a biblical flood were to come, she would willingly be shipwrecked in the deluge. Death. Yes, even death she would accept willingly. She would not even refuse death. In fact, there was no longer anything she refused. Not even the foot, nor the hand, nor the knee of Rocco, and then . . . then . . . everything. To the depths. Destiny wanted it this way.

The snow continued to fall for the rest of the night and for the rest of the night poor Rocco, under the red comforter, was compelled to lavish himself of the left and the right without respite, in equal measure, without slighting any-one—now Mecca, now Maddalena. Eliphas Levi recounted in *The Book of Splendor* that King David, in his time, did the same thing as Rocco, not under a red com-forter and not in the dark, but in the town square while the people of Israel applauded every embrace, like a goal scored at a soccer match.

THE SNOW AND THE WINTER PASSED. Spring came. The rain married the sun; flowers, plants and seeds in the fallow ground began to germinate. Mecca and Maddalena germinated as well. Both were pregnant.

As the months passed, this new situation did not escape the vigilant eyes of their neighbors, of the local women, but even more of the local men who, because of Caniuccio's imprisonment, watched over the two women with great care. Word went from mouth to mouth. The priest, scandalized, talked in church with-out naming names, of mortal sins, of lust, of divine sanctions, of Sodom and Gomorrah. Some of the faithful laughed knowing that, in accordance with a pecu-liar moral code, they had to do what the priest said and not what he did.

The ballads they knew were now enriched with a new song composed by Larizza and his cronies, the local town poets. This verse was sung with gusto by the peasant women in the fields, from the weeding and threshing of the wheat under the lion sun of summer to the gathering of the olives in winter, just as the stories of Orlando or Guerino had been sung in countless town squares in the past. Years later, someone remembered the refrain that praised the labors of Rocco, like that of Hercules.

Leave the one and do the other.   *Lascia e piglia.*
Leave the one and do the other.   *Lascia e piglia.*
First the daughter,   *Prima la mama,*
Then the mother.   *e poi la figlia.*

In order to avoid morbid curiosity, the two women no longer left the house. Undaunted, Rocco continued to meet his obligations and to assist the two women lovingly. When the women of the town, friends and neighbors, saw him pass by, they called to each other in turn to admire him as if he were superman. The only dark point of the story was the thought of Caniuccio, Mecca's imprisoned hus-band. But escape from prison wasn't possible, and Mecca could have peace for many years before her husband would be able to return home. Although she couldn't know this with certainty.

At that time, the letter carrier was a cobbler of some intelligence who went around in the inaccessible alleys and passageways of the town with the agility of a cheetah; with all due respect to the discretion of the postal service, he knew unfailingly the contents of all the correspondence before making deliveries to the legitimate addresses. In addition, he was as talkative as a jackdaw. Then one day, wishing to do his part in the story, and knowing that all the neighbors would be listening, he called out in a loud voice in front of Mecca's house, "Mecca Ponente, come outside. There is a letter for you from Porto Azzurro. Your husband wants to hear from you immediately."

And so it was. The diligent friend assigned to watch over Mecca in Caniuccio's absence had communicated to the imprisoned husband that his family would be enriched by two additions. He had not specified, however, whose work this was. It was the time when Il Duce was conferring rewards on those patriotic mothers who brought forth newborn "Children of the Wolf," in homage to Romulus and Remus.

Caniuccio, on learning the news in prison, was distraught. For some weeks he did not sleep day or night. He was tormented, not so much by the deed, as by the thought that there was someone in the town capable of not fearing him. This someone had to be either crazy or suicidal. He repeated to himself that to become the cuckold to wife and daughter at the same time had never been heard of in the whole history of the town. He was crazed. His mind whirled with proposals of vendettas. He would plunge the switchblade into the chest of his wife, his daughter, and that infamous one.

But the infamous one. Who was he? His "compare" had prudently not told him. Only Mecca could reveal this to him directly. So, taking courage, Caniuccio decided to write a letter in code to his wife to get around the prison censors without giving away the news of his disgrace, which would surely give the other prisoners the chance to mock him. He wrote his wife a very short letter, like that famous one of Caesar, adopting San Paolo the apostle as a phallic symbol. "Dear wife, let me know who made San Paolo walk in my house?"

When the God Neptune discovered that Aeolus had unleashed the stormy winds without his permission, he flew into a rage, threatening his deadly anger, but then instead he calmed the turbulent water with his trident. And everything ended there. Here, however, at this tempestuous news, a vendetta, blood must follow. Offended honor had to be washed with blood. There was no alternative. The death sentence was inevitable.

Punctually at the due date, Mecca and Maddalena brought into the world two beautiful baby boys whom Donna Ida, the midwife, never stopped praising from house to house. When the births were reported to the civic officer of the commune, Don Attilio Pastore, he couldn't touch food for two days. Thoughtful, rational and stubborn as he was, he could not establish the proper familial relationship of Mecca's child to the rest of the family. Was the boy son and grandson, brother and uncle, or . . . what else? Fortunately, Rocco had run for cover, marrying Maddalena before the happy event, thus resolving one of Don Attilio's difficult dilemmas. But this baby, the son of Maddalena, what relationship did he have to the child of Mecca, the grandmother?

"Gesu, Gesu," Don Attilio concluded without resolving the riddle. Better not to think about it. Better not to think about it.

Rocco continued as a shepherd. Mecca washed clothes, and Maddalena looked after the children. Not a cloud disturbed the family menagerie of wife, son-in-law, and mother-in-law. Until one day, according to Mecca, the envy of the neighbors prevailed. A general amnesty was declared following an auspicious event in the royal household, granting Caniuccio his freedom. A telegram to the mayor warned that Caniuccio would arrive in town any day. It was like a thunderbolt in a calm sky.

The word of Caniuccio's liberation quickly got around, and the news shook the town from its habitual torpor. Finally something new. At Mecca's house and in her little street, there was great agitation, a continuous coming and going of carabinieri, civil authorities, and curious bystanders. The mayor came, the political secretary, the parish priest, the womenfolk and the neighbors. Swarms of boys, seeing all the commotion, went wild, like at the Festa di Santa Lucia at the nearby Purgatorio church.

Everyone was certain, however, that the two stone faces of the Palazzo Perrone, involuntary guardians of that fine night, would, with the arrival of Caniuccio, become witnesses to a tragedy without precedent. Blood would run, so much blood it would dye the cobblestones red; all the puddles and mud mingling, as happened on New Year's Eve, when the pigs were slaughtered.

The mayor, for his part, took stock of the carabinieri without delay. He mobilized Filippo Cilenti and Matteo Frisara, the two municipal guards, to patrol Mecca Ponente's house night and day, with orders to dig a trench, if necessary, to preserve the safety of the family and the "Children of the Wolf." Filippo Cilenti, whose pronounced stutter gave him an authoritative tone, reassured the major of his diligence, showing him the bulky revolver he always carried in his belt, which had been loaded since the end of the First World War, but which, in truth, he had never taken from its holster. Matteo Frisara, notwithstanding his age, assured the mayor of his diligence and vigilance.

All the neighbors, as if anticipating an impending storm or procession of goose-stepping fascists, gathered in hens and offspring and withdrew courageously into their houses to observe these developments without being seen. They knew that Caniuccio was a stupid and dangerous scoundrel; that he knew how to handle a knife with the ability of a D'Artagnan; that he had no scruples at all, something that had been demonstrated on many occasions in the past, just imagine now, after so many years of perfecting the skill in the school of prison.

Thanks to Caniuccio, Don Ciccio Papapietro, the old carpenter, would finally have a good opportunity to sell those dusty caskets he had in his shop on the side of the Arch of the Towers, which he had never been able to sell because of superstition since the time of the Spanish flu epidemic.

Thus, curiosity in the town was raised to an agonizing pitch. "Has he arrived?" the neighbors asked anxiously of those passing by. No one knew anything. Only Vito the Red, also called "Sing Sing" (a man who bore a remarkable resemblance to Ho Chi Minh), ran by, oblivious to everything, as he had an urgent need to run to the town dump. Michele il Lupinaro, who, lacking eyebrows and hair and with that yellow face resembled the famous Chinese general, Chiang Kai-shek, cried out that he had learned with certainty in his town, Potenza, that Caniuccio would come that night. Caterina di Poppa, the wife of Ciccantonio, continued to knit her socks in the entrance of her house undaunted. "In my life," she said, "I've seen everything—the cooked and the raw."

Everyone, even if their house were far away, came to Via Palestra out of curiosity. Even Vito Vavalone, Rosario Capitanessa, Rocco Giuricicchio, Peppe Ruspone, Pietro Pipinaccio, Saverio Sciavardella, Velaso Annateresa, Luca Camplacasa, Rocco Cazzottola, Rocco Vito Recchiolungo, usually immune to everything, feigning indifference, passed through Via Palestra casting sideways glances.

Don Nicola Biscotti (who always knew everything, being from Potenza and the brother of a teacher) stopped in Mecca's neighborhood and announced with authority, "Don't pay any attention. They are all telling you tall tales. I know that Caniuccio will not come in the surrey of Nicola Vecchiarella or in Giolanno's, but in the new car of Antonio Maria LaCapra tomorrow."

Everyone was curious and everyone had something to say. Seated inside the house behind the open door, while the babies slept so innocently on the famous double bed, Rocco, Mecca and Maddalena waited resigned and in silence like those condemned to death, the fulfillment of their destiny.

The bells of the Ave Maria, which at one time were so festive, now seemed like a death knell. The clock tower announced the hours one after another in the heads of those poor souls, hours that never seemed to pass. Caniuccio did not arrive that day.

It was summer. The humid heat, mixed with the stench of garbage and manure in the streets, made the air heavy, almost solid. Clouds of flies swarmed in the street and inside the house, making the wait even more dreadful. Caniuccio arrived during the heat of the day, when everyone was inside behind closed doors—with rag shoes, the blue handkerchief of a rascal around his neck, graying mustache, his hat tilted forward, his eyes lowered, his face with the characteristic color of an ex-convict.

Old cronies, acquaintances, boys, and all the curious went to wait for him at the Trave Della Corda, the place at the edge of town where games were played and people assembled to carry San Antonio Abate in procession on his Saint's day.

Caniuccio crossed the piazza, the main street, the Arch of the Towers. Arriving at the entrance of the house, he thanked everyone, shook hands with them all and begged them to go away. Quickly, he pushed the half door open, and, as if he were trying to escape an invisible follower, entered suddenly. He slammed the door behind him with a great bang and pushed the rusty bolt closed with a piercing screech. The silence of a tomb followed. The wait became agonizing for the neighbors.

Filippo Cilenti and Matteo Frisara, the Mayor's armed guards, who were already at the place and ready, so to speak, to fire, having seen Caniuccio in such good shape, thought it best to withdraw from the front line and crouch even further away in the large doorway of Donna Lucrezia Fiore across from Luisa Capocaccia's house. They had families too and under such circumstances, it was better to be prudent. Not enough was known.

Nicola Damone derived his authority from being the town crier and the messenger for the office of the municipal tax collector. Extremely courageously, like all the others, he went to report the first name, last name, nickname and ages of all the protagonists to the authorities. The hours passed by slowly. Everyone was certain that a horrible tragedy was being committed in that house.

"But why doesn't anyone intervene?" the neighbors anxiously asked themselves from their secure positions. The guards, state police, carabinieri, the Mayor, the political secretary, the parish priest, where were they?

Too much time had passed, or it seemed that too much time had passed. "By now, it is done. The crime has been committed," they thought. Now that assassin, thirsty for vengeance and for blood, was arranging their corpses. But no one moved. They were all paralyzed, like those stone faces near the Palazzo.

A sinister creaking, the shrill and prolonged sound of the rusty bolt, made everyone turn his and her eyes toward Mecca's door. There couldn't be any doubt. That scoundrel had killed all of them and now was going to throw the victims onto the street. To obey the code of honor.

After the sinister creaking, Caniuccio appeared in the frame of the door. He stepped out onto the threshold. In his arms, on one side, he held the son of his . . . wife and on the other side, the son of his daughter, like two victory trophies. The innocent babies were beautiful, lively, and smiling.

Courageously, everybody came out from their houses and their respective places of refuge. Neighbors far and near ran from everywhere to enjoy the unusual spectacle. Caniuccio had revoked the code of honor. The nightmare was finished.

Rocco came out too. He elbowed his way into the crowd with the usual slow, rhythmic step of the shepherd, absorbed in thought. He set off again towards the cantina of Comare Paolina Giordano under the Arch of the Towers to fill the jug with the miraculous wine of that great occasion. In the hours ahead, however, each would eat, drink, and sleep in their rightful places. That winter evening and the snow were left behind forever.

Sanctifying Grace

Philip Cioffari

Fiction (2005)

WHEN DANTE O'BRIEN left Holy Redeemer Seminary in September 1959, he disappeared for a few days; then he showed up out of the blue one night to a standing ovation at the Parkchester Café. The regulars, all neighborhood guys, were shaking his hand like he was some long-lost buddy back from the war. Joey Vitello, known as Joey V to distinguish him from the other neighborhood Joeys—Joey B, Joey C, and Joey D—was tending bar. Beers on the house.

This was a Catholic area of the East Bronx—mostly Italian and Irish—and the celebration had nothing to do with disrespect for the Church or the priesthood. The Café happened to be in the Italian section where, unlike their Irish counterparts whose families seemed more willing to sacrifice their sons' virility to God's service, these guys were constitutionally opposed to living without the love of a woman, divine grace and the Holy See notwithstanding.

Besides, everyone knew what Dante had given up for those eighteen months upstate: Lorraine Cappadoccio. Sweet Lorraine. His long-suffering admirer since sophomore year in high school. Now that he'd been freed from the constraints of celibacy, the feeling was he'd soon be announcing his engagement.

During the ovation he stood shadowed in the doorway, hands in his pockets, head bowed, thin frame listing sideways toward the wall's darkly anonymous wood paneling. A helpless grin appeared and disappeared on his flushed face. If he could have turned around right then and walked out, he would have. But Joey V charged from behind the bar and ushered him toward a stool, the regulars mobbing him, whistling and shouting and pounding his back.

Neither Hump nor I, stranded at the end of the bar, could get near him for several minutes. One of the guys said something like, "So, what, priests don't eat? Look how skinny this kid is. Get him a meatball parmigiana before he fades out of sight." Joey B said, "Getting it regular again will put some color into those cheeks."

Tony Romano, who owned a butcher shop on East Tremont, pumped two quarters into the jukebox and shouted across the room, "So, what was it like up there?"

All eyes on Dante: waiting for him to sum up eighteen months of mystical solitude between man and his God, an intimacy the rest of us would never experience. He stared into his beer, drew his breath in a momentous pause, then delivered his response straight-faced with no apparent irony. "Different."

"Different," Tony echoed. His laughter rolled in waves across the room. "Least they didn't take away the kid's sense of humor."

Sinatra began singing about high hopes, the bowling machine clunked into action and one by one the regulars drifted away from Dante. Hump and I moved in: handshakes, pats on the back, welcomes. Joey V finished handing out beers, then joined us. We'd known each other since third grade and Dante had been the only one to leave the neighborhood. This was our first reunion.

Joey V raised his beer: "To the Renegade Club." That was how we saw ourselves in grade school. Outcasts. Living on the edge. Survivors in a cruel world.

Truth was, though, that despite his broad smile, Dante didn't look much like a survivor. Even allowing for the bar light, his face seemed unusually pale, broken out here and there in pimples. Never a fleshy guy, he seemed thinner than normal, something frail in the way his shoulders drooped inside his shirt. His eyes didn't look right, either. They had the narrowed, inward look that in later years I would see in the eyes of the dying.

Joey V leaned across the bar with a confidential head-tilt. "So what happened?"

"What do you mean?"

"I mean, what happened?"

A blush, a few stammered and unintelligible syllables, then Dante shoved his mouth into his glass and drank deeply.

"We heard you got out on Sunday. Where the hell you been since then?"

"Oh, that." Dante's smile made a fugitive dash across his lips. "No big deal."

"SOMETHING'S FISHY," Joey V said to me in the men's room several minutes later as, side by side, we paid our beer-drinking dues. "Something's not right."

"Think so?"

"*Know* so." He had a nose for deceit and though at times he seemed overly cynical I respected his unceasing efforts to unmask the treacheries of human behavior.

I should say here that the men's room at the Parkchester Café was no ordinary place. Small and cramped, yes, as you might expect, but at its center stood two huge and ancient enamel urinals. The walk-in urinals we called them because they were so oversized. Originally they might have been white or cream but over the years they had darkened to the color of coffee stains. Whatever it was—their size or age or inescapable man-smell or the enamel solid as an altar—the place became a shrine to masculine secrets, a place of revelation. In the time it took to relieve yourself, wash and dry your hands, guys were known to pour their hearts out, especially at moments of emotional distress. Joey V was no exception. He rattled on about how he could never figure why Dante wanted to be a priest in the first place, what with a girl like Lorraine in the picture. She wasn't the best-looking girl in the neighborhood, he observed, nor even the best-built; but she had the sweetest disposition, a smile that got his heart pumping and he confessed what anyone who hung out at the Café already knew: he'd been hitting on her—to no avail—since Dante left. What *had* been a secret until that moment, though, was how jealous he was of Dante because of Lorraine's unswerving devotion to him, despite her having to play second fiddle to the Almighty. That devotion must have touched Joey deeply, because under ordinary circumstances he would never have been interested in her. She was too small, too delicate for his taste. He preferred blondes and redheads, big-chested and flashy, good time girls who could match him, drink for drink, joke for dirty joke.

I zipped up and leaned away from the urinal, scrutinizing him: our leader since Renegade Club days, big man on the block, the guy most guys our age looked up to because of how many girls he'd gone out with—short term, of course, because he drove a chopped and blocked '59 Fairlane and because he was already out in the real world pulling down a decent salary while the rest of us were either still in school, like me, or working for minimum wage, like Hump. In the shadowy yellow light of the men's room he seemed to waver uncertainly between the urinal and the sink. His thick black hair lifted in imposing waves from his forehead but his squared, normally solid-looking jawline quivered and his eyes had momentarily lost their aggression.

Before the mirror he smoothed back his hair and stiffened his shoulders. "Dante boy's got some explaining to do." He turned then and yanked open the door, striding across the Café to take charge of things again.

At the bar he badgered Dante with questions. "So, you happy to be back or what? What's the deal?"

"I'm happy," Dante said. But looking at him you couldn't tell.

"You see Lorraine yet?"

"Not yet." After his third Rheingold, with the Moonglows singing *Sincerely* on the jukebox, he blurted out that he was going to ask Lorraine to marry him. "In a few minutes," he added, "soon as I work up my courage. I missed her when I was up there." He raised his glass and drained it.

Behind the bar, Joey V stood rock solid. Briefly his eyes narrowed and his face hardened the way it did when he was about to eighty-six someone. Then he broke into a grin and joined Hump and me, offering congratulations in advance.

IT WAS NO SURPRISE to anyone in the neighborhood when Lorraine accepted. The engagement party was set for Friday night at the Café. Joey V took charge of the arrangements. If he felt bested, he didn't let it show. Direct, manly action he could applaud, even if he was on the losing end. It was indecision, wishy-washy behavior, especially when it involved women, that tried his patience.

The four of us together again made it seem like old times. One afternoon Joey V appointed himself quarterback, as usual, sending us out for passes down the block alongside the Café. The seminary stint left Dante rusty: he'd forgotten how to negotiate the narrow street. You had to keep one eye on the ball and one eye on the cars parked on either side. Though Joey V threw perfect spirals, Dante would bobble the ball, weaving as he fought for balance *and* for a grip on the slippery pigskin. Once he veered into a yellow Bonneville and went down hard, but he managed to hold onto the ball and come up smiling, arms raised.

THE NEXT DAY we played stickball in our old schoolyard. After the game we hung out by the fence. Hump asked Dante if he was going to stop in to see Monsignor Fanelli, his sponsor for the seminary. Dante stared forlornly across the yard at the rectory. "Not right now."

"So when you gonna tell us what happened up there?" Joey V asked again.

Dante shoved his hands in his pockets and kicked a bottle cap across the pavement. He seemed ready to apologize for something. "Grace," he said.

"What about it?"

"I didn't feel it. Not once in eighteen months. I was studying to be a priest and I didn't even know what grace felt like."

"Grace?" Joey V said. He spread his arms and brought us together in a huddle. "*This* is grace."

Tough guy or not, his square-jawed face glowed with gratitude: something lost had been returned to him. This neighborhood and its memories were his world. I, on the other hand, had been more philosophical about change. You grow up, you move away for college or a job, you start a new life. That's just the way it was. Though I'd chosen a local college, Fordham, I already had one foot out of the neighborhood. I was making new friends, being introduced to worlds that beckoned from far beyond the Parkchester Café. As for Hump, I don't think the nature of change was an issue, one way or the other. He worked full-time for the A&P on Tremont, same job he'd held part-time in high school. Recently he'd been promoted to produce manager, though he would have been just as content to spend his life stocking shelves.

BY FRIDAY THE WEATHER had turned cooler, wind rattling the windows of the Café as we decorated for the party. Hump had called in sick for work and I had no classes till Monday so we worked steadily from noon on. Around three, Dante stopped in to help. This was *his* party, Joey V declared, and his only responsibility was to hoist his butt onto a stool, drink free beers, and tell us how it felt getting it regular again.

Dante's face flushed and he reached for his beer.

"Geez, man, you can tell *us*, your buddies. Better than Holy Communion, right?"

"We haven't done it yet," Dante said.

"Not rushing things." Joey stood on the ladder to hang a gigantic, crepe-paper heart from the ceiling and bobbed his head knowingly. "Not my style, but hey, you've got the weekend coming up."

"No, I mean we haven't done it yet."

Joey V teetered back on the ladder as if he might fall. *"Ever?"*
Dante's lowered head, his silence, answered for him.
"You've been going out since sophomore year."
"I know."
"So what'd you do all that time?"
"Kissed and stuff."
Joey V climbed down the ladder slowly, using his hand to steady him rung by rung. "Kissed and stuff, huh?"
"Yeah."
"Well, kiddo, it's never too late for love."
"But what if it is?" Dante rocked forward on the stool, legs dangling. His eyes raked us for reassurance. "We've waited so long. All that anticipation. I mean, she's going to expect *a lot*."
"And you're going to give it to her." Joey V clamped his arm around Dante's shoulders and hugged him. Then he shimmied his arms and slid his feet in a jive dance even the Shirelles would have envied.

THE CAFÉ HAD NEVER LOOKED so festive: scarlet, gold and blue streamers looping wall to wall, orange crepe-paper balls like fiery suns dawning above the ceiling shadows, heart-shaped balloons tethered to the bar. Around nine, Lorraine arrived with her sister. They wore matching satiny dresses, Lorraine's gold, her sister's red, the exact colors of the circles on Schaefer beer cans—an observation that Hump promptly made. Soon, to Lorraine's embarrassment, everyone was ordering cans of Schaefer and offering toasts. A quiet girl, thoughtful and intense and not accustomed to this much attention, she disappeared quickly into the ladies' room. At this point, Dante had not yet made an appearance. The man of God, Joey C quipped, had descended to earth and was now susceptible to the human failings of tardiness or perhaps vanity, if he had a grand entrance in mind.
The jukebox played the Harptones, the Dells, the Channels, the Earls. Guys took turns dancing with Lorraine who was so adept she could follow anyone, even lead-footers like Bobo Cifarelli and Joey B. On three occasions Joey V danced with her and each time she grew more agitated: he was the reminder that the night was advancing without any sign of her fiancé. Joey V was all charm—broad smile, broad shoulders—as he swirled her around the cleared space by the jukebox, talking into her ear, presumably amusing and reassuring her. For all his good intentions, I couldn't help but think this might also be his way of establishing himself as a standby, should Dante stumble or fall off the pace.
After the third dance he headed for the back room for another case of Schaefer. It was quarter past ten. Out the grimy window that faced Westchester Avenue he spotted Dante sitting on the steps of the church. He went to the door and motioned to Hump and me.

The three of us huddled against the window to peer through the section of glass he'd cleaned with his apron. From the steps, Dante stared blankly into the shadows of the El like a man whose future had suddenly quit on him.

"What's he doing?" Joey V asked.

A rhetorical question but Hump took it literally. "Sitting there."

Joey gave him a withering look.

"Praying?" Hump offered hopefully.

"For what? Everything he needs is right here." He had already turned away from the window, heading back into the bar.

By the time it took for him to tell Marty, the owner, he was stepping out for a minute and the time it took us to slip around the building and cross under the El on Westchester, Dante had vanished. First we checked the church—the doors were locked—then we split up: Joey headed west under the El, Hump went east, I searched the side streets. I remembered something he'd told me in his altar boy days. There was a way into the church through the alley alongside the schoolyard. You went into the boiler room, past hissing and clanking pipes, and up the back stairs of the rectory.

From the sanctuary door I spotted him in the church's dim nave: first row, left side, kneeling with his back straight, eyes raised to the altar. He looked marginally more hopeful than he had on the church steps. Quietly I slid into the pew beside him. This was the silence of eternity: heavy shadows, fluttering candles, the arms and legs of saints lifted in rigid supplication, frozen for all time. Finally he blessed himself and settled back on the seat. "I'm not crazy about her." The words seemed to slip out of the conversation he'd been having with the altar. "I love her, of course, she's a great kid. But I'm not crazy about her the way guys get over a girl."

"Maybe you need more time."

"You think so?"

"Maybe."

His eyes, misty with self-consciousness and hope, turned toward me. "Why do you think that?"

"Well," I said. The heavy silence, his expectation, made me feel under the gun. "You just got back. You've been living a different kind of life. . . . These things take time."

"I've known her almost four years. I've thought about this—*her*—a long time. In the Sem, I mean. Divine love and human love, the differences. The mind and the heart versus the body. I'm not cut out for this gritty stuff."

"What gritty stuff?"

"You know. Doing it. Those physical things. I'm not a priest and I'm not a lover. So what am I?" His eyes narrowed and his lips were drawn tight. He was working something out in his head. "There's this saint I read about, Christina the Astonishing, a nurse to medieval peasants. She loved them and took care of them but couldn't bear their smell. At her funeral her coffin lifted to the ceiling of the church to avoid the stench of her unwashed mourners."

"Sounds far-fetched to me."

He chewed his lip and bobbed his head. "Probably apocryphal. But you get the point, right?"

"I'm not sure."

"There's this distance between me and . . . I didn't feel grace in my vocation and I don't feel it with Lorraine. I mean I should, shouldn't I? I should feel something really good, shouldn't I, this being a Christian marriage ordained by God?"

The phrase *Christian marriage* seemed oddly sterile and cold in contrast to my fantasies of what married couples could do with one another each night in bed, but then I was inexperienced in these matters. At best I'd been to a few proms, suffered through a few dates here and there, nothing in any way long-term or serious. Basically, I'd kissed a few girls and held hands. Something akin to grace might have touched me on one or two of those kisses but so fleetingly I couldn't say for sure.

The silence seemed to fall upon us again like heavy mist. Dante stared catatonically at the row of saints flanking the altar. I checked my watch. Joey V and Hump would be wondering what the hell happened to me. "You want to pray a few more minutes while I hold off the other guys?"

He nodded gratefully. When I left, he was lighting a candle to the statue of St. Rita, patron of desperate situations.

"SO WHAT'S HE DOING?" Joey V wanted to know. "Praying to make the right decision?" We were standing in the street outside the church.

"He already made the decision."

I shrugged. "Now he's not sure."

Joey V shoved both hands into his hair and shook his head. "So what you're saying . . ."

"He's equivocating."

"Fuck equivocation."

"That's not the way he feels. He feels—"

"—What?"

"Equivocal."

Disgusted, he paced between the curb and the sewer. "I want to talk to him." He turned and started up the steps of the church.

"Door's locked," I said.

Dante was perched on the ledge of the alley, facing the El, when we came into the school yard. He offered an apologetic smile. "Hey," he said.

Joey V positioned himself directly in front of him. "What's the deal?"

"There isn't any deal."

"'Course there's a deal. There's always a deal." Arms folded, he waited, rocking back on his heels. "You leave Lorraine for the priesthood. Then you leave the priesthood for Lorraine. *Then* you stand her up on her engagement night. What's going on, man? Because I'll tell you, you're not interested, there's a bunch of guys lining up right behind you."

"Like you, you mean?"

"Not just me." Joey V stood his ground, refusing to go on the defensive. "Something happened up there, I can smell it." He stared until Dante lowered his eyes. "See?" Joey V hoisted his shoulders and looked triumphantly from Hump to me. "I *knew* there was something. I knew it."

WHAT HAPPENED "up there" was some guy, a fourth-year seminarian named Izzie, had been making advances. According to Dante, these advances were made over a three- or four-month period, becoming more and more overt until one Friday night in early September Izzie asked him to a dance at some riverfront bar in Poughkeepsie. Right after that, four days to be exact, Dante left the seminary. He'd been having his doubts anyway, and this assault on his manhood pushed him out the door. Too upset to come right home, he took a hotel room near Times Square and wandered the streets for a few days. "Maybe it's me," Dante said in an un-Dante-like whine in the school yard. "Maybe I really am messed up."

"No way," Joey V declared. "We've known you all your goddamn life. We would've known if there was something . . . *different,* wouldn't we?"

Hump and I agreed vigorously when he looked at us for back-up. Next thing he's hustling us into his Fairlane, saying Dante's got to deal with this once and for all. By that he meant we were going to drive to Poughkeepsie so Dante could "ram this Lulu Izzie's teeth down his throat." Dante neither agreed nor disagreed. In the back seat he sat with Hump and stared vacantly out the window. To my knowledge he'd never been in a fight in his life.

On the way up the Taconic, while we stopped for gas, Joey V called the Café to say there'd been a slight change of plans: the party would be rescheduled "very soon."

HOLY REDEEMER SEMINARY — a cluster of cut-stone, turn-of-the-century buildings — sat high on a bluff over the Hudson. It was after midnight when Dante, with Joey V a hulking bodyguard at his side, led us up the stairs of the dormitory down long, shadowy halls quiet as a cemetery. Seminarians were not permitted to lock their rooms so there was no obstacle to our confrontation with Izzie except that when Joey V threw open the door, the room was empty. On the chance he might be down the hall in the bathroom we hung around, Joey V eye-balling the Spartan furnishings — bed, dresser, crucifix — his nose in the air, nostrils pinched, as if he'd caught a whiff of something that died. Finally he said maybe Izzie had gone dancing, it being Friday night and all.

We drove toward the river. The bars seemed normal enough, if seedy. None of us was about to ask directions to a men-only, back-alley dive, not if our life depended on it. Dante said it was all right if we just went home and forgot about it. "No way," Joey V said. "Least we got to get you a girl."

Dante sank back in resignation against the seat. His face had a shut-down look, he wasn't happy at all, but there was too much at risk—not the least of which was his reputation—to resist Joey V's plan. And maybe, as consolation, he allowed himself the illusion that Joey was right, all that was needed to straighten out his life was to get laid, even if he couldn't take care of Izzie "once and for all."

Warehouses, darkly idle factories, empty streets. Two women who looked as if they'd been up for days without sleep stood in the shadows of an abandoned building. Joey V slowed down to take a closer look but kept on driving. He followed train tracks to a railroad yard at the edge of the river. Up ahead, a girl was crossing the yard, walking at first then skipping across the rails. "Hey," Joey said, pointing the car in her direction.

"She's just a kid," Dante protested.

The Fairlane moved along the tracks beside her. She was taking big steps across the rails, humming to herself, ignoring the car until Joey V leaned out the window, smiling. "Hey, can I talk to you a minute?"

She wore black pants and a thin, ragged sweater that had once been white. She stopped walking and stared across the tracks at us. "What about?"

"What's your name, honey?"

"Aggie, why?" Her face was small and round, partially hidden by curls.

"I want to give you something, Aggie."

She stood away from the car and kept her head lowered, as if she wasn't really interested. "What do you want to give me?"

"This." He held up a twenty and rubbed it between his fingers.

"What do I have to do?"

"Just take a walk here with my friend."

Bending down, she peered into the back seat. Dante was staring into his lap. "Where to?" she asked.

Joey V nodded toward the stalled cars at the edge of the yard.

She stared at the rust-colored freight cars then back at Dante as if she was calculating. "How long?"

"Not long," Joey V said, smiling away at her.

She looked over at the cars again then at the twenty. "That's it? Nothing else?"

"That's it."

Her eyes followed the line of tracks and it seemed she might be thinking to pass up the offer, but she stepped closer and reached for the twenty. "Okay."

"She's only a kid," Dante said.

"Hey, she's old enough to make a deal, she's old enough." Joey turned in the seat to push Dante out. "Think of it as batting practice," he said. "Lorraine is opening day."

They walked across the yard, fifteen or twenty feet between them, without looking at each other.

"Maybe this wasn't such a good idea," I said, watching them disappear behind the lines of freight cars.

"Yeah," Hump agreed. "The guy's guilty enough already."

"What he needs is to have his confidence built up. Either of you got a better idea?" Joey sang along to the Marcels' version of *Blue Moon*. For maybe five minutes he contented himself with the radio, using the wheel and the dash as the percussion for his one-man band. "All right," he said abruptly. "Let's see what Casanova's up to."

Before he opened the door I was outside the car, telling him that *I'd* go. The last thing Dante needed, whether his situation with the girl was going well or poorly, was to have Joey V burst in on him.

The night had grown a lot colder down here by the river. A wind came up, blowing dust in mist-like swirls across the glinting rails. I found them in the second line of cars, talking to one another. Aggie sat up in the open door of a boxcar, Dante on the ground below her. He jumped quickly to his feet, as if he'd been caught red-handed. "We going back?"

"Yeah."

"Okay, okay," he said, looking relieved. He stepped closer to the boxcar to say something to Aggie. She wore his windbreaker over her sweater. Up close like this, with her curls brushed away from her face, she looked even younger than before—fourteen maybe, fifteen tops.

"Your jacket," I heard her say.

"You keep it," he said.

As we moved between the lines of cars he told me her father was a drunk and a bully. She came down here sometimes, weekend nights especially, to sleep in one of the cars where it was safer. When we were out in the open again, walking toward the Fairlane with its lights on and motor running, he said, "You won't say anything—?"

"'Course not."

On the ride home Joey V asked for details but Dante kept his mouth shut. "A secure lover keeps his own secrets," I said.

Joey V gave me a sidelong look. "How the hell would *you* know?"

"I read it somewhere." Everybody laughed.

It was nearly three when we reached the Parkchester Café, dark and shuttered for the night. Joey V drove off in search of a parking place—in our neighborhood you sometimes had to park a mile or more from where you lived—and Hump headed home along White Plains Road. Dante wanted to go by Lorraine's house, in case she was still awake. I walked with him under the El. Her house was a brick two-family on Pugsley. Her light, second floor front, was still on. We stood outside looking at her window with its shade drawn, Dante rubbing his arms.

"Cold, huh?"

"I don't care," he said with a shrug. "Giving it to her, the jacket, made me feel something good. Really good."

"What are you going to tell Lorraine?"

He shivered again in the wind and laughed uneasily as if he already understood what I had yet to learn: that love was nothing like the automatic comfort it promised to be. "I wish I knew." He smiled—a hopeless, end-of-the-road kind of smile—and turned to climb the stairs to Lorraine's room.

THE SACRED AND PROFANE

POETRY

Luisa and Buffalo Bill

In memory of my grandparents, Luisa and Vito

John Addiego

(1993)

You wouldn't believe how his people live
they sleep with the goats
nothing to cover them but an old blanket
which he used to carry on his head
like a hobo look at him
asleep with his mouth open

my father was a civilized man
not like *his* bunch
when he was a barber cutting the hair in Chicago
he had the run of the block
those people couldn't speak a word
he used to warn me *don't marry*
no Calabresi they'll cut your throat
for a dime do you think I'm kidding

the old man here got in a fight once
can you imagine what kind of man
had to use a knife he couldn't use his hands
he kicks too you gotta watch

you don't get too close of course
now he's sick as a dog always sleeping
they don't know how to take care of themselves
they get old and lose their spoon
in the soup you know my brother
caught the tuberculosis the same year
that my father died I was sixteen
sitting by the bed for both of them
and *pow* they was out like the light
could they sing and play of course my uncle
was the one with the Irish harp
at the Orpheum Theater like it was made for him
the next day I was back at the leather tannery
because they didn't believe in feeling sorry

I used to help with the hair
Sweeping up or sometimes I'd sing
the men would give me a nickel
back in Omaha right after Chicago
that's when Buffalo Bill the cowboy
came through in a parade with his long whiskers
I was a little girl you wouldn't believe
I dragged stools on the sidewalk
and sold every seat for a dime.

The Concept of God

Kim Addonizio

(1995)

Years later, nothing inside the church
has changed. Not the dusty light,
not the white feet of the statues
or the boys in their pale smocks kneeling before the candles.
Not the cool basement, the paper plates of donuts
set out by the coffee urns.
Not the bathroom with its stall doors open
on a row of immaculate toilets,
blue water in the bowls,
a small wrapped soap on each sink.
Forever the two girls leaning against the wall
in the deep quiet, sharing a lipsticked Salem
    and watching themselves in the mirror,
forever the priest nodding in the confessional,
opening and closing his small window.
Always my father moving down the rows
of bored, sonorous voices, passing the long-handled basket,
my mother with his handkerchief pinned over her hair.
Always, too, his coffin before the altar, my brother
stammering a eulogy, the long line of parked cars
spattered with snow. Always this brief moment
when the candles shudder, then resume,
and the girl holding the cigarette peers more closely
into the mirror, startled for an instant
at how old, how much like a woman
it makes her look.

My Father at Eighty-five

Vince Clemente

(1995)

I find him
in the haze and drone
of the hospital ward, trace
every line in his sad face
back to his lower East Side boyhood:
his father's stables on James Slip
shodding horses,
the Fulton Market, where
a penitent monk
he logged in fifty years
weighing salmon in a scale.

I find him, as I ask
you find him:
pausing to catch his breath,
the sun up suddenly
over the East River,
the scale, a gold net
snares the fish, downstream
from Gloucester,
the salmon's back a million suns holds all the far galaxies.

These things my father saw
saw for fifty years
every day for fifty years
yet never told me so

God! How slow
love moves.

The Caves of Love

Jerome Mazzaro

(1996)

Lodged in the early morning, in dark pews,
away from the main aisle, each week they wind
sniffling and wheezing closer to life's end,
gray faces grown as doubtful as church dues,
where just their clothes, grown shabbier and odd,
and their own body smells increase each week,
as lighted, perfumed candles stall the reek
and incense curves man's worldly thoughts to God.

Listless and nasal, seeping as some mist,
the stale air grows more stagnant with their drone,
invading both my thinking and their own,
like some marred surface giving way to rust
as their own homes give way each year to rot,
the ruin offset, they hope, by stronger love
or obligation to brute force above.
They draw to trappings like an opiate.

Hobbled and humpbacked, bobbing as they move,
they seem as trolls or victims of long wars,
their outer forms betraying inner scars.
And winter does make this place seem a cave.
Light barely breaks in through the speckled air,
and echoes hollow in their each response.
A cave remembered from a legend once—
a Venusberg or hill or dragon's lair.

I try to think on them as they were young—
their parents beaming in a Sunday best—
bright children at a First Communion feast
eager to taste God with each pushing tongue,
cowed by the sisters as they must have been;
and how the aging sisters struggle hard,
failing to keep quick children on their guard
who follow them each year in one communion.

They pray for their own soul's recovery,
the hardy independence of the old,

and for lapsed children, missing from the fold,
cut off like lambs by gorse along the way,
knowing how all youth go to meet the world,
fresh with illusion, eager to begin,
and how a world's indifference shuts them in.
Each meek adjustment spots an inner mold.

It is a club for which I seem the priest,
where just the dying gain full membership
and only death can free one from its grip—
a horror club, whose restless coughs persist
and camphor makes one wish he'd never come.
But who can face a world devoid of love?
Quiet and anxious, keeping hopes alive,
I feel the dwindling number bulk like doom.

Linens

Rina Ferrarelli

(1998)

Plain weaves, twills and herringbones,
woven at home linen on linen, linen
on cotton. Some are still uncut—a band
of warp threads separating one napkin,
one towel from the other—but most are decorated
with needlepoint lace. My mother's older sister
had the broad back and strong constitution
to bend for hours, working the pedals, arms
stretching to send the shuttle scuttling through.
My mother, the more delicate one, the one
who wanted to get away, sat where the light
fell on her hands, and pulling out the weft threads
her sister had worked into a tight fabric,
restructured the space with floss, white on white
openwork borders, arabesqued windows.
Rough- or fine-textured, the linens I was saving
were meant to survive soaking in hot water
and ashes, milling on the rocks. I machine
wash them and when the weather is good,
hang them outside, the way women still do over there,
stretching them into shape while damp. Most
are holding up well; a few show signs of wear,
but not from use. It was keeping them safe in a trunk
for so many years that weakened the fabric.

LOVE AND ANGER

PROSE

The Two Uncles

An Addendum to Mount Allegro

Jerre Mangione

Memoir (1975)

THE DAY I RETURNED from Sicily, my father telephoned me to say that my Uncle Nino was dying and wanted to see me. My father had no great love for my uncle, but he urged me to come as soon as possible. I took the next plane to Rochester and went directly to the hospital.

In the waiting room, I found Uncle Nino's oldest crony, my Uncle Luigi, eighty-five years old and six feet tall. Usually, my uncle's powerful body was as impressive as the side of a mountain, but now it was sagging. Lately there had been too many reminders that he was living on borrowed time—his sister, who had died a few months before at the age of ninety-two; a Jewish neighbor with whom he had swapped stories for almost fifty years, until a week before his funeral. And now Uncle Nino, one of his oldest friends, the only one who was his match at *briscola*, was on his deathbed.

I had not set eyes on Uncle Luigi for almost a year but, when he embraced me, he had no words of greeting. His first words were those that had been gnawing at his soul ever since it became definitely known that his friend, Nino, could not live long. "I am packed and ready to leave," he said. "Anytime my call comes. After all, it's about time, isn't it?"

I argued with him: There was nothing seriously wrong with his health and all of his wits were intact. He was only suffering from discouragement. When he looked more discouraged, I asked him if he had ever watched a television program of that year called "Life Begins at Eighty," whose panelists were all octogenarians. "If you spoke English well enough, you could easily be one of them," I said.

"A shame they don't speak Italian well enough," he grumbled slyly. "It sounds like a silly program. How could life possibly begin at eighty? Second childhood maybe, but not life. Bear this in mind, nephew. Those of us over eighty years old who are sound in body and mind represent only about two percent of the population. That is a very small percentage. And that is why my bag is packed and I'm ready to leave."

Now that he had articulated his worry he brightened perceptibly, and was reminded of a "true story" about an old man he knew who was planning to marry a girl of eighteen. His relatives were aghast. One of them pointed out that in five years' time he would be eighty years old and the girl twenty-three. "Well, when that happens," the old man said, "I'll divorce her and marry another eighteen-year-old girl." It was an old chestnut of a story, one I had heard him tell before, but he was still delighted with it and, at the punch line, roared with laughter. Listening to the lusty sound of it, I had no doubt he would live to be a hundred.

Together we went up to see Uncle Nino. He was also roaring, but with the terrible anger of a man who is about to die against his will. I could hardly bear to look at him. He had always been small, but now he was down to seventy pounds and his wrists were so skinny you could see the bone structure. It was easier to look at his face, for in my memory it had always looked sunken, and always there had been the same high cheekbones, the same red and gray moustache bristling over thin, wry lips.

Now there was a tube stuck up his nose and held to the sunken cheeks with adhesive tape. Another tube emerged from a hole in his stomach where he had been operated on. His voice could only be heard intermittently, suddenly going off and on like that of a broken radio. Yet his lips kept moving, and his eyes darted with a rage that was brownish yellow like the rest of his bile-ridden body.

He paid no attention to Uncle Luigi, but he acknowledged my presence at once by speaking my name, and then quickly went into the theme of his anger: his pain was intolerable and no one was doing anything to help him, least of all the nurses and the doctors. "They want me to die in agony." He cursed them violently and motioned me to draw nearer.

"You are my nephew and my friend," he whispered. "The only friend I have left. You can do me a favor that will deliver me from my agony. I want you to buy me a poison pill. I have five dollars saved for it. Here, under my pillow. Bring me the pill and I'll give you the money."

"I'll do that, Uncle," I said. "But I don't have much cash with me. Could you give me the money now?"

I am a poor actor. He looked me in the eye and read what was in my mind.

"No," he screamed. "I know your game. You want to take the money away from me, so that I can't use it to buy the poison. You can't stop me. I'll get someone else to buy it."

His shouting brought the nurse. She was a strong girl twice his size, but obviously afraid of him. "Go away," he yelled at her, "or I'll tear this damn thing out of my nose." I learned that he had done just that several times, and fought the nurse with his fists each time she tried to put the tube back in its place. Earlier that day he had jumped out of bed and raced up and down the corridor, looking for the exit and shouting that he wanted to go home.

Had he gone home there would have been no one there to look after him. His wife (Uncle Luigi's sister) had been dead for four years, and he had insisted on living alone in the same apartment they had occupied for twenty years. He was no housekeeper, and within a short time what had been a delightful apartment was reduced to a nightmare of dirt and disorder. He had alienated most of his relatives by refusing their help and shunning them, claiming that the mere sight of them reminded him too painfully of the happy days he had known with his wife. This explanation infuriated the relatives, who said that in all probability he was reminded of his bad behavior as a husband.

They liked to point out that my aunt had supported both of them during most of their married life by working in a tailor factory sewing buttons. "She killed herself for him, so that he could live like a *galantuomo*." It is true that, except for conducting a small jewelry business from his home, which ended abruptly after a year when he was robbed of his entire stock, he never worked at any money-earning occupation. His days were spent playing cards with old cronies like Uncle Luigi, fishing for bullheads in Lake Ontario, and sitting in the local railroad station because he liked to watch people come and go. There were those who claimed that the attraction at the railroad station was not the travelers, but a blonde and buxom Polish waitress who let him feel her now and then. To a stranger he might have seemed like a useless person, but I knew him well enough to respect his power as a poet and philosopher.

No one could dispute his position as the family poet laureate, the inventor of the ingenious toasts, the speechmaker for important occasions—some made important only by the sound he brought to them. For this particular talent he was admired, though not generally liked. He lost his temper too often, especially at his wife, and his curses and profanities had a stinging eloquence that rankled long after they were uttered.

His behavior with children often enraged their parents. He seemed to enjoy frightening them or making them cry. He would pinch them, or toss them high in the air and pretend he was not going to catch them. Worst of all, he would threaten to carry off their house on his back to a secret place where it would never be found again. I remember, as a child, screaming with alarm each time he used this threat, believing implicitly in his power. Yet we children did not dislike him; he was no worse than an ogre in a fairy tale and far more fascinating than his wife, who bored us with her mundane concern over our health and welfare.

Probably because his imagination was as free as our own, we felt more closely related to him than to the other relatives, who were too steeped in their adult authority to be understood or enjoyed. Uncle Nino was the only adult among our relatives whom we sometimes addressed by the first name, and when we conversed with him we invariably used the informal *tu*, as though he were an equal. He must have gained some satisfaction in realizing that he, the childless uncle, enjoyed the confidence of his nephews and nieces more than their parents did.

Unburdened by any sense of authority, Uncle Nino knew how to listen to our problems without making us feel that the end of the world was in sight. And, often, it was thanks to him that we were saved from parental punishment. For no matter how guilty we might be, he would rush to our defense, arguing with a zeal and conviction that few parents could combat.

Remembering all this as I watched him in his torment, I was sorry I could not get him his poison pill. The nurse had left but he was still ranting, a scolding to the heavens as furious as any King Lear delivered. At last he leaned back exhausted, eyeing the room as though it were packed with enemies.

Uncle Luigi was getting worried. So far his old friend had paid not the slightest attention to him. Finally, he could no longer contain himself.

"Nino, don't you recognize me?" he asked anxiously.

The raging eyes rested on him: "Of course I do," he snapped. "You're eighty-five years old and you have the muscles of an elephant. I'm seventy-eight years old and I'm dying. What are you complaining about? Why do you have to be recognized?"

"I don't have to be recognized," Uncle Luigi said. "And it's not my fault that I'm eighty-five years old. I've had nothing to do with that. My valise is packed. I'm all ready to go."

"It's easy for you to talk like that," Uncle Nino retorted. "You're not in agony. You don't have tubes stuck up your nose and into your belly. Why don't you get me out of this Hell?"

"Nino," he pleaded, "what can I do?"

"You're eighty-five years old but you're a mountain of strength. You can help me escape from this place. That's what you can do. The pains will disappear as soon as I leave here. . . ." He tried to say more but his voice was gone. His lips kept moving and he did a frenzied charade with his skinny hands.

If Uncle Luigi understood the charade he gave no sign of it. "I've been ready to go for some time," he said. "I've had six children and twenty-two grandchildren. I have no unmarried daughters and my wife has been dead for a long time. There's really no reason why I should not go."

The nurse came in and whispered in my ear. My mother was downstairs waiting for her turn; either I or my Uncle Luigi would have to leave, since only two visitors at a time were allowed.

"Don't listen to her," Uncle Nino screamed. "She's the Devil in disguise."

The nurse retreated hastily. I explained what she had said, and held out my hand. His grip was surprisingly firm.

"Good-bye, nephew. If you can return, bring me a poison pill. I've got to get out of this inferno. If Luigi won't help me, the poison will."

"Don't talk that way," Uncle Luigi begged. "You will be well again and we'll have another game of *briscola*." He turned to me. "Nino has beaten me the last four times we have played. I want to play him again and get even."

As I went toward the elevator, I could hear Uncle Nino hurling Sicilian invectives at Uncle Luigi for wanting to get "even." "*Vigliacco*! Isn't it enough that you can come to my funeral?" he shouted.

"Look, Nino," Uncle Luigi cried. "What do you want with me? It isn't my fault that I haven't died yet!" I heard his voice break and I could imagine his huge frame limp with grief.

"Luigi! Carry me out of here. You are a mountain of strength. Quick, Luigi, before the nurse comes."

For a few moments there were no sounds from the room. All at once a fantastic figure that looked like a two-headed giant emerged into the hallway. It was Uncle Luigi carrying Uncle Nino piggyback. One of Uncle Nino's arms was wound around his neck; the other was whacking Uncle Luigi's ribs as though he were a horse. Uncle Luigi was lumbering toward the stairway exit, but long before he got there a nurse and two male attendants stopped him. Uncle Nino, who had torn away his tubes, put up a brief fight while Uncle Luigi stood by watching and (for the first time in my memory) crying. After they carried his friend back to his bed, he kept on crying.

The Prince of Racalmuto

Ben Morreale

Fiction (1979)

A MAN'S PRESENCE could provoke an anger in me that would last for days. His presence in my mind was an unanswerable offense because I did not know in what way I had been offended. I saw his face in the store windows I passed. I felt his presence in the flush of blood rising to my face and around to the back of my neck. All I would have to do was to take a few glasses of wine to anger me to such a point that only the most violent activity could, if not calm me, then exhaust me. And at such times I could not find the words either in English—which at that moment I could pronounce but not understand—or in Sicilian—which then seemed ugly in my mouth. Instead I stuttered. My anger increased as if it had found a force to feed on, so rapidly that it seemed to me like a small quick explosion with no middle, just starts, creating other starts and no ends. Explosions without end. That left me gasping with rage for want of an end to things—a resolution.

I felt a need for a Sicilian Vespers in my life, a drama in which I would kill everyone who could not pronounce a certain word. And there was the difficulty—why the explosions only had starts and no ends; I could not find the word.

For a moment I thought it might be my name. If my name were mispronounced, I'd kill. But in what language would this word be? I was faced with the absurd possibility of having my Sicilian Vespers using an English word—like *backhouse*.

So much of my time has been spent finding words in two languages, at times three, which would put an end to my rages. There was no understanding this inability to choose and this, too, added to my rage.

Nevertheless, I understood I could not work at my job with any comfort. The presence of people, the source of words, enraged me. But I had to make a living; that's why I came to this country. I, a man of princely blood.

I had no one to really speak to but my wife, my sweet bride.

Now this nice young man comes to ask me questions in this place. It's no use stirring *merda* or it will stink. Especially since it is so hard for me to put his words together. I don't understand him. I know he would not understand me, even if I could get the words out.

The first day he came he spoke endlessly, letting words out like beads from a broken rosary. They spilled onto the floor from his mouth, flew up the walls and rattled from the ceiling onto my head, and disappeared silently in my ear and left no impression. They had never existed.

I wanted to tell him of that day four years ago now—no, many four years ago—when I broke every store window bearing the emblem of the eagle gripping thunderbolts and the letters N.R.A., using the silver-knobbed cane I carried then. And tell him, too, I wanted to kill that goat-faced Irish cop because he could not pronounce my name. I, the Prince of Racalmuto of the Province of Girgenti, whose father and grandfather had owned four thousand acres of land containing salt and sulfur mines in which coins bearing the head of Marcus Aurelius/*Marco Aurelio* were often found.

The young man came and asked me, "In your family what language was spoken, Italian or English?"

All I could do after a great effort—God knows I tried—was to shake my head. I could not speak. I could not speak because each time the words rolled out of my mind, led by the three rounds of cheese, three black rounds: cheese/*formaggio* and *tumazu*, one in English, the other in Italian, and finally, *tumazu*, in Sicilian. They all three rolled out of my mind to the back of my throat and stuck there, the three of them, and only a gagging sound broke through my tongue. It happened with other words: backhouse/*bacazu*; a job/*'na joba*; the subway/*lu subeway*; dirty/*vastazu*. They all rolled out of my mind with no rhyme or reason, to get jammed in my throat in an ugly sound. I tried, but I could not speak after it happened. God knows I tried. I try to this day, even after all these years of having given up, sitting here, lying here, not saying a word, not answering while in my head there was a hemorrhage /*emorragia*/*'na murragia* of words. Words always rolled out of my mind led by those three rounds of cheese/*formaggio*/*tumazu*, to stick in my throat/*gola*.

About thirty years ago a nice young man came to see me and asked, "Can you tell me why you left Sicily?"

The words just rolled out of my mind: hunger/*fame*; bankruptcy/*fallimento*/*faillita*; hope/*esperanza*; something to look forward to. There was a massive hemorrhaging of words that clotted in my throat and not a word would come out. No use the young man explaining patiently by my side that he was preparing a book on emigration and wanted to ask the people who had taken part.

"Could you tell me," he repeated, "why you left Sicily?"

I could not answer with all those words in English, Italian, and Sicilian in my mouth like clots of people in a rush hour and my mind hemorrhaging words, words, words.

All I could think of in my rage of not being able to speak was the food I used to eat walking along the streets of Gravesend: cherries/*ciliegie/cirasi*; grapes/*uva/racina*; and marshmallows. I loved to eat marshmallows walking home to my wife, my sweet bride.

Suddenly, because I knew no Sicilian word or Italian word for marshmallow, this word escaped—marshmallow.

The young man repeated, "Could you tell me why you left Sicily?"

"Marshmallow, marshmallow," I answered. The young man left that day in great despair.

I was left with a rage that set my spinal cord vibrating like a crazy cord in the darkness where I could see these men who like sullen birds came to fit canvas shirts on me with long sleeves they always tie around my back. I am trapped, my spinal cord vibrating like a crazy cord/*'na corda pazza*, twitching to be touched by my tied-up hands. I could scream for the pain I felt and could not touch. I rolled on the floor against the wall hoping to touch my twitching soul. But even the walls, were soft, like callous pillows. All I could do was exhaust myself.

When I was first brought here, chained, with bars on my legs and arms—a mad dog, they called me—those sullen faces put that long-sleeved shirt/*la camisola di forza* on me and left me to my own crazy cord and to my own filth for days, after which they would come and wash me and the room with a fire hose.

I would be calm for days after that, until my wife came to see me, my sweet, gentle bride who was a piece of bread/*nu pezzu di pani*/a piece of apple pie. Who had a skin like spring rain, who spoke quietly with a smile in her voice, who took insults from everyone and returned politeness and goodness.

I could not speak to her. I would not. I couldn't even look at her and I would just sit there with my head bent looking away. Her words at home so soothing, here were stones aimed at my head and heart.

"*Decimu*/Tenth One," her words rose out of her mouth, "what pleasure it gives me to see you. How are they treating you? I brought you some lamb chops. I know I'm not supposed to, but it will do you good to have some tender meat/*carne.*"

Without lifting my head, I rolled my eyes up to catch a glimpse of my sweet bride. Her face was pale and her large brown eyes were like hazelnuts in the sun. I looked away and hung my head deeper. I felt blows raining down on me. I, the Prince of Racalmuto of the Province of Girgenti, had dishonored my sweet bride. I wasn't able to support her either in affairs or banditry.

I hear her voice to this day, "The children are fine, but they won't permit me to bring them."

Her words were stones and I hunched my shoulders to protect myself. "But they are all right. They send you kisses and embrace you."

I felt the vibrations low in back. I rolled my eyes upward and saw her crying. The words exploded out of my mind—"*Va tt'ne*/go away/*va tt'ne, va tt'ne*"—and stuck in my throat. "Go away" burst out in a furious roar. My sweet bride stepped back in horror. They came to see her out, those sullen men. I was left howling like a rabid dog/*'nu cane arrabiatu* because I could not get one word out of my throat.

Those sullen men returned to beat me limp and stuffed me in the shirt with the long sleeves. My spinal cord/*colonna vertebrale* had turned into a crazy cord/*'na corda pazza* and vibrated so. I thought I would break apart.

I knew my sweet bride should not come to see me in this condition. She was too nervous/*nervosa*/*nirbusa*. I knew that.

God knows how long it was. But she didn't come for a long time. Then a man from my village, a *paisano*, came and told me that she was taken to the crazy house/*lu manicomio*. My sweet bride was made to scrub floors in drafty grey buildings. She caught pneumonia/*polmonite*/*lu morbu* and died. My sweet bride died in a building not far from me, among people of whose language she knew not a word, not one word.

I did not speak a word for years after that. I, a former student of the College of Girgenti. I, who loved poetry/*poesia*. I did not speak for ten years because I knew my words, if ever they escaped, would be bits of broken glass and they would cut the throats/*sgnassero* of all those criminals. A real Sicilian Vespers, without a word to be pronounced.

We should not have moved to that part of the city with the foreboding name Gravesend/*Tomba di Termine*, with all those Polacks/*Polacchi*, Jews/*Giuda*, and Irish/*Airisci*. Not that they did anything to us. It was a tower of Babel/*'na torre de babela*. It was that subway ride to work, a tower of Babel on wheels. The Jewish mouths were spitting words into the air from the bottom of their throats. The Irish/*Airisci* dropped words that were soft insults. They mocked me with their haughty sound. I was glad to get to my machine in the cavern of a shop. It was a refuge. I made shoes. I, the Prince of Racalmuto. I had become a shoemaker, a stitcher. But it was a relief to work beside a man who was from a village not far from Racalmuto, a *paisano*. Only the thought of riding back in the evening made me brood and I spoke very little to my *paisano*.

For a while I tried to look like everyone else. I bought *The American Journal* and held it before my face. But those words just jumped off the back of the paper in that cattle car, and I was buried in an avalanche of words that would have killed me if I hadn't defended myself. I began looking for that one word which, if they would mispronounce, I would kill—my Sicilian Vespers. At first I began to mutter things like "marshmallow, jelly bean," the only words that would come out. I saw that people made room for me. They kept away. "Marshmallow, jelly bean." But it took so much energy that I arrived home to my sweet bride in our three rooms dark as caves because they were not on the sunny side of the street but on *la tramontana*, so exhausted I could barely eat.

How soothing were my sweet bride's words, her touch, our touching. Then all the words dissolved that were still clinging to me like barnacles from that cattle car. I was clean and free to sleep and face another day.

I had one thing to look forward to—we had one thing to look forward to: to make enough money so that we could return to Racalmuto to live, if not like a prince as I had been accustomed, at least as a gentleman/*'nu galantuomo*.

We became misers. We saved. We had spaghetti and bread without sauce. On Sunday maybe chicken wings. For lunch I brought an onion, a filthy sardine and some bread—miners' food. Little by little we put aside three dollars here, a nickel and a dime there in the savings bank. We went nowhere, saw no one and in the winter we sat in the dark to save electricity, looking out the window at the Jews, Polacks, and *li Airisci* quarreling in the streets.

Recently a nice young man came to see me. He said he was preparing a book. He asked me many questions: "What is your attitude towards Benito Mussolini? Do you: (1) love him, (2) like him, (3) feel indifferent to him, (4) dislike him, (5) hate him?"

The words came sweeping out of my mind again. "He makes me rage/*mi fa rabbia*, rage, rage/*rabbia, rabbia*. And they bottled up in my throat so tight I thought my eyes would pop. If I could have found that word he could not pronounce, I would have cut both his and Mussolini's throat.

My children, *Baldassaro*/Beni, and *Rosalia*/Rosy, had started school. It was a tall Irish assistant principal who announced, when my sweet bride took my son to school and said that his name was Baldassaro di Racalmuto di Licata, "Well, we'll call him Beni Legitt." Now who was she to do this, to change my child's name? She was taking everything else. She wanted their names also, my name. Because, soon after, my children stopped speaking Sicilian to me. I felt betrayed, cuckold/*curnutu*. They answered all my Sicilian in their English. This began a great confusion of words in my mind that made me stutter. I pleaded with them to speak to me in Sicilian, for the love of God and my sanity. But they sullenly refused. It was *Rosalia*/Rosy who cried one day and told me that the Irish/*li Airisci* children humiliated her if she spoke Sicilian in the streets to her brother. I was losing my children.

About twenty-eight years ago a nice young man came to ask me questions. "I will pronounce certain words," he said. "I want you to tell me how you feel about them. For instance, if I say cupcake. I want you to tell me if you feel: (1) pleasant, (2) good, (3) indifferent, (4) bad, (5) very bad."

For a moment then I felt if he pronounced *marshmallow* the dam would burst and I would speak like a poet.

Instead he pronounced *English* and then *Irish*.

The hemorrhaging of words began in my mind. How could I explain to him what those words in my head were telling me? "Your children are becoming American." And I had to admit that American was better—not that Sicilian was inferior—but that American was better, far better. Oh, America, you are not a cruel country, but a land without pity/*pietà*.

How could all those words escape? I was sent into another of those rages. They took me to a room where a machine was hooked to me that set up counter-vibrations so violent that they dissolved my very spinal cord, vibrating in me.

That Sunday forty years ago—as usual, I could not sleep. I dreaded the Monday subway ride, all the more because it seemed we were near the end of our calvary/*calvario*. We had put aside four thousand dollars/*quatru mila scudi*. We were planning to return to Racalmuto, perhaps in a year.

The end of the week when I returned in the rain, exhausted like a rat drowned in oil, men were milling in the streets shouting at one another, "Banks had to be

closed." In that tangle of words it took the Saturday and the Sunday to understand—the banks were closed because they had lost our money. My money, my
years of eating spaghetti sandwiches, a thousand rides in the midst of words
thrown at me like stones, of sitting in the caves of our three rooms like scared
animals—me, the Prince of Racalmuto of the Province of Girgenti.

I went the next morning to beat on the doors of the Dime Savings with the
hordes of people that had gathered there, clotted there, like the words in my
throat. We shouted. I shouted and cried until the veins in my neck stood out. We
threw stones until the cops came and I saw that goat-faced Irish cop looking at
me. I went home, running in short hops like a rabbit.

It wasn't that just then my sweet bride had received a letter from her relatives telling us that if we returned to Racalmuto I would be drafted into the army.
Mussolini had decreed it. No, it wasn't just that. But I did feel there was no way
out, nothing to look forward to. I had been had. I had been made a cuckold/
'nu curnutu. I, the Prince of Racalmuto—both my property and my children—my
future—had been taken. All in the time of a spasm.

I wasn't thinking of anything the day I put on my spats. My mind was hemorrhaging words. From the closet shelf I took down the cane with a solid silver
handle the size of a fist which I once thought I would take on princely strolls
along Fifth Avenue. And on that shabby street where my bank had closed I
smashed every window where I saw the face of the crippled/lu sciancatu president
they called Roosevelt.

I don't know how many store windows I smashed with my long elegant
strokes before the goat-faced Irish cop cornered me in a Chinese restaurant.

I'm not a small man, nor ugly. Many have told me I look like Dick Powell and
say I have the dignity of William Powell. So I slaughtered that goat-faced cop
who kept repeating, "Take it easy, boy. Take it easy!"

My first blow caught him on the side of the head. I saw him reach for his gun.
I did. My second blow with my cane hit his cheekbone and on the fifth blow the
cane broke in half.

When the squad cars came, the horde of men beat me to a pulp and yet I
never lost consciousness. I knew I had been defeated. I, the Prince of Racalmuto,
would be sold into slavery.

About twenty-three years ago a paisano who had taken care of my children
when my sweet bride was put away came to tell me he could no longer look after
my Baldassaro and my Rosalia. Times were bad, he said. They were being sent to
an orphanage.

Recently I heard on the radio, voices coming through my window, an avalanche of words, voices roaring free and abandoned. One high-pitched voice
detached itself and shouted, "Happy New Year. It's 1976." 1976! I don't believe
it. But I'm not sure. I'm not sure of much with all these words struggling in my
mind and throat led by CHEESE/FORMAGGIO/TUMAZU. To be sure of what's
in your mind it must come out in words, to judge their size and weight, their

quality. My words have been stuck in my throat so long they are beginning to rot. I know because of the strange odor in my mouth.

I am sure of one thing. I am of the class of '96. I was born in 1896 and I came to America in 1911 and I was brought to this place in 1934. My sweet bride is long dead. My children have been put away to grow up American. I will soon be eighty years old.

When I am gone that will be the end of us. What a waste of princely blood.

Wild Heart

Maria Bruno

Fiction (1992)

I HAD JUST FINISHED junior high the summer after President Kennedy died. It was the time of big hair and wild hearts. At least I had big hair. The biggest. I made it into a dime-store ritual, buying steel ratting combs, large velvet bows, three-inch bobby pins, steel clips to hold my peroxided spit curls in place. I stood in front of the mirror for hours ratting, smoothing, pinning, spraying my hive into a mound of perfection. I ratted it high until I looked like a shaman or an Egyptian goddess, pinning the velvet bow to my bangs as a final touch. Oh, I had heard stories: Once a girl from Long Island had found a rat in her hair with a litter of nursing babies; another out West housed killer bees; and still another in New Jersey had provided a much needed home to a vampire bat which was displaced when the girl's father reroofed the house. But in junior high we never listened too much to the rumors. And we didn't care too much about the environment then, either. Ozone layers be damned—we lived for Aqua Net. Big cans of it. We filled the halls with a sweet sticky mist, making our hair stiff like day-old meringue.

Boys were a mystery to me then. All the songs on the radio by the Shangri-Las and the Shirelles told me I needed one to be complete. I was determined to have a boyfriend so I wore tight straight miniskirts, mohair sweaters, and white fringed go-go boots. I bought a bullet bra for $1.29 at the dime store. My neighbor, Johnny Marino, told me bullet bras drove boys crazy even though they pinched and left circles on my breasts like the rings of an old tree. I bought packs of Lucky Strikes and blew smoke rings to the cruisers on Woodward Avenue. I practiced French kissing bottles of Grape Nehi. I outlined my eyes in black like Liz Taylor in *Cleopatra* and painted my lips with Maybelline's "White Lotus." I was pale, ghostly, cool—the coolest.

Johnny Marino was two years older than me. He was a year behind in school. He was what we used to call a greaser, an auto shop kid. He was an archetype of the times, I guess: a loner who smoked Pall Malls and wore leather and found solace in the debris of old Plymouths, music in the shaky hums of rebuilt engines. He didn't have the jock's butch cut, but longer hair that curled around his ears. And dark dark eyes. I never admitted it to anyone but I found him handsome.

He had always been a loner. In elementary school he never played kick ball or basketball; he would just stand to one side as if he wished he were somewhere else, as if there were some cosmic folly associated with our behavior that only he was privy to. You could ask any of the boys to go steady back then, announce it to the lunchroom, have one of your giggly friends go over and make a "going steady" deal. But no one to my knowledge ever announced their intentions for Johnny. By junior high he was considered dangerous. He listened to the Rolling Stones and smoked marijuana, growing his own in the back seat of his Fury. That's not all that happened in the back seat of his car, they'd say. No decent girl would or should go out with him.

By the time high school rolled around, I decided to seek popularity and defy the traditional stereotype of the Italian girls at Shrine of the Perpetual Guilt. It was rumored we were fast, dark and exotic. By the time we were sixteen we were expected to peroxide our spit curls, wiggle our hips like Marilyn Monroe and know, in the biblical sense, the back seat of every Ford Fairlane in suburban Detroit. But I wanted to head for higher ground. I had become enamored of the popular boys, the ones who looked squeaky clean, the ones who wore madras shirts and chinos and Bass Weejun loafers. I took down my uninhabited beehive and traded in my bullet bra for a plain cotton one, the kind a novice nun might wear. For the first day of high school I spent the night before sleeping on empty Minute Maid orange juice cans to make my kinky hair straight. I then reset it at 4 a.m. on brush rollers into what was going to be the perfect flip. For the next two hours I slept with the scratchy knowledge that I would be beautiful for my high school debut. In the morning, after an hour's ritual in front of the mirror, I sprayed my flip with half a can of Aqua Net Super Hold, making it point toward the heavens. My crown of ratted hair forever gone, I stood before the mirror staring, wondering who it was.

My mother further orchestrated my debut, all the while calling me her "good little girl." She bought me a white blouse with a Peter Pan collar, which I secured with my brand-new monogrammed circle pin. I talked her into buying me an outfit like the popular girls wore—a plaid skirt, a plaid vest and matching plaid Capezios. I traded those little blue bottles of Evening in Paris for the free samples of Shalimar I got at Hudson's. I put a plaid ribbon in my hair—I was ready.

But it was a typical first day of high school. I forgot my locker combination and I was late for biology. I had to pee but all the bathrooms were locked to thwart smokers, something I never had to deal with in junior high. It was Indian-summer hot; my circle pin was choking me, and I wanted to rip it from my throat. By 11:30, my perfect flip had fizzled, gone kinky, one side hanging lower than the other. I stood in the lunchroom holding a tray of Pizza Surprise and Tater Tots, my warm half-pint of milk curdling. My matching Capezios pinched my toes, and I could swear Muffy De Vries and Boo Egan, their blond flips still flipping, were sniggering at me. I had nowhere to sit.

Johnny Marino sat alone in the corner of the lunchroom. There was nothing on his tray, but he was drinking something; it looked like coffee. He must have swiped it from the teacher's lounge. He looked up and stared. I thought if I sat with him it might skew the direction of my entire high school career. But I knew he wouldn't say much, and I wouldn't have to say much to him so I sat down.

"Hey, Rosie," Johnny said. "Having a bad day?"

"You can't call me Rosie anymore," I snapped. "I want to be called Rosalie."
I didn't tell him I planned to dot the "i" with a big heart.

"Whaja do to your hair?" he asked, sipping his coffee. "I liked it better the other way."

"That was the old me," I said, struggling with my carton of milk, trying to get it open. I lopped the sleeve of my blouse into the Pizza Surprise. I started to cry.

"You wanna blow this popstand?" he asked softly. "Come on, let's go."

I knew if I went with Johnny my whole high school career could be threatened. I'd be picked last for the teams in gym, doomed to date the audio-visual boys, the greasers, or the guys with butch cuts and army fatigues who shot birds from trees. Rumors would run rampant: I went all the way—I did IT—you could score a home run off of me. No decent dates, no prom, even low SAT scores. My future loomed before me like a B movie: I'd have a two-year stint at a community college majoring in cosmetology or Travel and Tourism. I'd marry someone with a ducktail named Lance, a forklift operator for DeLuca's warehouse. We'd move into a trailer park in Livonia. I'd be watching *Another World* while presoaking Tiffany's and Lance, Jr.'s diapers in my Hoover portable washer. My big night out would be bowling at Yorba Linda Lanes. I'd wear a pink chenille bathrobe and fuzzy slippers and suddenly I'd look like Shirley Booth in *Come Back Little Sheba*.

"Come on," he said, and reached for my hand. We didn't even clear our trays. I was sure everybody noticed. Outside I took off my shoes and unfastened my circle pin.

I was completely indoctrinated with the movie-like scenario planted in every girl's brain that the Prince, the gorgeous Prince, would arrive some day and save me from a grim existence with boys who ate their boogers, lit their spaghetti farts with their fathers' butane torches, or tried to unsnap my bra during the intermission of the movies so all their friends, seated in the back row, could see. I wanted to be delivered from my frizzy hair, big feet, pendulous breasts and the chafing between my thighs.

I had this fantasy that I'd be at a formal dance unescorted. Muffy and Boo would be there in their pastel organzas, their silky hair framing their faces like golden auras. A tall blonde tuxedoed boy looking, I realize now, like someone straight out of Hitler Youth, arrives; he's new in town. His name is Skip. He takes one look at me, walks past Muffy and Boo, and even Wanda "Jugs" Del Florio, who it's rumored, let all the boys unsnap her bra and go "down there," and stands in front of me. I look up and swoon because his shoulders are so square, his jaw is so strong, his hand is so forceful. We glide onto the dance floor and the rest is history. No trailer park in Livonia for me. No ducktails or diapers or Yorba Linda Lanes. No Lance, straight off the forklift, wanting his meat loaf and mashed potatoes. It's Ivy League for both of us; our composite SATs astound our principal, Sister Immaculata, so much, in fact, that she erects a mini-shrine to us, complete with votive candles and holy water and an inscription sketched in gold by Capu-chin monks which reads: *MR. AND MRS. SKIP HOFMEISTER.*" The fantasy doesn't end there. Muffy and Boo go to an unaccredited community college and become keypunch operators and Wanda Del Florio takes a home study course and replaces Sister Immaculata as principal at Shrine of the Perpetual Guilt. Skip becomes a corporate lawyer and I become a famous novelist or a backup singer for Ray Charles.

"This way," Johnny said again as we finally found the path. He gripped my hand gently.

"Johnny, I have to get back, I'll miss algebra," I said. "Math is my worst subject."

"Come on," he said, moving quickly. "I have something to show you."

I suppose I should have been scared, considering the rumors and all. Some people said Johnny could unsnap a bra in three seconds, that he could French kiss and make you see God, that he carried ribbed condoms in his pack of Pall Malls, that he could recite all the lyrics to the Stones' "King Bee"—I'm a King Bee Baby / Buzzin' around your hive—while he removed your panties. But I was more worried about the nights of detention stretching before me; the call to my parents which would send my mother straight to the backyard to lay a flower at the ceramic Holy Virgin's feet; my reputation would be destroyed instantly, so that suddenly tough boys like Carmine and Rocco would be asking for my phone num-ber. Guys who would say things like "I want to live fast, die young, and leave a beautiful corpse."

Johnny stopped and knelt and pointed to a mayapple. It was already purpling, getting ready for fall.

"There's a trillium," he said, "and a jack-in-the-pulpit." We moved farther into the brush and stopped at a bare patch of earth.

"You know what this is?" he asked, looking up.

"No," I answered, feeling warmer. I unbuttoned the top button of my blouse.

"Bucks scratch here. Then they urinate all over it. Then they wait for the does."

"Wait for the does to do what?" I asked. I had no idea.

"To mate. To come for the males."

"Oh," I said, watching Johnny carefully. Was I in trouble here? I asked myself. Was he going to start hoofing his stiletto shoes in the dirt? Was he going to unzip, pull *it* out? Would I then be his forever? Would there be no Skip, no waltz across the dance floor, no Ivy League?

"C-can we go now Johnny?" I stammered. "I'm going to get detention."

It was then that he kissed me. Nothing dangerous. No Rolling Stones. No tongue. I didn't see God. He had more than three seconds and didn't reach for the snaps on my nun's bra. But I did feel my bare toes in the wet grass, the warm sun streaking the back of my neck, his hands around my waist. I could hear the cluck-ing of red-winged blackbirds in the low brush. His leather jacket felt hot next to my fingers. My heart raced.

"Johnny, I . . ."

"I know. I better get you back."

I looked into his eyes. He kissed me again. I smiled.

I wish I didn't have to tell the end of this story.

For some reason I never really spoke much to Johnny Marino after that day. Perhaps I felt it was too risky; maybe I just wanted to be accepted a little too much. Two months after my first kiss, Johnny quit school and enlisted. I began growing my hair long after that, ironing it straight with my mom's Steam N' Press. I bought a guitar and started to think less about Muffy and Boo and more about the world. I thought about Johnny on and off during my senior year until the day I heard he had died somewhere in the jungles of Vietnam. I often wondered if he was alone when it happened, separated from his platoon, off somewhere looking at the wildflowers.

Sometimes I wonder what he would think of the world today. He'd be forty-four now. Tabloid TV says President Kennedy used to sneak his mistresses into the back door of the White House; trilliums are on the endangered species list and there's a hole in the ozone layer. Sister Immaculata is still at Shrine of the Perpetual Guilt worried about hymens and the Madonna/Whore dichotomy; my daughter Francie attends public schools. She always wears black, and is noted for her tortured artist's clothing, powdered Kabuki cheeks and maroon lips. She treasures her thick brown hair, which leaps from her head like live wires. She never fusses with it. She questions everything and I love her for it. My mother, a widow now, spends a lot of time in the backyard with the ceramic Holy Virgin, planting red and orange poppies for my nephew who is stationed in Saudi Arabia where no wildflowers grow. I have gray hair and the natural curls flow to my shoulders. I'm on my second divorce. I never found Skip or even a close replica. I saw Wanda Del Florio the other day working at the 7-Eleven. She's married now and sends her children to Catholic school. She seemed bigger and more powerful than I remember. Her red hair flowed to her shoulders free from the ratting comb; she had Sophia Loren lips, and those large breasts, the objects of perpetual fascination years ago, were hardly noticeable under her uniform. After her shift, I bought her a Big Gulp and a chili dog and we sat on the curb waving at the cars going by.

"Remember how we used to do this all the time in elementary school?" she asked sucking on the plastic straw. "You know, at Wesley's Drug Store?"

"Yeah," I said, watching her, thinking she was so beautiful now.

"What happened? Why didn't we talk anymore?"

"I'm sorry," I answered. There was a silence.

"You believed everything they said about me, didn't you?"

"I guess so," I stammered. I felt fifteen again.

"A lot of it was true," she said smiling. "I have no regrets." She began to laugh.

Her eyes were as large and round as moons, her mouth open to gasps of laughter. I followed suit. And there we sat, arms entwined, howling into the air. For a moment I thought I saw Sister Immaculata drive by in her black car looking to see if our legs were properly crossed at the ankles. I flashed her the peace sign and hugged Wanda tighter.

Wanda and the 7-Eleven got me thinking about how I got Saturday detention after that day with Johnny, and how my mother and father both headed for the ceramic Holy Virgin and buried some peeled plum tomatoes beneath her rose covered toes. Johnny was suspended for three days; he rebuilt an engine in his driveway. Sometimes when I can't think of the world anymore, I think of Johnny Marino and the woods and the sun and the song of the red-winged blackbirds in the low brush. I think of the trillium, the way his mouth tasted, how the heat of his jacket felt between my fingers. I remember my wild heart.

A Conversation with Camille Paglia

Christina Bevilacqua

Interview (1992)

Camille Paglia teaches humanities at the Philadelphia College of Art. Her book Sexual Personae: Art and Decadence from Nefertiti to Emily Dickinson *was first published by Yale University Press in 1990. I spoke to her by phone in December 1991; what follows is about one-third of the comments she made during our conversation.*

Christina Bevilacqua: Having grown up Italian American and female, I was curious while reading your book to think about how someone else who grew up Italian American and female could have come up with some of the ideas and the way of presenting them that you did. I have a quote from an interview you did where you say, "My best sentences are written as if this is going to be the only thing left, just one sentence, 2,000 years from now, that's all that will be left. Someone will find this one sentence and in that one sentence you should be able to recreate it all. It's very Italian." I wonder if you could talk about what it means that that's a very Italian notion.

Camille Paglia: Well, a year or two ago, for the new edition of the *Princeton Encyclopedia of Poetry and Poetics*, I had done a history of love poetry, and I had been reviewing a lot of material from Greek and Roman poetry, and sometimes all that's left is one sentence, particularly very ancient, archaic Greek poetry from like 600 B.C. And I was struck by how only one sentence, one line from a poem can still speak. Here it is twenty-five hundred years later, and the thing is still so vivid, the person's personality and their love life; their emotional experiences still can telegraph over this distance. And the thing about living on forever and leaving your testament and your revenge, that is very like Dante. Dante's attitude I really understand completely, this thing where you're driven into exile by injustice, and you're totally alone and underestimated, but you're going to leave your testimony, and you're going to leave your view, your personality, and put your enemies in their place, and totally reorient the historical record so that your enemies are crushed and you triumph. There's something Italian about this. I have never met any other ethnic group who can think posthumously in the way Italians can. Italians are always talking about death. It goes all the way back, I'm convinced, to Etruscan culture, which was oriented around a burial cult. I've gotten in so much trouble in my life in academe by inadvertently saying things about someone who had died in a way that struck people as very rude or harsh or cold, but was just typically Italian. I can remember sitting around my grandmother's table, I was very tiny, and my uncle would say, "Eh, old man

Vincenzi dropped dead last night." "Oh yeah?" Just the way of talking about death is totally practical, pragmatic. There's none of this middle-class WASP hush-hush reverence. So I don't have any fear of death. It just seems like a practical thing that happens to you. I think the root of it is from Italian culture being oriented towards the land and, originally, farming. Usually rural people, even in America, have the same practical, non-pious attitude toward death—it's a factual reality. And that has been an enormous advantage to me in being able to talk about life. I was able to sustain myself over this long period when all my work was being rejected and I had been constantly rejected in getting a job. For some reason these reverses seem to crush other people, but I have this ability as an Italian to look at my work and myself posthumously, to say, "So I won't get any rewards or status from it now, but when I'm dead. . . ." Renaissance Italians—or Italian culture in general— they're very memorious. They remember with gratitude things done for them, and with anger the injuries and dishonor done to them. That's like a vendetta. It's making people nervous right now; they know I have this long Italian memory. People are afraid to say things about me in public, because I might show up on their doorstep, an Italian, you know . . . ? My parents' generation wanted to assimilate. My mother was born in Italy, came over at age six; my father was born here, but all the grandparents were born in Italy. And my parents wanted to blend in with America. But my generation, in the 1960s, we're the ethnic identity generation, and I totally have identified with my grandparents' generation.

CB: Describe the two, because I was curious about why you would relate to the earlier generation and what the influence was.

CP: To me, typical of my generation, the 1960s was a period of ethnic pride. That was when Blacks let their hair grow into Afros, and that sort of thing. I've had this conversation with Jews my age, and they'll say the same things; their parents also were trying to assimilate. I have a friend—when she goes to a restaurant her mother will say, "Shhh! You're talking too loud. People will think you just got off the boat." Our parents' generation wanted to be part of America. I'm very pro-America, but I have a great sense that I'm Italian, and I do not want to adopt a WASP style. As a matter of fact, I'd almost bend over backwards to retain my abrasive ethnic edge. But I'm sure my academic career was held back by the fact that I refused to smooth out my personality. My whole manner is revolutionary, because people can't imagine that anyone who talks this fast could have written such a deep and complex work, especially a fast-talking, small woman, a small Italian woman. You know, Gay Talese wrote me a beautiful letter, and he said, "Italians have not really penetrated very far into the intellectual establishment in America." Well, I've tried to say that I totally identify with being Italian . . . [laughs] . . . I force it down everyone's throat. I've been doing this for so many years, and suddenly I'm doing it in the media, and I'm delighted with it. In the European articles on me I'm this flamingly proud Italian-American Amazon; I make a big deal of that. I loved the energy and vitality and theatricality of my grandparents' generation, all the Italian relatives together having this great time. No one had any money, but the best part of my life is when all these people who had no money got together for these giant things with ham sandwiches and sodas and so on, giant weddings, you know. And now, when everyone's better established financially, a lot of that's gone, because that generation—the immigrants—has died off. The only place I see that kind of vitality today is in African-American culture. They have the huge extended family still, and they all get together and have the same good time that we used to have. So I just hate this American bourgeois culture where everything is low-key and passionless, sanitized. It's like people are embarrassed about the ethnic thing.

CB: In several interviews you've mentioned your admiration for Madonna; in one you state that, like you, she is a "hard-working, self-made Italian-American woman who sort of came out of nowhere." And you mention that, other than Geraldine Ferraro, Italian-American women have done very little. How would you characterize Italian-American women?

CP: The cliché has been that they're not assertive, and it used to be said that they were just trained to get married. That hasn't been my experience. And my father, who came out of World War II and went to college on the G.I. Bill, his attitude was quite avant-garde for how to bring up an Italian-American daughter: I should aim for the top and completely assert myself. He taught me to fight like a guy, and defend myself, and to be unconventional. That's not the normal way.

CB: No, not at all.

CP: No, but it simply is the case. You know, I admire [an Italian-American writer], and I think she likes to be all "Oh wow, I'm really Italian." But the name she publishes under is not—she just wants to blend in. I don't know. All I know is that the Jews have succeeded tremendously; they're just so prominent everywhere in the intellectual and academic world.

CB: But can you talk about the difference in educational expectations between Italian-American and Jewish-American girls?

CP: Well, of course Jewish tradition has been, going back thousands of years, very learning-centered. But sometimes in the Catholic tradition there's a monastic element. My mother's small town is just twenty miles from the great abbey where Thomas Aquinas was trained. You're much closer in Italy to the presence of the Church, everywhere visible to you. Something happened here toward the post-war era: Italians let go of their culture in the way that some Jews have. People are just wandering, soulless and empty; they don't even realize the incredible greatness of their own tradition. My mentor is Harold Bloom, who wouldn't let go of his ethnic . . . who didn't want at all to smooth out his Jewishness. But for some reason there are Jews like that, but we don't have those equivalents. Italians have divested themselves of their own ethnicity. In Black culture, even the ones who have risen into the middle class and above, even if their manner in the day seems almost white, when they return to their culture, there's a powerful culture, with music, dance, the Church, and so on. But—here's an example: my parents' generation, they're embarrassed by any mention of the Mafia. They think it's defamation. I think it's very interesting. Far from being embarrassed, I am delighted. I would love it if someone thought I was related to someone in the Mafia. To me the Mafia is a crystallization of traits that are Italian that go back centuries.

CB: Such as?

CP: The clannishness, the vendetta, the loyalty, the bloodbrother; this sense of practicality, making your way in the world, canniness, shrewdness. And I loved the *Godfather* pictures. The original two are among the few that actually capture certain things about Italian personalities. I cannot bear things like *Moonstruck* and *Prizzi's Honor*. I become apoplectic because of these clichés about Italians, and their complete lack of understanding of Italian anything. There's something Italian, Italian American in certain ways, that has a fierce, attack quality to it. So I think there is an overlap with the Mafia. But ninety-nine percent of Italians would not agree with me on that.

CB: You were talking earlier about the large family and your very fond memory of that. Now, you were raised by someone who didn't think along the lines of the status quo about, for instance, how an Italian-American girl should be raised. You were lucky that your father was someone who really had expectations that you would be an independent person. What about in families where that's not true; what about the down side of the clannishness of the Italian family, where to be different, or to want to go outside of what is expected is seen as a problem for the whole clan? What about the problem of individualizing yourself and being able to actualize yourself as an individual, and not as a part of this huge group?

CP: I still think it's a tension on me, and I think on most Italians, from what I can gather. It really is a problem, there really is a sense of outsiders and insiders. And I think that the toll is taken very much by the daughters. Like in Italy, it's still the case that if you're unmarried, you live at home, no matter what age you are. The idea that you would live apart in an apartment is just . . . [laughs] . . . it's not even possible. So it's the single daughters who end up nursing the parents. Even if you have a job you live at home in the family citadel. I still see a residue of that pattern. There's enormous pressure on the unmarried Italian daughters, and it has centuries and centuries behind it. And it's very difficult for the daughters to pull away, even mentally.

CB: That's something I'd like to ask you more about. You've talked about your father's expectations, what about your mother's? And did she also work?

CP: In the beginning she stayed home for three years with me. Then, my grandmothers were within a two-block area, so it was, for me, great—I just loved that. Many Black children have that, too, that connection with the grand-mothers, which I think is one of the greatest relationships you can have. And my mother, like my grandmother, earned a living by sewing at home. And then my mother went to work in a bank and became a teller, and then always worked, until very recently. She's retired. Now, my mother would've preferred that I be more conventional, there's no doubt about that. For example, I had no interest in sewing or cooking. So after fourteen years my mother finally got, when her second daughter was born, someone who wants to cook and sew, things like that; my sister has a gift for that. She's an art conservator, and her gifts are quite different from mine. She's great at music, painting, and all those things which I'm not into. And I got the verbal thing. But my mother would definitely prefer that I listen to social cues. But my parents generally spoke as one. I wasn't aware of a split, particularly. They had that, you know, just the firm. . . .

CB: The united front.

CP: Yes; absolutely. It was a very structured way of being raised. But at the same time they were very positive, encouraging me and things like that. But I think the women expected me to be a certain way that I was not being. So that's my earliest memory, going way back, my first sense of being sexually hetero-dox and a rebel. My sense of that goes back to my tiniest years when people tried to force me to do things I did not want to do, or to dress in ways I didn't want to dress, or to like gifts I didn't want to like. Like in particular, dolls. I just loathed them. And my first memory of absolute total human alienation, where I had a sense that I did not belong to the human race, was where I am a small child, the only child in this room full of people, all smiling with great expectation as this doll is being given to me, and my sense of the gap between my inner sense of loathing for this doll, and the beaming faces of these people, and me being forced to go through this charade of gratitude for something I did not want. Some people, I think, capitulate, and begin to play the social game. For some reason I just kept this burning flame of rage and rebellion inside of me; eventually it's going to lead to *Sexual Personae*. But I just had no sense of identification with this sex role that was being forced on me. And this was a time of the incredible 1950s blondes—Debbie Reynolds—I just cannot tell you how I felt about those blondes. There were so many, you could make a list of like twelve names, they all looked alike. And you're supposed to be this simpering, demure kind of a thing. And I was not that at all. I was just this Amazonian figure. What I was identifying with was my uncles, who had all gone to war, World War II and Korea. And there would be all this military equipment, helmets and so on. I identified with that, with the warrior mentality. I always did. I just have a sense from my earliest years of constant, constant social pressure to stop behaving the way I was behaving. Whatever I was doing was not appropriate, not acceptable for a girl. And at first people tried to get me to admit when I was going to get married, but then after a while they realized that I wasn't. And then I didn't get the pressure after a while. Aunts and so on, when I got into my twenties, realized that I was so career-oriented, which was unusual for then. I can't remember in high school that many women talking about careers the way I was intent on a career; I was intent on a career since I was six. I was going to be an archaeologist ever since I went to the Metropolitan Museum. I just had this scholarly vocation from preschool.

What's unusual about me is that I'm not just someone who has written this huge book about sex. I'm someone who is active as a person in real life. Normally someone who is a scholar is a thoughtful person who can sit still and study and write books; normally they're not hyperactive people who punch people. You don't have that combination, except in Italian culture. It goes back to the monks. The monks were studious and hardworking. At the same time they were very active; they worked in the fields. That was the monastic ideal, this combination of the contemplative and hard work. I think that's what's so odd about me. You don't normally get such an in-your-face person who can write as beautifully as I can. Norman Mailer tries to do it, and only a couple of people have realized the parallel between me and Norman Mailer. Norman Mailer's writing was its absolute best when he was using himself as the subject. And I think that's also very Italian, the absolute, unembarrassed egotism of my writing. I mean it's no problem; Italians are very assertive. Even when Italian-American women in the old days were trained to be silent, there still was a way of asserting your power in a very dramatic and theatrical way that I identify with strongly. Another thing about me that's Italian is this emotional truth thing, and that's a link that I see to African-American culture. Both Italian (not Italian-American, but Italian culture) and African-American culture are very music-centered and emotion-centered. And food, the preparation of food, and the extended family are the centers of life. The kitchen was a center of my grandmother's house; that's where everyone was all the time. It was, to me, the place where magic things were going on all day long; for days, these weird things are being cooked in huge amounts, and so on. When I meet somebody, I know whether I'm going to get along with them by their reaction to food. This whole thing about anorexia and bulimia is such a symptom of a culture falling apart. Food is the center—it's cooking, the heat, the fire; it's elemental, the hearth and so on. I'm very superstitious about that.

CB: I've read some of the interviews that you've given, and I'm listening to you describe this childhood with lots of people around, where you love being part of everyone doing something together, and not knowing what's going to happen next, where there's this kind of life-force. . . . But I want to ask you about some of the things that you write about Emily Dickinson in your last chapter, which I found the most interesting in the book. There's a sense of real solitude in that, and I'm not asking you biographically, "Do you spend a lot of time alone?" But there's an "alone" sense that also comes from the feeling that you described of being excommunicated and of being kept outside the mainstream, of your ideas not being allowed to be heard; there's this lone warrior, waiting or fighting for however long it's going to take. So there is on the one hand this description of being part of a large group, and yet you've chosen a profession in which there is a lot of solitary pursuit. Research and writing are things that you do alone.

CP: Well, I think the two are definitely related. The strength that I have in my aloneness is coming from my sense of identity that is actually very extensive. That is, I feel I'm related to this enormous group of people, and it goes all the way back to Italy. So I have this strong sense of identity coming from the sense of being part of this extended family. Even in Italy, you have this thing of the nun or the monk in the retreat—it's so Catholic, my solitary contemplative life; I could easily see how a hundred years ago I could've been a nun. What I really hate is the nuclear family. I think the nuclear family is a disaster. See, I feel that I have experienced in my lifetime this collapse of the extended family into the nuclear family, which was the 1950s. You know, the bourgeois, suburban, Father-Knows-Best, Donna Reed sitcoms enshrined this idea of the nuclear family. And more and more you hear these things about how ninety percent of families are dysfunctional, and I'm saying, that's right, the nuclear family is dysfunctional. The nuclear family was never meant to be—it's a horrendous, nightmarish imprisonment of the psyche. The proper relationship is to an extended family with many generations in it, and most of history has been that. I think that a lot of sexual problems today, a lot of psychological problems are coming from this new thing called the nuclear family. I felt like a prisoner in this new milieu, which wasn't just my family. The whole culture was forcing us to think in those terms in the 1950s. We have all these tract houses, with little plots of land around each one, everything exactly alike, every one looking and trying to be exactly alike. It took me about twenty years to realize that the claustrophobic tranquility of that period was unbearable to me. The 1950s came from the fact that our parents were relaxing—their whole life's been nothing but Depression, war, the rise of Nazism and Fascism, the camps, the bombs, and everything. And they were determined that they would protect their children from all the harsh realities of life that they had had to experience. So this is what happened. Essentially, they lied to us about the nature of life. And what we had was this pampered kind of affluent upbringing. What I'm doing in my book is bringing up from the cellar and down from the attic all the things that the 1950s bourgeois family had eliminated from the main floor. All the things that my parents did not want to talk or think about—all the unpleasant, barbaric, rawest, most brutal aspects of human experience—are in my book. I've opened the closet doors and brought all these things out. In the 1950s and 1960s I just felt like this person who saw things about the world, and no one else saw them. And if I would try to express them they would shock people, or no one would agree with them, so I kept things to myself. I long ago realized, probably as early as high school, that I could never fully communicate to anyone. What I was saying was so far in advance of what people were ready to hear, and the learning upon which it was based was so much in advance of what anyone, even smart people, had, that I gave up any hope of being understood. So that's why I identify with Emily Dickinson very strongly, with the way she tried to publish and succeed, and then she just kept to herself, and even though she is surrounded by her family, people didn't realize the extent to which she was writing until her poems were discovered after she was dead. So I had that feeling of just keeping going along, going along, going along. I mean I love solitude; I feel I'm most myself alone. And I think this is the lesson I'm going to leave for future women, the model of my life as I have lived it, a life that has totally spurned outside approval. I do not care about outside approval—of course I do, but I don't seek it. And I can, as a woman, tolerate hatred, and people underestimating me; I can tolerate any poverty and humiliation. I just continued because I had that Catholic thing, the vocation. You know, I feel that scholarship goes way back to the monastic period, where it's of the highest importance—the copying and studying of books and so on—it all goes back to Alexandria, to ancient Greece. So to me, the fact that I wasn't getting any academic recognition, well, if I would ever feel sorry for myself for even two minutes I would scorn myself. I would say to myself, you can't for one moment believe that those things are important, because an important book is one that speaks to the future, one that's read after you're dead—that's an important book. As I said about the fragments of the poems, these people are long, long dead, but all it takes is one thing that's emotionally true that you set on paper and it can speak to someone thousands of years later. You know the way books were lost and recovered, and the monks copied them in the Middle Ages? I just have this powerful sense of the transmission of scholarship over centuries, and of being part of that line that goes back to the Catholic Church. I feel very Catholic, even though I'm a lax Catholic.

CB: I was going to ask you to talk a little bit more about that; that's the other piece you say you have in common with Madonna.

CP: Yes. We're formed by the Church. And I don't like the way more and more sometimes it seems like she's disrespectful to the Church. When she's most thoughtful she says "The Church formed me," and speaks respectfully of it. She should. Because just because you're rebelling against it doesn't mean you should not speak respectfully of it.

CB: I'm interested because I was born in 1959, and went to Catholic school, and I remember nothing in the Catholic Church having to do with scholarship. I grew up at a time when the Church was trying to make itself more attractive to more people; for instance, they stopped saying the Mass in Latin when I was in first grade. I think probably a lot of that sense was lost.

CP: It changed radically. That's when the priests had to become friends with parishioners. They used to be required to have much more learning about the Bible; it was a much more austere religion. My father taught at a Jesuit school as well, so I also had the example of the Jesuits, who are very intellectual. So to me there was ever present the sense of the intellectuality and scholarship of the Church. Also, I was always interested in the past, and always had this sense of Biblical archaeology. Even in the missals, the prayer books, I'd root around and seek out the more scholarly aspects of Catholicism. I think that's just the way we were taught, early religious education. The Baltimore Catechism. . . . I don't know if they'd thrown that out the window by the time you had to be confirmed. Did they?

CB: I think so.

CP: You didn't have to, see? We had the Baltimore Catechism where we had these questions we had to memorize, and you had to memorize the answers. And the language that it was written in was so austere; I mean we just had this sense of the complexity of the theology of the Catholic Church. And all that is gone. It's gone and everything is casual, like folk mass, and the kiss of peace and all that stuff, yecch. Probably it's more authentically like primitive Christianity, the sense of the community of worshippers, everyone very humble. . . . But I identify with the majesty and grandeur of Roman Catholicism. All the things that people most stereotype that's negative about the Church are the things that I actually like best, like its haughtiness, that authoritative sound. The things that I rebelled against as a teenager are the very things that I think in some ways formed me. It gives you this philosophical perspective, allows you to see the universe in terms of this huge cosmic struggle between light and dark. And the hierarchy of the Church, the way it's so organized, I think gives you tremendous organizational skills. But I think that's also Italian. I think Italians have this practicality; you could see it in ancient Rome. There's no doubt in my mind that I have this ability that went into the writing of this book that's Italian—it's something genetic, and cultural, too. The book is an aqueduct, a structure that is transmitting the culture from ancient times to now. I'm showing the continuity, this water rushing down and so on. From my earliest years I remember my relatives commenting on structures. We have no snobbery about physical work; on the contrary, physical labor is considered ennobling. We are the ones who first made the transition; I mean, in Egypt, ancient Rome, the medieval period, the artists are unknown. But the idea that the sculptor, the dirty sculptor like Michelangelo has a divine ability that's inspired as much as any poet or man who works in words is something that the Italians did at the Renaissance; they made the painter and sculptor equal to the poet in cultural prestige. And I have this thing, this idea of a well-made driveway. I mean, my Uncle Albert can talk for twenty minutes about the proper way to pour concrete. . . .

CB: I can't believe it. I just spent Thanksgiving with my family, and three of my uncles and my husband sat around talking about concrete. . . . I can't believe it!

CP: The Romans are the ones who used concrete in a massive way for construction, it goes way back. It was the Romans who used concrete construction for baths, aqueducts, sewers. . . . I can remember from my earliest childhood, and even to this day, in Endicott we pass a road in upstate New York where everyone points out the window, "There's the curb your father laid in 1949." This is why in my book I could say how the George Washington Bridge is a sublime piece of art. The fact that I can see construction as an art form is coming from this Italian thing. But also, the organizational skills that go into construction—see, no one has commented yet about my ability in the book to construct this enormous argument that goes on for centuries; the whole thing is done like the huge arc of an aqueduct. And I just take enormous workman-like pleasure in these things. I have no writer's block—I don't have any of these neurotic things. And whenever I have a friend who has writer's block, I'll say to them, "bricks and boards, bricks and boards"; in other words, I try to convince them that the materials they're using to write—the notes they take and so on—are nothing but bricks and boards, and they shouldn't be so neurotic. It's just like you're assembling these bricks and then you construct it. One of my friends said to me once, "You know what you're like as a writer?" She had had no contact with this kind of Italian, but she got it exactly right. She said, "You're like, 'Hey, Joe, uh, unload the cinder blocks in the truck, you're done. Bring up the meatballs from the front seat.'" And I thought, she saw it, she understood. That's exactly my attitude. My organizational skill is like military talent that goes way back. We know that the administrative structure of the Roman Empire was adopted for the Catholic Church, and that's why the Church has such a magnificent international hierarchy, and why it works so well as an organization. Institutions, in their most efficient form, were invented by Rome. And I have this X-ray ability as an Italian Catholic to see the more efficient way of organizing things. And that is certainly operating in my book. So many chapters, different artists and authors—to marshal all that material, to organize it in this overarching pattern that goes from beginning to end, that's a practical engineering ability that I'm convinced is a genetic trait in Italians.

CB: I'll have to tell my uncles.

CP: Oh, please, yes—people get so passionate about concrete in my family.

CB: Well, it's very funny. My grandfather was a brickmaker, and my uncle is a ceramic engineer, and the other is a builder—we were just having this whole discussion about it. I can't believe there's another Italian family from upstate New York. . . .

CP: Oh! Read the book; the Italians are in construction. I'm sure it's cultural, but I'm also convinced that some cultural things are due to genetic traits. I believe in innate talents, too, and I think Italians have certain gifts that are transmitted over the centuries.

CB: I want you to talk about the chapter on Emily Dickinson. You say that other than to procreate, in order for a woman to create, she has to divide her mind from her body within herself. In one of your interviews you talked about feeling in the past the need to adopt certain behaviors in order to have men take you seriously intellectually so that they would not relate to you purely sexually. And that's again dividing your mind from your body. I wonder if you'd talk about this. Also, you just described your sister as having these talents for music and art. Do you see yourself as a creative person?

CP: Well, yes, I think so. I consider that I'm the first female writer of epic. This is the first female epic. Normally an epic is masculine. I consciously put all the literary characteristics of epic into this book: an epic is an enormously long story which takes in the whole of its own culture and has an epic hero; it has heaven and hell, the gods, and all those things. I even have an epic catalogue. I feel that scholarship should be an art form, and there should be personal things in it. So essentially, I'm the epic hero of this story, wandering in exile, wandering the world, alien, alone, looking for the secrets of sex, looking for the answers to these secrets and going everywhere, and then returning with these things, battle-scarred; and at first the message is rejected, and then accepted. So the whole thing is archetypal in a way. But there's no doubt that scholarship for me is not just something I do for a living. This is the way I learn about myself. Right from the start my intellectual interests were a way to explain myself, to explore myself and my own strangeness and maladjustment to the social norms. I think what the general reader is picking up in the book is exactly that, the self-revelation, and that's more like art than scholarship. But certainly it's supposed to be objective, to be about something, about the history of civilization. So it's not just autobiography. I feel it's very close to the Catholic Church; it's like St. Augustine's *Confessions* or something. You know, sometimes I feel that nineteenth-century belles lettres literature was so very interesting and lively because the critic is the person saying "I." A true critic is someone who is communicating to you the way art is having an impact on their particular sensibility, their particular imagination. They're able to vividly recreate that impact for you. I'm bringing back the idea of scholarship as belles lettres. The general readership wants to read about art, literature, but it's been totally blocked out by stupid pseudo-expert academic prose. It's all jargon-ridden, and it's everywhere. It's the worst. When people are reading my book correctly they're understanding the art, the artistry that went into the construction of it, and also the language. Also, I might point out that English is very new to my family. I mean, my father was born here, but my mother came over at age six, and didn't speak a word in English, and had to learn it. So I had a sense of discovering English as something new, and I'm sort of in love with English. My parents made a decision not to speak Italian at home so I would hear English from the earliest years, and that was a very wise decision. As a consequence, unfortunately, I was shut off from my grandparents' dialect, and I had great trouble understanding anything, because the dialect is so strange. I was shut off, in effect, from the language of my family. I mean, talk about the feeling of isolation! There was this huge family, but I didn't always understand what they were talking about. I was around them, basking in the family, but at the same time I was shut off in my own mental life because I couldn't understand them and couldn't communicate with them. My whole relationship was completely nonverbal. But they were so theatrical—the way they could act out things, I could follow what they were saying often. That's why I'm a good teacher, by the way; my body language is so Italian—I act out everything. For Italians—not Italian-American culture, but Italian culture— thinking is with the whole body. I think with my body, not just with my head.

I think that's what people pick up on in my writing, too; it's very sensory. People call it muscular writing; the rhythms are very physical. I get wonderful letters from the general readers, who say they just feel the thing sweeping them forward. They don't get stuck on all these points which these ideological academics get stuck on, like "It's nothing but I, I, I. . . ." "It's all generalizations. . . ." This is how you read a book?! You don't read a book like that, "Oh I don't agree with that." You allow the book to do what it's doing.

I think that one of the ways that I've been able to flourish as a writer, as a woman, is my attitude towards authority. Here I am, forty-four and I look back over my career and at the careers of others, the ones that seemed most promising in college and graduate school. In terms of production of scholarship it's interesting to see what happened. See, I'm very unhappy with what happens to women. I think that women are very much self-thwarted in many ways. I think that most women are too nice, and I don't think it's the way they were trained, I think that they are naturally empathic. Women naturally feel other people's emotions. And the kind of brutality it takes to destroy reputations, to attack the way I do—women rarely can keep themselves in that frame of attack; most women are forgiving or indulgent on some level. They don't want to make people suffer. But my attitude is that you have to have this powerful ego that's indifferent to other people's sufferings, if the people that you're making suffer are bad. I feel that people who are bad deserve to suffer. What I've noticed over time is that these very talented women I went to graduate school with have just gone, just drifted. And over the last couple of years I began to think about it in terms of their reaction to authority figures. And I conclude that to do really original work you have to be willing to topple the father figure. You have to be willing to attack, to destroy the father figures who came before you. If you don't do that, you can't make a space for you to do something new.

CB: I want to read a quote from the last chapter of the book, and ask you to respond. "Women do not rise to supreme achievement unless they are under powerful internal compulsion. Dickinson was a woman of abnormal will. Her poetry profits from the enormous disparity between that will and the feminine *social* persona to which she fell heir at birth. But her sadism is not anger, the a posteriori response to social injustice. It is *hostility*, an a priori Achillian intolerance for the existence of others, the female version of Romantic solipsism."

CP: Exactly. What I'm saying is that this idea, "Oh, Emily Dickinson, you know, she's in this patriarchy, she's shut in. . . ." I say, no—she *benefited* from having this horribly limiting patriarchy around her, from having this little frail nothing persona, with her physical appearance, her homeliness. All these things helped her because you've got this enormous gap between her inner hostile will and the way she was underestimated in her own time, the way she was limited in a prison by that patriarchy. The patriarchy produced the poetry, for heaven's sake. That's what I feel also. You will never get a book like *Sexual Personae* for a long time, again. Not with this new generation of women who have open to them so many options. I had no options available to me. I was enormously aggressive, and I had no place to put this aggression. I was too small for a lot of sports; I was fast and quick, but. . . . I could have liked weight training, I would have gone into sports. But you see then I would have drained off all the aggressive energy from the writing. And that's the thing today—girls have so many opportunities now. God, they can play lacrosse, soccer—I would have loved to just kick the soccer ball around, that would have been fabulous for me. And as a consequence they're not as angry. They don't have as much to be angry about. I can see clearly that having grown up in the repressive 1950s is what produced the crazy, obsessive intensity that would keep you doing this project for so long under such conditions of rejection. The presence of a patriarch can produce an enormously potent woman. It did in the case of Emily Dickinson, because she had that father running the scene; she never could escape him in that house. And the same thing with me. See, I don't have this idea of the flaw in men. I can allow for male strength and talents at the same time as I am totally rebellious against the authority of it. It formed me. It structures your personality. This is one of the paradoxes in my whole ideology. I'm a total rebel in terms of my attitude towards life; at the same time I can allow for strong men. My feminism calls for strong men, strong women. Which is, in fact, Italian. The Italian system. Enormously powerful personalities is what I come out of. You see, Italians don't whine, are not allowed to whine. Not in your traditional Italian family. You get clear no's. The Italian way of child rearing is very positive. Everyone pays great attention to children and thinks they're beautiful; at the same time they discipline them. What I cannot stand as an Italian is the way you have in America the tantrums in the grocery line. This would never be permitted in Italian terms, because ours is a shame culture. The child's an infant, and already "shhh!" in certain places—the Church, the restaurant, the public thing. You don't bring scandals to the family. You don't *scumpari*. You don't bring dishonor on the family.

CB: You maintain the *bella figura*.

CP: Yes. And I think that all kinds of neurotic behavior is produced by this wishy-washy parental upbringing where the child, by whining, can turn a "no" into a "yes." In my entire life you never turned a "no" into a "yes." That was unheard of. When the law was "no," that's it. And it would make you very angry, and you'll be simmering with anger and rage. But you would never raise your voice to the parent, no matter what you felt; there was the question of respect. So I think that the silence that's imposed on you, with all the simmering . . . your personality's being developed very powerfully. You're beginning a very powerful personality at the same time that you're being squashed and squelched. The consequence is that all this energy, this libido, is channeled, and it gets very intense. The end result is you get someone like me.

CB: Well, I was going to wrap up . . .

CP: I had one more thing, something that I didn't say about my mother's town, Ceccano. You know, my name is Camille, and I have a great aunt whose name is Camilla; it's a name in the family there. A strong sense of my identity comes from the fact that my mother's town goes all the way back to the earliest history of Italy, back to 600 B.C. The area was the Volsci; the Volscians were the fiercest of all of the enemies. When Rome moved outward to subdue all the tribes of Italy, the Volsci gave them the worst trouble. My mother's town is one of those Volscian towns. And Virgil has this Amazon named Camilla, who is the leader of the Volsci. So where did Virgil get this idea of an Italian Amazon, and why is she Volscian? In my opinion, Virgil knew someone from the town or region, and she was just very obnoxious, like me. I think it's genetic. There's an Amazonian thing that ascends there, that goes all the way back to antiquity. The Volscians are this very fierce warrior tribe. And it's no coincidence that I'm posing with a sword in *New York* magazine. You know, my grandfather that came over here, my mother's father, was so fierce, so intense. You could see the way he stands in photographs, so proud. You could just see he had this commanding thing; I could just hear his voice in the Roman period saying, "Yes, level Carthage! Destroy Carthage and sow it with salt!" It's that really assertive Roman voice that goes way, way back. And I just feel that this is the continuity of it.

Big Heart

Rita Ciresi

Fiction (1993)

HE CAME OUT OF THE BACK, his apron bloody. The butcher Mr. Ribalta had the biggest belly I had ever seen. When he leaned into the case to grab a handful of hamburger or lop off a rope of sausage, his stomach grazed the meat. I wanted to poke his fat, to see if my finger would sink into it like pizza dough, or press my ear against him, to hear his insides sloshing and grumbling. But I hung back from the meat counter until he crooked a plump finger and beckoned me forward.

"Oh, Swiss Girl," he called. "Yo-do-lo-do-lo-do-lay."

I always eyed his Swiss cheese. I wanted to take a chunk of it home and slip it between a wedge of sharp pepperoni and a slice of salty prosciutto on a seeded roll. But Mama refused to buy it. "I don't pay good money for holes," she said. She frowned when Ribalta reached into the case to cut me a sliver.

People said Ribalta had a big heart, but Mama was convinced that heart longed for only one thing: to turn her into a big spender. Every Saturday morning before we left the house for the market, she armed herself with a black plastic wallet stamped with a picture of the Leaning Tower of Pisa, a shopping list, and a green pencil stub she had pocketed after playing miniature golf at Palisades Park. Since my sister Lina thought she was too old for such outings, Mama took me—a mere nine-year-old who didn't yet know how to protest—as a witness. I was supposed to make sure Ribalta didn't try any monkey business, like doubling the wax paper or pressing his thumb down on the scale. Although Mama had patronized Ribalta for years, she still didn't trust him. "It's not like he's family," she said.

The market stood on a corner, the front windows lined with white paper, lettered in blue, that announced the weekly specials. Above the shop, behind windows hung with yellowed lace curtains, Ribalta lived with his mother. Mama called her Signora. For years I thought that was her first name.

In cold weather or warm, Mama and I found Signora out front, sweeping the dirt and litter off the sidewalk with a ragged broom that had lost half its dirty bristles. Signora reminded me of La Befana, the skinny old Italian witch who rode her broom over the rooftops on the Feast of the Three Kings, leaving toys for good children and coal and ash for the bad. She wore a black cotton coat over a flowered shift, and scuffed grey mules with no stockings. Her brittle ankles and calves were mapped with thin blue veins. Signora was practically bald, but what little tufts of grey hair she had left on her pink scalp she clamped around wire curlers fastened with big silver clips. She held her broom still just long enough to peer at us through her catglasses. When she was satisfied she had recognized us, she resumed sweeping.

Ribalta's shop officially opened at nine, but we always walked in a little after 8:30. Brass bells clattered as the door swung behind us. Mama headed down the first narrow aisle, stopping once or twice to inspect some canned goods that sat on the high wooden shelves. "Cheaper at the A&P," she announced loudly.

At the back of the store stood the gleaming white meat case, lit with fluorescent tubes that made the unit hum and vibrate. Behind the case was a swinging door, and behind that, the mysterious room where Ribalta butchered his meat while Radio Italia played. Mama went up to the counter and hit the silver bell on top with the flat of her hand. The radio went dead. We heard water running. Then Ribalta came out of the back, his breath heavy as he wiped his hands on a clean white cloth. He pushed his gold wire-rimmed glasses up on his nose. He was the only shopkeeper in our neighborhood who ever smiled at Mama.

Mama nodded back, her eyes on the case. Ribalta stocked it so the contents ranged from the reddest and rawest meat to the cleanest, tidiest rolls of processed food. First came the organs—bloody bulbs of liver, tough-looking necks, and limp hearts—packaged in clear plastic containers. Then came ground beef pressed in an aluminum tray, rump roast and flank steaks, coils of sausage, and a quilt of overlapping bacon strips. Cuts of pale pork and veal were followed by moist chicken breasts, and piles of stippled yellow legs and scrawny wings. In a separate section of the case, Ribalta kept logs of ham, coppacole, Genoa salami, and blocks of cheese.

Mama checked each item on her list against Ribalta's prices. Then she placed the list on top of her wallet and firmly crossed off some items with the pencil stub. "Here's what's left," she said. It always took Ribalta a long time to fill the order. Mama made him display each cut of meat, back and front, before she allowed him to put it on the scale. And when she said she wanted half a pound of something, she meant eight ounces, no more and no less. Ribalta knew better than to ask Mama if *a little bit over* was okay. He patiently lifted chop after chop onto the scale, while Mama watched the gauge waggle back and forth until it settled as close to the weight she had asked for as it would ever get.

After Ribalta had wrapped the meats in stiff white paper, tied each bundle with red and white string, and marked the price with a black wax pencil, he crossed his arms and rested them on his big belly. He knew exactly what Mama was going to ask for next.

"Any scraps today?" she said.

"For the dog, eh?" Ribalta held up one finger, meaning Mama should wait. He disappeared into the back.

I never understood why Mama kept up this charade. We didn't have a dog and never would. "Good for nothing except to bite and bark," Mama said, whenever I pleaded for one.

"If you hate dogs so much, why do you tell Ribalta we have one?" I asked.

"I tell him no such thing."

"But you let him think we do."

"I can't help the ideas he gets in his head," Mama said.

She waited impatiently for Ribalta to return with the scraps. He came back balancing a pile of metal pans. He displayed the contents to Mama and the haggling began.

"Veal bones," he said. "With plenty of meat. Chicken necks, close to ten of them."

Mama rejected the necks and offered fifteen cents for a bag of bones.

"Make it a quarter," Ribalta said.

"For those sticks?"

"These are beautiful bones. Juicy. Tender. Flavorful."

"Twenty cents," Mama firmly said.

Ribalta never said *done, fine,* or *okay.* He simply moved on to his next offering. "Giblets. Fresh this morning. And these hearts, I saved them just for you."

They went back and forth like that, until Ribalta ran out of scraps and Mama was satisfied she had bled him for whatever she could get. Ribalta stacked the white packages in a box. Then he winked at Mama and peered over the case at me.

"Oh, Swiss Girl," he said. "Yo-do-lo-do-lo-do-lay!"

He turned, wiped off a cleaver, and reached into the case to whack off a hunk of the cheese. He handed it to Mama. She frowned when she gave me the cheese. "Say thank you," she told me, before I could even open my mouth. To Ribalta she said, "You're too generous."

"Why not?" he replied as he wiped the cleaver. "Life is short." Then he came around the side of the case, carrying Mama's box. We followed him up the aisle. The strings of his apron stretched tightly across his broad backside. They were tied in a simple knot because there wasn't enough give for a bow.

Up in front, behind the squat glass counter, Signora now sat on a wooden stool. Ribalta lowered the box onto the counter and left Signora to figure the bill with a pencil and paper. Signora lifted out the bundles one at a time, and wrote down each price, totalling as she went along. Mama kept her eyes on that rising sum. Signora counted out aloud: *"Due piu cinque? Otto. Mi scusi, sette. Otto piu tre? Dodici. Mi scusi, undici."* Nothing would have made Mama happier than nailing Signora in a mathematical error. But Signora always caught her mistakes and confidently bellowed the sum the way a railroad conductor announced the next station. *"Sei dollari e sesanta due centi, per favore!"*

Mama opened her wallet and counted out the bills. Signora took them, recounted them, then reached below the counter for a rusty Maxwell House coffee can full of coins. With her gnarled fingers, she dug through the coins to make Mama change.

MAMA LEFT THE MARKET with a satisfied look on her face. But after a block or two, when the box grew heavy and she switched the weight from one hand to the other, she bit her lip and wrinkled her brow, convinced that Ribalta had gotten fat off her business and hers alone. "*Grassone!*" she said. "Thinks I don't notice that diamond ring."

On his right pinky, Ribalta wore a thin gold band studded with a diamond. Mama often remarked on it. "Who else do you know owns such a swanky thing?" she asked me. I shrugged. No other man I knew wore jewelry—not even a wedding ring—except the archbishop, who came to our church once a year to give confirmation. He wore a huge gold ring on his right hand that was supposed to hold a sliver of Christ's cross. On our way out of church, we all knelt down and pressed our lips against the cold, pale blue jewel. The archbishop wiped his ring with a little red cloth after each person had kissed it, the same way Ribalta wiped his cleaver before and after he cut me a piece of cheese.

Ribalta didn't go to church. Sundays, my mother and my aunts gathered together on the sidewalk after Mass and stared after Signora, who hobbled home alone. Then they turned back into a circle and began their attack against the butcher.

"What does the man eat, *pasta e fagioli* six times a day?"

"How can he breathe with a belly like that?"

"How does he move his bowels?"

"The size!"

"The smell!"

"They say he sings in a band."

"Fat as an opera singer."

"If he sings so well, why isn't he in the choir?"

"Have you ever seen him at Mass?"

"He should be there."

"He's a bachelor."

"That's his problem."

"He'll have a heart attack."

"He's unhealthy."

They blamed Signora. They said she spoiled him, babied him, cooked him whatever he wanted. They said that after she died, he would lose a little weight. Find himself a girl. Get married and have children. Why not? He was still young enough. He had a kind face. Most important, he owned a family business. In our neighborhood, that was the ultimate sign of having done well for yourself. The only thing better was getting in with the post office or phone company.

EVERY AFTERNOON when I fetched the newspaper off the front porch, Mama paused a few moments from her housework to scan the obituary page. One day she snapped the newspaper open and pointed to a picture with triumph.

"Ribalta's mother," she said.

I looked for the helmet of hairclips and wire curlers, the scraggly neck criss-crossed with lines, the silver catglasses and pinched cheeks. But the hair was full as a wig and the face smooth, as if air had been pumped into it.

"That's not her," I said.

"Stupid," said Mama. "It's an old photograph."

"The name's wrong, too."

"What? Gelsomina Ribalta, that's right."

"But you called her *Signora*."

Mama laughed. She spent the rest of the afternoon on the phone, repeating the story to my aunts. "Imagine, I had to tell the *bimba* it meant *Mrs.* How much more American can these kids get? I wonder who'll sit behind the counter now. He'll have to find some girl, and quick, too. Yes, tonight, at the Torino Funeral Home. Burial on Tuesday, the paper said."

For three days after the funeral, the shop was closed. A black ribbon hung from the door and upstairs, all the shades were drawn. The weekly specials remained the same. I made a sign of the cross as I passed on my way to school. I was frightened that Signora's spirit still lingered in the world, that I'd hear the swish of her broom on the sidewalk and the clatter of her bony fingers, sorting through the Maxwell House coffee can to make change.

On Saturday morning I stuck close to Mama on the walk to the store. When we arrived, the front door was locked. Mama pulled at the handle to test it again. Then she peered through the door. The glass grew foggy with her breath. A boy stood in the front aisle, stacking loaves of bread on the shelf. He turned. Mama rapped at the glass. The boy held up his wrist, pointed to his watch, and then went back to stacking the bread. Mama was astounded.

"The sign says open at nine," I pointed out.

"That sign has hung there for years. Signora always opened." Mama bit her lip, then rapped at the glass even harder.

"*Aspettino*," the boy called out.

Mama turned away. "Figures," she said. "A real *paesano*. Speaks no English. Lazy."

I could tell she wanted to knock even harder at the door, pull at the handle, and yell at him. But Mama held herself back out of respect for Ribalta. We waited two or three minutes in the cold before the boy came to the door. He was older than he seemed at first, about twenty, and short and erect, with muscled arms and a firm chest that swelled beneath the bib of his clean white apron. He had close-trimmed black hair and dark, liquidy eyes with long black lashes, high cheekbones, and a moist, pouty lower lip. A gold medal hung on a chain around his short, solid neck. I fell in love with him instantly.

"It's about time!" Mama huffed when he let us in.

He looked at us as if he didn't understand. Mama strode past him without even a nod. "Off the boat," she muttered, as I followed her down the first aisle. I turned back to look at him. Maybe he didn't understand English, but I was sure he caught the drift of Mama's loud *Cheaper at the A&P*. He stood with one hand on the counter and watched as Mama hit the bell on the meat case. Ribalta came out slowly, wiping his plump, squat hands. Radio Italia continued to play.

Two new things in one morning were more than Mama could handle. "You forgot to turn off your radio," she said.

"My cousin likes the music," Ribalta answered.

Mama looked back down the aisle at the boy. "That one there is your cousin? Funny, I don't remember him at the funeral."

Ribalta hung his head to show his sorrow. Then Mama got a hold of herself and rolled out her standard sympathy speech. "Torino did a wonderful job with your mother," she said. "She looked so peaceful. And Father said a beautiful Mass, don't you think? The flowers were lovely. I've never seen so many in my life. Sent by relatives?"

"I ordered most."

I could tell Mama was racking up the price of that in her head, adding it to the cost of the fancy coffin Signora had been buried in, and the white headstone that had an angel with outstretched wings. "A real tribute to your mother," she said. "I pray my children do the same for me."

"Not too soon, I hope."

"You never know, do you? God has his plan." She scanned the meat case. If she was hoping Ribalta would be running some specials to lure his customers back into the store, she was disappointed. She crossed about half the items off her list. "Start with the hamburger," she said. "That's fresh, I hope."

"I always sell fresh."

"Three-quarters of a pound, then."

I stood with my back to the front of the store. I felt the cousin's eyes on us. I was embarrassed by my childish red earmuffs and red wool mittens, by Mama's flat black boots and shabby wool coat. The haggling was long and intense that morning. I stood there awkwardly. I blushed when Ribalta called me the Swiss Girl and yodeled at me. I quickly ate the piece of cheese as we followed Ribalta to the front of the store. Mama's undisguised astonishment at what she found on the counter mortified me. Ribalta's cousin stood behind a cash register, a green metal box with smart red buttons.

"What's this fancy machine doing here?" Mama said.

"We're joining the modern age," Ribalta said.

Mama looked dubious. "Pencil and paper was good enough for Signora," she said. He watched the cousin carefully as he sorted through the box and rang up the paltry sums scribbled on the packages. When the insubstantial total popped up on little silver tabs in the window of the cash register, I wanted to die of shame.

Mama regarded the numbers suspiciously. "Is that it?" she said to the boy.

He pointed to the total. I turned my back as Mama drew the bills out of her Leaning Tower of Pisa wallet. The impatient way she held out her hand for the change annoyed me.

"Slow as molasses," Mama said after we left the store. "And sloppy, too. Packed the bones on top of the meat."

Just as Gelsomina Ribalta became known simply as *The Mrs.*, the boy became known as *The Cousin*. "So what do you think of Cugino?" my aunts polled one another, with little smiles on their faces. Too many muscles, they decided. Too long nails. He took forever to figure out the total and too long to pack the box back up. He was too handsome for a man. Good looks spelled trouble, you better believe it!

"Heartbreaker," my Aunt Fiorella pronounced him, nudging me. "Look out!" Then all my aunts cackled. I turned red, both from the shame of knowing that Cugino would never be interested in a silly girl like me, and from fear that Mama and my aunts would guess my secret. I had never been in love before, and I was sure it was written all over my face. But if Mama caught on to it, she said nothing. She was distracted by other things at the market. She made it her business to find out more about Cugino. The more Ribalta refused to be pinned down, the harder she hammered him.

"So where is this cousin of yours from?" she asked.

"Calabria."

"I thought your family was *Napoletano*."

"My mother's side, God rest them, yes."

"Oh, so this Cugino is from your father's side? But his last name isn't Ribalta? He's your father's sister's son, then?"

"Second cousin, actually."

Mama hesitated, then probed again. "I hear you sing in a band," she said.

"That's right."

"Your Cugino, he's in show business too?"

"He plays horn, yes."

"What sort of music—Sinatra, that kind of stuff?"

"We'll be giving a concert downtown—"

"Downtown!" Mama said, as if travelling five miles to the center of New Haven took Ribalta to a distant (and depraved) country. "You go downtown?"

"Just to Wooster Square. For *Carnevale*. Come hear us play."

Mama was taken aback. No one ever invited her anywhere. She looked down at her list, and for a moment I thought she truly was considering it. I imagined us standing in the square, bundled in our winter coats. Up on stage, Ribalta snapped his chubby fingers and crooned into the microphone. Then Cugino stood up from his folding chair, lifted his gleaming trumpet to his lips, and, staring me soulfully in the eyes, played a lilting solo that sent the audience into a frenzy of applause. People hooted and roared, knowing that the next day they would have to don black, go to church, and fast for Ash Wednesday. . . .

"I don't go to *la festa*," Mama said. "Too many people. The whole world is there." She paused. "Your Cugino's parents, they'll be there?"

"They're dead."

"Orphaned so young. How old is he anyway?"

"Nineteen."

"He'll be married soon," said Mama. "He has a girlfriend, I guess?"

"Not at the moment."

"You should fix him up. There are plenty of nice girls in the parish."

"We don't go to church."

"You should."

"What for?"

"To find God."

"God is in our hearts," Ribalta said.

"He's at Sunday Mass," said Mama. "And you should be there, too, with your cousin. Who knows? You both might meet a nice girl."

"We already have our favorite," Ribalta said, and smiled at me. "She's called the Swiss girl. Yo-do-lo-do-lo-do-lay!"

I prayed I would be Cugino's favorite. My mind was always on him. In the middle of a spelling bee at school, or during the Eucharistic prayer at church, I would feel warmth envelop me, and suddenly Cugino would be by my side, his thick fingers clasping my upper arms. We were rolling over and over again in a bed of grass, lying together on the beach as the waves lapped in on the sand. We kissed and embraced. . . .

Then I misspelled sacrifice and Sister Thomas made me sit down. I forgot to say amen after Father said *Body of Christ*, and he had to repeat it. I didn't care. I loved Cugino so much I hated everybody else: Sister and Father and all nuns and priests, my aunts, my mother and her wallet, even Ribalta. I was sure my heart beat louder and stronger than any of theirs. Only love was real, and mine was all for Cugino.

I desperately wanted to impress him. On the way to the store I tried to convince Mama to spend more money.

"Let's get some Swiss cheese today," I said.

"You'll get your piece for free."

"All my friends bring baloney sandwiches to school."

"Peanut butter isn't good enough for you anymore?"

"It sticks to my mouth," I said.

"So put on some jelly."

"We're almost out of jelly, I noticed this morning. We'd better get some at Ribalta's."

"It's cheaper at the—"

"Stop talking about the A&P!" I said. "Especially in the store."

"Who can hear me?" Mama asked. "Ribalta's blasting the radio in the back and Cugino *non capisce*."

"He understands from the way you say it."

Mama sniffed. "I've got nothing to hide from his type."

"Why don't you put your wallet in a purse?"

"Because I've got two hands."

"Don't you want a new wallet for your birthday?"

"This one works just fine."

"Aren't you tired of the Leaning Tower of Pisa?"

"When it falls over, you can buy me a new one."

I tried to wean Mama from haggling over the scraps. But the bargaining grew even more intense as the weeks went by. Mama was convinced Ribalta was offering her less of a choice. One minute she wondered if he was holding back on her; the next she was worried some other housewife was beating her to the best of the pickings. She insisted on leaving even earlier for the store to make sure Cugino didn't let anyone in before us. She stood outside the shop door, talking about him loudly as he stacked the bread. "It's that cousin," she said. "He probably steals the scraps and gives them to his friends."

"Ssh," I said. "He does not."

"He's taking Ribalta for a ride, believe you me."

"He is not."

"One of these days he's going to clean out that fancy cash register and be long gone."

"He won't leave."

Mama snorted. "That would break somebody's heart."

"It would *not*."

She looked at me. Then she laughed. "Oh, so you're wild about him, too?"

My face felt warm. "Am *not*," I said. I looked down at the dirty sidewalk. The word *too* resounded disagreeably in my ears. "Who else likes him?"

Mama snorted. "Are you thick in the head?" She gestured with a limp wrist toward the store. "*Tutti frutti* in there," she said.

I bit my lip. *Tutti frutti* was a phrase my father used to describe that strange, grinning man in the sparkling cape who played the white grand piano on Sunday night TV. I couldn't believe that Ribalta—and Cugino—was of the same ilk as Liberace. But when Cugino came to the door and Mama pushed past him, I noticed he wore something gold and sparkling on his finger—Ribalta's ring.

I kept my eyes on Mama as she marched down the first aisle, her fingers tightly clasped around her wallet. I hated her. She had killed my dream of being with Cugino as neatly and cleanly as Ribalta chopped the head off a chicken. I'd get her back. My heart pounding, I waited while she made her selections. When she was through, Ribalta folded his arms over his belly.

"Any scraps today?" Mama asked.

"For the dog, eh?" Ribalta answered.

My blood raced. "We don't have a dog," I announced.

Mama gave me a murderous look. Ribalta opened his mouth and nothing came out. He swallowed. In a sad voice that showed his disappointment in me, he said, "I know that," before he disappeared through the swinging door.

The moment he was gone, Mama smacked me soundly on the back of the head with her wallet. "That'll teach you," she said. "I'll never take you here again."

I turned and walked halfway down the soup aisle. The black letters on the Campbell's cans blurred. I was crying. Mama had put me to shame. I heard Ribalta come back and I walked down the rest of the aisle. Cugino, fortunately, was nowhere in sight. I went out the front door and around to the side of the store. The yard behind the market was blocked off with a high wooden fence. I peered over the gate.

Through the back window of the shop, I could see into the room where Ribalta did the butchering. It was illuminated with long fluorescent tubes that gave off a blueish hue. A huge refrigerator—five doors long—lined one whole wall. Above the triple sink hung knives as long as swords, cleavers that looked like they would fell a tree, and an assortment of scissors to trim and snip the meat after it had been sliced and gutted. From metal hooks on the ceiling, slabs of meat hung like punching bags waiting for someone to pummel them. On a wire stretched across the room, plucked chickens dangled, long, skinny, and naked as Mama's bras hanging on the clothesline. Radio Italia was playing opera.

Cugino moved around the room, then came out the back door carrying a bucket. He held it above his head as he came down the stairs. Then, from the back of the yard, trotted three lambs, their coats gray and covered with bits of grass. Their hooves sounded sharp on the frozen ground. They nuzzled up against Cugino's white apron, licking him and looking up at him with glassy, expectant eyes. Cugino waited until he had gotten to the center of the yard before he dumped the bucket. There, on the ground, lay beet stalks, shredded turnips, carrot and potato peels—and what little of Mama's coveted scraps that Cugino hadn't seen fit to put into a soup or stew. The lambs crowded in to feast on the mess.

Cugino looked up and saw me. He said something in Italian, broke it off, then beckoned. He came over and unlocked the gate to let me in. Cugino gestured that I should pet one of the lambs. I stroked the matted fur of the smallest, which had a black face and knobby knees.

Cugino gestured toward the lambs, then smacked his lips and rubbed his stomach. I screwed up my face to show I didn't understand him.

"*Per la Pasqua*," he said.

"Yes," I said. "Easter pets."

He smacked his lips and rubbed his stomach again, smiling. He kept grinning and gesturing, pointing first to the lambs, then to his belly. I noticed his teeth were crooked and his stomach was a little bit flabby. He looked like an actor in a silent movie trying to get a laugh. I wondered how I ever could have loved such an idiot.

"*Capisci, capisci?*" he asked. When I kept on staring at him, obviously not understanding what he was driving at, he grabbed one lamb by the fur on top of its head, held out one finger, brought it up to lamb's neck, and dragged it across, in the gesture of an executioner.

I took my hand away from the lamb I was petting. I couldn't decide who was more evil, Ribalta for butchering the lambs, or Cugino for telling me he was going to do it. Tears welled up in my eyes. Cugino looked confused. Then he reached out and took my hand. After all those weeks of dreaming he would touch me, his grasp felt tight and cold. I was about to pull away when Mama appeared at the gate, against the broad white backdrop of Ribalta's figure.

Mama tried to open the gate, then rattled it. She began to sputter incoherently. *What was this? Crazy nut! Drop her hand! Disgraceful! My daughter! He'd go to hell for this! Sick turkey!*

Ribalta's fat seemed to quiver as he gestured at Mama. "Calm down," he said, reaching over her to fumble with the lock. "Please be calm, Signora."

Mama made a fist and shouted something evil-sounding in Italian. Cugino dropped both the bucket and my hand and raised his fists at Mama. The lambs scattered. Mama gazed at the beets and turnips and the last of her scraps on the grass.

That was the final straw. When Ribalta finally popped open the gate, she marched in and dragged me out of the yard. "Family business!" she said to Ribalta as she pulled me down the sidewalk. "More like *funny* business you've got going on here. And you'll pay for it, just you wait and see."

ON EASTER, I refused to come down to dinner. I lay on my bed, trying to recapture the feeling of being in love. I tried to melt into a dreamy state, to smell the meadow and hear the waves. But it was useless. I couldn't get it back, no matter how hard I tried. I had lost Cugino, the same as Ribalta.

For Cugino was gone. They said Ribalta stuffed his pockets full of money and sent him packing. The butcher had his business to think of. Mama talked loud and word spread fast that something just a little bit fishy was going on over at that meat market, and never you mind what, although you could take a guess.

Knowing she wouldn't meet up with Cugino at the market ever again, Mama returned to Ribalta's on Holy Saturday and acted as if nothing had happened. She came back with a boxful of packages and reported, with satisfaction, that a very nice older woman—perhaps a relative of Signora's—sat behind the counter. She was quite pleasant and spoke good English, too.

As I lay on my bed, trying to block out the squeak of knives scraping against the plates, I heard Mama telling my aunts, for the umpteenth time, how she had bargained Ribalta rock-bottom low on the lamb. It was such a good deal she even bought some mint jelly. Why not? Life was short. "Try it," she urged them. "I got it on special. Delicious."

Permanent Waves

Kenny Marotta

Fiction (1996)

"WHEN WE MOVE TO MEDFORD," said Terry, "can Bobby drive me to work?"

Carmine looked at the girl. His wife always referred to Bobby DiFazio as the *compare*'s son; the children more frankly called him Terry's boyfriend. Carmine didn't speak of him at all.

"You think because you give permanent waves, you can do what you want?" he asked his daughter. For six months she had been doing shampoo and sets in a beauty shop off Hanover Street. Hanging down straight from its part, when it got to her ears her hair suddenly coiled itself into two motionless scrolls, like the wooden case of a mantel clock.

"Well," Terry answered back, "if *you're* not going to buy a car. I'm sure every other family in Medford has one."

"You'll pick up the bus at the corner and change at Sullivan Square," said Carmine. It was the route he had taken to his own job. Carmine had last touched a gas pedal in 1925, propelling his friend's father's car backwards into a brick wall.

"Just be thankful," he added, "I let you work in the first place."

But Terry wasn't the only one he had to deal with. The younger children wanted to know if they'd be getting bicycles, like their cousins who had moved. His wife Sara said she was thinking of getting a job in the fall, when Louis started first grade. After all, she said, once they were in Medford, Carmine wouldn't be walking home for lunch.

"What, are you crazy?" Carmine demanded.

If it was madness, it was epidemic. Since the war, Carmine's neighbors had thought of nothing but moving. They competed in their eagerness to leave the North End, giving up hot lunches cooked by their wives, sidewalks where the faces were familiar, clubs where a game of *scopa* could be had at any hour. He pictured his restless friends as G.I.s in a newsreel spilling out of the sides of ships, surge after surge, wading thigh-high through the surf. Few of them would have been content to stop even at Medford. They preferred to pitch their tents in land that had been marsh or pasture just yesterday.

Carmine's move was no part of that assault. He wouldn't have done it at all if it hadn't been for his brother Pete.

At their father's death, Pete had been left the two-family house in Medford, on the condition of taking care of their mother. Now, after ten years during which he had scarcely offered his mother a cup of coffee, Pete had been caught up in the wider frenzy. He was moving to one of the new suburbs—and he wasn't taking

Teresa. Nor was abandonment enough for him. He was keeping the house, renting out the upstairs. He had chosen as his tenant the grandson of Hilda, his late father's mistress.

"What's the surprise?" Carmine's wife asked him. "You said your father started taking Pete to her house when he was a baby. He's always treated Hilda like some sort of godmother. Just thank God he never invited her out to Medford."

"And how long will it be now," said Carmine, "with her grandson living there, wiping his feet on my mother's porch?"

Sara didn't argue, ready to acquiesce in anything that got her out of the North End. Otherwise, she would no doubt have mentioned the point Carmine's sisters had made when he tried to persuade them of Pete's criminality: that Teresa herself had not uttered a word of complaint.

As if Teresa had ever been known to complain, in all her painful life! Gaetano had left her alone for years to raise her family in Italy. When he brought her over, it was just to humiliate her, spurning her nightly for his American mistress. But Teresa had always held her tongue; not once had Hilda's name so much as passed her lips.

If Carmine alone had guessed the truth of Teresa's feelings, perhaps it was because he was the oldest. Only he had noticed the midnight sobs during the first months in America, and the morning redness of Teresa's eyes. With the years, she had learned to control even these symptoms. When Gaetano's last illness exiled him from all beds but his own, the careful obliviousness of her speech had given way to songs of praise for her husband and provider—a music painful for Carmine to hear, when he thought what it must cost her. More painful still was when, after the old man's death, these eulogies took for their subject Pete, the chosen of his father.

Carmine knew better than to contradict his mother. But he felt no such restraint towards Pete. The moment he had learned what his brother was planning, Carmine had called him up.

"Listen, Carmine," was all Pete would say, "Gerhart's a nice kid, a family man. Besides, I got a deposit."

So Carmine's decision to take the apartment himself had cost him fifty dollars off the top.

His friends at the club ribbed him about the move, predicting he'd be buying a boat and a barbecue next. Only to Rocco, with whom he had made many a novena, did Carmine tell the truth.

"I'm going to my mother," he simply said to the old man.

Rocco raised a hand in blessing, and took on his stubbly cheek Carmine's kiss of farewell.

Teresa received the news more stoically.

"Sure, Pete tell me you're coming," Teresa acknowledged with a shrug, the night Carmine went to Medford to tell her. Carmine had addressed her in Italian, but she replied in the English she had favored since her husband's death. Her broken expressions suited oddly with the somber dignity of her sagging face. You might have thought it was age that had hollowed her eyes and robbed her skin of its tautness, but she had looked this way as long as Carmine could remember. She was sitting beside her parlor window, where she kept watch on doings in the street.

"But that German boy," she asked, "where he gonna live?"

Her voice sounded only with idle curiosity. Even had Carmine seen her eyes, he knew from long experience they would have been as impenetrable as the black window to which she addressed herself.

"Now, Ma," he gently said, "you wouldn't like to live with strangers, would you?"

"Your brother tell me my husband know this boy," Teresa persisted. If features of such basset-like melancholy could be said to simper, Teresa simpered then.

"Sure, and Pa knew Patsy Morelli too, but do you want somebody making book upstairs?"

The moment Carmine spoke, he could have bitten his tongue. The topic of Gaetano's acquaintances was a dangerous one, so easily did it suggest that unmentionable woman. Teresa's simper was replaced by a frown, and Carmine turned away, to look at the wallpaper around him. The elaborate foliage, rolling endlessly in upon itself, had once been purple. Now it was brown as old bloodstains, on a setting of ivory-turned-yellow.

"You know what, Ma?" he said after a moment. "As soon as I move in, I'm putting up some new wallpaper for you. This stuff is falling off the walls anyway. It's been too long since anybody lifted a finger to fix this place up."

"Ah," replied Teresa, with her first smile of the day, "you like to mess your father's house. My son Pete, he say to me, 'Ma, I promise you, I never change a thing.'"

"WHY CAN'T YOU ALLOW HER HER MEMORIES?" Carmine asked his wife one evening after the move. "What else does she have to hold on to?"

"Holding on is right!" said Sara. In the last two weeks, Teresa had revealed the strength of her tenacity. She refused to permit the smallest improvement to the house. Every night, Sara met him at the door with a new complaint.

"And memories of what, tell me?" Sara went on. "It was Roberta put up those drapes." She gestured towards the latest point of contention with her mother-in-law.

It was certainly a puzzle. Even if she had had reason to feel nostalgic for her life with her husband, Teresa hadn't lived in the upstairs apartment since his death. Pete and Roberta had needed the space themselves, and evicted the downstairs tenant to make room for Teresa. Half the changes the old lady rejected were to Pete's innovations—a jerry-rigged vent for the stove, a china shelf that tottered on the wall—or to decay resulting from his poor stewardship.

Carmine knew it, too. His memories of the apartment, though less cherished than Teresa's, went back as long as hers. The Medford house was the first he'd seen in America, the one his wealthy father had brought them to. For Carmine, it had remained indelibly associated with the lingering effects of seasickness, the sounds of muffled weeping, and the silence of all the morning bowls of coffee and bread that Gaetano had not returned home to eat. It seemed to Carmine that he had not slept well until his own marriage when, reversing the usual process, he had moved into the Italian section downtown. He had wanted to be near his work and his wife's family; though born in America, Sara spoke Italian, too. He felt easier among the old men at the club, arguing over precedence and the rules of parliamentary order, than he'd ever felt among the Medford boys, who talked only of conquests and baseball.

"Ah, she's old, she forgets," said Carmine. But Teresa had no difficulty remembering the exact location of the pieces of furniture, once her own, that Pete had left behind in the upstairs apartment. The day of the move, Sara had transferred the heavy-looming bedstead to another wall, and taken a leaf out of the dining room table; they still hadn't heard the end of it. And though Pete's wife Roberta had served Teresa no more than four meals in ten years, the old lady apparently recalled every one. By their standard she criticized the daily lunches Carmine required Sara to provide her.

"Well," said Carmine to his wife, all other arguments failing, "why don't you go do some laundry?"

This was more of a concession than it sounded. Laundry had become Sara's chief solace. Entered by backless, steep stairs, the cellar was the only place to which Teresa wouldn't follow her. Carmine himself sometimes lent a hand, since the cellar was the coolest spot on a July evening. He wouldn't sit on the porch, whose loose floorboards and rickety railings he was not permitted to fix. He couldn't garden: neither Gaetano nor Pete had ever broken the soil of the backyard.

Besides, when he stayed to stifle in the parlor, he had to endure his daughter Terry's pouting. She claimed her life had been ruined by his ban on riding the bus alone at night, or getting lifts in cars. "I'm just going to the movies with Gloria!" she'd insist, or perhaps it was, "But I *always* spend Wednesday night at Susie's!"—as if she would have plastered her face with that much rouge for any Susie or Gloria.

If Carmine didn't feel up to handling damp linens—and sometimes, spread-eagling one of his shirts on the line, he felt as though he were laying out a corpse—he would step downstairs to visit his mother.

Teresa generally greeted him with the other side of the stories he'd heard from Sara. Usually he took the lash along with his wife, bearing as well Teresa's invidious comparisons to his brother Pete, who knew his father's heart so much better.

"And that's not all he knew," Carmine often thought of saying. But he always stopped himself.

After his latest talk with Sara, however, Teresa almost welcomed him into her parlor. The day's trials—including not only the curtains but several unprecedented shortcomings in her lunch—demanded an unburdening so urgent that Teresa seemed to forget he was connected to Sara. She frankly asked for his pity and indignation. His pleasure in this rare appeal may have been disloyal, but Carmine was thankful all the same. His gratitude, as it happened, led him a little too far.

"Ah, that is a shame," he commiserated about the salt in the soup. "I see, I understand. But you must remember my wife doesn't come from the *paese*: what can you expect of her?"

The admonition was playful, the overflow of a moment of happiness. How long had it been since he could address his mother in such conspiratorial terms?

In his foolish bliss, he did not observe Teresa's expression. Her nostrils were elevated, detecting the aroma of a criticism of her youngest son. Pete wasn't from the *paese* either. He had been born precisely nine months after the family's arrival in Medford—which was to say, about eight months after Carmine had guessed the truth about the blonde woman who worked in his father's front office.

"Besides," continued Carmine with a smile, presuming further on the atmosphere of good feeling, "how often did Roberta give you lunch at all?"

Teresa drew her shoulders up and her lips together. "Maybe," she said, "Roberta husband not so hot to poison the Mamma."

At this, Carmine awoke—though only to the throbbing of his own wound. "Ma! What a thing to say! After all," he added with a pout not unlike one of Terry's, "if you don't like what she fixes, you don't have to eat it."

"No? *Grazie*," replied Teresa with a nod. "Then thank God, I say bye-bye to those stairs."

He saw his error at once. Since the move, Sara had been talking of work again. "What else will I do when all the kids are in school?" she had said. "And how else will we put clothes on their backs, since your mother won't let me cut out my patterns on that dinner table?" The only answer Carmine had been able to offer her was the need to fix Teresa's lunch.

"Please, Ma," he said, backpedaling, "just tell Sara. She'll make whatever you want."

"Roberta, I don't have to tell," remarked Teresa—presumably revealing a fondness for take-out chop suey, the dish on which Roberta was reputed exclusively to feed her family.

That night Carmine could not sleep, his mother's words still rankling. But the next day he instructed Sara to cook whatever Teresa wished for lunch. He passed the morning in reminiscence of his own bygone hot lunches. At noon, he found the sandwich Sara had packed for him, took one bite, and threw it away.

When he got home to Medford, he might have assuaged his hunger with the dish Sara had fixed for his mother. The peppers and eggs sat congealed on the kitchen table, where they had been left in evidence. Teresa had refused to eat them—or, she had announced, any future lunch her daughter-in-law might provide.

"Yech, I wouldn't eat that either," remarked Terry, jabbing a finger through the bars of the parakeet's cage.

"Mary Cave called me," Sara said to Carmine. "I can start at Filene's the week after Labor Day."

HER HUSBAND'S ARGUMENTS meant nothing to her. If his mother didn't like it, Sara said, perhaps she could begin her crusade by talking her own daughters Lena and Mary into quitting their jobs. And would he rather, Sara asked, that she spend her time looking for other places to live? Before agreeing to the move, she had extorted this promise: if it didn't work out, they would move again, this time to a house of their own. She had saved a down payment doing war work.

So Carmine had no choice but to give in—though he knew what his mother must be thinking by the remarks she had made when Sara was sewing parachutes. This was his only route to her thoughts, in fact: once Teresa had stopped eating Sara's lunches, she also stopped talking to her son. She let him in when he knocked at her door, but that was all. He filled the silence alone, while she stared out her window; or he would occupy himself, when she stepped out of the room, in tracing the patterns of the bloodstains on the walls—and realize, after twenty minutes had passed, that she had gone to bed.

"She needs something to do," old Rocco advised him. "You should remember, those women in the *paese*, they weren't happy unless they were busy for the little ones."

Then Sara learned she'd have to work until four; but the kids were through with school by three-thirty.

"I guess you'll have to wait for something else," Carmine casually remarked.

Sara looked straight at him, not fooled. "I'm hiring Mrs. Feminella down the street."

"And what are you going to save," Carmine asked, "if you're paying half of it for babysitting?"

"What do you expect me to do?" said Sara sarcastically. "Ask your mother?"

He might have answered back, but the memory of Rocco's words brought him a better answer. He said nothing at all, leaving Sara to stew, and went to see his mother.

He had not yet told her of Sara's plan to work, but now he did so, with a full accounting of his efforts to dissuade his wife. He half expected one of the old rebukes—perhaps a query as to what man or men would be driving Sara home from her outings. But Teresa sat still, only raising a hand occasionally to touch her newly bare neck. Wordless in his company, Teresa had somehow let it be known that she wanted Terry to give her a summer cut. Carmine had told the girl she'd have to do it. Instead of the heavy mass gathered at the back, Teresa's hair was now a gray whirlpool of swirls and crests.

"So if you could be home in the afternoons," said Carmine, coming to the point, "it would be a help to her."

He put on a face of humble pleading, though it was little enough to ask. Teresa rarely left the house.

She began to bob her head slowly, as if she were considering it. After all, it was as Rocco had said: what more could a mother and grandmother wish for?

"It's just so the kids could know you're here if they need anything," Carmine added, lest the job seem too onerous. "Only a few minutes—"

Teresa cut him short. "And what," she said, "if my son need me?"

Although Teresa had three sons altogether, her conversation gave little indication of it. Carmine had grown used to this; but now, after so long a silence, he was somewhat irked that these should be her first words.

"And how would you know if he did?" he asked in return. "Has he bothered to visit you one time since he moved away? When I lived in town, I came to see you every week!"

Teresa didn't raise an eyebrow, but simply gave another pat to his daughter's handiwork. "Yes," she said, "ever week, and my Mamma tell me, when I'm a girl, the pain of the woman come only once a month."

"Well?" asked Sara when he got back upstairs.

"If you pay Mrs. Feminella more than fifty cents," said Carmine, biting off the words, "you're crazy."

By MORNING, he was repenting his harshness. No one knew better what his mother had suffered. If she balmed her wounds with a little pride, who could blame her? He accused himself still more in recalling that Teresa had sniffed a few times as they talked. It was just a summer cold she was getting over; but there was no telling, at her age, where things would lead.

When he got home from work, he knocked on her door to apologize. No answer came.

"How should I know where she went?" Sara said. "Probably down the street, to gossip with some old lady, and she got invited to dinner."

"Old lady who?" Carmine demanded. "My mother hates everybody on the block!"

It was Louis who spotted her from the parlor window. Carmine followed his pointing finger and saw her.

She hobbled a few steps in the August sun, then rested a hand on the fender of the next-door neighbor's car. Her skin had turned a dull pink, her ringlets drooped and adhered to her forehead. Carmine noticed nothing else before he had flown down the stairs to her side.

He touched her soaked sleeve, felt her breath come heavily.

"Lean on me, Ma," he said. She permitted him to guide her the rest of the way back to her apartment.

By the time he got Pete on the phone, Carmine could barely sputter. "You let her take the bus! With two changes! In this heat!"

"You're not kidding," Pete agreed. "Everybody in the office was sweating like pigs. But when I got home, she had already left. Roberta had told her to wait for me to drive her, but you know how Ma is. She thought you'd need her."

"You know, Carmine," his younger brother confided, "Roberta says Ma don't look so good as she used to. Maybe you should drop in on her now and then."

That evening Carmine found her propped motionless in a rocker, pale and shrunken inside her bathrobe. Still, he made himself say, "I hope you learned your lesson."

She compressed her lips, but he did not falter.

"I'm sorry to talk to you like this, but I moved here to take care of you, and that's what I'm going to do. If there's anywhere you want to go, just tell me, and I'll get you there."

"*Va bene*," Teresa answered, waving the subject away.

They talked a little of indifferent things. Then Carmine rose, placed a kiss on her brow, and told her he'd be bringing something special home tomorrow.

"*Va bene*," Teresa answered again. Only this time she added, "I'll be at my son's house."

Carmine managed to say, "Is he coming to pick you up?"

Teresa ignored the question. "The tomatoes break the bush. I put 'em in the jar. Roberta, she's not like your wife, she likes to make her family something good."

Carmine looked away, then turned back again. "If Sara sees you take a step into the street, she's calling a taxi," he said. "I told her." ("Or Bobby could take her, and me too, and we'd save carfare," Terry had put in, seeing her chance.)

"Though why you want to go out there, I can't think," Carmine added. "When Sara starts work, Mrs. Feminella will watch the kids."

This last remark was experimental. Sara had claimed Teresa's extraordinary trip was a threat, as if she'd rather walk herself to death than have to babysit her own grandchildren. But Teresa made no reply, and Carmine was satisfied. All the same, he felt some suspense when he knocked at Teresa's door after work the following day. Though it would cost him the taxi fare, he would have liked Sara to know she was wrong. If Teresa was guilty of any crime, it was surely an excess of maternal feeling for Pete—not any inhuman coldness to her grandchildren.

His knock went unanswered. When he got upstairs, his first remark to his wife was, "That Pete! Where does he get off, keeping Ma there so late?"

Sara glanced over from the sink. "What are you talking about?" she asked. "Your mother's been on her back porch all day, stringing hot peppers from the *compare*. Hear that?" Sara cocked her head towards the unmistakable sound of Teresa's back door closing.

"What are you looking like that for?" Sara said. "She hasn't cooked a meal for us yet, you won't have to eat them."

SO SARA WENT TO WORK, and Carmine's children came under the care of strangers. With the new call on Sara's time, his dinners grew as meager as his lunches. At least there was no pain in seeing the figure in the bankbook grow— except when Sara persisted in referring to it as a down payment.

He visited Teresa only to keep watch on her state of health. She got over her summer cold; but in early November she caught a winter one. He sat with her a few minutes one evening as she blew her nose into an old handkerchief. Aloof though his heart had grown, he could not help thinking of all the wakes where he had seen that lacy cloth—and of the far-off days when it was always ready in the pocket of her apron, as if her young life were one long wake.

Perhaps that was why he responded as he did when Sara mentioned, the next evening, that his mother was a little upset. Leaving for work that day, Sara had told the old lady that she'd have to be at home for the children.

"For heaven's sake, I didn't make her lift a finger!" Sara said, after his first explosion. "Five minutes before I had to leave, I find out they took Mr. Feminella to emergency last night, so what am I supposed to do? If she has a cold, she's not going anywhere. And nothing happened, she didn't have to lay eyes on the kids!"

Carmine let his silence answer her, and went down to his mother. She was breathing more noisily than last night, a wet cloth at her forehead.

"Ma," he said, touching her hand, "I promise you, this will never happen again."

"If God doesn't want me to rest," replied Teresa a little hoarsely, "then I'll work for *cristiani*."

"No, Ma." Carmine shook his head. "No one wants you to work."

Teresa smiled, from the other side of the grave. "That poor girl Roberta, she need the help."

Carmine's hand grew still atop hers. "Ma, you're not thinking of going there, in your condition?"

She did not reply.

"I'm calling him right now!" Carmine declared, standing up.

"Sure, he'll say no," Teresa answered with a shrug. "He don't like to see the mother work."

Feeble as she appeared, there was no shaking her purpose. She evidently planned to spend her life's last days in washing the toilets of Pete's new house, and polishing his floors.

"See what you've gotten us into?" Carmine asked his wife. "If I have to pay for taxis, too, you'll be losing money rather than making it!"

"What *I* got us into?" said Sara.

"And how else am I supposed to keep her from having a heart attack?" Carmine replied. "She's going to go out there every day now, and Pete's not going to use an ounce of gas for her. Do you know somebody else that has a car and nothing to do but drive all over creation?"

Just then Terry walked into the kitchen, some nylons in her hands. She couldn't wash a dish, but every sink in the house was full of her soaking underthings.

Sara looked over at her husband—and saw him looking back at her. That second was enough for the thought to pass between them. Then Sara turned away, perhaps because she could not bear the sight of his struggle with the angel.

"Sit down," she said to Terry. "Your father's going to talk to you."

EACH DAY BOBBY was to take Terry straight to work, then drive Teresa out to Pete's house. In the afternoons he would repeat the process, so that Teresa always interposed as chaperone. Those were the conditions. But Carmine could not fail to notice that the girl found reason to continue investing in lipstick. More than once he saw her take out her compact the moment she entered Bobby's jalopy. And her conversation at the dinner table became a recital of the boy's witty retorts to policemen, schoolteachers, and former bosses.

One evening, however, she was chattering not about these accomplishments, but about an aunt of Pete's wife Roberta. She and the boy had met her when they'd gone to pick up Teresa.

"What a doll!" said Terry. "She asked me where I work, and she invited us to her beach house this summer. When we left, she stood right by the door, and wouldn't let us go until we kissed her. You know how Grandma is, but even she got a kiss on the cheek."

"I didn't think Roberta had any aunts," Sara said to Carmine.

"No, I'm sure of it," Terry insisted. "They called her Auntie Hilda."

Carmine hardly sat still for Terry to answer his questions. The moment he had spoken them—had she met this Hilda before? Had she dared to talk to her?—he was on his way downstairs.

"Ma!" he called out, before she had a chance to get to the door. "Ma!" he cried, as if she were trapped in a burning room.

For a woman in flames, Teresa greeted him calmly. She was looking a little drawn, but so she had been since the start of her daily travels. He took her hand—it lay limply in his—and guided her to the sofa.

He told her that he would never have let her go, if he'd known this could have happened. Even Pete couldn't have meant it to be. He could imagine how she must feel, he said, but he assured her that it would never, never—

Then he stopped, her stoniness infecting him. Perhaps he imagined it, but the petrifying force seemed to be centered in the spot on her cheek that had taken Hilda's kiss. He could not keep his eyes from it.

"Ma, say something!" he cried at last, to break the spell.

"It was a little-a cold today," she said, removing her hand from his grasp. "But tomorrow, nize."

"Ma, you don't have to pretend with me," said Carmine, shaking his head.

"Sure," Teresa replied, "the man say, on the radio. Nize tomorrow."

Now Carmine himself grew a little warmer. "Look, Ma," he said, "you don't want your granddaughter exposed to someone like that."

"Like who?" Teresa inquired. She went on rocking, showing neither pleasure nor pain, like a hireling nursemaid at the cradle.

Carmine didn't trust himself to answer. Once back upstairs, however, he gave himself free rein on the phone with Pete.

"What's the big deal?" said his brother. "Remember, they're old ladies now."

"Yes, she's old, old," Carmine answered, "so let her be spit on in the gutter!"

Heart pounding, Carmine sent Louis down to invite Teresa to spend the night in her grandson's room. The boy could sleep on the parlor couch. Teresa would know that there was one family, at least, by which she was not spurned in her last days.

"She says 'No thanks,'" Louis reported. "And she wants to borrow Mother's Sapolio to bring with her tomorrow. She says Aunt Roberta is out of it."

When Terry entered the kitchen at her father's call, she was surprised to find him standing guard in front of the sink, as if the cleansers on the shelf above it were at risk. The strangeness of his stance was matched by his mutterings about how Aunt Roberta could buy her own Sapolio. At last he noticed her and said he had a message for Bobby DiFazio.

"Tell him," said Carmine, one hand gripping the sink's edge, "that starting tomorrow, you're back on the bus."

"And what?" Sara asked. "Am I supposed to strong-arm your mother into a taxi again?"

Carmine didn't look at her. Despite his hold on the porcelain, his body swayed slightly, as if to keep balance on an uncertain surface.

"She can walk," he said.

But Teresa went nowhere the next day, or the next. Each evening Carmine passed her front door, its panel of glass masked by a lace curtain, without a knock, without a glance. But he felt the presence behind it, throbbing like the last coal in the stove. On the third day he knew, even before Sara mentioned it, that she was gone.

"She left early this morning," Sara said. "I don't know where for."

Carmine said nothing, though the day was bitter, and the wind whistled through his father's window frames.

"I hope she's had more sense—" Sara began. But the words faded, pulled down by the undertow of Carmine's silence. He sat at the kitchen table, the newspaper laid out unread before him.

At last they heard a car door close. "That must be her now!" Sara said, rushing into the parlor.

Yes, it was Teresa, Sara called from the window, though it wasn't Pete's car. Then another door slammed; and Sara gasped.

"What?" Carmine said.

"Nothing," replied Sara, walking back into the room and busily moving pots from one burner to another. "It must be some friend of hers."

He watched her, dredging his memory. Then he remembered it: the day Sara had come with him on a call he had had to make to his father's office. Terry was an infant in her arms. When the blonde woman at the desk had told them to step right in, Sara suddenly guessed who she was and turned the child's face away.

At the sound of Teresa's front door opening, Sara at last met his eyes. The look held, and they listened. Another voice than Teresa's rose from downstairs, girlishly high-pitched and penetrating. Sara let go of the pot handle—there was no use pretending now—and sank into a chair across from her husband.

Teresa was apparently conducting her guest from room to room, as if showing the house for sale. Sara and Carmine followed the tour by ear. No words passed between them, until the buzzer sounded from their own front door.

"We won't answer," Sara said, and Carmine nodded.

But Teresa was not so easily stopped. When the buzzer failed to rouse anyone, she simply opened the door, and led her guest up the stairs to her son's apartment. They walked through the entry, paused in the parlor. They might easily have been seen standing in the dining room, if Sara and Carmine had looked. But they didn't turn their heads.

The visitor exclaimed, as she noticed the wedding picture hanging above the buffet, "There he is! There's your Poppa!" For she had evidently spotted Carmine through the kitchen door.

An introduction might have seemed naturally to follow these words, but Teresa led the way instead to the master bedroom. The visitor's whisper carried across the hall and through two rooms. "And is *this*," she breathed—and what else could she mean but Gaetano and Teresa's old *matrimoniale*?—"is this where he died?"

Teresa's answer must have satisfied her, for there came a long, racked sigh. Then footsteps in the hall. Teresa said, "The kitchen. My son. His wife." And she stood before them.

It had been fifteen years since he'd seen Hilda—and never at such close range, or with tears in her eyes. He supposed it was the years that had inflated her. He had never thought of her as resembling quite so much a balloon oddly cased in clothing, the buttons straining at what was required of them. Balloon-like in her lightness of foot as well, she pattered into the kitchen ahead of Teresa, and made short flights towards each of its attractions: the dinner on the stove, Terry's parakeet in the corner, the cherry-wood radio. The tears, evoked by the sight of her lover's deathbed, meant no lingering sadness; the liveliness of her interest in all around her proved that. They seemed only ornamental bright-nesses, like her ruby earrings.

Hilda stretched her arm toward him, a mortadella wrapped in fur, while Teresa explained how the kind lady, who had known her late husband, had driven her home from Pete's.

"You know how to drive?" asked Sara, finding her tongue.

"Oh, I've always had a little car," Hilda affirmed, the fingers of her left hand measuring a space two inches long. Her right hand, meanwhile, remained extended to her host, who continue to stare, motionless, towards Hilda's ears.

It wasn't so much the earrings that held him, though these were undeniably a match to Teresa's own best pair. It was instead the hair—no longer blonde, but golden—against which the red drops were set. The gold was of a brilliant, blind-ing hue, such as Carmine had seen nowhere except in magazine advertisements. It was arrayed about her ears in ripples and eddies, crests and swirls.

"My son," Teresa repeated, nodding, and looking not at Hilda but into Car-mine's own eyes, as if she were identifying him to himself rather than to her visitor.

When he made no move, and continued silent, Teresa turned to her guest and said, "*Scusa.* He's a—*come si dice*—a *stupido.*"

ALTHOUGH SNOW had been predicted, the following Sunday turned out so mild that Carmine's sister, who had come to visit, suggested a ride. She and her husband had been looking at model homes since summer, and sometimes Sara joined them. Carmine generally stayed home; apart from his lack of interest in new houses, he took no pleasure in automobiles.

Today, however, he consented to go along. After all, he was in the market now. The words that had passed between Carmine and Teresa, between Carmine and Pete, were all but a legal substitute for the breaking of the lease.

"I hope you don't mind riding over the wheel," his brother-in-law joked as Carmine got in at last.

He slid onto the padded bench. The engine started with a roar. Packed against his wife, Carmine closed his eyes, heard the salt wind whip against the glass, and surrendered himself to the lunge and bounce of the merciless rocking.

Perfect Hatred

Joanna Clapps Herman

Fiction (2000)

SOMETIMES for what seemed like no apparent reason Anna took a complete and intense dislike to someone the moment she saw the person. Another woman, Anna's age, moving into her line of sight wearing a blue business suit, might look at herself in a mirror approvingly when Anna thought that the suit was so straight it should be made of metal. Or a younger woman wearing a tight black dress and sunglasses might arrive at a dinner party contemptuous of everything that wasn't her. These episodes brought up a surge of hatred in Anna that surprised and satisfied her each time it happened.

Anna watched these strangers surreptitiously, so that she could position her virtue above theirs. Restaurants and hotel lobbies were among the best locations for these occasions.

Anna and Max were at Doc's, a small restaurant near Lake Waramaug in Connecticut. Surrounded by windows, the dining room felt like a sun porch. White cloths covered plain wooden tables. The only other decoration was a mix of odd chairs in various styles and shapes, some left in their original brown wood color, others painted a shade of green, evoking old schoolhouses and apples. This mix of plainness and design made you feel you were in a place of sophistication and unpretentiousness measured in equal parts. There was an air of modest ceremony to the room, congenial to appetite.

The room though was a minor pleasure compared to the taste of the food. It was a combination of Old World peasant food—vegetables, pastas, beans with the soft matrix of their juices combined, the gush, Anna liked to call it—and hip America at its most vital, lively touches of unusual combinations of herbs and legumes, as if they had been grown from seed that morning. Each bite brought these worlds together; deep, rich and ancient, fresh, new and young, a fine response to hunger.

Simple purity here in the white and green room. Food and drink along with the leisurely taking of measure and rank.

Doc's was quiet, only three tables with guests. The waitress, a young, chaste-looking woman with sandy hair, wearing jeans and a white linen shirt, pointed to a couple of tables. Most were still empty. They could have whichever they wanted. Anna hesitated. Max quickly chose the one nearest the kitchen. There were others by windows and this one was right across from the entrance. Anna resisted her impulse to overrule his choice.

They settled in, smug in their contentment. Above and behind Anna's head was a shelf that held wineglasses, bread and knives, stuff prepared for the night's service. Anna could see now that Max's choice of table was better than the one she would have made. The floor tilted slightly up at this end of the room and there was space around the table—it was in the clear. The room spread out in front of them. They would watch it fill.

"Can I open that wine for you?" The waitress arrived and handed them menus. She reached behind Anna's head to the shelf and, grabbing a corkscrew, opened the bottle efficiently, pouring for Max first.

Max lifted his glass to the waitress, toasting her service. Anna could see that Max had won her with that gesture. The waitress moved off skillfully to the door to greet other customers.

ANNA AND MAX had driven up from New York that night for an extended weekend of rest and reading. Their son Paul was on a school trip. They were free of all work and duty; even the renovations on the video store that they owned and Anna ran were behind them. Anna had been a schoolteacher for many years; "I'm sick of taking care of other people's children," she had said when they decided to start up the business. It had taken five solid years of hard work, catering to the needs of her Upper West Side neighbors. Sometimes Videoness felt like a settlement house for the overworked middle-class; Anna chatted with the children, recommended the right movie for a rainy Friday night and mentioned the best special at the Chinese restaurant next door.

Max, a college professor, worked on the books and helped out at the store on weekends. He often knew just which movie would please one of the customers. "*The Golden Coach* just came out on tape," he'd say, remembering that Mr. Rivet was a Magnani fan. "The color's not great, but who cares with that mouth of hers."

Anna was customer queen. She stood behind the counter, waiting for a moment when she could find a way to say something kind. She assured them that she was worse than they—that they were in this together. Young mothers arriving with small children on a rainy day provided Anna's opportunity. She knew they would begin by explaining their need for relief from these long days. Anna saw these moments as her opening. "When Paul was little I used to give him four baths on a rainy day. And I didn't care if he watched from *Mister Rogers* straight through to *The Young and the Restless*, as long as we both survived." She had no shame. She concocted details to suit whoever stood in front of her. It was her world. She invented and owned it.

It even looked like Videoness was finally going to make some real money. But they were tired. It had taken a great deal out of both of them these last years. They had taken a room with a fireplace at an old inn on a river.

AT THE DOOR OF DOC'S, two older gay men were making their entrance. The young waitress turned to them, gesturing with her hand: the room was theirs.

The slim one wearing the cravat was boyish-looking, even though his translucent skin was finely lined. One could see he had looked the same since he was seventeen, blond with brilliant blue eyes; his eyes had been his passport out of a box he had left behind. He fingered the silk at his neck as he looked around the room to see where they would sit. Then he strode across the dining room, settling in reluctantly at the table Anna would have chosen, just across from Anna and Max, by a window. His companion followed him.

The other man, who was older, had what had once been a large handsome head. Now his loose flesh had betrayed his beauty. His shaming body was carefully draped in fine wools, cotton and silk. He had the look of a deposed king who was sorry for all the trouble he'd caused, was filled with resignation. Anna liked him immediately.

The Boy had settled on a table as if he were granting a privilege, but it was a remark Anna heard the Boy address to his companion that made her feel a distinct dislike of him. "Whatever you do please don't tell the Monty story again." Then he looked around to check the room, and his eyes scanned past Anna and Max. Probably the Boy would have been Anna's object of disgust for the night if the *other one* hadn't arrived a little later.

Doc's was filling rapidly. In between sizing up the Boy and the Old King she and Max had been anticipating the drinking of their wine and conferring about what they would eat, a ritual they enjoyed as they watched the pageant. Looking over the possibilities in the menu, Anna could feel her appetite take shape.

A middle-aged couple stepped into the light. He was long, neat and bald. But it was the woman who caught Anna's attention. The woman, probably Anna's age, had on black crepe pants and a white silk shirt, with a gold necklace, two arrows joining together in a point. On her arm were noisy gold bracelets.

Her hair was chemically red, a rich bronze color that had no relation to actual hair. This hair was carefully coiffed into a large bronzed helmet of curls, curls lacquered for battle. She had the sculpted head of a Greek warrior. Her lips opened over her white teeth, which were set wide, and she had the relaxed look of someone who anticipates with easy assurance that her appetites will be satisfied. Even her walk annoyed Anna. The woman moved with a confidence so complete it could only arise out of arrogance. No one was worth that much.

"Thinks she's all that," Anna muttered, mimicking Sharif, their delivery boy from Videoness. Anna's object had just arrived.

The woman sashayed across the room, headed toward the Boy and the King sitting at the table across from Anna and Max's. Baldy followed demurely. Normally, friendship with an aging gay couple would have made Anna more kindly inclined.

The woman lifted her hand beneficently over the two men they were joining for dinner; conferring her presence upon them, she insisted on mercy: "John, can you forgive us?"

Max watched Anna. A story was being conceived. About the table, but especially about the woman. Max could see that Anna was making a swift character analysis of the woman's presence, but he'd have to wait until they were back at the inn to hear the full narrative.

ANNA AND MAX always chose what they ate carefully and with pleasure. With one dish from each course, they'd be able to taste everything. Max suggested they begin with mixed green salad with goat cheese, red onions, pecans and a citrus dressing. She was wondering if the pecans would go well with the greens and the goat cheese. But Max had suggested it, and Anna felt she had used up her large capacity for bossiness for the night, back at the inn. She was being more than usually cooperative to make up what she had done earlier.

"Yes, we'll have that to start," Anna agreed conscientiously. Max raised a hand to signal the waitress they were ready.

"How do you manage this menu?" Anna asked the waitress when she came over. She wanted to establish that they were the right kind of people, fans. "It's always splendid."

"Oh you know, we keep slaves in the kitchen chained to the stove," the waitress said cheerfully.

"He *is* good, isn't he?" The waitress smiled and continued. She meant the chef. "He plans the menu every week, and we get fresh deliveries every day."

"How about we have the polenta with Gorgonzola after that?" Max leaned across the table smiling at Anna.

At this dish too she hesitated. The polenta would be fried, which meant fat; but again she yielded; she was determined not to always have her way. Max guessed that Anna was still atoning for what she had done back at the inn.

THE INN HAD BEEN DARK when they arrived earlier in the evening. It was Wednesday and it was clear they were the only guests. The innkeeper, Lucas, had shown them to a room with a king-sized brass bed and a fireplace. But the brass of the bedstead was fake and the spread had many white ruffles. Anna had noticed that the rooms weren't locked, so as soon as Lucas and Max descended to register them she had slipped around the dim hallways, peering into the other rooms. She found a small quiet blue room with a fireplace and two chairs sitting in front of it.

When Max came back upstairs she began to hurry him around the rooms. "Wait till you see. Look here."

Max didn't like this particularity of Anna's. They had to buy the red plaid pillowcases. No, he couldn't have the white phone; it would look silly on his antique desk. That valentine's card would never do for his mother. She would think Max didn't love her. He found this trait of Anna's wearisome. But he knew it would eat at her all weekend if they were in the wrong room.

"Which one, Anna? Decide." They could hear Lucas ascending the stairs.

His thin mournful face appeared at the top of the stairs.

"Would it be a problem for us to stay in this room instead? I've looked around a bit." Anna indicated the smaller blue room, smiling apologetically.

Max joined in, helping her with his best courtly manner, the Old World behind his Bronx upbringing. "Would it be terribly inconvenient?"

The young man's shoulders sank just a little. "Well, we were supposed to have someone coming for that room in two days."

"Could we have it till then?" Anna pressed.

"It costs more than the other one," Lucas said sadly, "more than what I told you on the telephone."

"Oh, that's not a problem." Max and Anna stepped on each other's words, hoping to make up for Anna's transgression.

MAX WISHED she didn't care so much about these kinds of things. It meant life could disappoint her so easily. Why can't she relax and enjoy herself? he thought, as they sipped their wine.

The salad arrived, with lots of pecans. The greens were baby new, not a blemish on a single curled leaf. The dressing was tangy but delicate. The pecans crunched against the virgin greens. The wine was warming into its full taste. Anna took a long slow sip of wine.

The Greek rose now to make her way to the ladies' room. Head held high, she stopped to check herself in the mirror by the door. Her necklace was slightly askew. She centered the arrows to point directly at her sternum. But as soon as she turned away from the mirror the arrows shifted back to the left. Max watched Anna watching her.

"Don't you think we have to try the lamb sausage?" He pulled her attention back to their table. The menu said it was prepared with garlic, white beans with rosemary, sage, plum tomatoes and mushrooms. "Isn't Vincent's on Arthur Avenue the only place in New York that makes lamb sausage?" Max said.

"I always thought so," Anna said, picturing the window of Vincent's Meat Shop, the glare of the glass so transparently displaying the slaughtered animals hanging by their hind legs, their heads dangling just above the white enamel pans, the black fur cuffs around the white legs of those creatures reminding her again where lamb sausage comes from. She pushed the window out of her head.

The waitress arrived with their polenta now.

"This place is too much. Make sure you tell the kitchen we think the food is spectacular." Anna was at her most expansive. Max was laughing as she turned back to him. "I know you're dying to get into that kitchen, but I want to go back to the inn to read my *New Yorker*. So just don't belly up to the stove, like you did that time in Queens." The Greek returned to her table without episode. Even Anna seemed to be too involved with the pleasures of eating and drinking to notice her.

CLOSE TO STANDING ROOM ONLY NOW. One table cleared and three new people entered. This time an older woman with two young men. The sons? Anna liked her immediately. She was Goodwoman, tall, worn, filled with reality and exhaustion. Her hair was gray, a good cut, but only her fingers had combed it recently. There were circles under her eyes; her lipstick had been recently applied. In the car, after they parked, Anna thought, certain of her judgment. She wore a coat the color of dusk, and a terra cotta—colored shawl almost falling off her shoulder, unnoticed. She had an air of authentic grace and dignity. Both ample and contained, she was the real thing.

A young woman sitting with friends got up from her table as soon as she saw Goodwoman and went over to her. There was admiration, a furrowed brow conveying condolence. "How's . . . ?" There was a hesitating fascination with sorrow.

Although clearly tired, Goodwoman seemed tolerantly grateful for the young woman's concern. "Well he's . . . we think." Her sturdy sons stood there, in their good knit sweaters, sober disciples, staring into space. One was holding a bottle of wine; neither said a word. The young woman's friends also stopped talking and looked on, gravely observing their friend with Goodwoman.

"Is she a niece?" Max asked. He wondered where this older woman would fit into Anna's narrative of the evening.

"Can't be. The boys would be cousins. They're not saying a word to the young woman. Don't even know who she is."

Even the Helmet was looking at Goodwoman and the young woman. Anna wondered what the Greek could be making of this scene.

The young woman was aware only of Goodwoman, whom she admired and wanted to have a piece of, even if it was a piece of sadness. Goodwoman took this young woman's need of her into her emotional housing with a largeness of spirit.

"I wonder why the sons and the young woman don't know each other."

"Who could she be?" Max thought she might run the secondhand bookstore. Anna thought she might be a psychotherapist.

ANNA COULD HEAR Greek Helmet's escort, Baldy, saying, his head turned toward the Boy, "If you like movies, you have to admire this one." The King looked nervously around the table, ready to agree with whatever was being said. Max looked across the table. "So which is it?" They were always tuned in like this, no transitions needed. He leaned across the table conspiratorially. "It's probably *The Piano*," he said shaking his head.

"Yes, of course." Anna laughed. She wanted to hate whatever they thought was good.

There were no other clues. The King had found a small opening and was talking about Italy now and where they had to eat when they were in Rome. His jowls shook happily as he spoke. "There's a small gem in Campo di Fiori that you really shouldn't miss."

"Oh yes," the Greek said. "I've eaten there, but once you've eaten at the Hassler-Medici in Rome, everything else pales." The King sank back in his chair.

Anna and Max had both drunk a couple of glasses of wine by now. The polenta had come and gone; the lamb outdid the other dishes. The spice of the sausage against the beans cooked tenderly, but not into softness, was done just right, held together in a light sauce of tomatoes, garlic and herbs. They ate for pleasure, trying not to make themselves unpleasantly overstuffed. They had a room at the inn, food and wine. Satisfaction filled them. For the moment, a balance held. They were neither hungry nor stuffed; the beasts were in the dark; they were in the light.

"This is a feast. You guys are really amazing." Anna begged the waitress to take their compliments seriously, when she passed their table again.

Invoking other pleasures, they were remembering other great vacations by now. "The one on Martha's Vineyard when we borrowed Leah's house."

"That log porch in the Adirondacks."

"That room without the bath in Rome—remember?" They were back to their origins now.

Max's coffee came. The waitress asked if he wanted sugar. "I've got it," Anna said, smiling at her. She reached up to the shelf behind her head and got the small bowl with the Equal Max wanted. "What a great table," the waitress said. Max could see that Anna was really happy now, as if she had been given a prize. Approval from a waitress was the kind of thing that made Anna's day.

Although she wished she could find a way to smile discreetly at the King, she tried not to keep her attention from being drawn back to Greek Helmet. Why ruin the mood? Just then an older man got up from a corner table. Greek Helmet started waving to him. "There's Doctor Stan," she said in a stagy voice.

Another scene unfolding. Anna looked away, to take it in. It almost seemed to Anna as if the Greek Warrior wanted a larger part in the night's production. Was she making an attempt to attain Goodwoman's status? Is that what she had made of that scene? Anna asked herself.

The Helmet started calling out her acquaintance's name: "Oh Doctor Stan," she said, "yoo hoo." He was paying the bill. He didn't hear her. Everyone at her table stopped talking, waiting for this greeting to be acknowledged.

Her table waited quietly; they were all turned toward Doctor Stan. She called out to him again: "Doctor Stanley!" Still Doctor Stan didn't seem to hear her.

She leaned across the table and snapped her fingers, bracelets jingling, necklace dangling. "Doctor!"

"Oh hi," he said, finally, a distracted and dutiful greeting. He was fumbling to get his wallet out. The woman had to go on with it. Anna's heart beat a little faster.

The woman leaned slightly across the table and stretched out her hand for Dr. Stan to take. "How are you?"

"I'm fine." He looked back down to make sure he had left the right amount of money. Her hand didn't seem to exist. He made a small step backward, a graceful retreat, opening the air between them. Her chest leaned further across the table; her necklace banged into a wine glass, knocking it over, spilling wine on her shirt, the stain spreading across the white cloth. The King immediately began mopping up the wine. The others at her table looked away.

Why did Anna need these clandestine assertions of her worth with people she didn't even know? This predilection was as mysterious as it was uneasy. Anna felt sorry for the bald man, sad at her own pleasure.

Max counted the money out onto the table, leaving an excessively liberal offering. Anna checked the tip to make sure it was enough. "She has to protect the world from *me*," Max always laughed when he told friends she always did this. They stood up. The two of them saluted the staff as they walked by the kitchen. Doc's was hers.

Anna, moving toward the door waving goodbye to the waitress, bumped into someone coming into the restaurant. She turned to make her apologies, but the person had slipped past her and Anna found herself looking into the mirror instead; longing lay in her sagging jowls.

The biting cold air cleansed them as they walked to their car. The stars flashed their messages. The universe is infinite. It will continue. Even *you* will for a while. In the city there was no sky to soothe her.

Where did this Sculpted Head live? Was the Bald One someone Greek Helmet was dating, trying to impress? Had he liked her hair? Her imperious airs?

Max was singing, "In a small hotel, by a wishing well," content to wait for Anna to put the finishing touches on tonight's tale. Max had come to understand in his life with Anna that ordinary women write their stories on the breezes of backyard fences, on the currents of telephones, in murmurs in dimly lit bedrooms, daring only to tell public stories with incisive subtlety in private, but rarely the opposite. When they climbed into bed and Anna told Max her night stories, the world was shaped by what came out of her mouth. He drove along slowly down the dark roads. No real menace nearby, only dogs and stars.

LOVE AND
ANGER

POETRY

Inside the Inside of the Moon

Brian McCormick

(1991)

The night Neil Armstrong impressed the thin dust
On the moon, I made my meld in diamonds,
Playing pinochle, two decks cut and sussed
With my foster family, Italian
Americans, all now dead. Mom Vecchio
Fears treatment in ignorance, her breast black,
Malignant, eclipsing her aureole.
Her sixth grade schooling in science inexact
While on the TV screen Galileo
Is proved correct by golfing astronauts.
Armstrong's hop from module videos
To earth: Mom Vecchio lays down a heart.
She asks, "When is he going to go in?"
This puts a stop to the conversation.

Again—"When will he go inside the moon?"
"Inside the moon? He's on the moon's surface."
"I mean, inside the *inside* of the moon."
"Inside the inside of the moon?" Nervous,
I try to divine what she sees inside.
"Inside the inside where the moon-people

Live, the way we survive inside our sky."
She made her meld, her mind made wonderful
To me, that she could live inside a shell
Around the earth, the firmament made real
By faith in this Apollo miracle!
Planets, moons, traversed by NASA's angels,
Instantly transfigured, flown by foster
Love of God, she trumps with *Pater Noster*.

The phone rings. My brother sounds far away,
"Did I kill a black baby as a boy?"
Calling from his shelter in Rockaway,
The sunspot interference fades his voice.
"Did I burn it in the oven roaster
Because I went crazy, because I'm bad?"
Sea of Tranquility, golden visor!
"You're thinking of the oven used by dad,"
I said, "when he threatened to throw us in,
Clicked his heels, called us Jews, and lit the gas.
Now get some sleep, you're imagining things."
Invisibles explode us into space
The flag flaps in vacuum, and we salute
The black baby inside the inside of the moon.

Why I Drive Alfa Romeos

Kevin Carrizo di Camillo

(1993)

Because most people think it's the name of an Italian
clothier, or they spell the first part in Greek
and pronounce the latter in Shakespearean.
Because Alfas have the aura of a priceless antique.
Because the gauges read wrong and commit sins
of inaccuracy every other day of the week.
Because the logo is inscrutable: a man
swallowed by a snake and a cross, red as a cherub's cheeks.

But mainly because I drove an Alfa
around Nantucket this past summer.
Roads smoked with sand, Maria was with me.
Listened to the only music: Verdi's operas.
Engine kept tempo like an unflagging drummer,
driving towards the sun, ocean, and Italy.

Walking My Son on the Beach

J. T. Barbarese

(2003)

I smell like an engine housing
with my arms around his ribs;
his sweat tastes like her breast-milk
and something else—something his

and his alone. The tang of his hair,
the sweet cedar bark of his skin,
whatever my days have left out of me
in him has found a way in

and leavens the sweat that sweetens his cheek
and leaves it tasting of brine
and all the somethings drawn from me
as he was becoming mine.

The Skeleton's Defense of Carnality

Jack Foley

(2003)

Truly, I have lost weight, I have
lost weight,
grown lean in love's defense,
in love's defense grown grave.
It was some concupiscence
that brought me to the state:
all bone and a bit of skin
to keep the bone within.

Flesh is no heavy burden
for one possessed of little
and accustomed to its loss.
I lean to love, which leaves me lean
till lean turns into lack.

A wanton bone, I sing my song
and travel where the bone is blown
and extricate true love from lust
as any man of wisdom must.

Then wherefrom should I rage
against this pilgrimage
from gravel unto gravel?
Circuitous I travel
from love to lack
and lack to lack, from lean to lack
and back.

BIRTH AND DEATH

PROSE

A Marvelous Feat in a Common Place

Salvatore La Puma

Fiction (1992)

MY CAT WASN'T MUCH to look at and wasn't very polite either, having introduced herself the first time years ago when my apartment door had been left wide
open on a hot summer day, coming inside from the trash barrels in the alley where
she had lived up until then; but as a dead cat she looked instead like an apart-
ment-size black panther, standing gracefully poised, alert and pretty, preserved
with her white-sock feet firmly attached to a mahogany stand on the mantelpiece
in my living room.

My cat Bast was stuffed and mounted for me by my upstairs neighbor in the
apartment building, a butcher, after he'd shown me the stuffed sow that he keeps
in his own apartment. That sow was the first that he ever slaughtered, he said,
tears brimming from his eyes even now. To have my cat stuffed had cost me $385,
raising a lot of doubt in my mind about having her preserved, but money was
really of no importance in comparison to having my Bast back again. It was too
late anyway, there she was, beautiful as she hadn't been in life; and I had to write
out the check for the butcher who was waiting with a meat cleaver in his hand.

Physical beauty, as far as I'm concerned, has very little appeal. I go to great
lengths personally to be unattractive in order to discourage others from getting
too close—not taking regular baths, shaves or haircuts, eating to excess ice cream
and cookies. Of course Bast had more sense than to be concerned about my
hygiene, hers none too fastidious either, so we had, as lovers say, found each
other. She didn't interfere in the long quiet hours I spent on my treatise; I didn't

challenge her about all the hours she spent prowling the streets at night. In the morning's first light we were both delighted to meet again over her bowl of milk and dry cat food, and my bowl of apricots and granola.

Before Bast came into my life, I was content to work on my manuscript without conversation or the company of another living being, but after she arrived my work went much better than ever. When we had said "Meow" to each other, when she had curled up in my lap, sometimes sleeping with me in bed, Bast was like my muse, inspiring a new lyricism in my writing about the bed bug.

My lifelong ambition has been to write a definitive history of the bed bug over the millennia, which I'm now doing, having taken a sabbatical from the university where I'm a professor of psychology. The *cimex lectularius* is a bashful little thing that hates coming into the light where a vigilant sleeper might pick it off, and prefers its blood meal in the dark. Amazingly, it can live for as long as a year in an unoccupied bed on just the hope of a juicy behind getting in under the covers.

My thesis, which I intend to prove with historical research, is that the bed bug has shaped the world since before civilized times, making it what it is even today. For example, the bed bug, it might be said, has given birth to some of the most well-known personalities through the ages, when itching at night was commonly misinterpreted by men and women as raging carnal desire. In modern times there are instances, which I point out in my book, of the bed bug driving good and gentle souls to rise from their bed in the middle of the night for nefarious purposes.

My enthusiasm for the tiny creature had waned, however, ever since Bast didn't come back inside one morning two months ago. I went out to look for her and my heart broke when I found her dead in the alley. After my neighbor did his work, I sat here in my big chair day and night gazing at my dear stuffed cat on the mantelpiece like an objet d'art. When petted or spoken to about astrophysics or *Orchidaceae* (other favorite subjects of our past conversations) Bast, glassy-eyed, had remained unresponsive—until very early this morning. For the past few days I've been noticing that the level of dry food in the sack has been going down slowly. I suspected hungry mice. But this morning Bast smiles at me from the mantelpiece—and tells me with her eyes that she's been the one nibbling on the dry cat food.

Her smile of course immediately brings my intense reaction: my humming of Mozart to her, which in our previous good times together she responded to with the motor in her throat. It's exactly what she's doing now, purring loudly as she first hesitates, then crouching, jumps down from the mantelpiece in a wonderful high ballet-like leap right into my lap. "Bast, you've come back to life," I whisper, not wanting to frighten her with the shock of disbelief I feel but keep from my voice. As she always liked to do, Bast now rubs the top of her head on the point of my chin, then curls up contentedly.

It doesn't make an ounce of rational sense for a stuffed cat, despite the mythology of its nine lives, to be reincarnated before my astonished gaze. Am I imagining the impossible out of my grief for my deceased pet? Am I asleep and dreaming? I pinch myself, which hurts quite a lot, which doesn't really prove that I'm awake, but I assume so anyway. Now I look across at the mantelpiece and sure enough there is the wood stand that Bast was attached to, but it's vacant now. Bast isn't there. She's warm and gorgeous, not bony and threadbare as when she was alive the first time, curling up on my upper thighs as I sit in my chair. I'm forced to acknowledge that she has pulled off a marvelous feat in a common place, my living room.

Carrying Bast cradled like a baby in my arms, diamonds of light sprinkled on her glossy black coat, we go to the kitchen where I gently set her down on the table to wait while I pour out a saucer of milk for her. Crouching down, she laps it up—understandably acting like an animal who hasn't had a drink for quite a long while. "So, tell me, Bast," I say, my voice full of wonder, "how in the world did you accomplish this fantastic trick of coming to life again?"

Bast lifts her now pretty face to me, her yellow round eyes sending a message as if in digital zeros and ones, which my eyes, locking on to hers, can easily decode. Her explanation is simply that she now understands we are destined to be always together. And since I didn't also die to go where she was, she has had no other choice but to return to life, called back to be with me again by my deep sorrow at her passing.

Her eyes say that her death and departure occurred too abruptly through her own fault, always having been too impulsive, too quick to jump at things. With my own eyes I say to her—certainly, she has pulled off something quite remarkable by coming alive again, but I have to remind her that she still can't speak with words, nor can she hum symphonic melodies, so we both still have to rely on our eyes and vocal sounds to communicate with each other.

The day just evaporates around us, Bast eager to hear what little progress I've made in my research and writing, and I ask about cat heaven where, surprisingly, it turns out that cats have to hunt down every meal they have as in the days before they came into our homes. When night falls now, Bast jumps down from my lap to the floor and pads to the apartment door, showing me the way she wants to go as before, in her first life—whether to prowl in the night, sleep in bed, or for something tasty to eat in the kitchen. As most cat lovers, I think I've always understood her behavior, even as human behavior sometimes is very baffling to me. Tonight, however, I'm somewhat reluctant to allow her out of my sight after having been reunited for just twelve short hours. Still, the most one can do for a pet is to give it freedom to live a little of its life as it chooses, not enslaving the creature in exchange for a handful of food.

So I have to open the door for her, asking her plainly in my words and in a tone of voice she would understand that I'd like her to come back as soon as possible. I'll leave the door ajar for her. When she comes in she can sleep in bed with me. She turns to give me what I think is a tender smile while also beckoning me with a nod of her head to follow her a little ways out of the apartment, regardless that in my usual dress these last few months, I'm wearing soiled pajamas, buttons missing and held up with a safety pin.

Timidly, I take a few steps out of my apartment into the hallway and find by the wall a large brown box, the name pineapple juice company printed on the outside. Bast stops there and says, "Meow" in a way that invites me to inspect the inside of this reused box, even though my name doesn't appear written on it. Sitting back on her haunches as if she knows well enough what I'll find, she waits to be praised and stroked. I turn back the corrugated box flaps and find inside two small weaned kittens, one white and one black, mewing and pawing a towel put down for their soft bed. "You're acting just like their mother, Bast," I say to her, "but you can't be." Bast accepts my petting on her head and coat, then wanders down the hallway and out of sight. When she doesn't come home that night, or the next morning, I have to weep for a few minutes, but then find new happiness with my kittens Pharaoh and Sphinx.

Where It Belongs

Louisa Ermelino

Fiction (1992)

WHEN THE BABY WAS BORN, the mother asked the midwife to take the after-birth outside.

"I can't," Alfonsina whispered. "You got a girl. Don't you want her to stay home?"

The mother didn't. Armando was somewhere in the streets, already drunk, angry that he'd made a buttonhole.

"Take it outside," the mother said. "This is America."

"I can't," Alfonsina said. "Men go out of the house. No one wants a man who stays home, a *ricchione*, under his mother's skirts. You know that. A woman belongs in the house," she told the mother. "Let me put it down the toilet."

"Take it," the mother said again, "and dig a hole."

Alfonsina looked out the window at the lines of laundry.

"Don't ask me to do this," she said. "I'm too old now. I can't dig a hole so deep the dogs don't find it."

The mother leaned forward. "Take the money from the jar in the kitchen and get someone to help you. Pay them to dig a place and don't say nothing."

"But if someone sees?" Alfonsina said. "Everybody knows you got a girl. And Armando? What about Armando?"

Alfonsina pulled a handkerchief from under the sleeve of her dress and twisted it in her fist. The baby cried and the mother turned away.

"Take her," Alfonsina said. "Take your baby and forget this. You got a girl. Girls are always with you. You'll get more babies. You'll get sons."

The mother would not look. She would not take the baby. She would not be persuaded.

"Trouble," Alfonsina said. "You make trouble with this thing, I can tell you."

She went to the kitchen to find the jar. It was behind the tins of flour on the shelf covered in yellow oilcloth.

Alfonsina put the afterbirth in a rag and wrapped it in newspaper. She tied the package with a string. The things people want in America, she thought.

Downstairs in the yard, Alfonsina remembered the baby had no name, and she walked back up the stairs. The mother was sitting at the kitchen table. The sweater over her shoulder had no buttons. She was drinking wine.

"The baby has no name," Alfonsina said.

"Take some wine," the mother said, going to the shelf to get a glass.

"And the baby's name?" Alfonsina said.

"When I go to the priest. . . ."

"No," said Alfonsina. "I need it for the legal paper. This is America."

The mother poured the wine. "I don't know."

Alfonsina shook her head. "I come another time, but you don't wait too long. I need it for the paper."

She finished the wine and got up to go. "Don't forget," she said. "You tell Armando no if he tries to bother you. You just had a baby. You tell him Alfonsina says he can't bother you."

"He won't listen," the mother said.

"Ah," said Alfonsina. "If it was Donna Vecchio said it, he would listen. They all listen to Donna Vecchio. It falls off when they don't listen. You should have called Donna Vecchio for your baby."

Alfonsina opened the door. She was already in the hall when the mother touched her arm. The mother pointed to the package wrapped in newspaper.

"You swear to me, Alfonsina," she said.

"Yes, yes, I swear. Rest now or the milk won't come. And then where will you be? You and your mixed-up baby?"

When Alfonsina had gone, the mother picked up the baby. The baby was bound in strips of bed sheet, beginning under the arms and pulled tightly to the toes, where Alfonsina had tied a knot.

"You have to do this," she had told the mother, "to make the legs grow straight."

But now the mother unwrapped the baby and let the legs kick free. She sat in the chair by the window that looked out into the yard and the lines of laundry.

She undid her dress. She wasn't worried about the milk. With the other baby, the one that couldn't swallow, there had been so much milk that when the baby died, no one could make the milk go away . . . until Donna Vecchio had come with her powers of *afattura* and a paste of olive oil and parsley. Donna Vecchio would be angry that she wasn't called for this baby.

The mother tried not to be afraid. This was America. She tried not to be afraid of Donna Vecchio. She tried not to be afraid of Armando.

Armando, who had come to her brother's house in Brooklyn one day to ask for her.

"Yes," her brother's wife had said.

"Who is he?" her brother had asked his wife that night when she told him.

"He's *Genovese*," his wife had said.

"But what does he do?" her brother had asked.

"He's *Genovese*, I told you," the wife had said. "What are you worried about? The *Genovese* always make a dollar. The undertake, the butcher, all *Genovese*."

"She's a child," her brother had said.

"She's old enough."

ARMANDO HAD COME and taken her from her brother's house with the front yard in Brooklyn and brought her here to the building across from the horse stables. She had carried her own things.

Once she had gone to her brother, and her brother had said that he would kill Armando with a knife.

But this was America.

Could she see her brother in jail because of Armando? She had come back alone to the building across from the horse stables.

The mother sat in the chair by the window with her baby. She heard the men coming home from work and the children called in from the street. She heard them on the stairs and smelled the cooking from their open doors.

Outside the window the laundry had disappeared. Empty clotheslines crisscrossed the yard. The mother looked out the window to where her girl would go, not to hang laundry, and she waited for Armando.

Armando, who would come home and shout that there was no fire, that there was no food. He would try to bother her or he would be too drunk. He would not remember about the baby. She would not tell him.

If the sounds got too loud and the women got frightened, they would call the police. The police would come to the building across from the horse stables. They had come before, because this was America.

The men would not interfere. Behind the door was Armando's house. It would be the women who would call the police, and the police would come and make her open the door. They would make her let Armando in his house.

The men would nod. It was Armando's house. The women would stand in the hall with their heads covered. Some things do not change.

IN THE MORNING THE BABY CRIED. The mother went into the yard for wood to make a fire. She ate bread and drank coffee and sat in the chair by the window with her baby.

A policeman came. He asked the mother to come with him. She wrapped the baby, covered her shoulders, and followed him to where they showed her Armando with no blood in his face.

"An accident," the policeman said, "a fight. We don't know. Do you know?" he asked.

"I don't know," she told him.

"We'll find out," he said.

She knew they wouldn't.

When she came home, the women were waiting for her. They were waiting on the stoops and they were waiting by their open doors.

"Armando is dead," she told them.

Alfonsina came. She called out to the Virgin and Santa Rosalina. "I heard," she said. "I just heard about Armando." She took a package wrapped in newspaper from under her skirts. "I brought it back," she said. "We can do it now. We can flush it down the toilet now. You don't need no more trouble."

"Give it to me," the mother said.

Alfonsina crossed herself. She swore she would say nothing, and she left the mother and the baby and the package wrapped in newspaper that she had carried under her skirts.

Armando came into the house that night in the undertaker's box. He lay on the white satin inside the box in the black suit he was married in. The people came and gave the mother money folded inside envelopes. The women whispered and shook their heads. She was young to have no husband. Why didn't she cry?

The men standing in the corners talked of other things. Some of them watched her too closely. She was young, they thought. She would get lonely. Maybe, when some time had passed. . . .

THE PAID MOURNERS in black shawls moaned over Armando's body. They moved back and forth over him, shaking water blessed by the priest from their fingers. The water made damp spots on Armando's black wedding suit.

Donna Vecchio came. When Donna Vecchio came, everything stopped. Her hair was done in marceled waves. Her hairdresser lived in her house. Donna Vecchio had large breasts and short, bent legs. The envelope she gave the mother smelled of lavender.

"I'm sorry for your trouble," Donna Vecchio said. "And how is the baby?"

"Do you want to see her?" the mother said.

"The baby isn't mine," Donna Vecchio said. "You didn't call me for this baby. She isn't one of mine."

"But she is," the mother said. "She will have your name, Carolina. You will baptize her, and you will be her *gummara*."

Donna Vecchio smiled and held out her hand for the mother to kiss.

THE ROWS OF borrowed chairs were empty. The mother sat alone. She would sit all night to watch for Armando's spirit. When the spirit of the dead leaves, it looks for a sleeping body to enter. It enters through the mouth.

The mother wouldn't sleep, but would sit all night with Armando, with the sound of the ice melting into the pan underneath his black box. She would not let the baby sleep.

Underneath Armando's body was a block of ice, and underneath Armando's head, underneath the white satin pillow, was the package wrapped in newspaper.

And tomorrow they would bury Armando. They would put him in the ground with the afterbirth of the baby, in a hole so deep the dogs don't find it.

Unraveled

Paola Corso

Fiction (1996)

WHY MRS. NATOLI KNITTED in the cellar, poking away with those needles just to let it unravel, was beyond me. When her knitting got as far as her lap, she started all over again with the same loopy yarn. Watching her rip it out was like seeing someone yanking a bandage off.

I stayed with Mrs. Natoli most days because she liked the company and my big sister, Lisa, didn't. Once when I was five, my mother made Lisa and her friend play Barbie dolls with me. No sooner did we open up our cases when they dangled a leopard mink stole in my face and told me I could have it if I left them alone. Before I could say anything, they pulled out a matching leopard purse, so I took them both and left. It was worth it because nobody around here carried a purse that matched just one outfit.

I haven't played Barbie dolls with Lisa since, and I'm ten now. The twins my age on our street are never home because they swim in the river all the time since you don't have to pay like you do at the swimming pool. So I can't play with them or my sister. Don't know anybody else except Mrs. Natoli next door, being we just moved here from across the river. Besides, Mrs. Natoli's cellar is like a cave that feels way inside. The door is so thick, you can't hear any outside noises, at least the kind I don't want to hear—the twins giggling on their way to the river every morning, rolling a gigantic inner tube. They take turns with it, relay style. I wish my mom heard the part about them sharing because then maybe she'd let me go with them. She's always telling me and Lisa that she can't afford to buy two of everything no more. Nobody can since they shut the mirror works down.

For the longest time, I figured Mrs. Natoli only knitted with one ball of yarn because nobody left the house to buy her more. She was a widow who lived with her daughter, Rosetta, and son-in-law, Harold. I knew for a fact G. C. Murphy's sold yarns and threads across from the goldfish, but nobody in the Natoli family got out much because none of them had work. Every day, Mrs. Natoli knitted in her cool, dark cellar until the ball got smaller and smaller like a bar of soap melting so slow you couldn't see it happening. Rosetta, who smelled of baby powder, was hoping to get pregnant. She rested on the couch with tea bags over her eyes and the radio on so low all you heard was static that made her knees jiggle.

Harold called himself a science teacher, but my sister said he was a milkman until he smashed the delivery truck. Anyway, he practiced his science lectures with goggles on in front of the bathroom mirror and made me his audience. With every word he spoke, I fixed my eyes on the dribble in the crack of his mouth, waiting for him to swallow or spit it out. He pretended there was a camera in the medicine chest to record his every word and move. He even shifted me to the side once when I stood in his way. Said I was in the camera's view.

Harold told jokes about lab safety when he lectured. His favorite one went like this: "If you burn yourself, remember do not put butter on it. Do you know why? Because your finger is not a piece of toast."

I was so sure Mrs. Natoli only had one ball of yarn, but when I snuck a peek in her knitting tin while she was getting me a glass of mint ginger ale, I saw at least five more of the same color blue—as pale as toothpaste. Then I thought she had to do everything just perfect and kept ripping out her rows until the edges were measuring-stick even. When I got a good look, though, I noticed some rows were trampoline tight and some were as loose as the brown hairnet my mother wore to bed every night.

I thought it might help if I knew what her knitting was supposed to be. Trouble was, it never was big enough to tell, though it reminded me of a droopy tent about to collapse—the kind you pitch in the dark without a flashlight. I kept watching her blue ball of yarn spin slowly on the cement floor, a globe that was all ocean and no continents. Then Rosetta, her cheeks streaked with brown tea stains, came down and played some Dracula music on the organ. It was the same kind they blasted in church after Holy Communion to get you to bow your head. She held onto those notes for so long, they didn't go away even when she let up on the keys.

"You can stop knitting," she said, bumping the empty music stand.

"Oh, no, Rosetta. Not again," Mrs. Natoli said. She dropped the needles and yanked at the knitted yarn the way a sailor must pull at a rope on deck. She did this with her mouth open and her tongue drooping like a flag with no wind. By the time she finished, she had licked the pink lipstick clean off her lower lip. From then on, that's how I could tell she'd been unraveling.

My sister called me pasty face for spending so much time in Mrs. Natoli's cellar. Her smart mouth backfired, though, because my mom insisted Lisa take me to Sylvan Pool with her, since we won passes in some raffle and they had a lifeguard on duty. When we got there, Lisa offered me her cocoa butter if I let her swim to the deep end with her boyfriend, Oakie. She dropped the tube on my towel and ran to the pool. All he did was try to dunk her and splash water everywhere. Lisa was always afraid I'd tell on her because as soon as my mom dropped us off, she took off her one-piece suit and put on the yellow string bikini she was supposed to have thrown out a long time ago. I never told because I knew the only sister I had would be mad at me forever if I did.

Still, my mom could catch on if she checked Lisa's tan marks. That's why Lisa never let my mother in her room unless she had a slip on. She had to cross her legs too to hide the scar she made on her thigh. A thick capital O for Oakie that was perfect enough to show Sister Virginia, my handwriting teacher. If only she had used a ballpoint pen instead of a razor blade.

My sister wouldn't explain. Said I was a blabbermouth. The only secret she told me was about menstruation because when I asked my mother about it, she said to look it up in the big dictionary in my sister's room. Lisa said I'd have to wear a pad on my underwear to catch the blood. Then she explained the part about getting pregnant. I told her Rosetta next door wanted to stop menstruating and Lisa said Rosetta was never going to have her own baby.

"She wants one real bad."

"It doesn't work that way, Renata," Lisa said, getting close to the mirror to curl her eyelashes.

"Mrs. Natoli wants her to have one too. Just as bad."

"She can't," Lisa snapped. "There's something wrong with her."

"But Mrs. Natoli is always knitting. It must be for Rosetta."

Lisa pulled away from the mirror and looked at me. "She's wasting her time, Renata."

"Yeah, only because she rips it out," I said, waiting to see if Lisa would accidentally curl her lids instead of her lashes.

Now Lisa was applying mascara when she answered, "See. She knows."

"She starts over again though."

"She should stick to making hats and mittens," Lisa said, batting her eyelashes.

"It's not what she wants."

"I know that, Renata. I just mean she's good at it, that's all."

My mother had Mrs. Natoli knit my sister and me a hat and mitten set for Christmas. I loved mine. It was the only reason I liked winter at all. Lisa hated hers. She stuffed it in the back of her closet. My mom always told her to bundle up every morning before she left for school. My sister would lift her collar and give her the tiniest kiss on the cheek before she walked out the door. I didn't say anything to my mother, but I knew she met up with Oakie down the street and they'd walk to school together.

The day my sister told me about menstruation, I went to Mrs. Natoli's house looking for pads in the bathroom closet to see if Rosetta was pregnant. Harold was rehearsing that same science lecture on osmosis.

"Osmosis comes from the Greek word *osmos,* which means the action of pushing," he said, signaling his hands the way a traffic cop does with white gloves on. "The action of pushing. The action of pushing. So what is osmosis? Why, it's the diffusion of fluid through a semipermeable membrane until there is an equal concentration of fluid on either side of the membranc. An equal concentration on either side. Either side. Either side." His big white lab coat filled the mirror.

"You mean it spreads like magic?"

"Not magic. Science," Harold said.

"It don't take no scientist to do what you're saying, Harold. It's the same as relay style."

He adjusted his goggles. "Let me explain it to. . . ."

"Taking turns is the same as sharing," I interrupted. "Everyone around here needs to do that. You can't buy two of everything. That's what my mom thinks, anyway."

I began rooting under the sink for menstrual pads. I didn't see any and thought Rosetta must be pregnant. I stood up between Harold and the mirror and repeated the joke my sister told me.

"What's up tight, out of sight, and in the groove?"

"Cut," he snapped. "Not while I'm taping."

"Just guess if you don't know."

"Is there an equal concentration of fluid on both sides?"

"You're not even close, Harold."

"Is it on either side of the membrane?"

"You're so square. I'd give up if I were you."

He lifted his goggles. "You want me to give up?"

"A Kotex pad." I walked out to visit Rosetta upstairs and left Harold staring in the mirror with a wrinkled forehead.

"Harold's real scientific, isn't he?" I asked her.

"It's what he loves most."

"But what about you?"

"When I have a baby, I'll love it the most," she said, cupping both her elbows with her hands. "Did you know she's gonna look just like me?"

"You mean like twins?"

"Just like twins," she answered. "We're going to be so close to each other, you won't know where one of us stops and the other begins."

She kept staring at her wrist as if it were the neck of a baby and her knuckles were the tips of its toes, singing pieces of different lullabies that she strung together.

"Mama's little baby loves, don't say a word, put on the skillet, bring out the butter, go to sleep my little baby, when you wake you shall have shortening, shortening, hush little baby, shortening bread."

I took the powder from the coffee table, sprinkled white puffs on her arms and rubbed until it crawled under her skin. I knew the smell would keep her company until she had a real baby.

After that, I ran across the street to tell my sister she was wrong about Rosetta. My father was home awful early from work. He put his lunch bucket down, and he and my mother sat on the living room couch we never used unless there's company.

"Leave your sister alone. She's grounded," my mother said as I went up the stairs.

I gently knocked on Lisa's door.

"What?" Lisa said in that tone my father hates.

"Shhh. I'm not supposed to be here."

"I don't care."

"Guess who's expecting? This time for real."

"What is this? Some kind of joke?"

"Lisa, I want to tell you something."

"Tell me what?"

"Rosetta's expecting," I whispered.

"She's not the only one who knows how to get pregnant. I didn't even do anything wrong."

"Maybe you did the same thing as Rosetta."

"She always miscarries."

"Are you afraid you'll lose yours?"

"I don't want a baby, Renata. I have three more years left of high school."

"What are you going to do?"

Lisa finally opened the door, and I tiptoed in. "Mom and Dad are sending me to Aunt Nancina's camp for the summer."

I sat down on the bed beside her. "You're going on vacation up the river when you're grounded?"

"It's not a vacation, Renata. I'm being punished."

"You'll get to go swimming, won't you?"

"No way. I'm sick to my stomach."

"So? Stomachaches go away, right?"

Lisa put her hands on her head. "By that time, I'll be too . . . it'll be too cold."

"You're going to stay there in the wintertime?"

"I'll be there for months, Renata."

"Then you'll make hot chocolate with marshmallows."

"I'm not thinking about that." She leaned back on a propped-up pillow.

"You can take my Nancy Drew mysteries. I have the whole set now."

"Wish they'd let me take my stereo. That's all I want."

I looked down and saw Lisa had her big suitcase opened up on the side of the bed but very few clothes in it. I guess she had to buy new ones that fit. I offered to take up knitting for her. Make a gown like Mrs. Natoli was for Rosetta except I wouldn't keep unraveling mine. Lisa said she wasn't worried. She'd take one of Oakie's sweatshirts.

"He said he'd come and visit me after."

"How come?"

She paused before she said in a broken voice, "He's afraid he'd want to keep it."

"Lisa? Open that door!" It was Mom.

Lisa sprung off her bed and slit the door open a crack. "What?"

"Tell him he's not to ever call here again or set foot near this house! Is that understood!?"

"Yes. I heard you." She walked over to me. "I have to pack some more."

"Already? But I want you to stay."

"I'm leaving this weekend. They can't wait to get rid of me before I start to show."

I slipped out of her room, and she slammed the door shut. I pulled out the cocoa butter Lisa gave me at Sylvan Pool and knocked again.

"I have something for you."

"The answer is no! I don't want to play swapsies with your clothes, Renata."

"It's not that. It's something else. I promise."

"What?"

I could tell by her voice that she was still far away from the door.

"Please."

As soon as she opened the door, I slipped her the suntan lotion. "You'll use this more than I will." I prayed she'd take it so at least we shared something before she left.

"Thanks," she said, shutting the door so I couldn't work my way up to giving her a hug like I see the twins do sometimes. They hook their arms around each other's shoulder and walk with their feet in step—two right feet with red Keds and two left feet with red Keds. I showed my sister once and she said she wouldn't be caught dead doing the monkey walk.

"I bet you'd do it with Oakie if he asked."

"He wouldn't ask me to do that. He's not weird like you," Lisa would say.

I stood there, my eyes fuzzy. The wood on Lisa's door had no shine. It made my nose itch it was so dry. I began to wish Lisa hadn't taken the suntan lotion because I knew what would happen to it. She'd just bounce it on her mattress where it'd stay until she knocked it to the ground and then kicked it under the bed by accident. She could forget all about it and me. If I had that lotion in my hands now, I'd squeeze it out and smear it all over her door until it got good and greasy, until the doorknob was so slippery nobody would even try to go in to see her. Not even me.

I visited Mrs. Natoli the next day to see if Rosetta was as pregnant as my sister. She knew it was me even before I got there. Said my ting tongs slapped the gravel driveway, and everyone else's feet made a crunching noise. Because Mrs. Natoli's cellar was so dark, it always took my eyes a while to adjust, the way it does when you walk in late to a movie.

"Are you almost finished?"

She set her knitting down to get me a glass of mint ginger ale, which I especially loved when she took an ice cube, put it between a tea towel and cracked it with a spoon. Then I could have tiny chips floating in my glass like at the custard stand. She handed me my pop and picked up her knitting.

"I just started," she said.

"You start and stop a lot."

"I have to. I keep having to make it a different size."

"Who's it for?"

"My daughter."

"She's getting bigger, right?"

"We pray to God she does. She thinks she's pregnant and then she isn't. I keep hoping this is the last time I have to start this gown for her, but one minute she's blessed and the next she isn't. Each time, I say to myself, 'Guard your faith.' Then I go and picture my grandchild."

"Have you come close to finishing it?"

"I always have to rip it out and start over. Wouldn't you know, it takes no time at all to unravel."

"You're a fast knitter though, Mrs. Natoli. In fact, if what you do was the same as drawing a pistol, I'd pick you over John Wayne any day."

Mrs. Natoli didn't say anything, but her metal needles constantly made little noises like teeth chattering from nerves.

"Rosetta must really be expecting today."

"Doesn't matter what we expect though," Mrs. Natoli said, knitting with her eyes closed as if she were saying the rosary at the same time.

After she said that, I wondered if Rosetta was pregnant after all. Maybe my sister was right. It didn't seem fair, though, if what Rosetta wanted, she couldn't have, and what Lisa didn't want, she had to have. And no matter what, Mrs. Natoli hurried along her needles. I pictured her performing stunts the way a magician does so her knitting would suddenly appear or disappear. She'd sit on her rocking chair. Her assistants, Rosetta and Harold, would stand at either side. She'd start with easy stuff like knitting above her head and behind her back. Then Rosetta and Harold would blindfold her by putting her tea bags and his goggles on Mrs. Natoli's eyes. They'd hand her real big needles and real tiny ones. Rosetta and Harold would wheel in the clothes hamper from the bathroom, handcuff Mrs. Natoli and prop her knitting needles in her hands before stuffing her in the hamper. They'd spin it around and open it after the organ music stopped. She'd wear a pair of polka-dotted mittens she knitted with the handcuffs still on.

Her last trick required complete silence. Rosetta and Harold would each hand her what seemed to be ordinary knitting needles, but in seconds her knitting would get so long it climbed up the chimney, covered the entire outside of the house the way ivy does, spread over the grass, spilled into the street like a flattened wave, and scaled our house. When it was completely covered by her knitted sack, Mrs. Natoli would put down her needles and take a bow.

I looked down at Mrs. Natoli's knitting still shaped like a tent sucked in by the wind. I tried to picture it bulging and big enough to fit two people, but that was too much of a stretch. I had this idea to fill a bucket with water and get Harold to splash Rosetta, but he knew right away I was asking him to do something unscientific. I figured if it worked for my sister when Oakie splashed her in the pool, and they didn't even want a baby, it could work for Harold and Rosetta.

"Here. Rosetta needs splashing," I said, handing him the bucket.

"I'm in the middle of an experiment," Harold said.

"This has already been tested. I know for a fact it works."

He grabbed the bucket and suggested I record how fast water evaporated when I placed it in the sunny window versus the one in the shade, with the window closed versus open, with the bucket covered versus uncovered. He even drew me a chart with the red pen he clipped onto his lab coat pocket. I threw his scientific piece of paper in the wastebasket and thought of my own experiment, relay style.

I ran back to my house and tried to rub my sister's stomach, which I managed to do because I said her Madras plaid blouse was wrinkled. I pretended to flatten it out for her.

"You can't have my shirt," she said.

"I'm trying to fix it for you."

"I don't want to play your stupid games, Renata."

"We'll take turns."

"Don't touch me."

I held my hand out. She slapped it down, but not before I patted her in the stomach.

"I don't want you wearing my clothes."

"It's not for me," I pleaded.

"I don't want you looking like me."

"That's because you don't know how to share, Lisa."

"Yes, I do. Just not with you!"

I ran back to Mrs. Natoli's with my hand stinging from my sister's slap. Lisa's words stung worse, and if it weren't for me being in the middle of a relay, I would have thought enough about it to cry.

"Where's Rosetta?" I asked Mrs. Natoli.

She didn't take her eyes off her needles. "Resting on the couch. Why?"

"I have something for her."

"I'll give it to her."

"It's a surprise," I said as I went from the cellar to the living room. I found Rosetta asleep on the couch. She was white from the baby powder and her arm hugged one of the pillows. Her tea bags were all soggy as if she'd been crying. I pressed my hand on the middle of her stomach and held it there, figuring it would take a few minutes to pass through the pockets on her blouse, the handkerchiefs in her pockets, the thick elastic waistband on her pants, and the skinny one on her cotton panties before it reached her belly button.

I whispered in her ear: "The twins share all the time. My sister doesn't want to be twins with me. She doesn't know how to share, that's why. I've got to learn with someone. Might as well be you because you don't have anyone to share with either."

I went back to the basement. The cellar air smelled damp the way the sidewalk does the minute a few raindrops fall. The walls seemed to expand, making room for Mrs. Natoli's knitting. I swore I could hear them breathing but tried to tell myself it must have been the wind. There wasn't a breeze strong enough to budge a blade of grass outside. It made me think that something could grow in Mrs. Natoli's cellar. We just couldn't see it until it pushed through the cracks in the cement.

Harold went upstairs, and a few hours later, Rosetta came downstairs. She sat at the organ and began playing a song where her fingers looked like squirrels scampering across a telephone wire. It made Mrs. Natoli's toes tap. Mine too. Then she sang a lullaby, a loud one, and this time it made some sense.

"There's no trouble with twos, no trouble at all. You and me, we'll be mother and child, mother and child. As soon as can be, we'll be two. No trouble with twos, no trouble at all."

"It worked," I shouted, but nobody could hear me over Rosetta's voice.

I glanced over at Mrs. Natoli's knitting. It was the longest I'd ever seen it. She was three-quarters of the way done with a gown for Rosetta, and she hadn't ripped it out yet. Now her needles made the sound of two champagne glasses clinking for a toast.

"You're far along with your knitting. That means Rosetta must be expecting," I said.

"We're all expecting, Renata," she said in a cheerful voice.

Mrs. Natoli said she was about to start knitting the rows around the stomach. She said she would make them twice as wide as the other ones to make room for the baby. She leaned back in her chair. It's as if her eyebrows sat back and relaxed too. They weren't so bunched up anymore.

Then Mrs. Natoli did something she never did before. She opened the doors and let the sun in. My eyes darted through the blackness. I saw an old Victrola with the guts emptied out and filled with sheet music. A wad of blue wires flowed like veins along beams on the ceiling. Rosetta's organ, which pumped out music loud enough to circulate through the whole house, was curved and muscular. Angora hairs on a blanket grew long enough to run a comb through. Clothespins the same distance apart on a droopy line hung like discs on a spinal cord.

For the first time I didn't have to squint my eyes as I left Mrs. Natoli's cellar. Later that day, after supper, we drove Lisa to the bus station. For some reason, my mother sat in the backseat with me and my sister sat in the front with my father. It's almost as though my mother couldn't even trust Lisa in the car unless she could see what she was doing. I think she wanted a chance to find an apology on my sister's face without her knowing she was looking for it.

My sister didn't take her hand off the suitcase handle the whole car ride, and when we stopped, she lifted it up before my father could help. My mom got out of the car and kept her hands in the pockets of her pedal pushers the whole time. My father broke the silence.

"Take good care of yourself now," he said, stepping over to Lisa to give her a kiss on the cheek. "Say good-bye to your mother."

My mom didn't move. Lisa bobbed her head and kissed her on the ear, which was covered by the three-corner scarf my mom always wore the day before she gave herself a home permanent. My mom broke down crying and gave her a hug for as long as Lisa would let her.

"Call when you get there, you hear?"

My sister nodded and turned around toward the bus.

"Hey, what about me?" I shouted.

Lisa turned around and smiled. "I'm sorry. I forgot."

I grabbed my sister's hand and told her we could be pen pals.

Lisa hugged me with one hand and gripped the suitcase with the other.

"You write and I'll write you back," she said to me.

"Did you hear that, Mom? She's going to write me!" If she did that, I promised myself I wouldn't be mad at her anymore. Besides, this was something the twins would do anyway if they were separated from each other.

I wrote her my first letter as soon as we got home from the bus station. I told her the drive back was as quiet as the drive there. Dad suggested we stop for a root beer float at the custard stand, but Mom just took a sip of his. I ordered a single scoop of chocolate and a single scoop of vanilla just because I can never decide which one to get, they're both so good.

After that, I wrote every week, telling Lisa how long Mrs. Natoli's knitting had gotten. It was growing steadily. I knew because I checked every day. It practically covered Mrs. Natoli's knees and then began to drag on the floor, it was so long. I used up most of my writing tablet explaining all this to Lisa when finally she wrote back and said she was about to have the baby.

I wrote her right away and told her everything in a letter—that when I visited Mrs. Natoli, she had used up all the yarn in her tin and even had Harold break away from the camera to get her some more. He did when there was a commercial. Mrs. Natoli yelled to Rosetta to come down and try her gown on. She stepped up to a stool right through a strip of sunshine. Rosetta was covered in a web of blue that glowed so bright that I swore I could see right through her. Mrs. Natoli began tugging at the gown in places where it was too short. When she put her needles down to use both hands, the yarn dropped out of her lap and onto the cement floor. I reached to grab it for her, but it rolled out of my reach over to the cellar doors and up the stairs toward the backyard. At that point, Rosetta began spinning around like a ballerina, almost as though the force at the end of the yarn sent her in a thousand circles as the gown began to unravel. Her feet clawed the stool, her knees knocked, and her thighs shook like Jell-O salad. When the part around Rosetta's stomach was about to unravel, Mrs. Natoli pushed me out the door and yelled for me to stop it.

I followed the trail of blue yarn past the woodshed where it bounced across a bed of gravel then over dried-up rhubarb. My feet twitched with every stone in my sandals as I followed the blue ahead of me until it disappeared in the shadows of tulip trees. When I got closer to the river, the ground began to spring back from under my feet like a sponge. Beads of moisture trimmed everything green. The yarn was warm and damp now, pulsing with life.

I let it glide through my hand until I reached the end: the belly button of a baby. The newborn was lying on a patch of green moss floating on the river. Its skin was as smooth as a clean blackboard. Its hair stuck to its scalp. Its hands made tight fists. A bubble peeked through its open lips. I never held a baby this young before but knew enough to hold its head. I ran as fast as I could and would have gotten lost in the woods if it weren't for the trail of blue yarn to follow back to Mrs. Natoli's cellar. I couldn't wait to hand Rosetta her baby in a nest of yarn. Finally, she'd have a baby to love as much as Harold did his science. As soon as I walked in, Mrs. Natoli took a pair of scissors and snipped the yarn off the baby. Harold came out of the bathroom and took his goggles off. He couldn't wait to weigh and measure it.

Not long after I mailed the letter, I saw my sister on our front porch and rushed over to greet her. I asked her where her baby was, even though I was sure I already knew.

"What do you think I did? Let it float down the river? I gave it up for adoption," Lisa said as her eyes swelled up red.

"I thought you didn't want it."

"It still hurts, Renata. Oakie doesn't even care. He has a new girlfriend."

"I'm still here."

My sister nodded as her face broke out in tears, and I squeezed her as tight as she did me.

"Rosetta didn't miscarry this time, did she?"

I wanted to tell her how happy we made Rosetta, but it was too soon for that. I didn't know what to say to Lisa to make her stop crying, so I sat down with her on the glider. I was thinking of all kinds of things we could do together because we knew how to share now. She folded her legs up next to her stomach and locked her arms around them tight, so I pushed extra hard with the toes of my ting tongs, swinging for both of us until she let one leg dangle.

Mama Rose

Ann Hood

Memoir (1999)

MY GRANDMOTHER MAMA ROSE stood four feet ten inches, had ten children, twenty-one grandchildren, flaming red hair until the day she died at the age of seventy-five, and liked Elvis Presley, her hometown of Naples in Italy, "As the World Turns," and going into the woods to collect wild mushrooms. What she didn't like was me. This wouldn't have been a problem except that she lived with my family and so every day became a battleground for us.

Although my parents had technically bought our house from her back in 1962 when we moved back to Rhode Island, Mama Rose never really let it go. She had, after all, lived there since she was two and, except for three years in Italy recovering from a bout of scarlet fever, she never lived anywhere else. Despite her limited time in "the old country," Mama Rose acquired a thick Italian accent sprinkled with mispronounced words, her favorite being "Jesus Crest!" As an only child, the small three-bedroom house had suited her fine when she grew up. Until the day she died she had the same bedroom she'd had as a girl. The only changes were in her roommates: first her husband, then after he died her youngest daughter, June, and after June got married and our family moved in, I became her roommate.

Already slightly afraid of her, I begged for a different bedroom. "Where do you want to go?" my mother would ask me, exasperated. My father was in the Navy and after moving us back to Rhode Island was promptly shipped off to Cuba, an assignment that did not allow families. My mother had to find room for herself, my ten-year-old brother and me, who was five. Upstairs, my great-grandmother was still in the room she'd occupied for the last sixty years. My mother moved back into her old bedroom, the same one she'd shared with her five sisters. And my brother was in the tiny former storage room that my three uncles shared as children.

"Of course," Mama Rose offered, "you could sleep there." "There" was a beat-up green couch in the kitchen that Auntie June had slept on until her father died and she moved in with Mama Rose. To me, that couch held nightmares and ghosts. My strongest memory of it was when I was three and my Uncle Brownie died. Mama Rose lay there all day screaming and pulling her hair. I eyed the green couch and mumbled, "No thanks."

The nightmares came anyway. As I tried to sleep in Mama Rose's bed, the voices of my mother, my great-grandmother, my grandmother and my visiting aunts in the kitchen right outside the door told stories into the night. The stories were about children who spontaneously burst into flames, babies born with gills, and bad women in our neighborhood who put curses on people. Before everyone went to bed, they traded stories about the ghosts of Uncle Brownie and Auntie Ann, my namesake who had died years earlier at the age of twenty-three having her wisdom teeth removed. Auntie Ann usually came to them in the form of a beautiful bird. But Uncle Brownie appeared as a full-fledged ghost, wandering around our house whistling happily, kissing foreheads, and smiling as he flew out the window.

Finally everyone would go home and Mama Rose would come to bed. Already terrified, I'd press my trembling self close to her. "Jesus Crest," she'd say, "move over. I can't believe this girl. She doesn't give me any room." Then she would shove me to my side of the bed where I stayed, wide-eyed, waiting to spontaneously combust or for Uncle Brownie to put his cold ghost lips against my head. Most nights, after I finally fell asleep, I would wake up Mama Rose and me by letting out a bloodcurdling scream. "Jesus Crest," she'd say. "You almost gave me a heart attack. What is wrong with this girl anyway?"

When left to babysit my brother, younger cousin, and me, Mama Rose fried thick steaks for them and a hamburger patty for me. "I want a steak too," I would say. "That is steak," she'd tell me. "Now shut up and eat." "This is a hamburger," I'd insist, while my brother chewed his steak, moaning with exaggerated pleasure. I would wait up for my parents, then list her infractions: there was the hamburger patty, the way she let my brother watch the movie "The Bridge Over the River Kwai" instead of my beloved "Mary Tyler Moore Show," and how she held my cousin on her lap and told me there wasn't room for two. Mama Rose listened to my complaints, shook her head, and said, "That girl has a tongue she can wipe her ass with. She tells stories."

Why Mama Rose didn't like me was always a mystery. Perhaps, as my mother suggested, I was too much like her. As a child, Mama Rose had been beautiful and smart and witty. Aging was not something she did gracefully. "She didn't like having a pretty little girl around getting attention," my mother speculated. Too, as the family matriarch after her mother died, no one questioned her decisions or pronouncements. Except me. I would, in my way, badger her. Why don't we all still live in Italy? Why did you have so many children? Why did you choose the man you married? Why do we have macaroni every Wednesday? Mama Rose stood at the kitchen stove, frying meatballs, making spaghetti sauce—gravy, she called it—and answered my questions until finally she'd scream, "Look what you made me do! I put in sugar instead of salt! Jesus Crest! Shut your mouth already. Get out of here before I go crazy, before I have a heart attack!"

But where do you go when you don't have a room of your own? I would pick up a book and read at the kitchen table. And when that book was finished, I would write my own stories about a little girl with a mean grandmother, or a little girl chased by ghosts, or a little girl who travels back in time and meets another little girl who adores her and turns out to be the modern girl's grandmother as a child.

Then my grandmother would appear in her gravy-splattered apron and shout, "Get out of my sight! You're driving me crazy!" "You're driving me crazy!" I would yell back. "I hate you!" "Good," she'd say. "Now let me watch my story." She would go into the living room and turn on "As the World Turns." As soon as it finished, she put in a call to Angelo, her bookie, and played numbers based on dreams the family had had. Two hundred forty meant a dream about a dead person. Two hundred forty-eight a dream in which a dead person talked. If the dead person told you a number, it negated 248 and Mama Rose simply played the number she'd been given. "What was your dream?" I'd ask her after she placed her bet. "You again! Talking again! Shut up and leave me alone!"

Once, crying in the living room after a particularly big battle of wills, I overheard my mother and grandmother talking. "Ann thinks I don't love her as much as I do some of the others," Mama Rose said. "And she's right." I had sensed it all along; but having the proof of my suspicions only made me feel worse, and only made me try harder to please her. Nothing worked. Not asking what Bob Hughes and the shrew Lisa from her soap opera were up to, not sitting through hours of Lawrence Welk with her, or listening to her stories about "the old country."

We settled into an uneasy relationship. Mostly, we tried to ignore each other. With my brother away at college and my great-grandmother dead, we suddenly had rooms to spare, and I was able to move into my own room upstairs. But I still had nightmares that sent me out of bed and roaming the house. It was then, late at night, that Mama Rose and I often met. She would burst out of her room as I sat at the kitchen table, all the lights blazing, sipping milk. "What's wrong with this girl?" she'd say. "You're going to give me a heart attack." She questioned me about my dreams to determine if there was a number to play or a prophecy to heed hidden within them. Most of the time she deemed them worthless. "I'm old and I'm tired," she'd tell me, disgusted that not even my dreams were worth her time. "Go to bed. Go."

I entered adolescence, made friends, had dates, worked on school plays and the school newspaper which all kept me busy and out of the house. Mama Rose complained that I spent too much time on the phone. "That girl, all she does is talk talk talk." She complained that my friends were all noisy. "I can't even hear my story on TV." When I sat outside the house in the car with a date for too long she came out to the front steps and yelled, "Get in here, you *puttana*. All the neighbors are looking!" She stayed there until, embarrassed and reluctant, I went inside. "*Puttana!*" she told me as I pushed past her. "Whore!"

I went away to college. My nightmares stopped. On a Christmas break of my freshman year, I stood at the stove with Mama Rose as she made meatballs and gravy. She told me a story about a girl who used to live up the hill who had claws like a lobster instead of hands. She told me about the woman who could tell true love by looking into a candle flame. Hoping for peace between us, I asked her how she made meatballs. She shrugged. I asked her about having babies: did it hurt?

how long did it take? was it always the same? "Jesus Crest!" she yelled. "You and that tongue. Talk talk talk. Leave me alone." Hurt, I went upstairs and read until it was time to meet my father for lunch. While we were eating at a restaurant, my grandmother finished making a gallon of gravy, sat down in her chair, and died.

Years later, she came to me in my dreams. Always somber, dressed in black and wearing the hat she wore for special occasions, she would pretend to make up to me for all the things she'd done when she was alive. An irrepressible gambler in her lifetime, in death she brought me numbers to play. Eagerly, I bought lottery tickets. 6-15-21-12. Each time, I lost by a single digit. "She's still torturing me," I complained to my cousin Gina, one of my grandmother's favorites because Gina's father had died when she was only two and a dead parent immediately elevated your status. That same cousin got numbers in her dreams and always won.

Last summer, twenty years after she died, my grandmother came to me again in a dream. This time she took my hand and led me through hospital corridors. She held on tight. "Listen," she told me. "There's a spot on your father's lung. He needs to see a doctor." She whisked me past an Indian doctor who was shaking his head outside a hospital room. "He's a fighter," the doctor told me. "But there's nothing else we can do." My grandmother gave me a number: 410. Then she did something remarkable and completely out of character. She hugged me. "Go," she said. I did. The next day I made my father go for a chest X-ray, despite his disbelief in dreams and the power of dead grandmothers. The X-ray showed a spot; a CAT scan showed a whole tumor.

The prognosis was bad. The tumor was inoperable because of its location and size. We went from doctor to doctor until the Dana Farber Clinic in Boston came up with a treatment of intensive chemotherapy and radiation. The doctor they referred us to back in Providence to administer the treatment was Indian. "I don't like this," I told my cousin. I played 410 for months and it never came out. Not even close. At Christmas, hospitalized for pneumonia, my father had another CAT scan. The tumor was completely gone. "A miracle," the doctors told us. But they cautioned us to be wary, not optimistic. "It will probably come back." The 410, I decided then, had been days. My grandmother had come to prepare me that my father only had 410 days to live. I calculated from the day of my dream and landed in October, which seemed very far away.

At the end of January my father was back in the hospital with pneumonia again. The radiation and chemo had destroyed his immune system; the pneumonia was destroying his already diminished lungs. The doctors did not think he would live forty-eight hours. "He will," I said, confident in my grandmother's prophecy. He lived. Six weeks later another pneumonia struck and the doctors again were grim. "He'll make it," I said. The promise of those 410 days, though dwindling, gave me the courage to get through each new catastrophe. Twice in the middle of the night the hospital called me to his bedside. "It's critical," they said. "Hurry." As I sped down the highway, the strength of Mama Rose's hug brought me a calm that led me to the hospital and down the long corridor to his room, where each time I found him pulling through the emergency.

Then, on Easter Sunday, after almost three months in the hospital, he got yet another pneumonia. The doctor's prognosis was the worst yet: even if he survived this one, he told us, he would get another and die in a few days or a few weeks. The 410 days were beginning to be yet another cruel trick by my grandmother. The next day, sitting by my father's hospital bed, I looked at the date on the big wall calendar. 4/1 it said. Beside me, my father struggled to breathe through tubes pumping oxygen into his nose and a mask over his mouth and nose. The 410, I realized with dread, was a date. 4/10.

On April 10, my father's oncologist—the man from India—took us into the hall outside my father's room. "He's a fighter," he told us, and I knew what his next words would be. "But there's nothing else we can do." That night my father slipped into a coma from which he did not recover.

My father's original prognosis was grim. But because of my dream, he got treatment which gave us all more months together, and Mama Rose and I finally made our peace.

Cairns

Dennis Barone

Memoir (2003)

Tides wash all prints away except the fragments stones claim. It is the incomplete-ness of things that still hurts; that still haunts. Tears held back may break our bones, but names will never hurt us. From the corners of our eyes, stones. Stones in every beating vein. Hearts turned to stone and inscribed with a name. Small stones placed on other, larger markers. It is a way to remember.

The last time I saw Uncle Louis he sat quietly by a sunny window in the living room of my in-laws' apartment. My mother- and father-in-law had arranged a luncheon in Uncle Louis's honor, but almost no one spoke to him. He was in his mid-nineties and it was difficult to understand him. We made sure that he was comfortable, though, that he had everything he wanted, and then we turned to our conversations that took place elsewhere in the small and crowded room. On that occasion, as on several others, I did not ask him about his lifelong friend, Pietro di Donato.

When I had first met my wife's Great-Uncle Louis Ducoff my lack of knowl-edge kept me from asking about *Christ in Concrete*, the famous novel by his friend in which Louis Ducoff appears as the character "Louis Molov." My wife and I were both graduate students at the University of Pennsylvania, and Louis took a great interest in our work and in our lives. Just as Louis had been an inspiration to Pietro di Donato decades before, so, too, he encouraged our intellectual endeavors.

By the time of that afternoon luncheon I had finally read *Christ in Concrete*, but even then I didn't ask Louis anything about the book or its author. I busied myself in amiable conversation with Rabbi Bernard Ducoff. Every so often I would look over at Louis and think to myself that I should ask, I should ask some-thing. Then I'd check myself and consider how serene he looked with so many nephews and nieces and his son and daughter-in-law and grandnephews and grandnieces gathered about him, the sun catching the sandy strands of hair that fell toward his still handsome face.

A few months after that luncheon word came one evening that Louis had died. I think both my wife and I felt that we had lost a true soul mate as well as a great-uncle. As it turned out, the day of his funeral I had another commitment. Long before, I had been scheduled to read that day for the Oasis writers' group in Worcester, Massachusetts. I felt torn. I had missed my beloved Great-Aunt Mary's funeral—among other family events over the years—and sometimes I think that, yes, I could be a better son, brother, cousin, nephew, husband. I also felt a sense of obligation to Eve Rifkah and the reading that she had organized in

Worcester. I rationalized that Louis loved languages and literature. (He could speak a half-dozen and during his last years spoke Spanish more often than he spoke English.) He'd want me to give the reading. And so from Connecticut I went north to Massachusetts and Debbie, my wife, went south to New Jersey.

Debbie had become a correspondent of Hedley's, Louis's daughter-in-law, Michael's wife, and in the months after the funeral Hedley and Michael e-mailed Debbie photographs and genealogical information.

Meanwhile after a sabbatical semester during the fall of 2001, I returned to teaching at Saint Joseph College and offered a new course entitled "New York City and Italian American Narrative, 1924–2000." One of the books for the course was Pietro di Donato's *Christ in Concrete*.

In the fourth section of the third chapter of the novel Louis Molov tells the protagonist, Paul (an autobiographically based character), about his brother Leov whom the Czar's soldiers shot. Leov, Louis says, "was the most brilliant student in Minsk Gubernia. He was a poet. He wore his hair long, and he danced like the Russian winds. He loved everyone and was loved. He was quick and sympathetic. . . . He was a genius." Louis asks Paul if he would like to see a photograph of his brother Leov. Pietro di Donato described the picture as follows:

"Leov sat on a chair that was sideways. His left arm rested over the back of the chair and he held his left hand with his right. He looked right out from the picture. It was Leov at Paul's age. He had large dark eyes and rich dark hair. He was all Louis said."

Just by absolute sheer chance, during the week that my class read and discussed *Christ in Concrete* Debbie and I received an e-mail message from Michael. He had scanned some more family photographs for us, ones that Louis had always kept with him—from Union City, New Jersey, to Mexico City to Washington, D.C., to retirement in Florida to his final years back in New Jersey. I clicked on these images. I don't remember whether it was the second or the third image, but the moment I saw it I knew immediately who it was this treasured image revealed—"his left arm rested over the back of the chair and. . . ." For a moment I felt like I couldn't breathe. Never before in any of my study in archives or libraries did I feel so immediately an almost literal wind from the past blowing through time to the present. It was the brother killed by the Czar's soldiers, the brother left behind, the brother whose body had never been found, the brother described in *Christ in Concrete*. It was that picture. There on the computer screen was the photograph.

I made the best print of the image I could and brought it to my class. Now my plan was to maintain a professional objectivity; perhaps, not even to mention the fact that the model for the important character Louis Molov was my wife's late Great-Uncle Louis Ducoff. With the image in hand, however, I had to tell the class about Louis, about his brother Izzy, my wife's grandfather, who along with brother Max ran the stationery store mentioned by Pietro di Donato. I showed the class this amazing and startling photograph.

Louis Ducoff, the person on whom Pietro di Donato based a minor character in his novel, *Christ in Concrete*.

Leov's name was actually Moisha. The family left Starobin, Belorussia, soon after Louis's mother saw a soldier wearing clothes and a ring that belonged to Moisha. She confronted the soldier and he tried to make up some story, but she knew then and there that her son had been murdered and robbed and that her family had to leave the country. And so they traveled many, many miles hidden in a hay cart, and then they walked across the frozen, snow-covered river that formed the boundary with Poland. They took the train from that country to Paris and then continued on to Le Havre and from Le Havre sailed to New York. They stayed four or five days on Ellis Island and then they entered the great metropolis. The photograph, the description must prove that fiction can be fact, that this family legend was hard-lived reality. In America, Izzy had a son named Morris and Morris had a daughter named Deborah and she is my wife, my love.

In *Christ in Concrete*, Louis Molov tells Paul, a very youthful bricklayer who has all but given up on his schooling, "[. . .] the job is not freedom. Your wonderful brain is your freedom. . . ." I am sure that is what Louis Ducoff told Pietro di Donato on more than one occasion. I am sure because that is, in a sense, what he said to us: "Debbie, Dennis, your wonderful brains are your freedom."

Do tides wash all prints away except the fragments stones claim? The wind is not a veil but a bough that bursts forth, sudden, unaware: a bough in bloom and brilliant light. The wind blows fragrant blossoms far beyond fields of stone, far beyond our pain. The wind blows: something tangible, something real, it tousles our hair; and may it lighten our hearts.

I had two addresses of former residences of my grandfather and since I had planned to visit my father in Fort Lee, New Jersey, that day, I thought the trip down from West Hartford, Connecticut, would be the perfect time to stop in Stamford, Connecticut, and check these addresses out. The first address was on Atlantic Street, a busy main thoroughfare in the city. Where my grandfather's house should have been there stood the headquarters of Charles Schwab and Company.

The second address was just a short distance south: Taylor Street. But the address I wanted must have been plowed under and paved over long ago for the construction of Interstate 95.

I had one other place in Stamford to check out, the cemetery where my great-grandparents are buried. I had no trouble finding it—just southeast of the other locations I had sought out that day. I pulled in the gate, parked the car, and walked to the office. Inside an attractive woman who looked a bit like Morticia Addams asked if she could be of any assistance. I told her I came to see my great-grandparents' grave. I noticed that she had several incense candles lit, and I wondered if there might be a corpse or two rotting off to one side. I heard somber organ music and noticed a small boom box above her desk. She was very serious about her work.

I told her the date of my great-grandfather's death, and I told her his name. She took out an old ledger from beneath the desk and looked through it studiously, but without finding what should have been listed there.

"What year did he die?" she asked me.

"1955, I think." I repeated what I had already told her, but with less certainty this time.

She turned then to her computer. The cheap lavender incense candles, the black plastic boom box, the dusty old ledger, the dull light of the monitor screen, the intensity of this pale woman, it was all too weird for me and I bit my lower lip and tried so hard not to laugh.

I wanted to see this gravestone, this funerary monument, because I had seen a photocopy of a photograph of it and it is a large stone with the family name and crest engraved on it. On top of this stone, however, there is another stone in the shape of an open book. The photocopy of the photograph doesn't reveal what message the open book contains, what message it has to pass on to generations and so I thought this personal visit not only necessary, but also essential. What lesson does the past have for the present? What wise words did my great-grandfather choose to leave and to share *in perpetuity*?

The diligent cemetery worker found the location in her computer. Everything is on computer now, even death. What is the possibility for virtual cemeteries, I wondered? She wrote the location on a small slip of paper that she placed in my hand; then she said "L41" and I said, "Thank you."

I had no trouble finding my way about the cemetery. I, too, have some experience in their operation and maintenance. I used to work in one during high school and college, cutting the grass, keeping it neat and presentable. I had no trouble finding section L. (It was right after section K and right before section M.) I had no trouble finding the stone, the monument. It is a large stone. I could see it from far away. As I approached I could see the large block letters and the open book on top of the base stone. I paused and breathed deeply for a moment. What is the message, I wondered? What is the truth? I anticipated so much, so much discovery, revelation, and prophecy.

I walked on, closer and closer to my enlightenment. There sat the open book upon the upright slab and engraved inside the book—nothing. It is blank, an empty page. So that is what the past has to tell the present: nothing? So that is the great truth passed on to subsequent generations by my great-grandfather: there is no great truth? I wondered as I stood there still and astonished and befuddled gazing upon the empty stone. Or is it that the book is blank precisely because we must inscribe it with the story that is our own lives? We must do it for ourselves and not rely upon an inheritance of any kind? And this challenge, I decided, this challenge to write my own page is the greatest gift any ancestor could bequeath to future progeny.

And so this is my story. It begins in Connecticut (where I now live) even though it began in New Jersey (where I was born) and it ends in some yet undisclosed location. And because it began in New Jersey there is some persistent but half-hearted identification with the Italian-American experience. Persistent because my mother's parents were Norwegian, but they lived far away in California while my father's parents were born in Italy and lived nearby in Brooklyn; half-hearted because my father's father and his grandfather were not working-class immigrants. They were extremely well-read professionals. In one letter to my father, written when he was about to marry my mother, my grandfather says that his wife's parents thought that they were marrying their daughter to a wealthy doctor and that he had to ruin their illusion that all doctors are wealthy. I think he worried that my mother's parents might have been similarly impressed that they were sending their daughter off with a rich doctor's son and not just a smooth-dancing, fine-looking soldier. I think my grandfather wanted to be sure that there were no illusions.

But how could there be illusions when the war ended? There they were in San Francisco, a family of three now, confronting post-war reality in a small apartment on Turk Street. Ten years later I came into this world at Holy Name Hospital, Teaneck, New Jersey—the fourth and final child in this family.

And when I arrived that day in Fort Lee, New Jersey, for my visit with my father I told him of my adventure that day, about corporate headquarters and interstate highways. When I told him about visiting his grandparents', my great-grandparents', grave in Stamford he said, "What grave in Stamford? They're all buried in Brooklyn."

What's it all for? Here I am standing around freezing in this over–air-conditioned room, a black band on my arm while you lie now so still, slumber even, hardly breathing. I, too, saw a light that came and that's now receding into some dark station, some zone far beyond an old barn. What's it for? Here I am twiddling my thumbs, freezing. "Christ Died for Our Sins": white letters fading against a red wall; a structure leans each ephemeral year closer to the hay-brown lawn while you lie now so still, slumber even hardly breathing.

Into the computer I typed a ship's name. I clicked on the first site listed and then again I typed in the ship's name, and there it was. I read all about it, but wait—this couldn't be it. They came in 1899—my grandfather was only six or seven at this time—and this ship wasn't built until 1903. How could they have come to America on a ship that hadn't been built? The vagaries of history, I thought. The old adage "facts don't lie" is itself a lie.

Addition and subtraction, I thought, check your work. Perhaps there are other sites that list and describe these ships. So I returned to where I had begun and this time I clicked on the second site listed. Again, I typed in the name and there it was: not only the ship I sought, but also the answer to my conundrum. There had been in those years two ships with the same name but registered in two different countries, one built in 1903, yes, but the other built a decade before and so the vagary had easily been turned into a certainty.

But then again, I had always been told that they went from Italy to England and then to the United States, not directly from Naples to New York. This ship, however, made no stops in London or anywhere in Great Britain. I was not so certain, as it turned out, about anything at all.

Who was it that painted such oversized, bold lettering, visible from every tidy corner of this suburbanized farm? "Christ Died for Our Sins." What's it all for anyway? I stand around dumb, freezing. All these houses, boxes really, built to hide all this dying. A nameless soul painted those words, a borrowed charm maybe. And now you lie so still, slumber even: breathing? There are no horses, no fields, and no flowers, not anymore. These old red structures are, Usherlike, pointless, incessantly tossed into the tarn. What's it all for? Here I am standing around freezing while you lie now so still, slumber even, hardly breathing.

When I was young, snow for me differed from what it meant for my parents. For them it was a nuisance blocking the road to work. For me it was absolute beauty. But I yielded to the wisdom of their years or to the logic of their threats and I shoveled the snow. Mind you, I had no interest in sleigh-riding anyway, for I knew it was too soft. Furthermore, this freshly fallen powder was not the stuff of snowballs. This snow would produce meager puffballs that disintegrated in even the softest and slowest of throws. For our warlike projectiles we preferred to mix in a little of the pliable slush that came the day after a snowfall. By then the shoveling was long completed; the shoveling that broke the beauty of that wonderful world of puff.

Still, we would be the first ones to walk across and impact our footprints on a field of this white crystal stuff. As soon as we looked back at what we had done, we'd feel as if we had broken the heart and soul of the field. Perhaps, we thought, even when the first warmth of spring warmed the soil beneath, the shapes of our heels would still infringe upon it and what's worse we believed that such an infringement might hinder a seedling's reaching for the sun's bright light. We would return home and ask, "Must all things die?"

In the fireplace on Christmas morning we would put all the paper, boxes, and bows from all the gifts. On our television a Yule log would burn while invisible minstrels sang. Rarely would snow be falling as the fire crackled, the real one, in our fireplace. We learned after repeatedly wishing for white Christmas mornings that things rarely coincided quite as you'd like them.

Cleaning the fireplace was my job and I did not enjoy it. My nostrils filled with soot as I swept and pushed the ashes and dust and unburned wood and singed aluminum-coated wrapping paper down the dark hole, down to nowhere, to oblivion. Even on the coldest of windy days, I'd open the glass patio door to circulate and disperse the cloud of dirt and dust I kicked up with shovel and broom.

In one of the movies I am standing in a gray snowsuit on top of a snow fort. No one else is in the frame. I'm smiling, preparing to throw a snowball at the camera.

Once I almost drowned in snow. The snow was twice my height and powder, powder. I fell in it and swam in it. For a moment I felt like I couldn't breathe. It was in my lungs or so I thought. I swear, I almost drowned in the snow, but I didn't.

A cold slate-colored snow at Easter is more truthful than any make-believe TV snow at Christmas.

SNOW ON THE GROUND. *I'm holding flowers; kneeling by one carver's best marker. Shall I shovel now?*

MY MOM TOLD ME to go to church, but I came over here. I thought you'd be up, but you weren't. I threw some acorns at your window. The house looked dead.

I thought you'd be up by 7:30. I'll stop back, but if I don't, I'll try to get to the cemetery by twelve.

I WON'T BE ABLE TO MAKE IT. I have too much studying to do. Let Kevin take care of the north, south, and center. I like the way he cuts around the graves. You can cut the backfield with Danny's tractor. I was using it to move some dirt and I took off the blades, so you'll have to put them back on.

Back the tractor up, so you're right up to them. Then lower the hydraulic lifts all the way. Connect the big yellow thing. I forget what it's called. It turns the blades. Take the center hydraulic and connect it to the top yellow piece. That's a bitch. You'll have to lower it up and down, and so make sure the engine is on and the blade control is off. It's hard to tighten the centerpiece, but don't worry about it, just get it secure. Take the two-side hydraulics and connect them. They're easy, but make sure they're tight. After that, you're set, but it's not so easy.

Have fun and don't stop every time the Dead are on the radio.

With everyone crowded in space, we became also crowded by time. Star, Song of Solomon, you are limestone in New Jersey. Forgive me: my bike is almost flat. Aloha, Dairy Queen and Flamingo Golf. Many flowers bloomed and died. It almost became an obsession.

Card Palace

Christine Palamidessi Moore

Fiction (2006)

DENISE, A PETITE, dark-eyed woman with the gift of gab, inherited the Card Palace from her mother's brother Frank, who, like everyone else in the family, succeeded in keeping secrets. After reaching a certain age, the family stopped asking Frank if he was dating. In twenty-seven years, he had never answered yes. Frank was gay, and everyone held their breaths, hoping that he didn't like the boys who frequented his shop. Frank, a good man, was interested in baseball cards. He showed up at Easter with sweet cakes and wore Bermuda shorts to picnics.

He died from AIDS—though no one mentioned that detail at the funeral. After Mass, the family gathered at Mt. Auburn Cemetery and agreed the reason Frank was no longer with them was because his lungs finally had given out from all the smoking he did. Denise bowed her head—so did her teenage daughter—while attendants slid Uncle Frank's slate-gray casket into the ground.

The Nucci family, a confident group, never announced that they were perfect but believed they were. Denise figured their secret-keeping was a trait left over from the generations who believed in the evil eye, *bella figura*, and the duty of hiding possessions to protect neighbors from committing the sin of covetousness.

After the burial, the family drove their sedans to an aunt's house that smelled slightly of mothballs. Because Denise's mother was a widow, Frank left her and Denise the Card Palace and the dark house behind the shop with its fifteen treacherous concrete steps. Her mother politely renounced the gift. "Can you imagine in the winter? With my hip?" It was the first time she admitted to having arthritis. "Right against the street, too. No yard. No trees to filter out the traffic."

Lucky for her—and everyone, she said—a day after they buried Frank a pleasant man from Cambridge telephoned. "He read Uncle Frank's obituary, was sorry he passed, and offered me more for the shop than you could ever imagine that place is worth." She didn't reveal the exact numbers. "I'll deposit the proceeds in a high-interest CD until Jocelyn goes to college, or wants a big wedding," she said to Denise.

"Did the man say where he read Uncle Frank's obituary?" No one in the family had placed an announcement. "Maybe he just wants the inventory," Denise said. "Maybe I'll take the shop."

"No. Don't. It's junk, I tell you. Toys." Her mother swept her hand through the air. "My brother Frank never grew up. Never took responsibility. Never married."

Nonetheless, Frank had earned more money in the Card Palace than Denise took home by cutting hair in Newton Center. If she played her cards right—ha, ha—she could probably double or even triple the price the man in Cambridge offered her mother and send both herself and her daughter Jocelyn to college. The sacrifice would be living in Medford for two years.

"Are you kidding? Medford? Me? Girls tattoo their chests in Medford. I won't go." Jocelyn sat at the foot of her bed. "I can't leave my friends. How could you do this to me? I hate you."

"Grandma says you can stay here on the weekends. It'll be good. I'll be busy on Saturdays and wouldn't make lunch anyway," Denise said.

"You never make lunch! You don't know how to use a microwave. I even make your coffee." Jocelyn crossed her arms.

Denise didn't deny the accusations. "You're right." She smiled at her cute daughter. "You can see your Newton friends on weekends. Study during the week. I promise I'll learn to cook spaghetti—or grill cheese—and cook you dinner. Okay?"

"Why did I have to be your daughter?" she shouted. "Why couldn't I be like Sarah and Kristin and have normal parents and live in a normal house?"

"Everyone loves you. Stop whining." Denise put her arm around her daughter's slim waist. "We'll be okay, baby." She spoke softly. "You and me." Denise already appreciated the time she would have with Jocelyn when they moved to Medford. She would help her with homework in the evenings and savor the last few years of her daughter's childhood. She put her head on Jocelyn's bony shoulder.

"Mom, is there, like, even a subway stop in Medford?" Jocelyn asked.

"You can have a new bedroom set." Denise negotiated.

"I don't want a new bedroom set."

"A TV in your room?"

"Will you teach me to drive?" Jocelyn trumped the deal.

THE NUCCI CLAN had done quite well. Three of Denise's cousins practiced law; two were doctors. Her father's brother worked as a politician, and he invited them to black-tie dinners and ground-breaking ceremonies in and around Boston. Denise had planned on making something important of herself, too. At Tufts, she had studied archeology and completed the difficult courses—physics, biology, chemistry—and spent two summers in Maine, sifting through soil for remnants of ice-age bones. Distracted by her father's death and the dream of having a perfect family, she married after her sophomore year. A year later, her husband left, saying he didn't want to be married anymore. "Nothing personal," he said as he closed the door.

Denise sold their small house in Natick, moved back to Newton with her mother, and, while she was pregnant, studied hair styling in Waltham.

Beginning the day she was born, Jocelyn fit in. She flowed along in the family footsteps. She was quiet and did most everything right the first time, got A's, played first-string soccer, dressed neatly, and never wore tight jeans or showed her abdomen when that style became the fashion. Her thick, wavy hair resembled her mother's, and her blue eyes, wide face, and taut physical presence mirrored her absent father's edgy handsomeness.

No Nucci acknowledged that Denise's mother actually raised Jocelyn, but she did. After Denise completed her internship, she got a job cutting hair in Newton. She came home from the salon at six, ate the dinner her mother prepared, and either played with her daughter for an hour, plucked her eyebrows, gabbed on the phone, or went to the gym. At ground-breakings and holidays, Jocelyn and Denise cut a lower-tier *bella figura* next to the lawyers, doctors, and cousins in graduate school. Uncle Frank, however, favored Denise's company. In his well-pressed Burberry shirts and natty slacks, he sat next to Denise and chatted about food and his Card Palace. He was careful not to twirl his wrist. Right after a laugh, he coughed and waited a short moment before telling his Nice Niece Denise that his business was like entertainment and groceries. "The public never stops wanting what I have."

DENISE AND JOCELYN moved into Uncle Frank's half-brick, half-aluminum house, which perched like a pregnant bird on top of a street-level storefront, during the hottest week of August. As a housewarming gift, her mother bought Denise a LoJack. "You'll need it. Look, you have to park on the street." Denise owned a new RAV5, which she'd never allow Jocelyn to drive.

"You'll be hot here," her mother said. The house didn't have air conditioning, and a sticky scum from all those cigarettes that killed Uncle Frank coated the blades of his electric fans. Denise scraped the same brown gunk from the long leaves of a mother-in-law plant Uncle Frank had kept in the kitchen.

Embarrassed by her brother's slovenliness and perhaps because she did have a kind heart, Denise's mother hired cleaners and four men to paint every wall, ceiling, window sash, and baseboard a creamy white. The paint, the same color as Denise's car, covered up everything, thickly and pristinely.

Jocelyn claimed the entire third floor, a large, unfinished, dry-smelling room with its own bathroom. It had a claw-foot tub, and she bought thick red towels to hang over the faded brass racks hammered on the wall near the pedestal sink. Denise settled on the second floor bedroom with a small office. She redid the bathroom in crema delicata, covering the marble floor, counter, and walls. She spent quite a bit of money on the project and decided that would be where she would relax, stretch out, and pour her troubles down the drain. The kitchen, old-fashioned for sure, with a groaning refrigerator, wobbly linoleum, and a stove she had to light with a match, would suffice.

Uncle Frank might not have paid attention to where he hung his hat at night, but the Card Palace was a different story. The filing system was as impeccable as the glass showcase that lined the entire front room's east wall. Fanned next to baseball cards were balls, players' gloves, miniature ballparks, World Series tickets, and photographs. The showcase was temperature-controlled, lighted, and locked. Outside, the carefully painted cornice on the front of the store read "Card Palace 'dedicated to the innocence of youth.'"

The first day Denise rolled up the steel doors to do business, a dozen men, not boys, rushed in. They wanted Pedro Martinez cards. Denise knew nothing about baseball or baseball players—other than that the Red Sox played at Fenway Park and were forever disappointing fans at the end of the season. Martinez, the men said, was proving to be the best pitcher in baseball.

Five days later there was a run on cards for a third-base player. "His name spelled backwards is Ramon," a grown man told her as he forked over $1.50 for two Nomar Garciaparra cards and then actually spent another $139.00 on a sealed box containing a league-authenticated and signed baseball.

"He didn't know whose name was on the ball until he unsealed the box. Imagine gambling that much on a trinket," Denise confided to her daughter that night.

Jocelyn rolled over on her bed and asked her mother to leave her alone and to shut the door on the way out. "I'm tired. The light in the hall bothers me."

During the first month at the Card Palace, the telephone rang constantly. Denise received an offer a day from men wanting to come in and help her out for an hour or two, to catalog Frank's collection, to take anything she didn't want off her hands, and even to buy the Card Palace. She stupidly sold a baseball signed by Manny Ramirez for $100. The man who bought it convinced her the player was a loser. "He strikes out."

Every afternoon at two, the Medford police parked outside the Card Palace and stepped inside to check on Denise. Since Ted Williams had died that July, they suggested she auction Uncle Frank's Ted Williams collection. "You can make close to a million."

"What?" Denise dropped her jaw. The police showed her the three game-used and signed bats in Uncle Frank's showcase. "There's more here somewhere," the tall cop said. "That ball. Those cards over there."

"Ted Williams?" Denise asked.

"Yea. The family's pretty weird. The son dry-freezed his daddy's body." The Medford policeman shook his head. "Don't know if that makes what you have here worth more, or less. Never can tell what repulses the public. I mean, look at Manny. One day he's golden, the next day he doesn't sing the National Anthem loud enough and Boston puts him on their shitlist. Read the *Herald*."

Denise locked the shop, pulled down the steel door guard, and spent the night in her Card Palace, inspecting the showcase, opening the back room drawers, sifting through boxes for Ted Williams's paraphernalia. At seven-thirty, Jocelyn trudged down the rear hatch and helped Denise sort a few boxes. Hungry, she asked for money and walked down to the square to fetch a cheese pizza for the both of them. Denise's enthusiasm to discover what treasure they might have had rolled right off Jocelyn. Nothing made her smile, and Denise called her daughter's laconic attitude teenage angst, since she didn't want to label it depression.

"I hate this." Jocelyn kicked a box. "All of this baseball stuff." Denise pulled ten more boxes from a high shelf. "I miss Newton so much. My friends. All of them."

Denise interrupted her daughter. "Have a positive outlook. We could be millionaires. Understand? Uncle Frank's stuff is worth major bucks." She pleaded. "I need time to figure it out."

"Yeah. Sure." Jocelyn finished the pizza crusts and the slice Denise didn't eat. Her face looked flushed and puffy.

Over the next months, until Christmas, Denise inventoried and educated herself. Besides the complete 1960's Topps, Upperdeck, and Don Russ collections that Uncle Frank had stashed in the back, she found a dozen Hank Aaron cards, twenty Roberto Clemente cards from 1961, three sets of 1967 World Series tickets, and directions to a safety deposit box in a Medford bank. In the box, Uncle Frank had stashed two tobacco cards and a flip-top portfolio containing Ty Cobb, Walter Johnson, Babe Ruth, and a STILL NEEDED note for Christy Mathewson.

The 1909 Honus Wagner cards, Denise later learned, held particular value. Supposedly, Wagner didn't want his young fans to buy cigarettes and ordered his cards removed from the tobacco packages. Denise clucked and shook her head when she read this information. Protect the innocent? Honus Wagner must have been a great guy. Why wasn't there a role model like him for kids today? Her daughter had started to smoke, and she wasn't hiding her habit.

"Leave me alone. I don't want to gain more weight." Jocelyn struck a match to her Marlboro. Since August, she had been hanging out on the living room sofa, eating junk, and watching TV. Still, she wasn't fat—just chubby. Staying slim, however, wasn't a good enough reason, Denise argued, to blow smoke ten to twelve hours a day. Plus Jocelyn was looking sloppy—baggy clothes, tousled hair.

"Is this how the kids in Medford dress?" Denise spoke to her daughter in a solicitous, high-pitched voice, the voice she hated to hear herself use.

"Yeah, take me back to Newton and I'll be normal again." Jocelyn doused her cigarette in a glass ashtray.

"I hope you're not thinking of piercing your nose." Denise offered her daughter a slice of apple.

At bedtime, Denise followed Jocelyn upstairs to kiss her goodnight. She looked so cute in her floppy red flannel pajamas. Denise sat on the bed next to her.

"Don't worry." Jocelyn shrugged. "If I pierce my body, I'll tell you first." In the darkened room, she seemed happy to have her mother nearby and reached out for Denise's hand.

Denise rubbed Jocelyn's shoulder. "What's happening, honey? Tell me, baby, are your grades okay?"

"Of course." Denise admired her daughter for sticking it out, for not nagging her every single day, for handling her homework on her own so that she could get a grip on the card business.

"Do you have new friends?" She stroked her daughter's thick hair. Silence. She waited until a sudden dump of guilt crashed over her. Denise was so involved with the cards, she didn't know if her daughter had a new boyfriend, or understood calculus, or if she was still studying French. "Do you want to tell me anything?"

Jocelyn stared softly at her mother, as if Denise ought to know what she was thinking. Denise could see her daughter's eyes reach out to her as they had reached out in the hospital the day she was born. Remembering that day made Denise smile. They were going to have a wonderful life together, saturate each other, have fun together, love each other. Denise hugged Jocelyn and inhaled her musky, milky scent. "Soccer? You playing soccer? You're really good."

"Yeah. I guess I could check that out." Jocelyn patted her mother's hand before pushing her away. She sat up to light a cigarette. "Don't worry about me, Mom."

Denise followed the blue smoke shooting out of her daughter's delicate nostrils and imagined the damage it was doing to her lungs, the lungs she used to protect like a fierce lioness. "I don't think it's safe to smoke in bed, do you?" she asked.

"Would you rather I hang out in the bathtub?" Jocelyn snapped, which was an insult because that was where Denise spent most of her at-home time.

Denise sidestepped an argument. "Hey, I registered to take a computer class on Thursday nights. Want to come with me? We could do it together."

"Thursdays? Really? Every Thursday?" She shook her head. "I don't think so."

ON CHRISTMAS DAY, the entire Nucci family gathered at the Top of the Hub for an early afternoon dinner. Jocelyn agreed not to smoke, but she wouldn't wear a dress.

"You have such great legs." Denise encouraged her to show them off.

"No." Jocelyn tapped out.

"How about a different top—maybe a blouse instead of a sweatshirt?" Denise continued.

"I said no."

Denise stopped, realizing she might as well be talking to a two-year old. How, she wondered, had she made it through Jocelyn's toddler years? And kindergarten? Without her mother's help in elementary and middle school, it would have been impossible for Denise to do what she had had to do. But maybe, she thought—and didn't like the thought—if she had been more involved with Jocelyn then, she would be having an easier time now.

At the Christmas dinner Jocelyn slipped into a seat on the far-corner side of the table and didn't socialize. The tablecloth was long and no one could closely scrutinize her and her clothing. Denise talked even more than usual to cover up Jocelyn's being a wart. She was sure, however, that beneath their kind eyes, the family concluded that Denise and Jocelyn had made a mistake moving to Medford, that Denise had ruined her life by having had a child so young, and that they hoped they wouldn't have to bail her out of any unsavory dealings. It was a shame that her husband left her. There was something wrong with her. And her daughter. Just look at them.

After dessert—cherry torte—Denise stood to make an announcement. Boston spread out, like a miniature town, twenty-three stories below the huge windows. Snow scattered about. The room glowed with hundreds of tiny red lights. Denise tapped the rim of her wineglass. She wanted nothing more than for her family to be proud of her and to give them back something she had earned through inheriting Uncle Frank's Card Palace.

She cleared her voice. "There are three Goodwill things I want to share. First, I made a fifty-five-year loan of a bat Ted Williams used in 1942, the first year he won the Triple Crown. It'll stay on display at the Ted Williams Museum in Florida. Second, the Williams family has invited our family—all twenty-three of us—to a private Jimmy Fund banquet next March in Boston. We'll mingle with Red Sox and owners—I don't know who exactly." She bit her thumbnail. Denise didn't tell them that after fifty-five years the Williams Foundation would sell the bat and set up a special fund to support children who needed help buying sports gear—bats, balls, ice skates, tennis rackets. The Nucci family never considered sports as important as math and music and making money. They did like museums.

"I expect they'll ask us to make donations. Some of us might already have pledged money to that cause. However," she smiled. This was her final coup. "I just want you to know that this time, this year, I'll be taking care of it. All of it." Denise's voice shook. She had taken a risk, a bold one. Her uncle, who was readying himself and his troops to run for State Representative, sat nearby. He looked up at her with both suspicion and awe. She was nudging him out of his customary spot and doing it well. He was the first to applaud, interrupting an awkward silence.

Denise's chest filled with a power she'd never known. She felt self-expressed, independent, adult. It didn't matter that her daughter slouched at the corner of the table and hid her lovely face behind knotty hair. It didn't matter that they were living in downtown Medford. It didn't matter that Denise Nucci hadn't finished college, or that she didn't have a nobler job than buying and selling baseball cards.

At the March Jimmy Fund banquet, Roger Daubach, Cliff Floyd, and Doug Mirabelli signed three baseballs each for Denise, which they promised to match with double whatever she sold them for and donate it to the fund. Daubach, the first baseman, posed for pictures with Denise and croodled up to her. Later he asked if she'd like to go listen to some country-western with him.

Everything was too good. Denise made a poster of her and Daubach and put it in the Card Palace window with the signed baseballs. Medford kids were finally stopping by after school to buy grab bags filled with cards, gum, and candy. The Smithsonian bought her Cy Young card for a hefty price. The police, mailman, pizza delivery girl, local shop owners, Medford City Council, downtown dentists, and the inner circle of the Boston baseball world were her friends. The men who collected cards in their youth by playing a card-tossing game were now tossing their money to her. Gambling. Not at all like entertainment and groceries.

In April, Daubach invited Denise and her daughter to the Red Sox opening game. "Dugout seats," he said. "And if it rains, there's a reserved observation room for players' family."

"I won't go!" Jocelyn shouted. "You can't make me go." She slammed her bedroom door.

Denise pressed her cheek against the door. "Honey, sweetie, baby, what's wrong?" she cooed, attempting to soften both of their anger and confusion. "Can we talk?"

"Everything's wrong. Leave me alone!" Jocelyn said.

Denise imagined her daughter with her head buried in her pillow, the frustration she must feel, her lack of friends, and the loss of her childhood home. "Please, sweetie, let me in. Maybe you don't want to, but I have to talk."

"It's too late. Don't you get it? I hate you."

Teenage girls could be so cruel. "But I love you." Denise whispered into the crack of Jocelyn's door. "I love you so much."

Most recently, Jocelyn hid herself inside man-sized sweatshirts. The hems of her frayed jeans dragged on the sidewalk. She wore old sneakers with holes, even into the snow. "I'm sorry if it's my fault that you're unhappy." Denise was crying, too. "Maybe I made mistakes." She pressed her cheek flatter against Jocelyn's door. "I want you to be happy. I don't know what to do. Will you open the door? I'm sorry."

"No. Leave me alone."

"We have enough money, sweetie, to move back to Newton, if you want," she whispered. "We don't have to live here anymore." It was her final offering. Denise really didn't want to go backwards—to be her mother's daughter again, to live where she used to live. "If you don't want to live with grandma, we can buy our own house," Denise said. "I'll do anything and everything for you."

"It's too late," Jocelyn screamed.

The next afternoon, when Jocelyn returned home from school, Denise sat in the living room, a room they rarely used anymore, since in the evenings they each retreated to their bedrooms.

"Hey. Hi." Denise motioned her daughter to sit beside her on the overstuffed ivory sofa. "Come look." She handed Jocelyn a red remote control, which operated a new, flat-screen TV. "Let's watch something together." She wanted to put her arm over Jocelyn's shoulder, but didn't. She would wait for Jocelyn to make the first move. "We can order Chinese later. What do you think?"

Jocelyn managed not to hide her excitement. "Wow! I like it."

"We can sit downstairs together more often now."

"I guess." Jocelyn flipped to the MTV station.

"I bought a couple of games, too. But I don't want you to neglect your homework, okay?" Jocelyn, entranced by the large images, didn't answer. "Okay?" Denise asked a second time.

For a handful of nights, mother and daughter did sit on the ivory sofa, as if it were a boat they each wanted to steer in the same direction. The big TV, both a buffer and a gate, drew them towards each other carefully, slowly, and with needed interruptions, but they never stayed touching, as if a full-fledged hug might topple them over. Jocelyn stayed on her side of the sofa, munching snacks and laughing a lot. Denise didn't complain about her daughter eating too much and gaining more weight. She brushed her own thick hair and tied it on top of her head and hoped her daughter would ask her to do the same to hers. They wore cozy chenille robes even though the weather was warming up. Stubborn green grass poked through the cracks in the concrete steps leading up to their house. Sometimes they watched baseball. Jocelyn resented the game, because of the cards. She said the cards had taken her mother away.

When Jocelyn agreed to watch, Denise cooked her a hot dog in the microwave, put it in a bun with lots of ketchup, and let her sip half a cup of beer.

On the first evening in May, Jocelyn said she needed to get to bed early. She took a Power Bar with her up to the third floor. At first Denise worried the novelty of the new TV had worn off already. Then she panicked, thinking she had failed again. Then she realized she needed a break, too, and that was all Jocelyn needed.

Denise moved her ThinkPad into her bedroom, packed four pillows between herself and the headboard, and said, "This is exactly why they're called laptops." A glass of red wine waited on the bedside table. She tuned the radio to 89.7, to *Eric in the Evening*, and listened for a few minutes to a Herbie Hancock tune before opening the Excel program.

The past year she had transferred Uncle Frank's handwritten records onto computer files, as well as her own sales data, and the publicly auctioned sales of other cardtraders. Now Denise could track the value of her merchandise. If she found two Christy Mathewson cards in good condition, she would own two complete sets of the first men initiated into the Baseball Hall of Fame. Serious collectors would pay upwards of a million for a set. That evening she ran a probability program to determine for how much she could sell her incomplete sets of the Hall of Fame men versus auctioning the Cobb, Johnson, and Babe Ruth cards individually. If Uncle Frank were alive, she knew he'd hold on until someone in the business died. He would snatch a Christy from a widow. Denise poured a second glass of wine, a Merlot.

At 11:46, Denise heard Jocelyn fill the upstairs tub. Why wasn't she sleeping? Tomorrow was a school day. Plus, she was sure she had bathed earlier. Denise went back to her numbers.

If she wanted out of the business, she could auction the three cards and have enough to invest, live modestly, and send herself and her daughter to college. She could sell the house, too, the Card Palace, and start yet another life. But what life, and where? Soon she'd be thirty-six. In a year and a half, Jocelyn would be gone and out of the house. Then again, if Denise stopped selling cards and baseballs, she'd stop being invited to Red Sox games and getting red-carpet treatment. Did she really want to be an anthropologist? Work for her uncle on Beacon Hill? Denise shook her head.

Jocelyn was making a lot of noise upstairs. Reluctantly Denise put on her robe and stepped quietly up the sisal-carpeted steps. Maybe her daughter was sick, which would be unusual. Since they'd moved to Medford, Jocelyn had stayed as healthy as a horse: no flu, strep throats, or monthly cramps.

Denise pushed open her daughter's bedroom door, figuring she could lay a cold washcloth on Jocelyn's forehead and give her aspirin. The lights were on. The bedclothes, thrown back, were stained with blood. Jocelyn must have gotten her period. But so much blood?

Denise tapped on the bathroom door. "Are you all right, baby?" She had to repeat the question.

"I think so," Jocelyn quietly answered.

"What is it, honey?" She tapped lightly on the door again. "Cramps?"

Jocelyn made a gurgling noise, as if she was drowning, but Denise wouldn't open the door without being invited in.

"Are you sick, baby? Throwing up?"

"Yes. Yes," she shouted.

"Get it all out, you'll feel better," Denise said, as all mothers say to their children.

"I will, I will, mamma." Jocelyn sounded scared.

"Can I come in?" Denise asked.

"Almost, not yet." She could hear Jocelyn hold her breath and let out a long howl.

Denise heard crying, and it wasn't Jocelyn's crying. In a split-second her entire being filled with a clinging-to-life desperation. She had a single desire. She must take care of her child.

On the floor, a puddle of blood expanded along the cracks of the linoleum, inching towards a pile of crumpled red towels. Jocelyn slouched in the bathtub naked up to her breasts in red water. A tiny head floated between her breasts. A tiny, tiny head covered with downy black hair. Denise recognized the head. It looked like her own baby's. A tiny fisted hand, with nearly transparent fingers, searched to find its mouth.

Jocelyn looked at her mother, with tears and a smile, caressing the baby between her breasts. "I guess this is a surprise, isn't it?"

"Don't worry." Denise kneeled on the floor and kissed her daughter's face, dipping her hand into the warm red water, touching the new life, telling them all not to worry. "Everything is all right."

They wrapped the new baby girl in a clean towel, flushed the afterbirth down the toilet, and drained the tub. Denise soaked up the blood from the floor and stuffed the dirty towels in the washer. Jocelyn dressed in clean clothes and tied her hair up in a neat bun. Her mother made her a peanut butter sandwich and poured her a glass of milk. While they waited for the ambulance, Denise and Jocelyn curled against one another on the sofa and watched the baby sleep. Nothing else mattered: just that they were together, above board—the three of them feeling like one. For a moment the baby opened her dark eyes, which looked ripped from the sky, to let them know she was a piece of heaven that they had caught in the Card Palace.

When they heard the ambulance coming, Jocelyn, Denise, and the baby, whom they thought they would name either Christy or Francesca, descended the long row of concrete steps. The sun hadn't come up yet. They rode to the nearest hospital, which was in Malden, to register the birth.

BIRTH AND DEATH

POETRY

Planting a Sequoia

Dana Gioia

(1991)

All afternoon my brothers and I have worked in the orchard,
Digging this hole, laying you into it, carefully packing the soil.
Rain blackened the horizon, but cold winds kept it over the Pacific,
And the sky above us stayed the dull gray
Of an old year coming to an end.
In Sicily a father plants a tree to celebrate his first son's birth—
An olive or a fig tree—a sign that the earth has one more life to bear.
I would have done the same, proudly laying new stock into my father's orchard,
A green sapling rising among the twisted apple boughs,
A promise of new fruit in other autumns.
But today we kneel in the cold planting you, our native giant,
Defying the practical custom of our fathers,
Wrapping in your roots a lock of hair, a piece of an infant's birth cord,
All that remains above earth of a first-born son,
A few stray atoms brought back to the elements.
We will give you what we can—our labor and our soil,
Water drawn from the earth when the skies fail,
Nights scented with the ocean fog, days softened by the circuit of bees.
We plant you in the corner of the grove, bathed in western light,
A slender shoot against the sunset.
And when our family is no more, all of his unborn brothers dead,

Every niece and nephew scattered, the house torn down,
His mother's beauty ashes in the air,
I want you to stand among strangers, all young and ephemeral to you,
Silently keeping the secret of your birth.

É si riuniscono, questi vecchi . . .

LindaAnn Loschiavo

(1997)

And they assemble, these old men this day,
Prepared for preservation of respect.
Economy of passion scaled correct
For male Americans will be outweighed
By sons of Italy who've come to lay
Il nonno mio to eternal rest.
July air tense with recollections checks
The speed of prayer in Latin's cushioned sway.
Too young for gravesites, I imagine this,
His shadow far too heavy for their praise
To tow where I won't follow. Winds whip up
My want. *He can't be gone!* Sleep is dismissed,
Distracted. Night turns dangerous, grief glazed,
Fears filed beyond where living souls can touch.

Grandmother in Heaven

Jay Parini

(1999)

In a plume-field, white above the blue,
she's pulling up a hoard of rootcrops
planted in a former life and left to ripen:
soft gold carrots, beets, bright gourds.
There's coffee in the wind, tobacco smoke
and garlic olive oil and lemon.
Fires burn coolly through the day,
the water boils at zero heat.
It's always almost time for Sunday dinner,
with the boys all home: dark Nello
who became his cancer and refused to breathe;
her little Gino, who went down the mines
and whom they had to dig all week to find;
that willow, Tony, who became so thin
he blew away; then Julius and Leo,
who survived the other by their wits alone
but found no reason, after all was said,
for hanging on. They'll take their places
in the sun today at her high table,
as the antique beams light up the plates,
the faces that have lately come to shine.

ART AND SELF

POETRY

Cape Clear

Peggy Rizza Ellsberg

(1994)

Here wind stops forever and rain stops forever
And nothing appears in the far pure blue always
And there is silence, a crystalline stillness,
And so you write, "In the beginning."

As a fish moves through water, though having no word
For water, you are lost here in the mysteries
Of "clear" and "blue." Long, sea, God—you lose
Yourself in the thought of being, and yourself

Without it is intolerable. What is clear
In this place is vast and rocking. It is
the ocean coming to a child not yet
conceived, in a huge embrace.

Language Lesson

Grace Cavalieri

(1995)

It was a day much like this,
grey, with drizzle,
my mother took me visiting,
which was a big event.
She didn't drive a car,
seldom went out.
How did we get there?
My father, perhaps, who
worked in a bank nearby.
He must have dropped us
by this large white house
with grand pillars.

I can't imagine why
we were wanted there
but I met a boy my age.
I suppose that was it.
Get the toddlers together,
Ready to learn to play.

I assessed the toys,
and took my pick,
a brand new trike, and
oh how it went,
as shiny as it looked.
My new playmate ran crying
filled with envy and
complaint:
Me wants the bike
Me wants it now.

I stopped. The wheels froze
on the rug as I looked
at my foe
      "ME wants the bike?"
I felt the sweet pleasure of

superiority, the first ache
of it, age three.
There would be no contest. I
could play as long as I liked.
I had him by the pronoun.
It was the happiest day of my life.

Lizard-Tree

Peter Covino

(1998)

Here in our garden you are
a gnarled, spindly intruder,
the transplanted heart
of an old conjure woman.

Nourishing you is no easy task:
the fastidious pruning
and insecticides, the plastic covers
for the cold. You ward me off

with claws three inches long
and shriveled fruit: poisonous
lemons whose fragrance
still haunts the yard.

How will I know you are dead—
when you no longer dart around me,
when the hiss of the wind subsides.

Athletes of God

Grace Cavalieri

(1999)

The first time I saw my American poems translated
I just stopped and studied
the hieroglyphics on the page,
tiny scribbles of black ink
saying twice
what was said before.
Then I knew
I would not leave this world
without loving some of it . . .
nothing reduced to a single truth . . .
all of one blood,
our words, music and lives coming together.
It was not that the stars had fallen down—
It was more that we didn't need
the lamp which had gone out.

How separate we are in the dark
after the poem is gone.

Libretto

Mary Jo Salter

(1999)

Libretto. That's the first Italian word
   she wants to teach me: "little book."
This afternoon (but why are we alone?
   Were Daddy and my brothers gone
all day, or has memory with its flair
   for simple compositions air-
brushed them from the shot?) she's set aside
   just for the two of us, and a lesson.

On an ivory silk couch that doesn't fit
   the life she's given in Detroit,
we gaze across the living room at the tall
   "European" drapes she's sewn
herself: a work of secret weights and tiers,
   hung after cursing at her own
mother's machine. She lets the needle fall
   onto the record's edge; then turns

to pull a hidden cord, and the curtain rises
   on Puccini's strings and our front view
of shut two-car garages, built for new
   marriages constructed since the war.
Well, not so new. It's 1962
   and though I'm only eight, I know
that with two cars, people can separate.
   He went away; came back for more

operatic scenes heard through my wall
   as if through a foreign language. Muffled
fury and accusation, percussive sobs:
   they aren't happy. Who couldn't tell
without the words? *Libretto.* On my knees
   the English text, the Italian on hers,
and a thrill so loud the coffee table throbs.
   I'm following her finger as

we're looping to a phrase already sung
   or reading four lines at a time
of people interrupting and just plain
   not listening, and yet the burden
of the words is simple: Butterfly must die.
Pinkerton will betray her, though the theme
rippling before him like a hoisted flag
   is the Star-Spangled Banner. Mother, why
would a Japanese and an American
   sing Italian at each other?
Why would he get married and not stay?
   And have a child he'd leave to wait
with the mother by the screen with her telescope
   for the ship of hope? Why, if he knew
it wouldn't last, did he come back to Japan?
   —But I'm not asking her. *That's men*

is her silent, bitter answer; was always half
   her lesson plan. *O say can you see . . .*
yes, now I can. Your dagger's at the throat
   and yet I feel no rage; as tears
stream down our faces onto facing pages
   fluttering like wings, I see you meant
like Butterfly to tie a blindfold over
   a loved child's eyes: the saving veil of Art.

For it is only a story. When the curtain
   drops, our pity modulates
to relief she isn't us, and what's in store
   for you, divorce and lonely death,
is still distant. We have our nights to come
   of operas to dress up for,
our silly jokes, our shopping, days at home
   when nothing is very wrong and in my chair

I read some tragedy in comfort, even
   a half-shamed joy. You gave me that—
my poor, dear parents, younger then than I
   am now; with a stagestruck, helpless wish
that it wouldn't hurt and that it would, you made
   me press my ear against the wall
for stories that kept me near and far,
   and because the hurt was beautiful

even to try to write them; to find that living
    by stories is itself a life.
Forgive whatever artifice lies
    in my turning you into characters
in my own libretto—one sorry hand
    hovering above the quicksand
of a turn-table in a house in Detroit
    I can't go back to otherwise.

Books, how silent you are

John A. Tagliabue

(2001)

Books, how silent you are, you
   tell me
nothing this gray day. All lined up,
   no phoenix
flies from your vowels. All those books of
   "wisdom"
East and West; their lovers they wrote
   their words
with such passion, they with the motion of stars,
   they with
the motion rich course of rivers, though
   they knew
their own body would turn to dust, put word
   on page
with absolute need. Dear loneliness of words, dear
   sadness of
sisters, dear mysteries of parents, dear astronomers
   of planets,
you sleep for a time, but when we awaken you'll
   persist in
giving the communal cosmic cooperative vitality of the
   sacred sign.

Requiem for a Practical Possum

Michael Palma

(2001)

The gray fog tapping at the windowpane
Had come to spend the night.
The teacups tinkled on their saucers
For want of knowing
Anything else to do.
In the yellow lamplight
The old man's magic head
Tottered on the thin stretched neck
As he slipped into a fissure
(Be merciful to me O Lord)
In the cloud cushion that had just appeared
On the parlor rug.

The pages long behind him now,
Everything still within.
Brown river, rose garden at the root,
The rooms of solid women
(Let my cry come unto Thee),
Long evening walks
Through crooked Cambridge streets,
Dusk inking the stretched sky.
Past the blackboards and the brickyards
To the edge of the known world
Where the vast gray corrugated ocean called
With a human voice.

Stonetowered London, coldfingered rain,
The boneless multitudes unheeding
The smell of their damnation.
The daring clenched inside him,
The sudden cleaving,
The long letting go.
The firelicked shadows on the wall,
The scraping of taut nerves
(Wrapped in a burning sheet of sin)
And poetry, the strange

Images churned from a misery that changed
The taste of the air.

The bowlers, the umbrellas,
The barricade of books.
An owl's hard stare back into the camera
(And always there the one he had done in).
The podiums, the stadiums,
The arrangement of response.
A slight cornered smile as he stooped
To slide a flat hand over a flat book.
Arm linked in arm at last
And blinking eyes
In the sunlight, where a pair of ragged claws
Had become a rock.

The gray fog settled, wrapping the hour,
As the old man napping gently
By the fire (not the fire
That leaps to swallow up the lost)
Has done with his dry breathing.
Now he has climbed into that bower
He soiled tweed knees in sober search of,
Or he has fallen into that hole
He dreaded most,
Or worst of all
He has suddenly found himself to be a nothing.
He chose not to tell.

Self-Portrait as Woman Posed on Flowered Couch

Clare Rossini

(2001)

She thought her education would come
All at once, as it did
For Saul, lucky boy, trailed by lightning
Until the right moment,
Crawling out from under his horse
With a new name and obsession.

But daily the weather comes around,
And he who claims to love her
Is still there in the morning,
Buttering toast,
Calling her yet
Another nonsensical name.

She imagined the battles of the soul
Fought out
In the old high style, leaving her
Dappled with virtue.
But she finds that she's infected
With a mild self-love;
She's the would-be martyr
Who dreams of the executioner's knife
And wakes praising heathen gods
In her safe bed.

What will educate her
To the mirror and the clock,
All those exigencies?

Like a flower,
She colors in the moment.

Meanwhile, the anger of God
Waits in the cupboards, ready to fill the house,
Upbraiding the meek
Philodendron, astonishing
The dust on the sills.

Happenstance

Joseph Salemi

(2005)

I hardly knew the camera flashed and blinked;
One random moment, totally unplanned,
I passed before the shutter's eye—it winked.

A frozen second I stood there unmanned,
Thinking some purpose lay behind the act,
But seeing that the photo was in fact
Simply an aimless, accidental slip,
I walked on. Why presume to understand
Exactly what made some unconscious hand
Come to position just in time to flip
A lever, press a button, click a switch?

Life has some fragments that make up no whole:
Mere vagaries of errant drifting which
Capture chance images like leaves in coal.

War Song

Rachel Guido deVries

(2005)

Like ideas through curtains
poems lift their diaphanous heads
and I look through them. Beyond
their growing wisdom, a worm
turns his head, or perhaps his tail, slowly,
as though gazing into a mirror of grief.

In the garden, amidst the violets
and chrysanthemums, blooms as big
as fists rise, and the haunted cries
of the-not-yet-buried rise too,
a tender agony of parting. Open
hands reach up from new holes.

Someone plays a flute carelessly,
devouring the last of the blue air.

ABOUT THE AUTHORS

Domenico Adamo (1888–1964) descended from a family of dialectical poets. He left his birth-place, San Mango d'Aquino, in Catanzaro province, for a six-year apprenticeship in Naples, returning in 1908. He set up shop and married, but left his family in 1912 to seek prosperity in the United States. In 1923, a year after the fascists took power in Italy, he returned to Italy for his family. However, his antifascist writings had put him in disfavor with the authorities, and early in 1924 he fled to America, an exile. The poet Riccardo Cordiferro says of Adamo: "He was born a poet; consequently he writes without any pretense of creating art. But how many beautiful poems he writes and how much ardent passion he imbues in the verses that spring from his heart!" Joseph D. Adamo (Adams) is the translator of his father's work. He is an author himself, as well as an editor and literary scholar who now dedicates himself to oil painting at his studio and gallery in Painter, Virginia.

John Addiego is a writer living in Portland, Oregon. His poetry has been published in *Kansas Quarterly, Epoch,* and *Ohio Review,* as well as numerous other small journals.

Kim Addonizio's paternal grandparents, as far as she can ascertain, emigrated from the province of Avellino around the beginning of the twentieth century. Addonizio is the author of four poetry collections, most recently *What Is This Thing Called Love* (W. W. Norton). Her other books include two novels from Simon and Schuster, *Little Beauties* and *My Dreams Out in the Street.* Her work has been honored with a Guggenheim Fellowship, two NEA Fellowships, and the John Ciardi Lifetime Achievement Award. She is online at www.kimaddonizio.com.

Carol Bonomo Albright has been editor-in-chief of *Italian Americana* for almost twenty years. Recently under the direction of Christine Palamidessi Moore, she initiated a website supplement to the journal. It can be found at www.Italianamericana.com. She is active in literary and historical associations and was a two-term vice president of the American Italian Historical Association. She teaches Italian-American Studies at Harvard University Extension School and has been a visiting lecturer at Harvard University. In 2004 she coedited an annotated edition of two of Joseph Rocchietti's works, written in 1835 and 1845 (making one of them the first Italian-American novel). She coedited an anthology, *Italian Immigrants Go West,* and was series editor of *Italian American Autobiographies.* "Washington Square," a section of her memoir, was published in *Our Roots Are Deep with Passion.* She wrote essays for the landmark publication *The Dream Book: Writings by Italian American Women,* for *Voices of the Daughters,* and for *Social Pluralism and Literary History.* She has published articles and reviews in the *Journal of American Ethnic History, PMLA, LIT,* and *MELUS.* She has received numerous grants and awards, including being named an associate fellow of the Danforth Foundation of Higher Education and receiving a university-to-community outreach grant from that foundation.

Tony Ardizzone is the author of seven books of fiction, including the novel *In the Garden of Papa Santuzzu,* from which "Lamb Soup" is excerpted. His work has received the Flannery O'Connor Prize for Short Fiction, the Chicago Foundation for Literature Award, the Milkweed National Fiction Prize, the Pushcart Prize, and two fellowships from the National Endowment for the Arts, among other honors. He is the Chancellor's Professor of English at Indiana University, Bloomington. His father's parents came to the United States from the town of Menfi in the Sicilian province of Agrigento.

J. T. Barbarese is the author of four books of poems, most recently *The Black Beach,* and a translation of Euripides' *The Children of Heracles* (University of Pennsylvania Press, 1999). His published poems have appeared in the *Atlantic Monthly,* the *Georgia Review,* and *Poetry* and have been anthologized in *The Italian-American Reader* (Morrow, 2003) and *The Poetry Daily Anthology.* He has published short fiction in *Story Quarterly* and the *North American Review* and essays and literary journalism in *Tri-Quarterly, Sewanee Review,* and *The Columbia History of American Poetry* (1993). He is a second-generation Italian American whose paternal grandparents were both from Nereto in Abruzzi and whose maternal grandparents were Neapolitan and Piedmontese.

Dennis Barone is the author of twelve books, including *God's Whisper* (a novella from Spuyten Duyvil, 2005) and *North Arrow* (stories from Quale Press, 2007). Recently, he prepared a collection of poems by Emanuel Carnevali, *Furnished Rooms,* for which he wrote an afterword. His father's parents were born in Italy and moved to America as young children; his mother's parents were Norwegian.

Christina Bevilacqua, who interviewed Camille Paglia, is the director of programs at the Providence Athenaeum Library in Rhode Island. She is a graduate of Bard College and received her M.A. from the University of Chicago.

Maria Bruno is an associate professor in the Department of Writing, Rhetoric and American Studies at Michigan State University. She has published more than forty short stories and creative nonfiction essays in *Ms., Women's Words, Earth's Daughters, Spectacle, Korone, Italian Americana, Midway Review, The Feminist Teacher, Feminist Parenting, New Directions for Women, Sin Fronteras, The Salt Reader, Waystation,* and the *Red Cedar Review.* Her stories have appeared in the anthologies *Bless Me Father, The Time of Our Lives, Breaking Up Is Hard to Do, Women's Friendships,* and *The Strange History of Suzanne LaFleshe.* Her screenplays *The Black Madonna,* a semifinalist in the Moondance International Screenwriting Competition, and *Virtually Yours* were optioned by Rearguard Productions of Los Angeles, California.

Mary Caponegro is approximately third-generation Italian American on her father's side. Her ancestors came from Canna, in the province of Cosenza in Calabria, and Arpino, near Rome. She is the author of *Tales from the Next Village, The Star Café, Five Doubts, The Complexities of Intimacy,* and (in Italian) *Materia Prima.* Honors include the General Electric Foundation Award, the Rome Prize in Literature, the Bruno Arcudi Award for Fiction, the Charles Flint Kellogg Award in Arts and Letters, and a Lannan residency. She is currently Richard B. Fisher Family Professor of Writing and Literature at Bard College.

Grace Cavalieri's parents came from opposite ends of Italy. Though her father's family was originally from Trieste, Angelo was born in Florence and lived in Venice. Her mother, Anna May, was of the Zoda family from Villalba, Sicily. Her parents met and married in Trenton, New Jersey. Grace is the author of several books of poetry and twenty-one produced plays; she produces and hosts public radio's "The Poet and the Poem" from the Library of Congress. She holds the 2006 Bordighera Award and a 2005 Paterson Prize for Poetry. Her poetry commentaries are heard on MiPOradio.com. and iTunes.

John Ciardi remains the most influential Italian-American poet-critic in America. Well known for his translation of *The Inferno,* he has published numerous books of poems, such as *The Lives of X, Person to Person: Poems,* and *The Strangest Everything,* as well as books about poetry, such as *How Does a Poem Mean?* Several posthumous volumes of his work have recently appeared from the University of Arkansas Press. He was the director of the Bread Loaf Writers Conference for many years.

Philip Cioffari has a Ph.D. in literature from New York University. He is professor of English and director of the Performing and Literary Arts Honors Program at William Paterson University in New Jersey. He is the author of a collection of short stories, *A History of Things Lost or Broken,* and a novel, *Catholic Boys,* both from Livingston Press. He is a second-generation Italian American. His feature film, *Love in the Age of Dion,* which he wrote and directed, won Best Feature Film at the Long Island International Film Expo 2006. His grandparents came from the Campania region: from Calitri in Avellino province and Luzzano in Benevento province.

Rita Ciresi is director of creative writing at the University of South Florida and the author of five award-winning works of fiction that address the Italian-American experience, including *Pink Slip, Blue Italian,* and *Sometimes I Dream in Italian.* Her father was born in Termini Imerese, Sicilia, and her grandparents on her mother's side came from outside Naples.

Vince Clemente's books include *John Ciardi: Measure of the Man, Paumanok Rising: Writers in a Landscape,* and seven volumes of poetry, the latest of which is *Sweeter than Vivaldi.*

Paola Corso is a native of Pittsburgh, where her Calabrian immigrant father and grandfather found work in the steel mills. She is the author of *Giovanna's 86 Circles and Other Stories*, a John Gardner Fiction Book Award Finalist and a Best Short Stories selection in the *Montserrat Review*, as well as a book of poems, *Death by Renaissance*. A Sherwood Anderson Fiction Award recipient and New York Foundation for the Arts poetry fellow, Corso is a writer-in-residence in Western Connecticut State University's M.F.A. Program. She lives in Brooklyn with play-wright Michael Winks and sons Giona and Mario.

Antonio Costabile was born in Tolve, Provincia di Potenza, in the Basilicata region. He was a practicing lawyer and a serious amateur historian of the region. Mr. Costabile had a reputation in the district as a gifted storyteller. He died in 1994.

Peter Covino was born in Sturno (Avellino), Italy, and immigrated to the United States when he was three years old. Currently he is an assistant professor of English and Creative Writing at the University of Rhode Island. He is also the author of the chapbook *Straight Boyfriend* (winner of the 2001 Frank O'Hara Prize), as well as the poetry collection *Cut Off the Ears of Winter*, New Issues, a winner of the PEN/Osterweil Award for emerging poets, and a finalist for the Thom Gunn Award. New poems have appeared in recent issues of the *Colorado Review*, *Gulf Coast*, *Interim*, and the *European Poets* anthology due from Graywolf in 2008.

Rachel Guido deVries is a poet and fiction writer. Her most recent book of poems is *Gambler's Daughter* (Guernica Editions, 2001). Her novel, *Tender Warriors* (Firebrand, 1986), recently celebrated twenty years in print. A new collection of poems, *The Brother Inside Me*, was published by Guernica Editions in 2007. Her first children's picture book, *Teeny Tiny Tino's Fishing Story*, is forthcoming. Her grandparents came to the United States from Sicily and Calabria. A past recipient of a New York Foundation for the Arts award in fiction, she lives in Cazenovia, New York, where she teaches and is a poet-in-the-schools.

Kevin Carrizo di Camillo is the author of two books of poetry, *Why I Drive Alfa Romeos (and Other Excuses)* and *Occasionally Yours (and Others)*, both from Typographeum Press (1997, 1999). With Lawrence Boadt he edited *John Paul II in the Holy Land* (Stimulus Books, 2005). Winner of the Foley Poetry Prize from *America* magazine and published in *Daedalus*, *Notre Dame Review*, *James Joyce Quarterly*, *National Poetry Review*, *Prairie Fire*, *Slipstream*, and *La Valle del Tirino* (Italy), he is an editor at Paulist Press and an aspirant to the Order of Deacons in the Latin Church. In his fourth year of battling cancer, he is a fourth-generation Italian American, his paternal great-grandparents having hailed from Villa Manga, and Calascio, L'Aquila, in the Abruzzi.

Poet, translator, and essayist **W. S. Di Piero** was born in South Philadelphia, Pennsylvania, in 1945. His six collections of original poetry include *Skirts and Slacks* (Alfred A. Knopf, 2001), *Shadows Burning* (TriQuarterly Books, 1995), *The Restorers* (1992), and *The Dog Star* (1990). His books of translation include Euripedes' *Ion* (1996); *The Ellipse: Selected Poems of Leonardo Sinis-galli* (1983); *This Strange Joy: Selected Poems of Sandro Penna* (1982), for which he won the first

Raiziss/de Palchi Book Prize; and Giacomo Leopardi's *Pensieri* (1981). His three collections of essays are *Shooting the Works: On Poetry and Pictures* (1996), *Out of Eden: Essays on Modern Art* (1991), and *Memory and Enthusiasm: Essays, 1975–1985* (1989). A recent collection of poems is entitled *Shadows Burning*. His honors include fellowships from the Guggenheim Foundation and the Ingram Merrill Foundation and a grant from the Lila Wallace–Readers' Digest Fund. He lives in San Francisco and is a professor of English at Stanford University.

Albert Di Bartolomeo's maternal grandparents were born in the Abruzzi, although knowledge of the specific town died with his grandmother. His paternal grandparents were also born in Italy. He earned his master's degree in creative writing from Temple University. He is the author of two novels, *The Vespers Tapes* and *Fool's Gold*. He has written for *Reader's Digest*, the *Philadelphia Inquirer*, *Philadelphia Magazine*, *American Woodworker*, *Italian Americana*, *Salon*, and other publications, and his work has been anthologized in *Chicken Soup for the Soul* and *Human Ecology*. He received a Pennsylvania Council-on-the-Arts Award and currently teaches at Drexel University and the University of Pennsylvania.

Peggy Rizza Ellsberg is a first-generation Italian American. Her father was born in the province of Syracusa, where his parents were lemon farmers. Vague tales are told of his orphaned Northern Italian father, separated from his identical twin at birth and reunited with him eighty years later in America. His mother was Calabrian. All of these family members came to the United States through Ellis Island in 1910. An outbreak of smallpox on the boat resulted in the death of her father's older sister, whose burial at sea he witnessed.

Louisa Ermelino has written three novels, *Joey Dee Gets Wise*, which was a Barnes & Noble DISCOVER selection; *The Black Madonna*; and *The Sisters Mallone*, all of which celebrate the power of women, her Italian-American ancestry, and her New York City neighborhood. She's a second-generation Italian American of "mixed" heritage. Her father's family is from outside of Genoa, and her mother's family is from Avellino, which made for an interesting and wonderful combination of culture and cuisines. She has worked at *People*, *Time*, and *Instyle* magazines and has taught in the creative writing program at Columbia University. She is currently the reviews director at *Publishers Weekly*.

John Fante began writing in 1929. He made contact with H. L. Mencken, who became his literary mentor. Fante published his first short story in 1932. His first novel, *Wait Until Spring, Bandini*, was published in 1938 and was the first of his Arturo Bandini series of novels, which also includes *The Road to Los Angeles* and *Ask the Dust*. A prolific screenwriter, he was stricken with diabetes in 1955. Complications from the disease resulted in his blindness in 1978 and, within two years, the amputation of both legs. He continued to write by dictation to his wife, Joyce, and published *Dreams from Bunker Hill*, the final installment of the Arturo Bandini series, in 1982. He died on May 8, 1983, at the age of seventy-four.

Rina Ferrarelli came from Calabria, Italy, at the age of fifteen. She was awarded degrees in English from Mount Mercy College (now Carlow University) and Duquesne University, and she taught English and translation studies at the University of Pittsburgh for many years. She has published a book and a chapbook of original poetry, *Home Is a Foreign Country* (Eadmer Press, 1996), and *Dreamsearch* (*malafemmina* press, 1992), and three books of translation, her most recent of which is *Winter Fragments: Selected Poems of Bartolo Cattafi* (Chelsea Editions, 2006). Her poems have won numerous prizes, including the international Sandburg-Livesay Award, at both local and international competitions. She has received an NEA grant and the Italo Calvino Prize from the Columbia University Translation Center.

Vincent Ferrini was born in June 1913 in Massachusetts, the son of Italian immigrants. He received his formal education in local schools and continued his learning through a self-initiated program of study. Ferrini's first book of poems, *No Smoke* (1941), was written while he was employed at General Electric's Lynn, Massachusetts, plant. Much of his poetry focuses on social issues relating to his factory experiences with GE and other large companies. In the early 1950s he edited a small magazine entitled *Four Winds*. For many years, Ferrini was a close friend of the poet Charles Olson (1910–1970) and had numerous acquaintances in literary circles. He was poet laureate of Gloucester, Massachusetts, and published more than twenty volumes of verse. Mr. Ferrini died in early 2008.

Jack Foley's poetry books include *Letters/Lights—Words for Adelle, Gershwin, Exiles,* and *Adrift* (nominated for a BABRA Award). Foley's *Greatest Hits 1974–2003* (2004) was published by Pudding House Press as part of a by-invitation-only series. His critical books include the companion volumes *O Powerful Western Star* (winner of the Artists Embassy Literary/Cultural Award 1998–2000) and *Foley's Books: California Rebels, Beats, and Radicals.* His radio show, "Cover to Cover," is heard every Wednesday on the Berkeley, California, radio station KPFA and is available at the KPFA Web site; his column, "Foley's Books," appears in the online magazine *The Alsop Review.*

Sandra Mortola Gilbert is the author of seven collections of poetry, most recently *Kissing the Bread: New and Selected Poems 1969–1999, The Italian Collection,* and *Belongings.* She has also published a number of prose works, of which the latest is *Death's Door: Modern Dying and the Ways We Grieve.* With Susan Gubar she is the coauthor of *The Madwoman in the Attic* and its three-volume sequel, *No Man's Land,* while also coediting *The Norton Anthology of Literature by Women.* A professor of English emerita at the University of California, Davis, Gilbert is the mother of three and grandmother of four. She divides her time between Berkeley and Paris, but her lineage is mostly Italian: Her father was born in Paris to a Russian mother but his father's family hailed from Ruta in Liguria; her mother was born in Sambuca, Sicily—where Gilbert devoutly wishes that a Golden Sala can still be found!

Dana Gioia is an internationally acclaimed and award-winning poet and critic. A native Californian, Gioia received a B.A. and an M.B.A. from Stanford University and an M.A. in Comparative Literature from Harvard University. Gioia's poetry collection, *Interrogations at Noon,* won the 2002 American Book Award. His 1991 book, *Can Poetry Matter?*, is credited with helping to revive the role of poetry in American public culture. An influential critic, he is also a prolific literary anthologist and a longtime commentator on American culture and literature for BBC Radio. Dana Gioia has been Chairman of the National Endowment for the Arts since February 2003. He and his wife, Mary, have two sons.

Mr. Gioia's modesty precluded his publishing his own work in *Italian Americana* while he was poetry editor. But, given the imprint he put on *Italian Americana*'s poetry, we felt that one of his poems should be included in this anthology.

Daniela Gioseffi is a second-generation Italian American whose ancestors were born in the province of Foggia in Puglia, Italy. She is an American Book Award–winning author of fourteen books of poetry and prose, the latest being *Blood Autumn (Autunno di sangue): New and Selected Poems*. In 2003, Feminist Press reissued her feminist classic, *Women on War: International Writings*, originally published by Simon and Schuster. She has won two New York State Council for the Arts/NEA grants in poetry, a PEN Fiction Award, and The John Ciardi Award for Lifetime Achievement in Poetry, 2007, as well as a Lifetime Achievement Award from the Association of Italian American Educators, 2003. She has read and presented her work widely on campuses and at international book fairs throughout the country and Europe, as well as on National Public Radio and the BBC. She was recently featured on the Library of Congress Radio Show "The Poet and the Poem."

George Guida is a second- and third-generation Italian American on his mother's side and third- and fourth-generation on his father's side. Both sides of his family trace their roots to Prata di Principato Ultra, a small village near Avellino; his maternal grandmother's family emigrated from the Santa Lucia district of Naples. Guida's publications include *Low Italian*, a book of poems; *The Pope Stories*, a chapbook; and *The Peasant and the Pen: Men, Enterprise, and the Recovery of Culture in Italian American Narrative*, a book of critical essays. He has written on topics ranging from Louis Prima to "The Sopranos" to the teaching of Italian-American studies. His work appears in a variety of journals and collections. In addition to writing, he teaches English at the City University of New York and Italian American Studies at Stony Brook University, serves as secretary of the American Italian Historical Association and treasurer of the Italian American Writers Association, and produces and hosts the Intercollegiate Poetry Slam at the Bowery Poetry Club.

Joanna Clapps Herman has recently coedited *Our Roots Are Deep with Passion*, a collection of nonfiction, with Lee Gutkind. She has published in *Massachusetts Review, Kalliope, Crescent Review, Critic, Inkwell, Woman's Day*, and *Italian Americana*, in addition to many other periodicals. She has two prizes for fiction, the Bruno Arcudi Fiction Prize for her short story "Perfect Hatred" and the Anne and Henry Paolucci Prize for her story "Falling." She has been published in the anthologies *Don't Tell Mama: The Penguin Book of Italian American Writing* and *The Milk of Almonds*. She teaches creative writing courses in the Graduate Writing Program at Manhattanville College as well as at the Center for Worker Education at City College, CUNY.

Ann Hood has published seven novels, including *Off the Coast of Maine* and *Ruby*, and the story collection *An Ornithologist's Guide to Life*. Her most recent novel is *The Knitting Circle*

(W. W. Norton, 2007). She has won a Pushcart Prize and a Best American Spiritual Writing Award, as well as the Paul Bowles Prize for Short Fiction. Her essays and stories have appeared in publications such as the *New York Times, Good Housekeeping, Bon Appetit, O* magazine, and the *Paris Review.* She lives in Providence, Rhode Island.

Salvatore La Puma received the Flannery O'Connor Award for his collection of short stories, *Boys of Bensonhurst.* His latest collection of stories is *Teaching Angels to Fly.* His last novel, *A Time for Wedding Cake,* is available in paperback.

Native New Yorker **LindaAnn Loschiavo** has volcanic blood on both sides. Her maternal grandparents are from Naples, a whisper from Vesuvius. Her paternal side hails from the Aeolian Islands—her grandmother is from Lipari and her grandfather Giuseppe Lo Schiavo grew up on an active volcano, Stromboli. She is a second-generation Italian American; her parents were born in New York City. During World War II, the military altered her father's surname to "Loschiavo." A lifelong journalist, Loschiavo has won prizes for her nonfiction and her formal verse. Her bilingual remembrance "Return of the Native to Stromboli" has been reprinted at least a dozen times.

Brian McCormick is a poet and fiction writer who has published in *Harper's,* the *Atlantic, Zzyzzyva, Yarrow,* and other journals. He was a fellow at the Djerassi Foundation and the tuitioned John Ciardi Scholar at Bread Loaf Writers Conference.

Gerard Malanga is a first-generation Italian American. His father is from the village of Bella, Potenza, in the region of Basilicata. His mother's family originated in Salerno. He is the author of a dozen books of poetry spanning a forty-year period, the latest being *No Respect: New and Selected Poems 1964–2000* (Black Sparrow Press). His poetry appears regularly in many important American literary periodicals, including the *Paris Review, Partisan Review, Literary Imagination, Raritan,* the *Yale Review,* and the *New Yorker.* He is a contributing editor to the Italian literary magazine *Storie* (Rome). His website is gerardmalanga.com.

Gerald Mancini has traveled widely in Italy and Sicily and has twice been a visiting artist at the American Academy in Rome. His grandfather Antonio Calamandrei was born near San Casciano in Val de Pesa, and his grandmother Adalgisa Biseo was from Genoa. He is almost a first-generation Italian American, his mother, Marie Calamandrei (who taught Italian at SUNY Binghamton), having been born in 1914—three months after his grandparents arrived in America. A new collection of his poetry, *Trouble Light,* is forthcoming in 2008 from West End Press. He is at work on a book about Italian wine and film.

Jerre Mangione wrote *Mount Allegro,* a memoir; *A Passion for Sicilians: The World around Danilo Dolci*; and *An Ethnic at Large: A Memoir of America in the Thirties and Forties,* among others. He published *La Storia: A History of the Italian Americans over Five Centuries,* often used as a textbook in Italian-American studies courses.

Kenny Marotta is a first-generation Italian American on his father's side and second-genera-tion on his mother's. His father came from Anzano di Puglia, his mother's parents from Pie-traperzia in Sicily. He was born in Malden, Massachusetts, and received a B.A. from Harvard and a Ph.D. in English literature from Johns Hopkins. His novel, *A Piece of Earth*, was published by Morrow in 1985; Guernica Editions published a collection of related short stories and a novella, *A House on the Piazza*, in 1998. He has published stories, reviews, and articles in vari-ous literary journals and was most recently coeditor of *Re-Creating The American Past: Essays on the Colonial Revival* (University of Virginia, 2006). His stories have won the Aniello Lauri Award (1993) and *Italian Americana*'s Bruno Arcudi Literature Prize (1996). *A House on the Piazza* was selected for the 1999 Books for the Teenage List, New York Public Library. A teacher and freelance editor, he lives in Charlottesville, Virginia.

Michael Maschio is a novelist living in New York City. His books include *Robert Lombardi, The Trespassers, The Mirror, Joseph De Angelo, The Flag Trilogy, Dust of Life,* and *Sarah Bravo,* all unpublished. He is a third-generation Italian American whose ancestors were from Ischia and Naples.

Jerome Mazzaro is a first-generation American. His parents came from Avella in the Com-pania, which was mentioned by Vergil in the *Aeneid* (7:740). He is the author of four books of poetry—*Changing the Windows* (1966), *The Caves of Love* (1985), *Rubbings* (1985), and *Weather-ing the Changes: Poems* (2002)—as well as of several books on contemporary poets and poetry. His poems have appeared in the *Hudson Review,* the *Literary Review,* the *Nation,* the *New Repub-lic, Poetry* (Chicago), *Salmagundi,* the *Sewanee Review, Shenandoah,* the *Southwest Review,* and the *Yale Review.* In addition, he has published widely as a scholar. He was awarded a Guggen-heim Memorial Fellowship in 1964, and in 1979–80 he was named Hadley Fellow at Benning-ton College. Among his works are *Six Poems* (1959); *The Achievement of Robert Lowell* (1960); *Juvenal: Satires* (1965); *The Poetic Themes of Robert Lowell* (1965); *Changing the Windows* (1966); *Transformations in the Renaissance English Lyric* (1970); *Modern American Poetry* (ed., 1970); *Pro-file of Robert Lowell* (ed., 1971); *Profile of William Carlos Williams* (ed., 1971); *William Carlos Williams: The Later Poems* (1973); *Postmodern American Poetry* (1980); *The Figure of Dante* (1981); *The Caves of Love* (1985); *Rubbings* (1985); *John Logan: Collected Poems* (coeditor, 1989); *John Logan: Collected Fiction,* ed. (1991); *Mind Plays: Luigi Pirandello's Theater* (2000); *Robert Lowell and Ovid* (2001); *War Games* (2001); *Robert Lowell and America* (2002); *Weathering the Changes: Poems* (2002); *Memory and Making* (2003); and *Unlocking the Heart: Sincerity in the English Son-net* (2004).

Christine Palamidessi Moore began her writing career in radio and advertising. During the 1980s she covered New York City's independent film and video industry. St. Martin's Press published her novel *The Virgin Knows* in 1995. Her memoir "Grandmothers" is engraved in granite at the Jackson Square train stop in Boston. She teaches writing at Boston University. Her short story "Card Palace," which is part of this collection, won *Italian Americana*'s Salva-tor and Margaret Bonomo Fiction Prize. Other awards include the Barbara Demming Award for Women Writers and an Urban Arts Award. She was the guest editor for the Foods of Affection issue of *Italian Americana*. Her grandparents were from Lucca. She is a second-generation Italian American and holds both American and Italian passports.

Ben Morreale published several novels in the 1970s, including *A Few Virtuous Men: A Novel of Sicily* and *Monday, Tuesday . . . Never Come Sunday*; in 1997, he published *The Loss of the Miraculous*. He coauthored the book *La Storia* with Jerre Mangione.

Lucia Mudd was born in Waterbury, Connecticut. While she cherished the sweet apricot nectar dialect of her Tolvese and Aviglianese grandparents, she eventually studied standard, sparkling mineral water Italian with the beloved Maria Sandi and Laura Pizer at the Cambridge Center for Adult Education in her new hometown and was thus able to translate Antonino Costabile's story, published here in this collection.

Camille Paglia, the scholar and culture critic, is the University Professor of Humanities and Media Studies at the University of the Arts in Philadelphia. Her books are: *Sexual Personae: Art and Decadence from Nefertiti to Emily Dickinson*; *Sex, Art, and American Culture*; *Vamps and Tramps: New Essays*; *The Birds*; and *Break, Blow, Burn: Camille Paglia Reads Forty-Three of the World's Best Poems*. Her next book, a study of visual images and a companion book to *Break, Blow, Burn*, is under contract to Pantheon Books. Professor Paglia is a contributing editor at *Interview* magazine, where she was a cofounding contributor and columnist for six years, beginning with its debut issue in 1995. Her *Salon* column returned in February 2007. Professor Paglia's mother and all four of her grandparents were born in Italy: Her mother was born in Ceccano in Lazio; her father's family is from Benevento and Avellino.

Michael Palma was born in the Bronx in 1945. Three of his grandparents had emigrated from Italy, his paternal grandfather from Benevento and both his mother's parents from Raccuia, Sicily. In addition to his own poetry (*The Egg Shape*; *Antibodies*; *A Fortune in Gold*), he has published translations of ten modern and contemporary Italian poets, as well as a fully rhymed translation of Dante's *Inferno* (Norton, 2002). He has received the Italo Calvino Award, the Raiziss/de Palchi Book Prize, the Olindo De Gennaro Poetry Prize, and the Raiziss/de Palchi Translation Fellowship. He serves as the poetry editor of *Italian Americana*. He is an elector of the Poets' Corner at the Cathedral Church of St. John the Divine in New York City. He lives in Bellows Falls, Vermont.

Joseph Papaleo was a central figure in the development of the Sarah Lawrence College writing program and was mentor and friend to generations of students. He taught there from 1969 to 1992. He wrote two novels and numerous short stories during his long career as chair of the creative writing program at Sarah Lawrence.

Anne Paolucci is a poet living in New York. In 1976 she launched the Council on National Literatures and is still series editor of its two publications, *Review of National Literatures* and *CNL/World Report*. Her academic credentials include dozens of books, articles, and reviews.

She was president of the Pirandello Society of America and wrote *Pirandello*. Her numerous awards include prizes as a poet and playwright.

Jay Parini is a poet, novelist, and critic who teaches at Middlebury College. His latest volume of poems is *The Art of Subtraction: New and Selected Poems* (2005). His latest novel is *The Apprentice Lover* (2002). Parini has written biographies of John Steinbeck, Robert Frost, and William Faulkner. In 2009, Yale University Press will publish a volume of his essays called *Why Poetry Matters*. Jay Parini's grandparents were immigrants from Rome and Genoa, arriving in the United States at Ellis Island between 1908 and 1912. Parini himself has lived in Amalfi and has spent a good deal of time in other parts of Italy. He is currently editing a volume of essays by Italian writers on writing.

Clare Rossini's grandparents were born in Guamo, outside of Lucca. She remembers the Italian proverbs her father passed along, including "Quel che non ammazza, ingrassa" ("What does not kill you, makes you fat"). In 2007 the University of Akron Press published her third collection of poetry, *Lingo*. Her poems have appeared in such venues as *Poetry*, the *Kenyon Review*, *Poetry Daily*, and the *Best American Poetry* series. Among her awards are fellowships from the Bush Foundation, the Maxwell Shepherd Foundation, and the Connecticut Board of Culture and Tourism. She teaches at Trinity College and in the M.F.A. Program at Vermont College. She lives in West Hartford with her husband, Joseph Byrne, and son Francis.

Joseph Salemi has published *Nonsense Couplets* and *Formal Complaints*. He teaches in the Humanities Department at New York University and in the classics departments of both Hunter and Brooklyn colleges.

Mary Jo Salter is the author of six books of poems, most recently *A Phone Call to the Future: New and Selected Poems* (Knopf, 2008). Her earlier books include *Open Shutters*, a *New York Times* Notable Book of the Year for 2003. A playwright and lyricist, she wrote, in collaboration with the composer and jazz pianist Fred Hersch, the song cycle *Rooms of Light*, which premiered at "Jazz at Lincoln Center" in 2007. She taught for many years at Mount Holyoke College and is now professor in the writing seminars at Johns Hopkins University.

Felix Stefanile was born in 1920 in Long Island City, New York. He was educated in the public schools and at CCNY. A World War II veteran, he found employment after the war in a series of clerical jobs until 1950, when he began his eleven-year stint in the New York State Department of Labor. There he eventually became a middle functionary in worker's claims and entitlements. In 1954 he and his wife, Selma, started the poetry magazine *Sparrow*, which is now one of the oldest poetry journals in the United States. His essay "The Imagination of the Amateur," which expresses his ideas on independent literary publishing in American history, was published in 1966, gained him a National Endowment for the Arts Prize in 1967, and has been anthologized. In 1961 Purdue University invited Felix Stefanile to serve as visiting poet and lecturer for one year. At the end of his tenure the university asked him to stay on as a member of the English faculty. He taught freshman composition, survey courses, and a poetry writing class that drew campus-wide attention. In 1969 he was appointed to a full professorship, and in 1973 he was awarded the Standard Oil of Indiana Prize for Best Teacher. His poetry awards include the Emily Clark Balch Prize of the *Virginia Quarterly Review*, 1972. In 1997 he was the first recipient of the recently established *Italian Americana* John Ciardi Award for lifelong achievement in Italian-American poetry. His poetry books include *The Dance at St. Gabriel's*; *In That Far Country*; *East River Nocturne*; *A Fig Tree in America*; *The Patience That Befell*; and *River Full of Craft*. His translations are *I Were Fire: 34 Sonnets of Cecco Angiolieri*; *The Blue Moustache: Some Italian Futurist Poets*; and *Umberta Saba: 31 Poems*.

Rosalind Palermo Stevenson was born in Syracuse, New York, and lives in New York City. She is a second-generation Italian American; her grandparents on both her paternal and her maternal sides were from the Naples region of Italy. Her fiction and prose poems have appeared in numerous literary journals and anthologies, and her novella "Insect Dreams" has been published in the 2007 contemporary novella individual book series (Rain Mountain Press). "The Guest," which appears in this anthology, was awarded the Anne and Henry Paolucci prize for Italian-American writing and was selected as *Italian Americana*'s best story of 2005.

Professor John A. Tagliabue, a member of the Bates faculty from 1955 to 1959, was the author of six books of poetry, including *New and Selected Poems: 1942–1997*, published in 1998.

Alexander Theroux is the author of three novels (*Three Wogs, Darconville's Cat,* and *An Adultery*), two collections of poetry (*History Is Made at Night* and *The Lollipop Trollops*), and several other books.

Tina Tocco is a former editor-in-chief of *Inkwell,* Manhattanville College's literary journal. A 2006 graduate of Manhattanville's Master of Arts in Writing program, she is an editor, creative writing adjunct, and writer-in-residence. Her poetry can also be seen in upcoming issues of *Cricket* and *Inkwell*. She is currently working on a young adult novel. She is a third-generation Italian American; her family is from Gugliano, a village outside Naples, and from the outskirts of Bari along the Adriatic Sea.

Lewis Turco is a poet. *Awaken Bells Falling: Poems 1959–1967* is one of his numerous books of poetry. His *Book of Forms: A Handbook of Poetics* is a classic in the field of poetry. Among his critical works is *Visions and Revisions of American Poetry*. He taught at Bread Loaf Writers Conference for many years.

Robert Viscusi has published the novel *Astoria* (American Book Award, 1996), the long poem *An Oration upon the Most Recent Death of Christopher Columbus (1993)*, a poetry collection entitled *A New Geography of Time* (2004), a critical history entitled *Buried Caesars, and Other Secrets of Italian American Writing* (SUNY Press, 2006), and numerous essays on Italian-American literature and culture. He is the Broeklundian Professor and executive officer of the Wolfe

Institute for the Humanities at Brooklyn College, where he teaches American and Italian-American literature. He is president of the Italian American Writers Association and has held fellowships from the NEH and the Calandra Italian American Institute.

William Foote Whyte was awarded a fellowship by the Harvard Society of Fellows and began three years of residence in the Boston area. During his tenure as a junior fellow he embarked on research in the North End Italian neighborhood. He lived in the neighborhood and developed close friendships with young men from Italian immigrant families who, in Depression-era conditions, hung out on the street corners of the North End. Angelo Ralph Orlandella, one of the "corner boys," became one of his best friends and a key informant on urban slum conditions and gang activities. The Society of Fellows at the time prohibited fellowship holders from pursuing doctoral degrees, so Bill Whyte decided to move to the University of Chicago for his sociology Ph.D. The manuscript describing "Cornerville" became his Ph.D. thesis and was published as a book in 1943, *Street Corner Society* (still in print from the University of Chicago Press, now in its fourth edition). Among his many honors was election to the presidency of the American Sociological Association in 1981.

Tony Zurlo's Italian grandparents claimed to be descendants of Marco Polo. That claim inspired Tony to go to China to research this story. Today he lives in Texas, where he has polished his skill in telling tall tales. No one besides Zurlo and his grandparents (who are no longer living) knows if the story "Marco's Marcoroni" is true or not. He is currently researching the influence of Chianti on Christopher Columbus's ambition to sail west in search of a water route to China so he could corner the Chinese green tea market. Zurlo was a Peace Corps volunteer in Africa.